THE LIBRARY
ST. MARY
ST. MARY

P9-CDD-723

STORIES FROM CHINA'S PAST

The Chinese names and terms are romanized according to the
Pinyin system.

Design: Gordon Chun
Photography: Chris Huie, Joe Samberg, Li Jiping, and Lucy Lim
Copy Editor: Cate Brady

Typography by Wilsted & Taylor, Oakland, California
Printing by Cal Central Press, Sacramento, California

Copyright © 1987 The Chinese Culture Foundation of San Francisco
All rights reserved

Published by the Chinese Culture Foundation of San Francisco

Library of Congress Catalogue Number 87–70422
ISBN 0–9609784–3–7 (paper)
ISBN 0–9609784–4–5 (cloth)

STORIES FROM CHINA'S PAST

Han Dynasty Pictorial Tomb Reliefs and Archaeological
Objects from Sichuan Province, People's Republic of China

An exhibition organized by

LUCY LIM

Executive Director/Curator
The Chinese Culture Center of San Francisco

in cooperation with

The Sichuan Cultural Department
People's Republic of China

Foreword by
ALEXANDER C. SOPER

Introduction by
RICHARD C. RUDOLPH

Contributors:
KENNETH J. DeWOSKIN
GAO WEN
LUCY LIM
MARTIN J. POWERS
WU HUNG
YU DEZHANG

中華人民共和國

四川漢代畫像磚與考古文物展覽

EXHIBITION SCHEDULE

Chinese Culture Center of San Francisco — April 11–May 31, 1987

Museum of Fine Arts, Boston — July 1–August 16, 1987

University of Michigan Museum, Ann Arbor — September 8–October 25, 1987

Walters Art Gallery, Baltimore — November 20, 1987–January 10, 1988

Herbert F. Johnson Museum, Ithaca
(Cornell University) — January 26–March 13, 1988

Frederick S. Wight Gallery
(University of California, Los Angeles) — April 3–May 22, 1988

Phoenix Art Museum, Phoenix — June 18–August 21, 1988

CONTENTS

CHINESE CHRONOLOGY

Xia Dynasty	c. 2100–1600 B.C.
Shang Dynasty	c. 1600–1027 B.C
Zhou Dynasty	1027–256 B.C.
Western Zhou	1027–771 B.C.
Eastern Zhou	770–256 B.C.
Spring and Autumn period	772–481 B.C.
Warring States period	481–221 B.C.
Qin Dynasty	221–206 B.C.
Former (Western) Han Dynasty	206 B.C.–A.D. 8
Wang Mang Interregnum	A.D. 9–23
Later (Eastern) Han Dynasty	25–220
Three Kingdoms	220–280
Western Jin Dynasty	265–316
Eastern Jin Dynasty	317–420
Northern and Southern Dynasties	420–581
Sui Dynasty	581–618
Tang Dynasty	618–906
Five Dynasties	906–960
Song Dynasty	960–1279
Yuan Dynasty	1279–1368
Ming Dynasty	1368–1644
Qing Dynasty	1644–1911
Republic of China	1911–1949
People's Republic of China Founded	1949

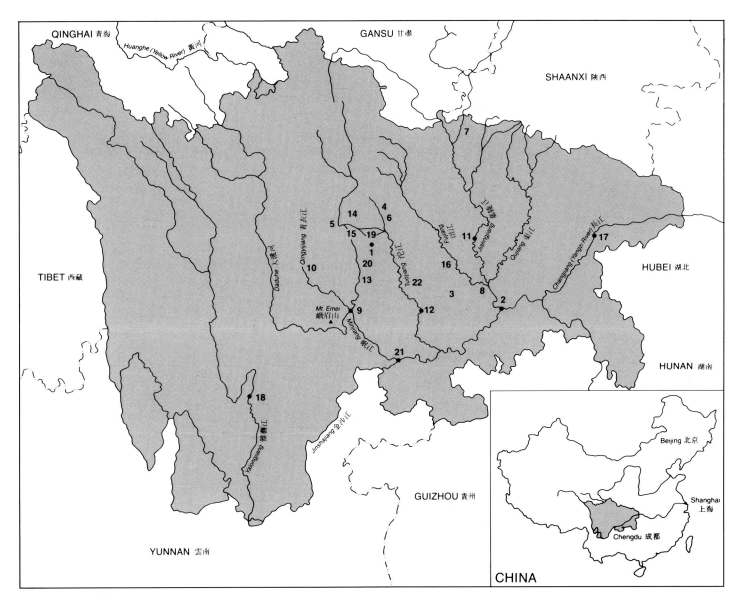

SICHUAN
四川

1 Chengdu 成都

2 Chongqing 重慶

3 Dazu 大足

4 Deyang 德陽

5 Dujiangyan 都江堰

6 Guanghan 廣漢

7 Guangyuan 廣元

8 Hechuan 合川

9 Leshan 樂山

10 Lushan 蘆山

11 Nanchong 南充

12 Neijiang 內江

13 Pengshan 彭山

14 Pengxian 彭縣

15 Pixian 郫縣

16 Suining 遂寧

17 Wanxian 萬縣

18 Xichang 西昌

19 Xindu 新都

20 Xinjin 新津

21 Yibin 宜賓

22 Ziyang 資陽

LENDERS TO THE EXHIBITION

SICHUAN PROVINCIAL MUSEUM
四川省博物館

CHONGQING MUSEUM
重慶市博物館

CHENGDU MUSEUM
成都市博物館

LESHAN MUSEUM
樂山市岩墓博物館

XINDU COUNTY CULTURAL BUREAU
新都縣文物管理所

GUANGHAN COUNTY CULTURAL INSTITUTE
廣漢縣文化館

LUSHAN COUNTY MUSEUM
蘆山縣博物館

PENGSHAN COUNTY CULTURAL BUREAU
彭山縣文物管理所

FUNDING ACKNOWLEDGMENTS

The Chinese Culture Foundation of San Francisco gratefully acknowledges the generous support of the following funders toward the exhibition project "Stories from China's Past" which includes a touring exhibition, catalogue, symposium, and educational programs:

MAJOR FUNDING IS PROVIDED BY

National Endowment for the Humanities

WITH ADDITIONAL SUPPORT FROM

National Endowment for the Arts

San Francisco Hotel Tax Fund

George Frederick Jewett Foundation, San Francisco

The Dillon Fund, New York

California Council for the Humanities

California Arts Council

Walter and Elise Haas Fund, San Francisco

Asian Cultural Council, New York

The L. J. Skaggs and Mary C. Skaggs Foundation, Oakland, CA

Charles Ulrick and Josephine Bay Foundation, Inc., New York

Chevron U.S.A. Inc., San Francisco

C. C. Wang, New York

Han Suyin, Lausanne, Switzerland

Jeannette Shambaugh Elliott, Tucson, AZ

PUBLICATION OF THE CATALOGUE IS ALSO ASSISTED BY

The J. Paul Getty Trust, Los Angeles

Weyerhaeuser Family Foundation, Inc., St. Paul, MN

Mrs. Paul L. Wattis, San Francisco

This exhibition is supported by an indemnity from the Federal Council on the Arts and Humanities.

The Chinese Culture Foundation also thanks the following individuals for their generous contributions:

SPONSOR

Andrea Comel di Socebran, San Francisco
Marshall B. Coyne, Washington, D.C.
Jane R. Lurie, San Francisco
Mr. and Mrs. Duncan L. Matteson, Menlo Park, CA
Mr. and Mrs. Art T. Wong, Los Altos Hills, CA

SUPPORTER

Dr. and Mrs. Clyde Wu, Dearborn, MI
Lillian Chin, London, England
Mr. and Mrs. Collin Fong, Sacramento, CA
Dessa and Wendell Goddard, San Francisco
Frederick L. Gordon, San Francisco
Doctors Maurice and Frances Sachs, Carmel Highlands, CA
Mr. and Mrs. Stanley S. Tom, San Francisco

CONTRIBUTOR

Alice Boney, New York
Mr. and Mrs. John B. Bunker, San Francisco
Calvin and Alice Chow, Hillsborough, CA
Daniel E. and Vyolet L. Chu, San Francisco
Julienne Shiu-Yan Lau, Palo Alto, CA
Hok Pui and Sally Yu Leung, San Francisco
Eva Lowe, San Francisco
Dr. and Mrs. Rolland C. Lowe, San Francisco
Mrs. Robert Seller, San Francisco
Bea and Chaney Wong, San Francisco
Florence Sue Wong, Piedmont, CA
Ming and Sallie Wong, Oakland, CA
Mae C. Woo, San Francisco
Mr. and Mrs. Thomas Yee, Oakland, CA

PREFACE

We at the American Consulate General in Chengdu, Sichuan, are most pleased that this outstanding exhibition of archaeological treasures from Sichuan province will tour the United States in 1987 and 1988. "Stories from China's Past," an exhibit of funerary reliefs, stone and pottery sculptures and other artifacts from the Han dynasty, is the first exhibition in the United States to feature the early art and culture of Sichuan province. Sichuan, China's most populous province, has been primarily known to Americans for its delicious, spicy food. But with this exhibition from 2,000 years ago, more Americans will also become aware of Sichuan's long cultural history and the important role that the province has played in the development of Chinese civilization.

The American Consulate General in Chengdu is the newest American Consulate in China. We are proud to be a part of the expanding relationship between the People's Republic of China and the United States. This exhibition of cultural treasures from Sichuan is an impressive example of our growing relationship in the area of cultural exchange. I sincerely congratulate the Cultural Department of Sichuan Province and the Chinese Culture Center of San Francisco on this fine exhibition and extend my best wishes for a successful American tour.

William W. Thomas, Jr.
Consul General

Consulate General of the United States of America
Chengdu, Sichuan
People's Republic of China

前 言

"四川漢代畫像磚與考古文物展覽"，是中美兩國建立外交 關係以來，四川省第一次赴美展出。雖然我們遠隔重洋，但是我 們願將這些古老文物，藝術珍品，呈顯在廣大美國人民的面前，為中美文化交流史上增添新的篇章。祝中美兩國人民的友誼像長江、像密西西比河一樣，暢流不息，萬古長存！

杜　天　文　　　高　文

四川省文化廳，中華人民共和國

The Sichuan Cultural Department is pleased to present this exhibition of Han dynasty tomb reliefs and archaeological objects from Sichuan province for viewing by the American public, organized in cooperation with the Chinese Culture Center of San Francisco.

Chinese tomb reliefs dating from the Han dynasty (206 B.C.–A.D. 220) have been found in various provinces including Henan, Shaanxi, Shandong, and Sichuan. Those excavated in Sichuan show a rich diversity of subject matter. In general, Han tomb tiles found in north China emphasize pictorial scenes derived from historical sources, mythology, and folklore while those from Sichuan, in marked contrast, bring realism to the art form with vivid representations of everyday life.

Among the items included in this exhibition are some rare and outstanding relics of ancient Chinese cultural history unique to Sichuan regional art. Among them are the lively pottery figure of the storyteller/entertainer, the flutist, the female figure holding a mirror; the stone figure playing the *qin* zither, the stone sculptural base decorated with figures in a landscape scene, the stone house; the magnificent pottery horse; and the spectacular bronze "money tree." Many of the tomb reliefs are newly excavated finds, shedding light on the regional art and culture of Sichuan in remote southwest China during the Han. These archaeological treasures have never been displayed in any Western country.

We sincerely hope that this exhibition will promote the friendship and understanding between the United States and the People's Republic of China and that it will contribute to further research in the study of Chinese art, history, and culture. We take this opportunity to convey our warmest regards and sincere thanks to many American friends and colleagues who have generously given support to the project in various ways.

SICHUAN CULTURAL DEPARTMENT
PEOPLE'S REPUBLIC OF CHINA
Du Tianwen, Chief
Gao Wen, Head, Cultural Relics Bureau

ACKNOWLEDGMENTS

On behalf of the Chinese Culture Center of San Francisco, I would like to thank the Sichuan Cultural Department for their enormous assistance in organizing this exhibition project. This is the first time that an exhibition featuring the Han regional art and culture of Sichuan is presented in the United States. We are indeed very grateful to the Chinese government and the Sichuan museums for lending these rare art works and cultural objects for viewing by the American public. In particular, we thank Mr. Jin Feng of the Cultural Relics Bureau, Ministry of Culture in Beijing; Mr. Du Tianwen and Mr. Gao Wen of the Sichuan Cultural Department and their staff. Many people in the Sichuan museums have contributed to various aspects of the work involved. Although they worked behind the scene, this project would not have been possible without their cooperation.

Cultural Counsellor Xu Jiaxian of the Embassy of the People's Republic of China in Washington, D.C. facilitated this cultural exchange for us, as did Vice-Consul Li Mosu of the Chinese Consulate General in San Francisco and members of their staff. We are also very grateful for the help of Ambassador Hu Dingyi and his wife, Madame Xie Heng, who are now at the Chinese Embassy in London, England.

This project has received generous support from many funding organizations and individual donors. I am very grateful for their generosity, and for the kindness and good advice of the many people involved. Many colleagues and friends have provided invaluable encouragement. I am particularly indebted to James Cahill, Thomas Lawton, Wu Tung, Jade Snow Wong, Phyllis Wattis, Jeannette Elliott, Jane Lurie, Alice Boney, Wilma Wong, and Han Suyin.

We thank Gordon Chun for his fine services in designing the catalogue, poster, brochures, and the exhibition installation; Chris Huie, Li Jiping, and Joe Samberg for their photography; and Cate Brady for copyediting the catalogue. I would also like to thank Ellen Casazza and Matthew Chanoff for their assistance in coordinating the catalogue. Dr. Catherine Witzling and Carol Stepanchuk assisted me in compiling the bibliography. To all of them and many others, I express my sincere gratitude.

Lucy Lim
Executive Director/Curator
Chinese Culture Center of San Francisco

Pottery Female Figure Holding Mirror
65 cm. (25½") h., 35 cm. (13¾") w.

COLORPLATE 2

Detail of Storyteller/Entertainer Pottery Figure
67 cm. (26¼″) h., 26 cm. (10″) w.

Pottery Figure of Storyteller/Entertainer
67 cm. (26¼″) h., 26 cm. (10″) w.

COLORPLATE 4

Pottery Figure of Flute Player
60 cm. (23½") h., 35 cm. (13¾") w.

Stone Figure of *Qin* Zither Player
57 cm. (22½″) h., 40 cm. (15¾″) w.

Stone House
58 cm. (22¾″) h., 40 cm. (15¾″) w.

Pottery House
62 cm. (24½″) h., 47 cm. (18½″) w.

COLORPLATE 8

Detail of Bronze "Money Tree"
153 cm. (60¼″) h.

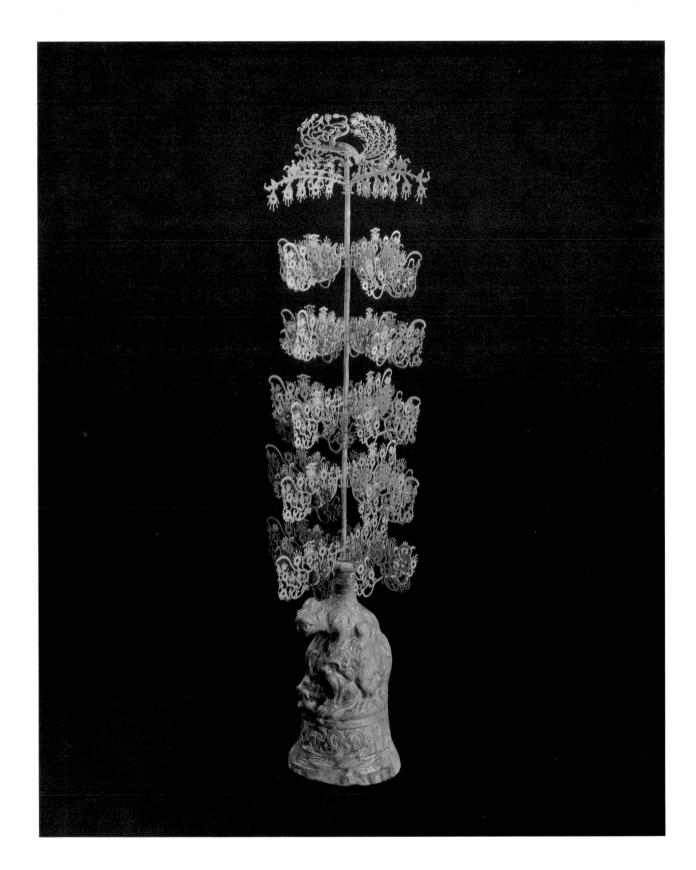

Bronze "Money Tree" with Pottery Base
153 cm. (60¼") h.

Stone Sculptural Base for "Money Tree"
46 cm. (18″) h., 102 cm. (40″) w.

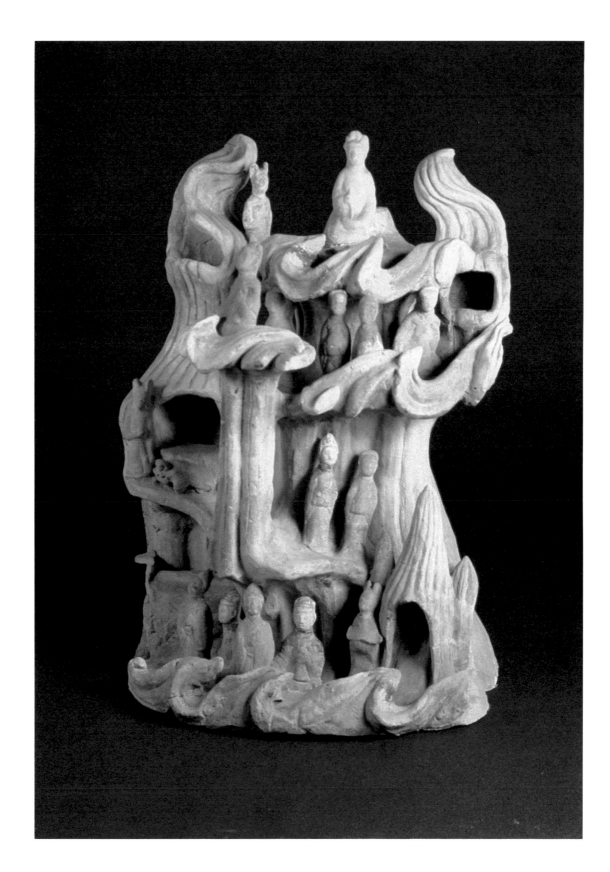

Pottery base for "Money Tree"
60.5 cm. (23¾″) ht., 42 cm. (16½″) w.

Pottery Figure of Horse with Saddle
95 cm. (37½″) h., 78 cm. (30¾″) w.

Pictorial Tomb Relief of "Hunting and Harvesting"
39.5×48 cm. (15½″×19″)

Pictorial Tomb Relief of "Hulling and Winnowing Grain."
28×49.5 cm. (11″×19¼″)

Pictorial Tomb Relief of "Collecting Rent"
25.5×44 cm. (10″×17½″)

Pictorial Tomb Relief of "Feasting and Entertainment"
39.5 × 48 cm. (15½" × 19")

COLORPLATE 17

Pictorial Tomb Relief of "Sundry Show"
28.5×47.5 cm. (11¼″×18¾″)

Pictorial Tomb Relief of "Drummers on Camel"
33.5×41.5 cm. (13¼″×16¼″)

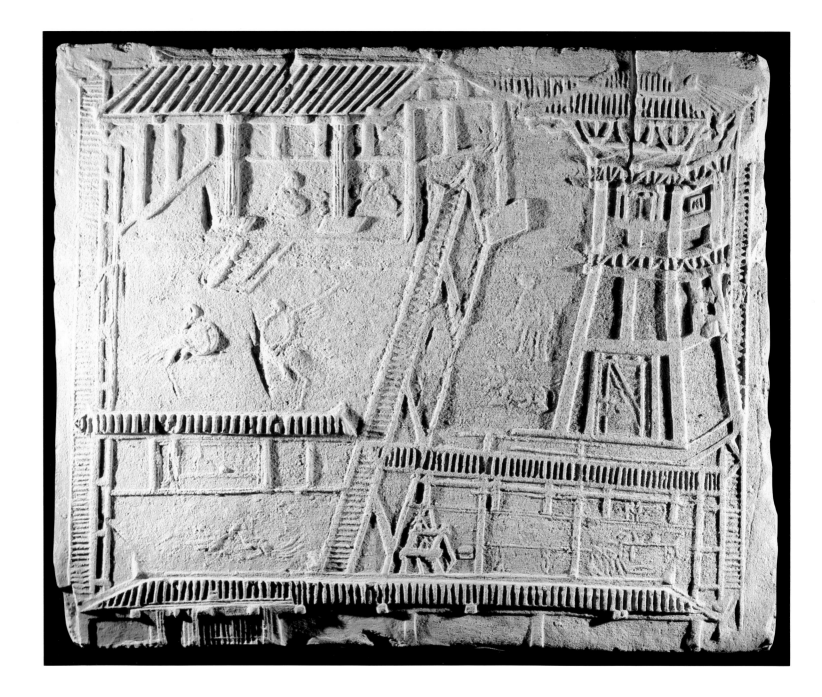

Pictorial Tomb Relief of "Courtyard"
39.5 × 47 cm. (15½″ × 18½″)

Pictorial Tomb Relief of "*Que* Pillar Gate"
39 × 48 cm. (15½" × 19")

Pictorial Tomb Relief of "Armory"
33.5×41.5 cm. (13¼″×16½″)

COLORPLATE 22

Pictorial Tomb Relief of "Mythological Deity 'Xiwangmu'"
40×46.5 cm. (15¾″ × 18¼″)

COLORPLATE 23

Pictorial Tomb Relief of "Moon Deity"
28.5 × 48 cm. (11¼" × 18¾")

FOREWORD

by
Alexander C. Soper

The belief in the dignity of man and the importance of human achievements has been one of the longest held premises in the history of Chinese culture. The connection between this immemorial ideal and the world of art has been two-fold. On the one hand, it has encouraged a concentration on man and his works as the noblest and most useful function of the art of painting. On the other hand, it has stimulated the emergence of the individual artist toward an ever greater awareness of his own importance as a creator.

What gives this situation a special interest for the historian is the fact that the interrelationship between the three elements—the humanistic ideal, the figurative art, and the artist—has been a complex and changing one. The kind of painting that was directly supported by humanistic values had a relatively short life span—short by Chinese standards—of around one thousand years. Its primacy was lost by the end of the Tang dynasty, circa A.D. 900, in an age when painting as a whole was still pursued with a high degree of creative vigor. The artistic personality gathered strength and definite outlines more slowly, and rather than suffering from the decadence of its old companion figurative art, was freed thereby for fresh advances.

At least from the time of Confucius on (circa 500 B.C.), Chinese thinking showed in various ways a growing preoccupation with the theme of man. Some of the very factors that made the declining Zhou dynasty a time of troubles—the breakdown of an orderly class structure, the waning of routine practices and predictability in human relationships, the general alternation between uneasy peace and crisis—here proved a potent stimulus. The final centuries of the Zhou dynasty, in which men could use their own talents to rise to prominence, brought a new individualism. The literature of the time records this new awareness by an insistence on the names of memorable individuals of the present and past. Some were the half-mythical heroes of long ago who had led the struggles out of barbarism. Many were the actors in historical episodes, both good and bad. Some had been teachers; some, hermits who rejected society; others, great craftsmen in the arts. Still others had won their small share of fame merely by saying something worth remembering.

At the same time the idea of man was raised to a new dignity. Two centuries after Confucius, his follower Mencius began to explore the mysteries of psychology. When he taught about the problems of government, he gave the highest importance to the factor of human emotions. All of this growing pride emerged in its most grandiose form in the claims of mystical thinkers. Man was for them the microcosm on which the whole of the universe was patterned. All creation existed to nourish him. The great man, who developed his powers to the fullest degree, might raise himself to become an equal partner with earth and heaven.

It is clear that art was slow in coming to terms with this grand new theme. The traditional forms, which we know in the ceremonial bronzes of the earlier dynasties, had been built out of a world of the imagination into which man had been admitted only as magician, worshiper, or sacrificial victim. Most of the more modern forms of art that began to appear from the time of Confucius on were created primarily for display, as part of the luxurious ostentation of court life. Their appearance was determined largely by abstract qualities—by spacing, by the movement of lines—that drew naturally on nonhuman subject matter.

The first marked change of direction in Chinese painting occurred in the first age of empire. During the Qin and Han dynasties the new scale of human achievement, the spectacular successes of the imperial armies, the greatly increased power of the government, the unprecedented splendors surrounding the ruler, and the general increase in wealth gave a new authority to the humanist vision of human grandeur. Imaginations were fired as never before. The major Han poems are rhapsodies on the size and magnificence of man's works, torrents of words that almost burst through the limits of coherence in their attempts to describe the capitals, palaces, banquets, entertainments, and hunts—even in one case the wonders of a single palatial building.

This exalted matching of fact and fancy was still possible only in the medium of words, however. The Han painters were far too limited in their knowledge of how to present the real world to cope with more than fragments of the spectacles they saw. Instead, the decisions that set a new course for painting were adopted for more sober and utilitarian reasons. Early in the process of consolidating the empire, the Han rulers and their advisers came to realize the potential value of Confucianism to the stability and efficiency of their regime. Confucian ethical teachings were made the basis of the state educational system, designed to train a loyal and responsible civil service. Doubtless because the Chinese mind was better satisfied by concrete examples than by mere exhortation, the training laid great stress on moralizing stories drawn from history or fable. Since it was a cardinal principle that family relationships were an invaluable preparation for life in the outside world, very important roles were assigned to the propaganda that dealt with the two most difficult family problems, the son and the wife. For the son, who must be persuaded to accept his inferior status cheerfully and with love, there were collected examples of filial piety toward father, mother, or elder brother. For the potentially discontented or wayward wife, there came into being a canon of female virtues, illustrated by stories of the ladies who had demonstrated these qualities conspicuously in their own lives.

The discovery that this sort of instruction might be aided by the medium of painting seems to have been first exploited in the imperial palace. Much that we are told about Han art has to do with wall paintings of this sort

in palace apartments. It was an emperor of the first century A.D., when the Han regime reached its high point of decorum and ethical discipline, who was the first to be remembered as an admirer of the newly developing art. He is said to have maintained a picture gallery of his own and to have commissioned his historians to cull through the books for examples of behavior, good or bad, that might profitably be translated by his painters into pictorial lessons. The Han impulse to systematize eventually organized the separate demonstrations into a painted "Mirror of History"—to use the Western phrase—to show and explain all that had been important in the past, from the primeval separation of heaven and earth through the interregnum of monsters and myths into human history with its never-ending clashes between good and evil, wisdom and folly.

The texts that tell us about the major Han paintings make it clear that the regime encouraged one other subject of humanistic importance, the portrait, for equally functional reasons. Here a decision that was to set another precedent was made in 51 B.C. to celebrate the conclusion of the Han empire's bitter fighting against the Hun hordes in the steppe country to the north and west. As an official acknowledgment of indebtedness, the portraits of the generals and councillors who had contributed most to the triumph were painted and placed in a special building of the palace, the Unicorn Pavilion.

About the Han painter himself we know very little; hardly more than the names of the masters who worked at court have survived. The texts do suggest one side of the advancing status of the art. The painters named during the Former Han were merely master craftsmen who specialized in one field or another. The same type of expert continued to serve thereafter, of course, but the persons about whom the most is said in Later Han tended to be in some sense gentlemen amateurs, men of breeding and education who held other governmental posts beyond those in the state workshops. The case of one of these, a scholar of the second century A.D. who served as governor of a province, is particularly telling. He is said to have painted for his own tomb a picture in which he entertained as guests the three worthies of former times with whom he felt the closest sympathy. He doubtless had no very precise idea of the hereafter and so looked forward merely to a general liberation from the narrow confines of this life. But where the majority of privileged Han Chinese dreamed of breaking bounds in the most obvious way, of flying across the sky to visit the stars, or seeking out paradises at the ends of the earth, he asked instead for the freedom to enjoy the richness of human accomplishment through the ages; much as a Renaissance poet in Italy might have dreamed of a meeting some day with Petrarch, Dante, and Virgil. The idea was clearly an unusual one, or it would not have been recorded in a history of painting, but it reveals a humanistic enthusiasm that could on occasion transform even the conventional forms of art, turning what was often a mere instrument of governmental policy in directions that were personal and moving.

We know a great deal more about Han pictorial art than is revealed in written sources. Much has been preserved in the tombs, where the walls have been decorated with paintings, pictorial tiles, or stone engravings, using figure subjects that clearly perpetuate the interests and, to some extent, the style of lost Han paintings done for the living. Our knowledge of this art has been greatly extended by recent Chinese archaeological discoveries, which show it in much greater variety and with a broader geographical and chronological coverage than had hitherto been suspected. We now possess, from mid-second century B.C. tombs of a noble family in the south, outside of Changsha, fascinating paintings on silk, in both the vertical and horizontal formats, the former devoted to death and the afterworld, the latter to the deceased's living guards and household servants, the instruments of their power. At the opposite extreme, the graves of well-to-do farmers of the second or third cen-

turies A.D., contain quick linear sketches of the activities that made up the farmer's life, outdoors and in. Some of the decorated tiles from Sichuan included in the present exhibition show line drawings of the extensive buildings that might make up the country homes of rich landowning families (plate 20). On others, with a shift out of realism into fantasy, we find the favorite Sichuan goddess of endless life, Xiwangmu, with her almost comic court (plates 61, 62, and 63).

It must be admitted that most of the tomb art that testifies to the triumph of the human theme does so at a fairly routine level. The great majority of such illustrations are concerned with stressing the social and economic status of the deceased by enumerating his carriages, retainers, and body-servants, his material possessions, and the entertainments that he and his guests enjoyed (plates 47 and 48). Fortunately the best known of all these Han tomb decorations, the mid-second century A.D. stones from the Wu family shrine in Shandong, are much more rich and varied in subject matter than the rest. Perhaps because they originated in the one corner of the empire that was scholarly and conservative beyond all others, the former homeland of Confucius and Mencius, both the craftsmen and the patrons responsible seem to have been sophisticated to a degree surpassed only at the Han capital.

Inscriptions tell us a good deal about the individuals who were buried in the Wu family plot between A.D. 145 and 167. One served at a middle level in the imperial palace, another at a key garrison post in the far west. One member of the family, Wu Liang, differed in being a scholar immersed in the lore of the past. The set of stones executed for his tomb shrine is more learned and systematic in its subject matter and organization than any of the others. There, if anywhere, we are justified in seeing visible evidence for the look of the great "historical" cycles painted for the imperial court, on palace walls, at much greater size.

One of these slabs, which served as the entire gable wall for the small shrine chapel, gives us an object lesson through its hierarchical layout (figure 17). The scheme begins in the pediment with the supernatural realm of Xiwangmu and her fantastic court. In the next frieze below history is epitomized by the single figures of celebrated rulers, running chronologically from right to left. The second tier shows paragons of filial piety or wifely virtue, performing their well-remembered acts. Well below, beyond a conspicuous border, are illustrations of deeds of violence, political assassinations, and heroic gestures of defiance against blameworthy rulers. The bottom tier apparently depicts scenes related to the life of the deceased, picturing the carriages that might visit him in his lifetime or attend his funeral.

All this is portrayed with the great economy of means seen throughout the Wu pictorial stones, perhaps in part through a deliberate conservatism. The engraving technique, permanent but infinitely less flexible than painting, permitted little elaboration and no subtlety. What the lost monumental paintings of the time may have possessed to make their themes more plausible and moving can only be imagined today.

Foreword

INTRODUCTION

In the early planning stages of this exhibition it was suggested that I write the introduction to this catalogue because I went to Sichuan forty years ago, studied the tombs *in situ*, collected rubbings of the reliefs that decorated them, and later published a book on them. It was also suggested that I include a brief account of my work and impressions there from late 1948 to mid-1949. So I have compiled the following from loosely kept diaries, correspondence, and memory. While I was on the staff of the Royal Ontario Museum of Archaeology from 1945 to 1947, I was led to make a subject index to the rubbings of the Wuliang tomb reliefs in Shandong by Henri Maspero's article on daily life in Han times, and this familiarized me with the formal, stiff, repetitious, and somewhat uninteresting style in that area.[1] My interest in the Sichuan reliefs, however, was brought to life by Paul Pelliot's 1945 lecture in New York in which he stressed the great difference in style between the southwest (Sichuan) and the northeast regions of China.[2] From the few published Sichuan rubbings available then, this difference in both style and subject matter was so exciting that I dreamed of going there to make a large-scale study of the tomb reliefs and the cliff tombs in which many are found. The opportunity to do so came unexpectedly, with an invitation to start a Chinese and Japanese program at UCLA in 1947, and appointment the next year as a Fulbright Research Fellow to study archaeology in China. In addition, the university supplied funds for me to buy thousands of books for the start of a scholarly Chinese library; this pleasant task subtracted from research time but added distant places to my original itinerary.

In Beijing in October 1948 I was amazed to see many examples of both old and new subjects rendered in a very free and dynamic style in some Sichuan rubbings shown to me by Dr. Wolfgang Franke.[3] I became intrigued by these rubbings, decided to study the original reliefs, and by the year's end moved to Sichuan for a six-month stay. In Chengdu Professors Wen Yu and

Feng Han-yi kindly helped me start a general study collection of Sichuan rubbings.

In January 1949 I made a leisurely trip down the Min River valley, with detours from the main roads, to study as many cliff tombs and reliefs as possible. I was surprised at the hundreds of tomb openings visible high on the red sandstone cliffs around the Jiading area, about ninety miles south of Chengdu. Here I studied almost two hundred tomb shafts cut straight into the cliffs and acquired a number of new rubbings. Returning upstream, I studied another group of cliff tombs of completely different design and acquired additional rubbings around Xinjin, about thirty-five miles southwest of Chengdu.

Wen Yu and I started to study some of the most interesting rubbings and planned to do a book about them, but due to the imminent change of governments I had to leave China before our work was finished. I completed this book a year after my return to Los Angeles. While it was in press, I was asked by the Chinese Art Society of New York to exhibit some of the rubbings I had brought back and to lecture on them in April 1950.[4]

I brought home the rubbings needed for the book and many others of particular interest intended for future publication. Many were used in my archaeology classes, perhaps unwisely, for most were stolen from my university office in 1970. It was a heavy personal loss that still rankles, but the sight of long-familiar tiles and rubbings, plus many new art objects, all graciously loaned by the People's Republic of China for this exhibition, somewhat assuages that sense of loss. Moreover, they vividly recall pleasant memories of my Sichuan sojourn and that exciting trip of discovery along the Min River so many years ago. During the forty years since I studied the cliff tombs, more reliefs and grave goods have been found and much new research has been done, correcting old errors, including some of mine, and giving us a much

by
Richard C. Rudolph

better understanding of the life of the people of this area in Han times.

The relief illustrations on the tomb tiles and rubbings, the sculptural burial objects, and the reconstructed Yangzishan tomb model in this exhibition narrate the fears, hopes, beliefs, and the everyday life of the people of Sichuan province over two thousand years ago. Somewhat larger than France, Sichuan lies in remote southwest China next to Tibet, about a thousand miles away from the better known ports and resorts along the Chinese littoral. In remote times formidable mountains on its borders discouraged large-scale intrusion from the northerly Chinese states of the middle Yellow River basin and its alluvial plain. Even the eighth-century poet Li Bo versified on the difficult road that led to this region.

> Eheu! How dangerous, how high!
> It would be easier to climb to Heaven
> Than walk the Szechwan Road.
> . . . .
> How the road curls in the Pass of Green Mud!
> With nine turns in a hundred steps it twists up the hills.
> Clutching at Orion, passing the Well Star, I look up and
>   gasp;
> Then beating my breast sit and groan aloud.
> I fear I shall never return from my westward wandering;
> The way is steep and the rocks cannot be climbed.
> . . . .
> It would be easier to climb to Heaven than walk the
>   Szechwan Road,
> And those who hear the tale of it turn pale with fear.
> Between the hill-tops and the sky there is not a cubit's
>   space;
> Withered pines hang leaning over precipitous walls.
> Flying waterfalls and rolling torrents blend their din,
> Pounding the cliffs and circling the rocks they thunder in a
>   thousand valleys.
> Alas, traveller, why did you come to so fearful a place?[5]

Introduction

Sichuan is underlaid with very thick deposits of red and yellowish sandstone, commonly used for tomb construction and building purposes. Perhaps the most agriculturally productive area of all China is a tableland in eastern Sichuan, covering the whole region around and between the metropolitan cities of Chengdu and Chongqing and known in the west as the Red Basin. The ubiquitous red stone and earth caused it to be so named by the noted geologist and geographer Ferdinand von Richthofen, who spent five years making studies of this and other provinces and trade routes a century ago.[6]

Agricultural production in this naturally fertile area reached peak efficiency due to the skill and dedication of Li Bing, China's greatest hydraulic engineer and onetime governor of Sichuan. Around 250 B.C. he diverted, dammed, and otherwise brought under control the four rivers (*si chuan*) flowing from the north in order to supply the whole Red Basin with ample irrigation. The field crop results of his efforts are shown in a number of tiles with related illustrations.

The salt and iron industries, among others, also flourished here at an early date and were a source of income for the entrepreneur and a source of revenue for the government tax collector.[7] Complex technology for salt recovery was gradually developed because solar evaporation was impractical due to the typically cloudy weather and to the limited quantities of brine that seeped to the surface from deposits of rock salt beneath the heavy layers of sandstone. This technology is illustrated in several versions of salt recovery on tiles found in vaulted brick tombs, of which one version is represented in the exhibition (plate 14). The scaffold on the left serves for boring the well and raising the brine, which flows by gravity from a raised hopper through bamboo pipes to an evaporating oven with five large boilers (in the lower right of the scene). In the clearest version of this scene, four or more rigid lines, resembling the brine conduits, lead into the oven. Because pockets of natural gas were often found when boring for salt, it seems reasonable to conclude that these were bamboo pipes, with clay-tipped tuyères, which constantly fed gas into the oven. In the absence of contrary evidence to date, it appears that these illustrations may show the earliest use of gas as an industrial fuel.[8] It would have been impractical to stop the boiling at night, so gas also may have been used for illumination, as it was at a later date. Nineteenth-century sources stress the size and short life of the evaporating basins, factors that thus created a constant demand for iron.

A valuable source of information on the region's industries, products, natural history, and other topics is the *Huayang guozhi* (Records of the kingdoms south of Mt. Hua), a historical geography of southern Shanxi and northern Sichuan compiled in A.D. 347.[9] For example, it records salt wells in the Red Basin as early as 127 B.C. and the drilling of twenty wells and use of gas from "fire wells" to evaporate brine in 67 B.C. in present Quionglai county, which is still an important center for salt production. It is not surprising then that in this same location tiles narrating salt recovery were used in the interior decoration of complex and relatively costly brick tombs—perhaps for the burial tombs of salt barons whose heirs could well afford them.

Much more was manufactured in Sichuan than just heavy industry items like salt and iron with their ancillary requisites. Three luxury-type products in particular—book knives, lacquerware, and fine textiles—were sold or traded far beyond their point of origin. Book knives, such as the one hanging on the belt of the scholar in the lower right in the pictorial tile "Lecture Scene" (plate 34), were used on the wooden or bamboo writing tablets (held by several other scholars in this tile). Sichuan is reputed to have placed a high value on education in Han times, and this scene eloquently substantiates this reputation. The knives were especially designed to shave writing errors from the tablets, and evidence shows that they were also used to make palimpsests from unwanted tablets. Typically they were short iron knives with a flat, fixed ring and bore inscriptions and decorations inlaid with gold (figure 4). They were called "golden horse knives" because of the frequent use of a winged flying horse decoration, but a flying phoenix and tiger were also used for decoration. The gold inscriptions, some as long as thirty characters, generally date them to the Later Han period, give their origin as Guanghan, adjacent to Chengdu, and sometimes name the responsible artisan or official, suggesting government control.[10] No wonder historians recorded their use as

important gifts and poets praised their beauty, for they must have been elegant additions to the tools of any scholar.

The lacquer tree is indigenous to Sichuan, among other places in the south, and its refined and colored sap, impervious to water when properly applied and dried, is used both for preservation and decoration. Oversized coffins and furniture, delicate wine cups, hair combs, writing brush cases, chopsticks, and many other items have survived in fine condition (after correct treatment) for over two millennia of burial in wet tombs. Lacquer techniques were well developed in the Warring States period and further improved during Han times. Well over half a century ago superb and historically important examples of lacquerware from Sichuan were found in tombs at the Chinese outpost of Lolang, now Pyongyang in North Korea. Some have long inscriptions that give specific dates in the first century, Shu prefecture as the place of manufacture, and names and titles of artisans and officials responsible for the various steps of production in the government workshops. The systematic archaeological survey of the People's Republic of China over the last four decades has brought to light thousands of objects that in one way or another have been treated with lacquer, and some of the finest were made in Sichuan. Its high-quality luxury goods were in demand by the Han imperial household, and many of the lesser aristocracy and officials must have followed this fashion. This was illustrated by a landmark excavation in 1972 at Mawangdui in Changsha, when the first of three family tombs dating from the second century B.C. was opened. This tomb contained a hoard of important grave goods, the majority like new, and also the remarkably well-preserved body of Lady Dai, who had court connections. Inscriptions on a large number of the 184 lacquers, many of exquisite design, proved that they were made in Chengdu.[11]

Textiles, the third of the Sichuan luxury exports mentioned previously, were probably among the luxurious store of clothing and bolts of silk in Lady Dai's tomb, for Sichuan's brocades and other fabrics were as famous as its lacquers. While the variety and extremely fine quality of textiles in her tomb are indeed amazing, it should be remembered that several millennia of textile development preceded the second century B.C. A half-cut cocoon of a silkworm (*Bombyx mori*) and clay impressions of a coarse fabric—both found in Neolithic sites—and advanced weaves in patterned silks seen in patina on Shang bronzes bear witness to early origins and rapid progress. A few fourth century B.C. pictorial bronzes show women picking mulberry leaves, the food on which silkworms are nurtured. A mulberry branch appears on a Xinjin relief depicting the story of Qiu Hu and his wife (plate 55). Scenes of weaving looms and mulberry picking, though rare, have been found in the Sichuan reliefs (plates 10 and 11).

Numerous historical records mention that an advanced textile industry flourished in Sichuan during the Han, and some of its regional specialties were in demand far away. Even the license, if any, may not be inappropriate in the *fu* prose-poem on Chengdu written by Zuo Si at the end of the third century B.C.

> Inside the market walls and gates
> Are the artisans' homes.
> In detached rooms of countless houses
> Weavers' shuttles clack harmoniously together.
> Shell-brocade is elegantly fashioned,
> Its colors rinsed in the river's waves.
> Yellow Sheen lined up in tubes
> Is worth more than baskets of gold.[12]

Reliable records frequently mention *Shujin*, or Shu brocade, and the one named by Zuo Si must have been only one of many variations of this involved type of weaving. The translator states that Yellow Sheen is "an especially fine cloth," and perhaps it is the one said to have reached India at an early date. A report written in 126 B.C. by Zhang Qian, a Han court official, says that he saw *Shubu*, or Shu cloth, in Bactria and that the locals imported it from India. Both of these renowned materials must have been prominent in the wardrobes of the official and moneyed classes for whom these reliefs were made. Featherweight gauzes, like those that once clad Lady Dai, were probably used for the flying scarves and flowing gowns of the dancers who entertained them.

Naturally other parts of the country were also prosperous at times. But Sichuan was generously blessed with a rich variety of natural products, had the most fertile soil, was free from the scourge of droughts, had a favorable cash flow from its exports, and was the home of some of the wealthiest families known in Han times. All of this is reflected in the reliefs and grave furnishings from this area, as well as in the evocative lines of Zuo Si. Even allowing for some hyperbole in his rhapsodic description of Chengdu's commercial area, his image of its atmosphere, affluence, and metropolitan character seems credible.

> Its shop rows stand a hundred layers deep,
> With thousands of stalls nestled neatly together.
> Goods and wares are heaped in mountainous piles;
> Delicate and lovely crafts are amassed in stellar profusion.
> The men and women of the capital
> Are splendidly attired, gaily painted.
> Merchants hawk and barter, hoard and sell,
> Haggling back and forth, dickering left and right.
> Their unusual products are unique and strange,
> Rarer than anything in the eight directions.[13]

Editor's Note:
Dr. Richard C. Rudolph is the author of *Han Tomb Art of West China*, written in collaboration with Wen Yu and published in 1951. It is the first book to introduce the Sichuan Han relief rubbings to Western readers.

NOTES

1. Henri Maspero, "La vie privée en Chine à l'époque des Han," *Revue des arts Asiatiques* 7 (1932): 185–201.

2. *Archives of the Chinese Art Society of America* 1 (1945–1946): 23.

3. Wolfgang Franke, "Die Han-Zeitlichen Felsengräber bei Chiating (West Suchuan)," *Studia Serica* 7 (1948): 19–39.

4. R. C. Rudolph, "Han Tomb Reliefs from Szechwan," *Archives of the Chinese Art Society of America* 4 (1950): 29–38.

5. Li Bo, "Shu Dao Nan." The excerpts quoted are from Arthur Waley, *The Poetry and Career of Li Po* (London, 1969), 38–40.

6. Ferdinand P. W. von Richthofen, *Baron Richthofen's Letters, 1870–1872* (Shanghai, 1890), 115 et passim.

7. For an excellent treatment of this problem and related industries, see Nancy Lee Swann, *Food and Money in Ancient China* (Princeton, 1950).

8. R. C. Rudolph "A Second-Century Chinese Illustration of Salt Mining," *Isis* 43 (1952): 39–41.

9. Chang Qu, *Huayang guozhi* (compiled in A.D. 347), Congshu Ji-cheng ed., ch. 3, 31, 35.

10. T. H. Tsien, "A Study of the Book Knife in Han China (206 B.C.–A.D. 220)," *Chinese Culture* 12, John H. Winkelman, trans. (1971): 87–101.

11. Yu Weichao and Li Jiahao, "Mawangdui yihao Han mu chutu qiqi zhidi zhu wenti" (Some questions about where the lacquers excavated from Mawangdui tomb no. 1 were made), *Kaogu* 6 (1975): 344–48.

12. D. R. Knechtges, *Wen Xuan or Selections of Refined Literature* (Princeton, 1982), 1: 361.

13. Ibid., 359.

*Stories
from
China's
Past*

A BRIEF OVERVIEW OF THE HAN TOMB RELIEFS FROM SICHUAN

by
Gao Wen
(translated by
Jessie Bunnin)

Sichuan, in southwest China, has been inhabited since ancient times. In 1951 railway construction workers in Zhiyang county accidentally unearthed a female skull dating back forty thousand to ten thousand years. During the sixteenth century B.C. Sichuan came under the rule of two clans, the Shu and the Ba, and was divided into two separate states, from which the very distinctive "Ba Shu" culture developed.

Our particular concern is with pictorial tomb tiles and tomb bricks, building materials used in constructing the tomb chambers of the nobility of the Han dynasty. Interest in this art form has been evident since the seventeenth century, when work in collating, researching, and recording Sichuan Han tomb tiles began. It was not until the 1950s, following the growth of interest in Chinese cultural and archaeological undertakings, that excavations of Han tomb tiles in Sichuan increased rapidly and came to attract the attention of the cultural, archaeological, and art worlds. Systematic research work, however, did not get underway until a decade later. This essay, a reflection of recent exploration and scholarly research, explores the characteristic themes and artistic styles of the Sichuan tomb tiles.

During the early years of the Han dynasty, after the reign of the two famous emperors, Han Wendi (179–157 B.C.) and Han Jingdi (156–141 B.C.), economic growth reached its height. Sichuan was especially noted for its abundant natural products and thriving economy. The rivers and weirs in the region gave this area the name *Tianfu zhi guo*, "the land of abundance." The birth and development of the art of pictorial tomb tiles in Sichuan provide a cultural and artistic reflection of the social and economic conditions of the time. Following in the wake of economic prosperity and a rich diversity of cultural activities, this art form grew naturally and inevitably out of the tradition of wall paintings and the elaborate funeral practices of the period.

During the Han dynasty, people were painstaking in their observance of the ancient custom of having elaborate funerals. The feelings of the time were described in *Lun Heng* by Wang Chong (A.D. 27–97): "Death is but another form of life. We weep for those whose funerals are solitary. The desolate souls are without companions. The tombs are tightly shut and there are no cupboards for the cereals and grain. That is why figurines are made to wait on the dead and food is stored in great quantity to appease their souls." This custom of elaborate burial was widespread at all levels of society. The ruling classes were buried with all the luxuries they had enjoyed while alive, including wooden figures representing their servants. The common people were forced to borrow from every possible source in order to bury their dead, causing, in some cases, the downfall of homes and bankruptcies. In *Hou Han Shu*, Ban Gu (A.D. 32–92) described this custom as having reached the stage where "it could not be stopped by either the law or the rites." A passage from *Yen Tieh Lun* (compiled in 81 B.C.) also condemned the practice: "While the parents are alive, the children fail to love and respect them. Yet once the parents die, the children indulge in a show of extravagance. They do not feel grief in their hearts, but because they spend heavily on an elaborate funeral, they are praised for being filial children. They are honored and glorified by the world."

The Han people were particularly fond of wall paintings and wall carvings. The reign of Han Zhangdi (A.D. 76–89) was described as a time "during which residences of military officers were filled with carvings and decorations. Drawings of mountain spirits, sea gods, strange beasts and monsters are in bright display, sending foreign invaders away in fear." Wall painting was so overwhelmingly popular that it could be found in royal palaces, official residences, grand houses of the nobility, and academic institutions. The popularity of wall painting on *yangzhai*, "dwelling houses of the living," led to wall painting on *mingzhai*, "dwelling houses of the dead." The subject matter of *yangzhai* art comprised ancient famous persons, martyrs, strange beasts and creatures, and warriors. These latter, painted on doors, were shown wearing short jackets and wide trousers and carrying long swords. *Mingzhai* art has the same subject matter and clearly mirrored *yangzhai* art in form and content. It was through carefully wrought decoration, according to patterns derived from art for the living, that Han pictorial tomb reliefs in Sichuan came to be created.

DECORATIVE PATTERNS

Han tomb tiles may be divided into four different types: square, rectangular (strip-shaped), decorative, and chronological/character tiles. Square tiles measure about 42 centimeters in height and 48 centimeters in width. Most of the pictorial tiles referred to in this essay belong to this category. Since 1950 several hundred square tiles have been excavated from the suburbs and environs of Chengdu. These tiles, which are of the clearest, best quality and have the most complex designs, encompass eighty different kinds of subject matters and modeling.

The rectangular or strip-shaped tiles do not conform to a uniform standard because their work surface is in the shape of a narrow strip. In general rectangular tiles have a simpler content and a more uniform composition than square-shaped tiles, although sometimes their compositions are quite complex.

Decorative tiles resemble strip-shaped tiles in dimension. Their mainly decorative forms normally embody one of the following patterns: a diamond pattern, a geometric pattern, a checkered pattern, a cloud pattern, and a pattern resembling the calyx of a persimmon. The majority of the tiles excavated over the past thirty years belong to the latter two patterns. Approximately ninety-thousand decorative tiles have been discovered, covering about two hundred varieties. Many of the decorative patterns on the tiles were derived from the Shang and Zhou dynasties. The decorative tiles were placed continuously along the tomb walls, thus forming a complete design.

The chronological/character tiles differ little from strip-shaped tiles and decorative tiles. Their distinctive feature lies in the carvings found on one side of the tiles or on their top end. The carvings refer to either the reign title of the emperor or other chronological characters which are often surrounded by a decorative border. These tiles are highly prized by scholars because they provide a basis for archaeological dating.

Because the tomb tiles were made from molds, tiles made from the same mold are often found at different sites. The representations on these tiles were carved by two different methods. The first is the bas-relief (low-relief) method by which the tableau is raised above a flat surface. The picture to be represented was first drawn in outline and a thin layer of the surrounding surface cut away. The contours of the foreground were carved to add depth. Colors were applied to enhance a three-dimensional effect. This method of bas-relief carving was mostly used in the portrayal of human forms. The second method, that of line representations, employed straight or curved lines above the surface of the tile to form simple pictures. Generally, representations of fish, flowers, birds, and architectural objects were executed in this way.

The pictorial tomb tiles, primarily bas-reliefs, have provided much information on these aspects of life during the Later Han: the life of the common people; the life of the nobility; music, dance, and entertainment; art and architecture; myths and folklore.

LIFE OF THE COMMON PEOPLE

The most remarkable group of Han tomb tiles from Sichuan portrays the major productive activities engaged in by the common people: namely, the tasks of sowing, harvesting, fishing, making wine, producing salt, and hunting. These depictions provide a realistic evocation of daily life in Sichuan during the Han and give significant information to assist research into ancient agricultural practices.

Rice cultivation was highly successful in western Sichuan during the Han dynasty. Many historical documents mention the fertility of the land and the abundance of the harvest. The poet Zuo Si described the richness of the land in *Shu Du Fu*: "Ditches spread out like arteries, criss-crossing everywhere within the borders of the field. The millet crops are as dense as clouds and the rice stalks are as luxuriant." The "Weeding and Planting" pictorial tile (plate 1) excavated from Xindu county reinforces the literary description. The scene shows two connecting water fields. The right field looks like a shallow water pond, teeming with domestic fowl, fish, and lotus seedpods. Two farmers work with scythes raised high. The left field shows a lush growth of rice seedlings. Here two farmers lean on long poles and weed with their feet. This method of weeding may still be seen in some farming villages of Sichuan today.

"Hulling and Winnowing Grain" (plate 8) shows an open balustrade-like building, a granary, raised on wooden poles. (In rainy and damp Sichuan, this kind of granary prevents moisture from harming the grain while allowing free circulation of air.) The farmers are hulling grain by using the *dui*, a trip-hammer operated by foot pedals. During the Han dynasty, mortar and pestle as well as various kinds of *dui*, powered by foot, domestic animals, or water, were used for this purpose.

The plain of Chengdu is exceptionally rich in water resources. The intersecting rivers and canals not only promoted the growth of rice crops but also the cultivation of lotus and taro plants. The pictorial tile "Lotus Pond" (plate 4), excavated from Deyang county, presents a scene of a wide pond. Swarms of ducks fly overhead on either shore, while the lotus gatherers glide easily in their boats amidst the swimming ducks and lotus blossoms. In 1978, the pictorial tile "Picking Lotuses" (plate 5) was uncovered from Xindu county. The latter picture shows schools of fish in the lotus pond interspersed with water fowls, crabs, and snails. A luxuriant growth of lotus leaves drips with the dew drops, and in the lower left corner, a dragonfly rests on a lotus leaf. The lakes and ponds depicted in the pictorial tiles "Picking Lotuses," "Rafting," "Fishing," and "Hunting and Harvesting" (plates 5, 7, 6, and 9) recreate vividly the waterland atmosphere of Chengdu plain.

Salt mining and iron smelting were major industries during the Han dynasty. The salt-mining industry was particularly well developed. Literary texts recorded that many households possessed salt wells as well as fruit orchards. Wine making also progressed considerably during the Han dynasty. In earlier times sprouts of plants were used for making wine; yeast came into use in the Han dynasty. Several tiles portray city markets and wine sellers (plates 16 and 17), giving us a vivid picture of thriving business. The growth of agricultural and handicrafts industries vigorously increased the trade in local products and led to prosperity in the commodity economy. Pictorial tomb tiles depicting this aspect of life have also been found.

LIFE OF THE NOBILITY

Han pictorial tiles were generally found in the burial chambers of the powerful and wealthy, often portraying the lifestyles of the tomb owners and their ostentatious way of living. *Liluan Pien* recorded the scale of their wealth: "The homes of the rich consist of several hundred buildings. Their fields and properties cover the countryside. Their slaves and servants number thousands. Their trading boats and carriages surround the four corners of the earth while uninhabited residences and overflowing storerooms occupy the cities." The tile "Feasting and Entertainment" (plate 48) shows court officials and noblemen dining and drinking to the accompaniment of entertainers, musicians, and dancers. Ban Gu described the extravagance in *Dong Du Fu*: "Thousands of gifts are in the audience chambers. Excellent wine is poured into countless cups. Gold jars and jade goblets are arranged according to rank. The choicest delicacies are on the table while [the nobles], like gods, feast on sacrificial animals."

Other scenes depicted on the tomb reliefs show nobles riding in carriages (plates 28, 29, and 30). Sometimes musicians played ancient military songs as they traveled (plate 51). A company of men would clear the roads while mounted escorts followed behind. Several carriage scenes are included in the exhibition, one being a long procession represented on the wall of Yangzishan Han tomb number one (see Appendix).

MUSIC, DANCE, AND ENTERTAINMENT

During the Han dynasty the aristocrats looked upon music and dance as a class privilege and incorporated these two elements into ceremonial rites as well. Music and dance were commonly performed at banquets and festivals. Not only emperors and kings had imperial dance and music troupes; most court officials and rich merchants possessed entertainment troupes as well, thus explaining why so many entertainment scenes are depicted on the tomb reliefs. Scenes of dancing often show accompanying musicians, and many show song and dance together. Names of the dances were often determined by the content of the lyrics; consequently, it is difficult to give suitable titles to the music and dance patterns found on the tomb tiles. Dancers commonly had long sleeves and swirling scarves (plates 47, 48, and 49). Han Feizi (third century B.C.) wrote: "Long sleeves are an aid to dance as wealth is an aid to trade." Many light, fluttering steps were enhanced by the use of long sleeves. Another common characteristic was the use of drumbeat to reinforce the rhythm of the dance.

Baixi ("hundred shows") is a form of entertainment comprising a variety of performing acts, with acrobatics as one of its important components. Many fine acrobatic displays are shown on the pictorial tiles. "Sundry Show" (plate 49) is a fine example. "Drummers on Camel" (plate 53) is another variety of *baixi*. Representations of camels had been found previously on lacquerware excavated from Changsha, Hunan province, and in sculptural carvings found in Shandong and Gansu. Recent excavation in Xindu county uncovered the first pictorial tile from Sichuan depicting the camel (plate 53), which provides evidence for research into the relationship between northwest and southwest China during the Han.

ARCHITECTURE

In ancient China, grand and imposing architectural structures were in existence by the Qin and Han dynasties. They are described in the texts and visual evidence is provided by several Sichuan Han tiles. The tall tower shown at the top right of the tomb relief "Courtyard" (plate 20) was apparently a common structure during the Han dynasty, appearing frequently on Han tomb reliefs and in the form of pottery models. This scene represents a residential building. Han architecture had a specific type of watch tower. An annotation in *Han Shu* describes it thus: "The *jiaomen* refers to entrances with a high tower on top for observation. The building itself is called *jiao*; those which are particularly elegant are called *lijiao*. *Jiaoche* means a military chariot with a turret for observation." Another source, *Ji Jiu Pien*, records: "The regulation during the Qin and Han dynasties was that within every ten *li* a pavilion must be erected. The pavilions have a high tower for the purpose of observation."

Que "pillar gate" (plate 21) is a construction peculiar to Han architecture. It is often represented in Sichuan Han tomb tiles. *Que* were erected in palaces, city gates, entrance doors, and tomb sites. More than 30 percent of the extant Han tomb *que* are found in Sichuan. Various references in historical documents explain that the tomb architecture imitated constructions for the living. Tomb sites without actual *que* "pillar gate" at their entrances would often have representations of the *que* inside the tombs.

Since 1950, tomb tiles representing armories have been found in more than ten locations. During the Former Han, not only the central government constructed armories, but also a few wealthy families possessed armories for their own weaponry. These extremely exalted families were, however, rare. By the Later Han, as a result of the growing power of tyrannical groups, private armies increased rapidly and private armories multiplied as well. The tile "Armory" (plate 19) was excavated recently from Xindu county in Sichuan. Weapon racks are portrayed in this tile and others found in Chengdu.

MYTHOLOGY AND FOLKLORE

Mythology and folklore are fully represented in Han pictorial tiles. Stories of the mythological figures Xiwangmu, Fu Xi, Nü Wa, and the sun and moon deities were frequently mentioned in ancient texts and at the same time widely circulated in folk tradition. These figures, together with mountain spirits and strange beasts, were common themes portrayed in Han tomb tiles, copper mirrors, and wall paintings. (See plates 63, 64, 65, and 66.)

"Dragon Chariot" (plate 68) is a tile uncovered within the last few years. Three dragons, or *zhi* (a dragon whose horns have not yet grown), pull a chariot in which a driver and a supernatural being sit. Three stars shine in the space outside the chariot. The chariot wheels are in spirals, giving the dragon chariot the appearance of fleeing in space. The treatment of the subject suggests the rider to be the Sun god who however is always described as riding a chariot pulled by six dragons. A verse from *Chu Ci* refers to a Sun god "riding through the vastness of the mist in the East, holding fast six dragons situated to the extreme east." Some scholars have wondered whether the rider could be the River god, He Bo. But according to *Shan Hai Jing*, He Bo rides with two dragons. Qu Yuan's lyrical poem about the River god also describes him as riding on a water chariot with two dragons. Because the chariot in this tile is pulled by three dragons, the identity of the rider cannot be determined without further research and evidence.

INDIAN AND BUDDHIST INFLUENCES ON THE ART OF SICHUAN

Buddhism and Indian culture influenced the content of Sichuan art, including Han pictorial tiles. Even before Han Wudi (140–86 B.C.) developed the route from Sichuan through Yunnan province to India, contact had been established between the two countries. The Chinese emissary Zhang Qian, while traveling to the West, came across fabrics and bamboo work that had been made in Sichuan, brought to India, and finally taken to the Western locales where he found them. In Sichuan there are a few important works of art from the Han dynasty that show the influence of Buddhism. One example is the image of Buddha carved on the lintel in the Mahao cave tomb in Leshan, Sichuan (see Appendix). The Buddha sits cross-legged, his right hand held out in the characteristic "have no fear" gesture. His forehead is marked with a protuberance, and a halo surrounds his head. His attire is not of the common Buddhist style, nor is it Indian, but rather it closely resembles the attire of the Han Chinese people.

Another example to consider is a pottery "money tree" base found in a Pengshan cave tomb. Two dragons with jade discs in their mouths decorate the base, above which is a Buddha image seated in an upright position. This Buddha also has a protuberance on his forehead, and his right hand appears to be raised in the "have no fear" Buddhist gesture. The folds of the robe are clearly delineated, and an attendant stands on either side. (See editor's note below.)

A third item was found in a Han tomb discovered in 1974 in Xialushan county. A bronze Buddha statuette, a pottery jar, and a bronze vessel were unearthed from the tomb. The statuette measures 14.1 centimeters in height and is seated in a kneeling position. It is characterized by a high-bridged nose and a stern facial expression. The forehead has a protuberance, and the hair is tied in a knot. Both arms hang down. The body is marked with lines, its lower portion being unclear. The torso is bare. The statuette is supported by a stand made up of four animals with curved limbs and heads turned back. They seem to resemble either lions or tigers. The base is circular in shape, its sides decorated with a pattern of pointed leaves. The whole structure is extremely unusual. The statuette was perhaps made by the Buddhist Hinayana sect and has been tentatively called a "bronze Buddhist statuette of the Later Han."

These examples confirm that there was a link between China and India during the Later Han and perhaps even before the Han period. Buddhism was considered to have spread into China from India through the northwest route of the Silk Road. These Buddhist images discovered in Sichuan point to the possibility that perhaps other routes existed and they offer important material for the study of early Buddhism in southwest China.

Editor's note:
The pottery "money tree" base depicting a Buddha image found in Sichuan is now in the collection of the Nanjing Museum. The author's article arrived too late for us to include any photograph of the object. It is illustrated in figure 8 of Wu Hung's article, "Buddhist Elements in Early Chinese Art (2nd and 3rd centuries A.D.)," *Artibus Asiae* 47, no. 3/4 (1986): 263–352.

Han Tomb Reliefs

FORM AND CONTENT IN EARLY CHINESE PICTORIAL ART

by
Lucy Lim

In its form and content Han art marks a departure from the art of the Shang and Zhou (circa 1600–221 B.C.) represented by the ceremonial bronze vessels adorned with semi-abstract, zoomorphic motifs. Imbued with enigmatic, otherworldly concerns, these were ritual artifacts created for the nobility who used them for ancestor worship and in sacrifices to the gods. They were also emblems of power and status and, during the Zhou, were given by the feudal princes as gifts. The bronzes were buried with the owners when they died. Many of the extant examples were excavated from the royal tombs. Human images rarely appear in the decorations of these bronzes and, when they do, they are usually in the form of a mask-like face whose meaning is ambiguous and obscure. In short, the aesthetic idiom of these monumental vessels is formal, awesome, and mysterious—hinting of religious and symbolic significance incomprehensible to us today, although various scholars have attempted to interpret their meaning. (Some of the most magnificent pieces were introduced to American audiences in the "Great Bronze Age of China" exhibition organized by the Metropolitan Museum of Art in New York, which toured the United States from 1980 to 1981.)

Decorative designs that allude to the real world began to appear in the so-called "pictorial bronzes" of the late Eastern Zhou around the fifth to third century B.C. Among these bronzes are scenes of people engaged in mulberry picking (figure 1), fishing, and hunting. These scenes are usually divided into registers, and the compositional elements, especially the silhouetted puppet-like figures, are rendered in profile as disparate units without any relationship to each other. The aesthetic approach is basically conceptual: the "idea," or concept of the scene, rather than its reality, is represented.

Han art marks a turning point in early Chinese art. Human figure gradually came to be the predominant subject, visible on pottery and stone reliefs, remnants of mural paintings, and fragments of silk paintings that have been recovered from the tombs. Our knowledge of Han art is primarily based on these extant archaeological materials, which served as *mingqi* burial objects to provide for the needs and comfort of the deceased tomb owner in his life-after-death. Although textual sources describe the grandeur of the wall paintings that decorated palaces and public buildings of the time, all these buildings have long since been destroyed. According to the literary descriptions, the wall paintings portray famous historical figures, meritorious officials, Confucian paragons, and virtuous women, along with images of strange beasts, sea gods, and mountain spirits.

The court dominated painting during Han times and organized it as part of the bureaucratic system. Along with other luxury crafts, painting was specialized for efficient production. The humble artisan was at one extreme and at the other was the *taichao*, an expert or master painter who waited personally upon the emperor and who may well have been able to work in a more independent and experimental vein. This explains the uneven quality of many examples of Han art, since a piece of art work may sometimes have had several artisans working on it, supervised by the master painter. During the Former Han (206 B.C.–A.D. 8), when official patronage of the arts for secular purposes began, painting was an art of persuasion, dictated by the Confucian moral viewpoint whose underlying principle was "to encourage good and censure evil." With the scholar-official class in control of the government and Confucianism well established as the orthodox political ideology in the second century B.C., painting became a vehicle for the Confucianist bureaucracy to consolidate and legitimize its power; it was also useful in maintaining the proper social relationships and upholding traditional Chinese culture.

Figure painting proved to be most effective in promoting the Confucian ethical code. The art commemorated figures and events considered exemplary by Confucian moral standards, while it sought to admonish and to restrain by illustrating moral ills. Hence, didactic in purpose, figure painting during the Han was mostly done under official auspices. The moral attitude that prevailed is made abundantly clear in the early Chinese texts. Because painting was a court-dominated art, a stock repertory of themes probably developed for the Han artisans to follow. As suggested by the texts, portraits at this time were not necessarily done from life; in many cases an image was produced only after the death of the person, although occasionally actual models were consulted. The richness and complexity of Han pictorial art as well as the influence of Confucianism may be glimpsed from the stone carvings of the famous Wu Liang shrine in northern Shandong province, the homeland of Confucianism. Those from other regions of China are less orthodox in their style and content but are representative of specific regional traditions.

A subtle difference distinguishes the artists of the Former Han from those of the Later Han (A.D. 25–220). The earlier men were "professional" painters—artisans connected with the official workshop, the *Shangfang*. Although "professional" painters still continued to make up a vast majority of the practitioners, there had come into existence the so-called gentleman painter: holder of high office and often of noble rank, no longer a craft specialist but an artist talented in many arts, sometimes a notable scholar. Brief accounts of these individual Han masters are given in the *Lidai minghuazi* (Records of famous paintings) compiled by Zhang Yanyuan in A.D. 845. The manner in which these artists are recorded shows that Chinese gentlemen-painters were already in existence by the Later Han and had risen in social status. They were perhaps the precursors of the later eleventh-century literati painters.

Changes in the political and social environment of the Later Han undoubtedly created a freer and more independent artistic milieu for the artists. The archaeological materials recovered from the Later Han tombs reflect new directions and achievements. In general the art of the Later Han shows a heightened concern for expressiveness and spatial effects. The free and natural disposition of figures in their setting was no longer confined to any base line. Certain compositional devices were used in many of the Han pictorial scenes (and are visible in the Sichuan reliefs in the exhibition) to create the feeling of a three-dimensional environment: the extensive use of the diagonal line and the overlapping of forms are intended to suggest recession and perspective (plates 14, 48, and 51, for example). Figures are interrelated through their postures, rendered frequently in three-quarter views and contraposto poses, and by their psychological interaction. They are depicted as a cohesive unit, conversing with each other or engaged as a group in their activities (plates 33, 54, and 55). The formula of a "space cell" unit in which figures and objects are confined within a defined, measurable area are used increasingly (plates 34 and 47). Swirling scarves and curving hemlines, as well as the turning and twisting postures of the figures, enhance the sense of liveliness and movement that the Han artists aimed to impart. These stylistic traits are particularly evident in the Sichuan pictorial representations of dancing and entertainments (plates 47, 48, and 49). The continuous, precise, fine-line drawing style, called the "silk thread" line, appears to be the prevalent tradition in Han painting and its use was later brought to perfection by the master figure painter Gu Kaiji in the fourth century A.D. Thin, raised relief lines employed in several Sichuan reliefs (plates 20, 36, and 63) suggest the influence of this traditional technique. This linear style emerged as early as the Eastern Zhou, visible in rare remnants of painted silk fragments from that period. Other descriptive lines were also used in Han pictorial art: broad and thick lines were used to define contour, while a more sophisticated calligraphic line, whose brushwork fluctuates in breadth, is occasionally seen in the more expressive ink-and-brush paintings that decorated the tombs (figures 14 and 19). An outstanding example from the Han is preserved in a beautiful tile painting of conversing figures, kept in the collection of the Museum of Fine Arts in Boston (figure 15).

The figures portrayed in Han art are usually generalized types with no distinctive individualized features. The stooping posture becomes a pictorial convention to indicate old age, such as in the "Collecting Rent" relief from Sichuan (plate 26) and a painting from Mawangdui (figure 18, detail). The status and role of figures are often defined by their size and the type of clothing they wear. At times, especially in the surviving fragments of tomb paintings that employ the more flexible media of ink and brush, these figures attain an expressiveness and grandeur that speak eloquently for the Han artists who were bold enough to experiment, risking occasional failure. For example, ambitious attempts to render perspective sometimes resulted in distortion, as in "Courtyard" (plate 20). As a result of such experimentation realism burgeoned during the Han, but it was not until later in the Tang dynasty (A.D. 618–905) that naturalism was fully mastered in Chinese art.

Realism was a matter not only of technique but also of subject matter and attitude toward that subject matter. Regional variations notwithstanding, the subject matter of Later Han art indicates a shift to more intimate, everyday scenes that are less formal and pompous, and there is an ever-widening interest in human activities as the art gradually strips itself of hortatory concerns and textual prescriptions. The interest in everyday activities is particularly evident in the Sichuan pictorial reliefs, remarkable for their informal style and highly illustrative content. They are in effect visual narratives that tell us stories from China's past, specifically the daily life of Sichuan during the Han: its farming and fishing activities, industry, transportation, music and entertainment,

mythology and folklore, and the religious and philosophical beliefs that motivated the creation of these wonderful tomb furnishings. Because they are well preserved and form a coherent group, the Sichuan materials render an analytical study possible, being significant not only for their aesthetic quality but also for their authentic documentary value.

SOCIAL VALUES AND AESTHETIC CHOICES IN HAN DYNASTY SICHUAN:
Issues of Patronage

by
Martin J. Powers

Over the past two decades the study of patronage has become a standard approach to understanding how human values take shape in the material forms of art. As the potential of this approach has unfolded, the meaning of the term has changed. Not so long ago the term *patronage* referred to the enlightened support of talented artists by farsighted benefactors. But in recent decades students of art history have discovered that the true story behind the production of art can be far more complex and interesting. Patrons' fears, ambitions, and conflicts of interest, as well as their love of beauty, can affect profoundly the kind of art works they promote. This broader understanding has led historians to investigate more thoroughly how an art work comes into being: not simply how an artist got the idea for a work but who paid for it, who commented on it, who was expected to look at it and why. By answering such questions, scholars have shed much light on the relationship between artistic taste and other kinds of values. Through research of this kind we have gained insight into the sometimes paradoxical mix of noble thoughts and petty schemes that gave birth to the works of art we admire today.[1]

In retrospect it seems only natural that art should issue not merely from lofty intentions but from the full drama of human experience. For if we but concede to art the power to express human values, we may question whether any work could be viewed neutrally in a world where the interests, dreams, and schemes of different people are forever in conflict. Certainly in ancient China few harbored illusions about the neutrality of art. From almost the earliest times that art entered into the historical record, we find references to art deeply entangled in debates about luxury consumption and social responsibility. From such references we learn that artistic taste was no mere ornament to life but both a mark and a method of success.[2]

THE RISE OF NEW PATRONAGE GROUPS DURING THE HAN DYNASTY

That matters of taste were debated at all in Han times makes the period a watershed in the history of Chinese art. Before this time very few people had anything to say about art at all. Of course, pre-Han intellectuals early on criticized the showy displays of opulence attending the homes, carriages, and especially the funerals of the rich and noble. Grand in scale and rich in detail, the lavish funeral had been the mark of wealth and nobility since the dawn of history. But despite objections to bald displays of wealth, the texts do not suggest that any other values might be expressed in art other than wealth and nobility. A vessel or carriage could be plain (for commoners) or ornamented (for the rich and noble), but little else. One suspects this was so principally because at that time the rich and noble were the only people with the means to enlist the artist's imagination.[3]

By the second century A.D., during which time the many inventive works in this exhibition were made, the numbers and kinds of people soliciting work from artists were greater by far and the kinds of art patrons favored correspondingly varied. The imperial court, of course, was a significant consumer, supplied by a variety of specialized bureaus responsible for the production of paintings, precious novelties, buildings, clothing, and the still important funerary articles at the capital. Similar, though smaller, operations must have functioned at the various kingly courts. We can expect also that the imperial in-laws (consort families) and the families of eunuchs—nonroyal elites attached to the court—were not stinting in their acquisition of artifacts. But in addition to these groups, people of more limited means were acquiring decorative handiwork and even monumental sculpture. Of these, local merchants and scholar families, or literati, were by far the most important, and it is these groups who likely were responsible for the thousands of engravings, stamped tiles, and mortuary artifacts whose production flourished in Han times. Some of these new patrons of art, though wanting noble or official rank, were financially secure; others could ill afford to purchase an artist's time and talent but did so anyway. They managed by purchasing monuments through subscription (in league with others), by saving money over time, or by going into debt.[4]

What had happened? How was the persuasive power of art wrested from the hands of the nobility and why would ordinary people go to such lengths to purchase what they really could not afford? The full story is complex, but if forced to summarize, one could explain these changes largely in terms of three interrelated historical trends: the decline of the old nobility, the establishment of empire, and the rising importance of public opinion. The decline of the nobility and the rise of empire were two sides of the same coin. The imperial coffers were filled with taxes from ordinary citizens rather than tribute from vassals. Noblemen, with their own sources of income and personal armies, were of little use and a clear threat to the efficient functioning of the central government. This is why, only a few generations after the founding of the Han dynasty in 205 B.C., most of the nobility from pre-Han times had been eliminated on one pretext or another. A few kings were granted small fiefs as a source of royal blood should the emperor fail to produce an heir, but even these were kings in name only, for their lands were administered by officials dispatched by the central government. Other wealthy and powerful families of all sorts, such as imperial relatives or great merchants, were forced to live in the capital area under the watchful eye of the central government.[5]

The weakening of hereditary political status opened up new opportunities for the lesser rich, those families solid enough to pay taxes but too weak to contest the law. Men from these "middle-income" families comprised the rank and file of the new bureaucracy, for an official salary was theoretically within reach of anyone with a command of Confucian learning. Citizens were not slow to recognize the implications of the system, and we are told that the numbers of men devoting themselves to the classics increased dramatically, "for this, indeed, was the way to appointments and profit." Despite the egalitarian character of the system, we should not imagine that most Confucian scholars were sons of paupers—education is acquired more easily by the wealthy—but they were not very rich either, for they both feared and despised the truly affluent.[6]

Not only scholars but plowmen and tradesmen benefited from the lapse of the hereditary system of political rule. We read of farmers abandoning the plow and heading for the markets where one could make a living as craftsman, shopkeeper, druggist, fortune teller, or the like. There are hints of watchmen moonlighting as brokers and of students earning their way through school by selling books or washing dishes.[7] The establishment of empire had ushered in an age of unprecedented social mobility. As ordinary citizens moved up the social scale, they began to appropriate for themselves some of those things formerly enjoyed by the rich and noble.

In olden times the rafters were not carved and the hut thatch was left untrimmed. People wore plain clothes and ate from earthenware. They cast metal into farming utensils and shaped clay into containers [that is, artisans manufactured useful items]. Craftsmen did not fashion novel, clever articles. . . . Nowadays manners have degenerated in a race of extravagance. Women go to the extreme in finery and artisans strive to make exceptionally ingenious items. Unadorned raw materials are carved and strange novelties prized.[8]

This passage and many others like it describe the typical signs of a society undergoing an increase in social mobility. People were no longer satisfied with plain homes and practical utensils because they no longer needed to remain in the same social slot all their lives. As hereditary divisions in status began to erode, the distinction between "noble" and "common" was supplanted by the more negotiable distinction between "rich," "middle income," and "poor." The implications of this sleight-of-hand for art consumption were profound.

In pre-Han times a commoner could not hope to become noble simply by purchasing a ceremonial vessel. By the first century B.C., however, many did hope to make their way into higher social circles by acquiring the material attributes of another group. "When the husband is honored at court, the wife pushes her calls into the higher social circles. . . . No wonder that even paupers and cripples entertain vain hopes of quickening their pace."[9] When we read of the poor wearing "gay coats without lining" or "silk trousers over hempcloth underwear," we cannot but suspect that these thin veneers of success were intended to purchase membership in some higher status group.

The new market for luxury goods signaled a fundamental change in the meaning and function of art. For the old nobility, who were born into their station, exquisite bronze vessels, carved rafters, and embroidered clothing were little more than signs of hereditary status. But the local merchants and village hopefuls who began to purchase luxury goods hoped to die in a higher station than what they knew at birth. For men and women such as these the accoutrements of luxury were less a symbol of rank than a means of acquiring status in the eyes of their communities. They hoped that the anonymous public would accept these tokens of status, thereby increasing their influence in the community. The magic of public opinion provided a potent stimulus to the market for luxury goods.

What about funerary monuments? Did public opinion affect the market for these more ambitious works of art? The answer is yes, to an even greater degreee. While villagers trimmed their thatch and decorated rafters in hopes of acquiring a touch of class, would-be bureaucrats carefully cultivated their public image for a contest with much higher stakes. Should a young man gain a reputation in his community as possessing Confucian virtues (learning, frugality, filial devotion), he might hope that the local officer from the Bureau of Merit or the local magistrate would recommend him for employment in the prefect or commandery. A truly outstanding candidate might be recommended to the central government.[10] Many young men had accomplished as much

with little more than a village education, a reputation for piety, and, perhaps, some personal connections. But even with a little help from friends, it was wise to cultivate an image consistent with the official criteria for recommendation—there were stiff penalties for the recommending officer should the candidate's conduct prove unbecoming. But how did a young man go about convincing the public of his learning, frugality, and filial devotion?

Clearly the mastery of one or more Confucian classics was a minimum requirement, such as illustrated by the pictorial relief of the "Lecture Scene" (plate 34). We can be sure that the opinions of village teachers and local scholars were critical to most men's early careers. But learning was in itself no guarantee of a reputation for piety. And since in Confucianism frugality is nearly synonymous with piety, sporting fancy tableware or donning silken britches like other village hopefuls would be but little help to the aspiring bureaucrat. No, for impressing one's peers with acts of piety there were many good reasons why the funeral—not the marketplace—was the ideal forum. First, there would be an audience, for in all likelihood the ceremonies would be attended by anyone of consequence to the family. Second, there would be many occasions for exhibiting devotion—the wailing, the wearing of mourning garments, the offering of gifts or prayers. Third, the food and entertainment provided to the guests and the many opportunities for sympathetic conversation certainly could not hurt a man's relationship with local power brokers. Finally, and perhaps most importantly, the casket, the tomb, the tower, or the shrine would remain as a physical monument—a document—of the filial devotion of the survivors. For these monuments stood not only as reminders of the deceased but also proclaimed just as surely the financial sacrifice undertaken by the patrons of the work. And just in case someone might miss the point, inscriptions on monuments sometimes recount their cost and other pious acts of the survivors in considerable detail. The eulogy for the shrine of An Guo, dated A.D. 158, is a prime example. After a brief sketch of An Guo, his virtues, and manner of death, the inscription turns to details about the survivors:

Too soon did [An Guo] leave his parents and three younger brothers! His brothers Ying, Dong, and Qiang, together with his parents, overcome with grief, diligently carried out their duties. His brothers were earnest in fulfilling the requisites of filial piety, outstanding in conduct and sincere in comportment. Such are the things in which the gentleman takes delight![11] His brothers were harmonious in working together; they kept the house in good order, serving their parents obediently. Thinking constantly of An Guo, and full of grief, they were unable to bear parting from the tomb, and constructed a grass hut so as to live nearby. They also built a mound and planted towering cypress trees there. Morning and evening they offered sacrifices, with varieties of tasty foods. They ceaselessly provided him with offerings of seasonal food, serving their big brother as though he were still alive. The family used its savings to build this shrine, commissioning the famous artists Wang Shu, Wang Jian, and Jiang Hu from Gaoping to do the work. . . .[12]

This portion of the inscription—the litany of pious acts by the family—takes up four times as much space as the description of An Guo's virtues. The survivors, not the deceased, are described as paragons of filial virtue, almost as though An Guo's eulogy were actually a *curriculum vitae* for his brothers. Indeed, it might have been so. "Filial and pure" was the rubric under which most young men entered the bureaucracy, and properly respectful interment of one's elders had been made a requirement for public office only decades before this inscription was written.[13] Even as early as the previous century an outspoken social critic complained that little could be achieved by those accused of stinting on the funeral: "People condemn those who do not fulfill the rites and are full of praise for those who piously fulfill all the rites. He who is praised by the people finds support in all his enterprises, while he who is disliked meets with opposition whatever he says or does."[14]

This passage, with many others of Han date, gives a dramatic glimpse of the enormous impact of public opinion on the lives of local elites. Because of its influence on social mobility, public opinion was, for the ambitious scholar, a temperamental goddess, dispensing fortune as easily as ruin, feeding hungrily on burnt offerings of local gossip. Since the fate of a clan rested on its public reputation, families hoping to climb the ladder of success had a powerful incentive to invest in funerary art.

If public opinion was the goddess of Fortune, she was also patron of the arts, for it was largely through the parade of the arts that upwardly mobile clans could display their success, their learning, and their piety for all to see and, more importantly, talk about. Small wonder that families were willing to invest so much in the funerary ceremonies and monuments. We read, for instance, that the funerals of the rich would feature performances by acrobats, dancers, and professional singers. Middle-income families, unable to match this, would settle for the music of drums, zithers, and reed organs. The rich would bury their dead in embroidered, multicoffered caskets, while middle-income families would make do with fine, hardwood coffins. In every sphere of consumption—food, houses, carriages, clothing, and even feminine companionship—the rich had their marks of success, while families struggling up the social scale offered their own distinctive claims to higher status. Among these claims funerary monuments surely held a commanding place. "Nowadays the rich will fashion earth into man-made mountains, plant trees to make a forest and build terraces and kiosks with connecting pavilions and multi-storied viewing towers [as monuments to the deceased]. Those of middle income will erect offering shrines with screens and walled memorial towers with wooden screens."[15]

At the time this passage was written (first century B.C.), it is not clear if middle-income families decorated their offering shrines and towers with pictorial reliefs, but by the first and second centuries A.D. this practice seems to have become de rigueur. It is not difficult to imagine why this fashion should have evolved. Pictorial decoration—whether painted, engraved, or stamped—could accomplish at once several benefits for ambitious clans. It could document the achievements of the family by illustrating the attainment of official rank by the deceased. It could bear witness to the learning of the deceased or other clan members. And it could offer the community a rough gauge of the financial sacrifice made by the clan in the interests of filial devotion.[16] In brief, the role of public opinion as the engine of social mobility made it both a source and an object of funerary art, an art that flourished in many provinces of China throughout the first and second centuries A.D. of the Later Han.

REGIONAL VARIATIONS IN FUNERARY ART AND ITS PATRONAGE

Pictorial funerary decor did not flourish evenly throughout the empire. Large numbers of tomb reliefs have been found primarily in the greater Shandong region (modern-day Shandong and northern Jiangsu), Henan, Shaanxi, and Sichuan.[17] These areas had both enough material and sufficient numbers of prosperous citizens to support this industry. But this is where the similarity ends. In numbers of engravings produced, and especially in style and preferred subject matter, the various regions differed widely. Perhaps the most marked differences are those separating the greater Shandong region in northeast China from the rest of China. In stones from Nanyang and Shaanxi, for instance, it is common to find sinuous, animated figures running about among scrolls (figure 24). These designs were not inventions of Later Han artists but were derived from the tradition of cloud and animal imagery common on bronze and lacquer artifacts of the Former Han (figure 22). The artists of Sichuan were more innovative in many respects and were less bound to the decorative cloud scroll. Their depictions of lively, sinuous figures with trailing sleeves and fluttering scarves (plates 47, 48, and 49), however, show stylistic links with the traditional art of the Former Han. In Shandong this tradition disappeared during the first century A.D. Although cloud patterns recur there during the second century A.D., these are unlike the distinctive, sinuous patterns of the old tradition.[18]

How does one explain these differences? I would suggest that the evolution of regional styles had much to do with the importance of local patronage during the Later Han. Local patronage, after all, would tend to favor local craftsmen. A family willing to exhaust its savings or go into debt could not easily afford to import art works or artisans from other provinces. One might have expected that this would be the normal situation, but in fact it signaled an important shift away from Former Han conditions of art consumption. Most of the bronze and lacquer artifacts we find in Former Han tombs were made in workshops owned and operated by the central government. Many of the lacquerwares found at Mawangdui in Hunan, for instance, were made further west in

Sichuan. It is not known where the beautifully painted caskets of that tomb were made, but instances are known where such items were donated by the imperial court and sent to provincial nobility. Since imperial shops all over Han China adhered to similar patterns and standards, it is difficult to assign such items to a particular region by style.[19] During the Later Han, in contrast, all the evidence points to local craftsmanship. For some monuments, such as the Wu shrines and An Guo's shrine, inscriptions tell us that the artists were local, but even where inscriptions are lacking, the geographical limits of various styles leave no doubt as to the regional character of the work.

Since local artists would have inherited certain traditions of representation from their predecessors, it should be possible to recognize traces of pre-Han regional traditions in Later Han art. Indeed, this may explain in part the stylistic rift between Shandong and the rest of China. In pre-Han times, from about the fifth century through the third century B.C., the region now occupied by Sichuan, Hubei, Hunan, and parts of Henan, Anhui, and Jiangsu was under the control of the powerful southern state of Chu. The bronze mirrors and lacquer articles of Chu are noted for their beautiful and ingenious "cloud scroll" patterns and exotic animal imagery. After the unification of China the tradition of Chu art (and literature) continued to flourish at the capital and in regional courts.[20] Since the Chu tradition was native to southern China and was influential at the imperial court in the west (Shaanxi), it is not too surprising that its traces can be seen in the art of Nanyang, Shaanxi, and Sichuan. Since this tradition originated outside of Shandong, it was easier for Shandong artisans to develop independent styles.

The simplicity of this model makes it attractive for explaining regional differences. However, it is an insufficient explanation, for the impact of patronage was not limited to the selection of local styles over imported models. The Han public was highly sensitive to tokens of wealth, status, learning, and piety—in short, all those social values that could influence the fortunes of ambitious families. Just how sensitive the public was is difficult for us to appreciate today, but contemporaneous sources provide some glimpse of the strong language inspired by matters of taste in Han times.

AESTHETIC CHOICES AND SOCIAL VALUES DURING THE HAN

Confucian humanists had early on drawn a correlation between the luxury consumption of the rich and the misery of the poor, but by Former Han times the language of criticism had grown much stronger. Toward the end of the second century B.C., one critic complained of "the frozen and hungry lying on the roads, shoulder to shoulder" and the "punishment and death of the innocent." The source of this misery, according to the writer, could be traced to "the building of great palaces and houses with massive rafters and door pillars . . . elaborately decorated and carved" and various other artistic extravagances. This line of criticism continued into the early first century B.C., when scholars from Shandong expressed their disapproval of intricate cloud and animal designs on architecture and luxury articles, insisting that such luxuries were a prime cause of social injustice—"when the people are extravagant, cold and hunger will follow."[21]

Up to this time the imperial court had, on the whole, maintained a taste for architecture heavily ornamented with those intricate designs despised by scholars. By the early first century A.D., however, the court had so thoroughly embraced the views of the Shandong scholars that it too rejected traditional signs of ostentation. The architecture and ceremonies of the Former Han were dismissed as "extravagant," while those of the Later Han emperors merited adjectives like "symmetrical," "solemn," "majestic," "dignified," "frugal," "restrained," and "simple." Confucians were no longer content merely to criticize the old cloud and animal imagery but now began promoting a new set of aesthetic standards adapted to their own interests. It is notable that the earliest funerary engravings from Shandong, which appear at just this time, lack any trace of cloud and animal designs and embrace instead tokens of classical learning. But not everyone abandoned the luxurious styles of the past simply because the scholars pigeonholed them as immoral.

To many, the look of luxury associated with the old tradition survived at Nanyang, a great commercial center famous for its rich merchants and court favorites. And further east there were the kings, many of whom cultivated a taste for the extravagant. One such personage was King Kang, a man reputed to be fond of palaces, pavilions, and beautiful women. A memorial to him from a loyal officer exemplifies the clash of aesthetic/moral standards being debated at all levels at this time: "Your servant hopes that his great lord shall reform and [adopt] frugal [habits], follow the classical canons, reduce the number of slave girls [in the palace], the number of horses and carriages, the amount of royal land, the [scale] of parties, the amount of land set aside for royal use [at the expense of farmers], and establish ceremony and decorum [in the court]." From these suggestions it is easy to infer that King Kang embraced all those values— social and aesthetic—that Confucian pedants most despised. We are told that he respected his advisor's words but was unable to change his habits.[22]

The controversy over elaborate ornamentation versus tokens of frugality remained current into the second century A.D. The social critic Wang Fu (mid-second century A.D.) devoted portions of several chapters to the subject. Like many scholars before him, he regarded commercial enterprise and novel ornaments as but two species of artifice, each of which was detrimental to a healthy society. "If the ruler wishes his citizens to prosper then he must treat farming and silk production [that is, the major media of tax payments] as fundamental and commercial enterprise as peripheral. Craftsmen should treat products of practical use as fundamental and clever ornaments as peripheral. Merchants should treat the circulation of goods as fundamental and the sale of novelties as peripheral. . . . Those who are pious should treat caring for their parents as fundamental and competing for a reputation as peripheral." Numerous memorials throughout the second century kept the issue alive. Indeed, most references to art in Han literature occur in the context of this ongoing debate.[23]

Why were scholars so vocal in their opposition to elaborate art styles and why were merchants, courtiers, and royalty so attracted to these styles? One might be tempted to dismiss the frequent complaints of scholars as Confucian prudery, but this would be losing sight of what was a major social issue of the time. The debate over extravagant art was, in fact, nothing less than a debate over the distribution of resources—which kind of activity should be rewarded most, the acquisition of wealth in the market place or the acquisition of knowledge? The scholars were in direct competition with other groups working through the commercial sector for society's resources as well as for influence at court. It was for this reason that something so apparently trivial as the eunuch penchant for ornate poetry and calligraphy drew such a vehement response from a prominent statesman of the late second century A.D.:

There has been an edict ordering imperial artists to make portraits and eulogies of thirty-two men for [the walls of] the Hongdu Academy, including [the eunuchs] Le Song and Jiang Lan. I have learned from the classic the *Zhuan* that "whosoever the ruler raises up must be recorded. If those recorded are not imitated then future generations have no way of learning from them." Now Song, Lan, and the others are all cheap, vulgar people who get into power through family relations or by currying favor with powerful families; they are nothing but sycophants and opportunists. Some donate a prose-poem [a highly ornate style of poetry] or some stylish calligraphy and thus are raised to the status of court attendants and have their portraits painted. But although they hold the brushes they do not keep the records and their words do not correspond to what they think. They [actually] have others do their calligraphy for them and thus fake quantities of works, and for this they all receive special favors from the emperor! These are the dregs and castoffs of humanity! Those who know what is happening keep their mouths shut and the whole world sighs at the injustice of it.[24]

What so infuriated the author of this memorial was the fact that Song, Lan, and other eunuchs were receiving official honors in exchange for presenting products of art rather than showing evidence of classical learning or administrative competence. Here, as in many other memorials of the time, the eunuchs and other "venal" social groups are associated with ornate styles of calligraphy, literature, and art.[25] These art forms signified wealth and status to eunuchs, merchants, and possibly a majority of villagers and so were treasured by these groups. Scholars resented these signs of achievement in part because they could not utilize them.

If we take into consideration the political and social motives underlying aesthetic choices during the Han, we might expect to find two kinds of funerary art fostered over time: one for members of the commercial sector, showing a preference for tokens of material opulence and another for scholars, favoring tokens of learning, piety, and frugality. This theoretical contrast is borne out to some extent in the work typical of Nanyang and Shandong. Nanyang was famous throughout the Later Han as a stronghold of rich merchants, eunuchs, and imperial favorites. The great families of Nanyang were famous for overt displays of wealth but showed little concern for Confucian precepts. The funerary engravings of that region, in keeping with the character of the clientele, favored those elaborate cloud and animal designs (figure 24) associated in Han times with the rich and noble while slighting classical subjects.[26]

Shandong, on the other hand, had always been a center of Confucian learning, and there themes drawn from the classics dominated the iconography of funerary monuments, while cloud and animal imagery appeared late and in a distinctly secondary role. Given the aesthetic and political issues prevalent in Han times, these differences in the archaeological record might well be attributed to differences in the attitudes of local elites—how they tolerated or rewarded signs of opulence and tokens of learning. A close analysis of the art works of Sichuan can tell us much about local social and aesthetic values and in this way serve as a window into the souls of its owners and makers.

REGIONAL CHARACTERISTICS OF THE ART OF SICHUAN

If, putting aside scholarly caution, we were to caricature the patrons of Nanyang as profligates and those of Shandong as pedants, we should have to describe those of Sichuan as liberals, for there we find the widest tolerance for those extremes that elsewhere in the empire suffered some degree of exclusion. In the art of Sichuan there is room for joy and room for labor; there is lust for money and thirst for knowledge; there is a place for exactitude and a place for exaggeration; most importantly, perhaps, there is a tolerance for the ordinary and even the ugly.

Unlike Nanyang, where classical subjects were scarce, the art of Sichuan was not indifferent to learning. Classical subjects did not enjoy special favor, but heavenly omens and stories such as Confucius meeting Laozi (plate 54) or Qiu Hu and his wife (plate 55) are not unusual.[27] The Shandong scholars would have approved of these subjects, but they might have been shocked by the open delight taken in scenes of commerce and industry in the Sichuan reliefs (plates 6, 8, and 14). Salt processing was a thriving industry in Shandong, as in Sichuan, and some patrons of local monuments most likely enjoyed revenues from this activity. In Shandong, however, there is no pubic admission of such on the walls of tombs or shrines, while salt-mining scenes appear in several tiles from Sichuan. Some of the Shandong reliefs refer to activities in the iron industry, another lucrative source of income, but the material message of these scenes recedes under layers of moral meaning conveyed by miraculous portents of virtue.[28] Never in northeast China do we find an entire composition devoted to depicting people engaged in commercial exchange such as in the lively scenes of city markets visible in the Sichuan reliefs (plates 15 and 16). There the hawkers, the shopkeepers, and even the consumers and their children constitute the very essence of the scene.

The Sichuan pieces displayed in this exhibition are mostly free of the moral overtones so characteristic of the art of Shandong. Although it is known that the scholars who paid for decorated shrines and tombs in Shandong typically collected rent from tenants, unambiguous depictions of such activity are lacking. In the Sichuan pictorial representation the exchange of wealth is portrayed in a natural, genre-like scene. There are inscriptions in Shandong that speak of money, but in terms of the sacrifice suffered by the family rather than income.[29] It was probably the high standard of Confucian morality in Shandong that encouraged imagery alluding to charity rather than trade and industry. In Sichuan, however, the various scenes of trade and industry show that labor and money were not considered cause for embarrassment but were treated in a natural, open manner in tomb decorations.

There is much in the art of Sichuan to suggest that the physical effort germane to labor not only was accepted as natural but also perhaps was even admired, such as in the scenes of "Sowing," "Hunting and Harvesting," "Hulling and Winnowing Grain," and "Salt Mining" (plates 2, 9, 8, and 14, respectively). The farmers stoop and the reapers stretch in a manner illustrating the effort required, while the spindly-legged salt miners plod slowly and uneasily under the weight of their sacks. The Shandong impulse to edit away and delete the ignoble features of daily life is entirely absent in Sichuan.

The Sichuan people's acceptance of the ordinary is evident also in a greater tolerance for sexuality. This is perhaps most obvious in the charming "Kissing" scene (plate 40), a carved relief *in situ* in Sichuan, whose match could not be found in all of northeast China. The contrast becomes even clearer in illustrations of the story of Qiu Hu and his wife, for this story is illustrated both in Sichuan and in Shandong reliefs. The Shandong relief depicts Qiu Hu's wife with an eye to her virtue, completely neglecting her physical beauty and sensuality (figure 13). She is clad in a voluminous skirt that covers the contours of her body entirely. The Sichuan representation shows the virtuous beauty wearing a shapely gown that clings to her hips as she leans on one foot, revealing her lovely, curvaceous form (plate 55). As she turns to pick mulberry leaves, her sleeves flutter in the wind, revealing her naked forearms. The thick, voluminous clothing worn by Qiu Hu attests to his financial status and success. He swaggers past the beauty with a confident wave of hand that befits a man of means. The psychological detail of this scene is so rich that it is difficult to believe that its main purpose was to promote modesty in women.

These special features of Sichuan iconography and style tell us that local standards of piety, modesty, and frugality were less severe than in Shandong, the homeland of Confucius. Unlike the Shandong reliefs, the Sichuan reliefs show little concern with images of charity and sacrifice, although they do occur occasionally (plate 25). Education did matter to local elites, as illustrated in the "Lecture Scene" (plate 33). It is notable, however, that this composition shows an actual classroom with teachers and students engaged in a learning process. In Shandong, although signs of learning abound in many reliefs, references to classical texts are the usual means of documenting education.[30]

In Sichuan many images combine the extraordinary and the ordinary. In this context the occasional exaggeration takes on the character of fantasy. In portraying the storyteller/entertainer pottery figure (plate 42), the artist heightens—even exaggerates—the distinguishing features of this dwarfish figure: his bloated paunch, his loose and wrinkled pants, his sloppy chest, and especially his grimacing face. It is the exaggerated, comic features of the storyteller that give him an extraordinary quality bordering on fantasy, a quality akin to the freaks in Fellini's films or the comic characters in Shakespeare's *Midsummer Night's Dream*. Ignoble characters like this never occur in the art of Shandong and, indeed, were explicitly criticized as unworthy of attention by scholars of the late second century. Such figures are unique to Sichuan. This same blend of the ordinary and the ethereal lends charm to the musician figures displayed in this exhibition (plates 43 and 44). The open, childlike face of the flute player is unpretentious, without the pomp and reserve one would expect to see in famous scholar musicians of the period, such as the scholar Cai Yong. These are not stereotyped tomb ornaments but highly individualized figures. Their telling eyes hint at a marvelous world of imagination and fantasy, of great sweetness and spiritual depth, the very world to which music transports the viewers.[31]

Why did these special qualities flourish in Sichuan and not in Nanyang or Shandong? While we can infer something about local attitudes towards wealth, labor, and learning from the art objects in this exhibition, we know very little about why these attitudes should have been tolerated or rewarded in Sichuan. But it is perhaps not too bold to suggest that some of the qualities we have noted—the delight in fantasy and the tolerance for things as they are—had roots that may be traced far into the past. There are, at least, many passages in the *Zhuang zi* (fourth to second century B.C.), that great Daoist work of southern literature, in which the qualities of imagination and tolerance for the real are reminiscent of the art

works of Later Han Sichuan. Typical of this sensibility is a passage in which a badly misshapen cripple is asked if he dislikes the lot to which he was born. His answer, a wonderful mix of the vulgar and the fanciful, the pitiful and the sublime, is spoken in a spirit that may be said to typify many objects in this exhibition: "No, why should I dislike it? If the Creator were to transform my left arm into a cock, I should be watching with it the time of the night. If he were to transform my right arm into a crossbow, I should then be looking for a bird to bring down and roast. If he were to transform my buttocks into a wheel and my spirit into a horse, I should then be mounting it, and would not change it for another steed."[32]

NOTES

1. Examples of patronage studies in European and Chinese art include Michael Baxandall, *Painting and Experience in Fifteenth Century Italy* (Oxford, 1972); Michael Baxandall, *The Limewood Sculptors of Renaissance Germany* (New Haven, 1980); James Cahill, *Parting at the Shore* (New York, 1978); Wai-kam Ho, Sherman Lee, Lawrence Sickman, and Marc Wilson in *Eight Dynasties of Chinese Painting* (Cleveland, 1980); Francis Haskell, *Patrons and Painters: Art and Society in Baroque Italy* (New Haven, 1980).

2. For an introduction to the Han economy see Michael Loewe, *Everyday Life in Early Imperial China* (London, 1968), ch. 12; Martin J. Powers, "Artistic Taste, the Economy and the Social Order in Former Han China," *Art History* 9, no. 3 (September 1986): 295–305.

3. For early critiques of extravagance see the *Mo Zi* (fifth century B.C.), available in Burton Watson, trans., *Mo Tzu: Basic Writings* (New York, 1963), 65–77; *Mencius*, bk. 1, pt. 2, ch. 2, in James Legge, trans., *The Chinese Classics*, 3d ed., 5 vols. (Hong Kong, 1960), 2:153–54; see also a chapter in *Lü Shi chunqiu ji shi* (The annals of master Lü), compiled by Lü Buwei (d. 235 B.C.) (Taipei, 1975), 10.4b–8a. Huan Kuan (active first half of first century B.C.), *Yantie lun* (Shanghai, 1974), 28.64. Esson M. Gale, *Discourses on Salt and Iron* (reprint, Taipei, 1973), 109. For a review of the role of ritual vessels in pre-Han religion and politics, see Lester James Bilsky, *The State Religion of Ancient China*, 2 vols. (Taipei, 1975), 1:81–100.

4. Hans Bielenstein, *The Bureaucracy of Han Times* (Cambridge, 1980), 50–55, 67–68; for examples of Emperor Ling's artistic consumption see *Hou Han shu* (Beijing, 1965), 78.2530–2532. For a review of the kinds of patronage practiced by the Han literati, see Martin J. Powers, "Pictorial Art and its Public in Early Imperial China," *Art History* 7 (June 1984): 142–51.

5. T'ung-tsu Ch'ü, *Han Social Structure*, ed. Jack Dull (Seattle, 1972), 165–67, 185.

6. Ban Gu (b. 32–d. 92), *Po Hu T'ung* (Discussions in the White Tiger Hall), trans. Tjan Tjoe Som, 2 vols. (Leiden, 1949), 1:143. See also Loewe, *Everyday Life*, ch. 3.

7. Ch'ü, *Han Social Structure*, 347, 375, 385–86; Cho-yün Hsü, *Han Agriculture*, ed. Jack Dull (Seattle, 1980), 192–95; Powers, "Artistic Taste."

8. *Yantie lun* 3.7–8; translation based upon Gale, *Discourses*, 21.

9. *Yantie lun*, 9.21, 28.64; Gale, *Discourses*, 58, 109.

10. For details on the Han recruitment system see Bielenstein, *Bureaucracy*, ch. 6.

11. The passage translated "such are the things in which the gentleman takes delight," like many portions of this difficult inscription, is open to other interpretations. For instance, it could be translated more specifically to mean "the gentlemen [of the region] all approved [of their behavior]." Since *jun zi* usually takes a more general meaning, I have translated it that way here, but either interpretation reflects the family's concern with public opinion. On funerary art and funerary practices see Yang Shuda, "Handai sangzang zhidu kao" (A study of funerary customs in Han times), *Qinghua xuebao* 8/1 (1932): 26 ff; Robert Thorpe, "Mortuary Art and Architecture of Early Imperial China" (Ph.D. diss., University of Kansas, 1980), 221–28; Powers, "Pictorial Art," 142–46.

12. Li Falin, *Shandong Han huaxiang shi yenjiu* (A study of the Han dynasty engravings of Shandong) (Jinan, 1982), 101–2.

13. *Hou Han shu*, 39.1307.

14. Wang Chong, *Lun heng* (Critical discourses), 4 vols. (Beijing, 1979), 4:1455; translation based upon Alfred Forke, in *Mitteilungen des Seminars für Orientalische Sprachen* 11 (1908): pt. 1, 123.

15. *Yantie lun*, 29.69.

16. Lien-sheng Yang, "Great Families of the Eastern Han," in *Chinese Social History*, trans. and ed. Sun Zen E-tu and John De Francis (Washington, D.C., 1956), reprinted in *The Making of China*, ed. Chun-shu Chang (New Jersey, 1975), 122–23.

17. Li, *Shandong Han huaxiang*, 60–62.

18. Hsio-yen Shih, "Han Stone Reliefs from Shensi Province," *Archives of the Chinese Art Society of America* 14 (1960): 49–64; Hsio-yen Shih, "I-nan and Related Tombs," *Artibus Asiae* 22 (1959): 277–312; Richard C. Rudolph, "Han Dynasty Reliefs from Nanyang," *Oriental Art* 24 (Summer 1978): 179–84; Wen Yu, *Sichuan Handai huaxiang xuanji* (Selected Han dynasty reliefs from Sichuan) (Beijing, 1956); Richard C. Rudolph and Wen Yu, *Han Tomb Art of West China* (Los Angeles, 1951).

19. Yu Weichao and Li Jiahao, "Mawangdui yi hao Han mu chutu qiqi zhidi zhu wenti" (Various problems concerning the provenance of the lacquer articles excavated at Mawangdui tomb number one) in *Mawangdui Han mu yenjiu* (Studies of the Han tombs at Mawangdui) (Hunan, 1979), 358–64; *Hou Han shu*, 78.2521 and *zhi* 6.3152.

20. The contents of royal tombs at Mawangdui and at Mancheng, Hebei, testify to the persistence of Chu traditions in the courts of Han times, and the poems of Ban Gu refer to a familiar type of intricate ornament in the imperial palace. This is not too surprising considering that the founder of the Han dynasty, Liu Bang, was a man of Chu. Even the poetic form favored at the Former Han court, rhyme-prose, was derived from the poetry of Chu. *Mawangdui yihao Han mu* (Tomb number one at Mawangdui), 2 vols. (Beijing, 1973); *Mancheng Han mu fajue baogao* (A report on the Han dynasty tombs of Mancheng), 2 vols. (Beijing, 1980); Burton Watson, *Chinese Rhyme-prose* (New York, 1971), 2–9; for a description of palace ornament in the Former Han, see Ban Gu, "Liang du fu" (A poem of two capitals), in *Wen xuan*, compiled by Xiao Tong (501–531) (Hong Kong, 1974), 1.6–8; Xiao Tong, *Wen xuan*, trans. David R. Knechteges (Princeton, 1982), 119–24.

21. *Huainan jizheng* (Collected commentaries on the Book of the Prince of Huainan), compiled by Liu Jiali, (Shanghai, n.d.), 8:3b—

5b; translation based on Evan Morgan, *Tao The Great Luminant* (reprint, Taibei, 1966), 82–83. *Yantie lun*, 1.1; Gale, *Discourses*, 3.

22. Xiao, *Wen xuan*, 1.3–4, 2.17, 18, 21, 23, 3.52, 54, 57, 58, 60, 68; Knechteges, *Wen xuan* 157, 161, 169, 173, 255, 261, 267, 269, 277, 301; *Hou Han shu*, 42.1431–32. Nanyang merchants were already famous in the Former Han and remained so during the Later Han. Li Jiannong, *Xian qin liang Han jingji shi gao* (An outline of pre-Qin and Han dynasty economic history) (Beijing, 1962), 212; *Hou Han shu*, 15.573, 56.1823, 67.2212.

23. Wang Fu, *Qian fu lun* (Discourses of a hermit), annotated by Wang Jipei (b. 1775) and collated by Peng Duo (Beijing, 1975), 1.15–16. There are many references to art in the histories, among which are *Hou Han shu*, 54.1778–80, 78.2510, 78.2521, 78.2522–23.

24. *Hou Han shu*, 77.2499.

25. This is one of the major points of *Hou Han shu*, *juan* 78.

26. Unambiguous references to Confucian subject matter are extremely rare in published rubbings of engravings from Nanyang. There are three which might be considered as illustrations of heavenly omens, all of which seem to be of the early Later Han dynasty in date and one is dated to the reign of the Confucian enthusiast Wang Mang. See Shan Xiushan, Chen Jihai, and Wang Rulin, *Nanyang Handai huaxiang shike* (Han dynasty stone engravings from Nanyang) (Shanghai, n.d.), figs. 57, 58, and 67.

27. Wen Yu, *Sichuan Handai huaxiang xuanji*, figs. 28, 36, 40, and 43, among others; Käte Finsterbusch, *Verzeichnis und Motivindex der Han Darstellungen*, 2 vols. (Wiesbaden, 1971), vol. 2, figs. 100, 385, 391, 408, and 436.

28. For the iron-smelting scene see Fu Xihua, *Handai huaxiang quan ji* (A collection of Han dynasty engravings), 2 vols. (Beijing, 1949), 1:94.

29. Wilma Fairbank, "The Offering Shrines of Wu Liang Tz'u," *Harvard Journal of Asiatic Studies* 6 (1941): 1–36, reprinted in *Adventures in Retrieval* (Cambridge, 1972), 50; Li, *Handai huaxiang*, 102. There is a very clear illustration of rent collection at a site called Dahuting in northern Henan. The tomb in which it is found, however, is unusually lavish and unlike the monuments of the scholar-gentry in structure, pictorial style, and iconography. It resembles closely a tomb in Bo County that belonged to the fabulously wealthy clan founded by the eunuch Cao Teng. Tombs of this sort cannot be considered together with those of the Confucian scholar-gentry.

30. Edouard Chavannes, *Mission archéologique dans la Chine septentrionale*, 2 vols., plus atlas (Paris, 1909); Bertold Laufer, *Chinese Grave Sculptures of the Han Period* (New York, 1911); Martin J. Powers, "Hybrid Omens and Public Issues in Early Imperial China," *Bulletin of the Museum of Far Eastern Antiquities* 55 (1983): 1–55.

31. *Hou Han shu*, 60B. 1991–92.

32. Wang Fuzhi (b. 1627–d. 1679), annotator, *Zhuangzi jie* (An interpretation of the Book of Master Zhuang) (Beijing, 1976), 6.65; translation based upon James Legge, trans., *The Texts of Taoism*, 2 vols; Max Müller, ed., *The Sacred Books of the East*, vols. 39–40 (reprint, New York, 1962), 1:248.

MUSIC AND VOICES FROM THE HAN TOMBS
Music, Dance, and Entertainments in the Han

by
Kenneth J. DeWoskin

The Han dynasty flourished two thousand years ago, yet scholars are in the process of reconstructing a detailed picture of the daily life of that remote period. Burial objects, pictorial decorations, and both well-known and recently discovered classical documents offer varied perspectives on Han life. A sizable fraction of Han texts and pictorial art is devoted to representations of music, dance, and entertainments, a fact well illustrated by the archaeological objects, tomb reliefs, rubbings, and other artifacts in this exhibition. These ancient and enduring relics capture the most fleeting of all arts—music and dance.

Music and dance are prominent in records of China's past. Confucius, by the account of Han-dynasty and earlier texts, used music and dance as a basic instrument of self-cultivation. He was described as being personally attached to his *qin* zither, which in later Confucian ideology came to be considered the inseparable companion of the gentleman. Dancing was a regular activity for the community of disciples that surrounded Confucius. The harmony of the Confucian music illustrated a harmony among the community members that reached beyond their verbal interactions. At the same time their music cultivated individual skills for achieving internal harmony in life.

A number of archaic literary sources, including the ceremonial texts *Ili* and *Zhouli*, describe the types of ritual dances, the officers of the court charged with perfecting them, the selection of young dance students, and the teaching of dance for both ritual and entertainment purposes.[1] The *Commentary of Zuo* contains narratives of musical entertainments provided by hosts for their visiting guests. It describes these entertainments in convivial settings, and it stresses the distinctly regional nature of song, instrumental music, and dance. Finally, it expands on an important theme in classical Chinese thought—the power of music to shape and to reflect the moral qualities of the people who produced it.[2] The music of a well-governed state is upright, orderly, and not overly stimulating. Complexity is eschewed, and a deliberate, steady pace with gravity of expression is most highly prized. It is a music of great sonorous bells, massive stone chimes, zithers of tone so subtle they border on the inaudible, and pipes true to the pitches of nature itself.

The Han dynastic histories record how the Han founder, Gaozu, had not even dismounted his chariot after the conquest when he ordered the court elders to reconstruct and refine the practices of court ritual that were lost during the preceding Qin dynasty.[3] This commission doubtless included the reconstruction of the Zhou pitch system, the dance, and the calendar of ritual practices that prescribed mode-keys and music for each festival in the annual calendar. In addition to the literary sources, the splendid materials recovered from the Han tombs provide ample information on the importance of music, dance, and entertainments during the Han. Many of the archaeological pieces in this exhibition have been excavated in Sichuan during the last two decades; they are authentic visual documents for the emerging research on Han life and culture.

Han culture inherited a legacy of ritual music from its archaic predecessors and labored hard to reconstruct it by replicating the accurate instruments and recovering the proper pitches. But as the Han unfolded, what became most characteristic of Han music and entertainments was their eclectic nature. The Han empire expanded the boundaries of a central administration beyond what it had ever been previously. The silk route was open for traffic. A network of administrative, military, and trade links to several frontier areas facilitated the transmission of culture to the court and throughout the empire. As a result, musicians with their instruments, conjurers and jugglers with their props, and dancers with their costumes circulated from region to region and had relatively easy access to the emperor's court, the palaces of the nobility, and the entertainment areas that sprang up in Han urban centers.

When viewing the relics of music, dance, and entertainment from Sichuan, we should remember that they are tomb goods. Westerners commonly think of the tomb as a silent vault. The ancient Chinese tomb was anything but that. The Sichuan Han tombs, for example, were richly staffed with sculpted figures of jesters or storytellers, *xiao* flute players, *qin* zither players, and dancers with flowing robes. The walls were decorated with tomb tiles depicting orchestras, dancers, jugglers, acrobats, feasts, processions, and military bands. Yangzishan tomb number one, with its lavish furnishings and decorations, is a stunning example, represented in the exhibition by a reconstructed model decorated with pictorial reliefs on its walls (see Appendix). Reflect on typical Western associations with tombs in order to appreciate how different was the broad cultural context of ancient Chinese burial practices. In the words of Thomas Gray ("Elegy Written in a Country Churchyard"):

> Can storied urn or animated bust
> Back to its mansion call the fleeting breath?
> Can Honour's voice provoke the silent dust,
> Or Flatt'ry soothe the dull cold ear of death?

HOW STORIES ARE TOLD IN HAN TEXTS AND TOMB TILES

Before the discovery of the many archaeological objects from the Han tombs, our knowledge of the Han relied almost entirely on literary texts that had been transmitted continuously from Han times. A major source of information on every Chinese dynasty is the dynastic history, a compendious document that includes essays on institutions and practices of the time and biographies of rulers, major figures, and miscellaneous characters. Both the *Shiji* (Records of the Grand Historian) and the *Han shu* (History of the Former Han) contain anecdotes on music

and dance during the Han. Since the discovery of the tomb tiles, scholars have returned to the dynastic histories for help in interpreting the iconograpy of the reliefs.

The dances described in the dynastic histories are specifically connected with historical events. Shortly before the establishment of the Han, Liu Bang—who later became the dynastic founder Han Gaozu—was locked in a struggle with the powerful general Xiang Yü. Once Liu Bang's key general, Xiang Yü had become an emerging rival for the throne by 206 B.C. Xiang Yü invited Liu Bang to a banquet at Hong Men, where there unfolded an attempt to assassinate Liu Bang. Xiang Zhuang, a follower of Xiang Yü, offered to perform a sword dance for entertainment. But Xiang obviously had an ulterior motive.

Xiang Zhuang entered and proposed a toast. When the toast was finished he said, "Our lord and the governor of P'ei [Liu Bang] are pleased to drink together, but I fear that, this being an army camp we have nothing to offer by way of entertainment. I beg, therefore, to be allowed to present a sword dance." "Proceed," said Xiang Yü, whereupon Xiang Zhuang drew his sword and began to dance. But Xiang Bo also rose and danced, constantly shielding and protecting the governor of P'ei with his own body so that Xiang Zhuang could not attack him.[4]

The Hong Men banquet became a popular theme for later fiction and drama, and it was probably attached to dances and pictorial representations as well.[5] (See figure 14.) The story contains all the ingredients of a dramatic tale, including action and a well-known historical episode. By the Jin dynasty (A.D. 280–420), scholars had already associated the sword dance mentioned in the Han texts with a series of scarf (*jin*) dances, in which the swirling scarves were substituted for the whirling sword. A number of Sichuan tomb reliefs of the first and second century A.D. show dancers swirling, with billowing sleeves and ribbon scarves trailing their energetically out-flung arms (plates 47 and 49).

Han literary and historical records are sharply skewed toward the events of court and the interests of the elite. Since the writing system was in the hands of the educated elite, this is not surprising. A popular Han dynasty courtier poem, the *fu* (rhyme-prose or rhapsody), was often written at the request of the ruler or another patron on formal occasions. Many survive and provide detailed descriptions of the finery and elegance of feasts and entertainments. *Fu* on entertainment dances were written by Zhang Heng and Fu Yi of the Eastern Han.[6] Both *fu* are framed as entertainments prepared for the pleasure of the king or patron on the occasion of the feast. Zhang Heng's *fu*, for example, is prefaced with the following: "In ancient times there was a guest watching dance in the kingdom of Huainan. He thought it very beautiful and wrote the following rhapsody." This particular view, of the guest watching a performance on a formal occasion, is much like the view we have on the Han tomb tiles.

Much less is known about popular dance and entertainments from the written record, but some references to them are found in the Han dynasty *fu*. Zhang Heng wrote a pair of *fu* on the two Han metropolises Luoyang (east) and Chang'an (west). In the one on the western metropolis, Chang'an, he describes the emperor's visit to a large public entertainment arena. Here again, although the performances are in a popular milieu, the view is through the eyes of the emperor.

> He went down to the broad arena with a far-ranging view
> And observed the wondrous feats of competitive games.
> Wu Huo hoisted cauldrons;
> A Dalu climber shinnied up a pole.
> They "rushed the narrows" and performed a swallow dip,
> Their chests thrusting at the sharp spear tips.
> They juggled balls and swords whirling and twirling,
> Walking a tightrope, meeting halfway across.
> Hua Peak rose tall and stately,
> With ridges and knolls of irregular heights,
> And divine trees, magic plants,
> Vermilion fruits hanging thickly.
> They assembled a troupe of sylphine performers,
> Made panthers frolic, brown bears dance.
> The white tiger plucked the zither;
> The azure dragon played a flute.
> . . . .

> A sacred mountain, tall and rugged,
> Suddenly appeared from its back.
> Bears and tigers climbed on, grappling one another;
> Gibbons and monkeys leaped up and clung to a high perch.
> Strange beasts wildly capered about,
> And the great bird proudly strutted in.
> A white elephant marched along nursing its calf,
> Its trunk drooping and undulating.
> A great sea-fish transformed itself into a dragon.
> Its form writhing and wriggling, twisting and twining.
> . . . .

> Amazing magicians, quicker than the eye,
> Changed appearances, sundered bodies,
> Swallowed knives, exhaled fire,
> Darkened the arena with clouds and mist.
> They drew on the ground and created rivers,
> That flowed like the Wei, coursed like the Jing.[7]

In its entirety this prose poem provides a panoramic description of the arena entertainments, which included musicians, singers, magicians, acrobats, and costume dancers, as well as strong men, strange foreigners, exotic animals, and scenic props. The poet establishes a deliberate interplay between the real and the imaginary; it is often impossible to tell what is a genuine thing and what is a prop, what in reality is an animal and what is a costumed dancer.

In the Han pictorial tomb tiles the same subject and the same license in representation may be found. Large birds, strange ape-like creatures, dragons, and sea fish are represented with forms that lie somewhere between the creature and the dancer. While we might assume the more bizarre of these to be actors, they are portrayed by the sculptors as fully beast. Birds have scrawny legs that could not conceal a human dancer's legs. There is no clear indication of an actor or dancer in costume. This degree of absorption in the imaginary context of the performance, by both the poet and the sculptor, actually reduces the value of the materials as evidence for reconstructing the actual scene. But it enhances the aesthetic and dramatic appreciation of the performance. In other words, we cannot ascertain whether an ape was portrayed with a full-body costume or a minimal costume—for example, a tail. But we can ascertain the theatrical impact: how the performance was able to create wonder and amazement and to absorb the viewers into the context of the performance.

Recent archaeological work has uncovered a wealth of tomb materials to complement the texts. New materials appear just as discussion gets underway on the previous finds. Tomb reliefs from the southwest, primarily Sichuan, and the northeast—Yi'nan, for example—contain numerous representations of music, dance, and entertainments, ranging from simple banquets to elaborate feasts. The Sichuan finds include some striking figures made of pottery and stone, some over two feet tall, portraying images of Han storytellers and musicians with their apparatus in hand (plates 42, 43, and 44).

HOW ENTERTAINMENTS WERE SET IN THE HAN

The Hong Men banquet exemplifies the convivial use of music, dance, and other entertainments during the Han. Many of the Sichuan pictorial reliefs depict scenes of feasting and entertainment, frequently with performers outnumbering the guests. The number of guests shown in the scene may not necessarily represent the number of guests enjoying the performance. The artist may have wished to focus his representation on the music ensemble, as suggested by the composition of several scenes. In pictorial evidence ensembles of four or five performers appearing before an audience of one or two are not uncommon, but written records make clear that such banquets were likely to have a large number of guests.

The historical records of the Hong Men banquet generally corroborate what the pictorial reliefs show. Dancing was a common entertainment at feasts. That Xiang Zhuang apologized for the lack of entertainment provides insight into what was normally expected at a feast—music and dance. The tomb reliefs present host and guests at feasting scenes viewing dancers, jugglers, and acrobats, with drummers and other musicians in attendance (plates 47 and 48). The Hong Men account is useful not only because it explains how the sword dance may have originated but also because it depicts how such a gathering proceeded, including a description of the seating arrangements for guests. The formality of such

functions is suggested in the tomb art from Sichuan and other Han sites as well. Details of something as basic as the seating arrangements might have had political as well as ritual and ceremonial significance. In other words, the correct ritual arrangement is the background for changes that imply subtle political significance. In one incident Han Prince Dai (later known as Emperor Xiao Wen) indicated his willingness to become emperor by agreeing, after much urging, to face south. At the Hong Men banquet Liu Bang sat facing north, which indicated his intention to follow Xiang Yü.[8]

If we are to judge the degree of skill imputed to the performers by both the texts and the pictorial tiles, they must have been professionals, supported primarily by their skills and trained by family or by owners. Pre-Han and Han texts indicate that many musicians were slaves. Wealthy families in the Han often kept male and female slaves as entertainers.[9] These slaves were sometimes of the minority tribes and their usefulness as professional performers was undoubtedly due to the prevailing interest in non-Han music. Before the Han some slaves may have been intentionally blinded in their early years to make them stronger musicians, but there is no indication this practice was current in the Han. Entertainers were buried as sacrificial victims with their masters during the earlier Shang and Zhou dynasties, as late as the fifth century B.C.[10] This practice ceased by the Han. Instead, sculpted figures or figurines were substituted for humans and buried with the tomb owner.

The pottery house with musician and storyteller figurines inside (plate 46), an unusual discovery from Sichuan, suggests that music was performed informally as well, as an individual leisure-time pursuit. But such entertainments in a less formal setting are less extravagant. Since figures of performers playing alone or in duos have been discovered in the Han tombs, we might assume that amateur performance was practiced as well. For amateurs, a *qin* zither was more suitable, say, than a set of *pan* disc-drums that required more skill to manipulate. The *qin* was known as an instrument well suited to personal cultivation and personal enjoyment.[11] The stone figure of the *qin* zither player in the exhibition appears completely absorbed in his music, as if oblivious to the outside world (plate 44).

Commonly portrayed in the feasting and entertainment scenes are a pole drum and a scarf- or sword-dancer, usually accompanied by musicians on an assortment of the "seven voices"—that is to say, metal, gourd, skin, silk, bamboo, stone, and pottery instruments. Such scarf-dancing scenes tend to be more serene (plate 47). In contrast, the "sundry show" pictorial tile (plate 49) depicts a *pan* dancer, a table balancer, and a ball juggler performing together in a circus-like fashion, with several different acts proceeding simultaneously. Generally, the settings for the performances are divided into two categories: the indoor feast scene and the outdoor arena or festival scene.

The Han histories describe costumed animal dancers and processions as part of an annual, scheduled festival cycle. Strange animal-like figures appear in many Han pictorial tomb tiles. The most important examples are from Yi'nan in northeast Shandong province, not Sichuan. They are a central component in Han entertainments, and an occasional figure of this type appears on a Sichuan tomb relief (plate 48). The most significant scheduled festival in the yearly cycle was the "Great Exorcism," or *Dano*, beginning on the *La* day and inaugurating the New Year. The Great Exorcism involved driving away demons, pestilence, droughts, and other lingering evils to sanctify the observances for the New Year. The expulsion rites, which included costumed dancing and processions, are described in detail in both the *Hou Han Shu* (History of the Later Han) and Zhang Heng's *fu* poems on the western metropolis, the latter cited previously.

According to historical records, animal dancing was a major event during the New Year ritual "Great Exorcism." In the key procession 120 young palace guards dressed in red and black form a large hand-drum troupe. An exorcist wearing a four-eyed bearskin headdress leads another group of palace guards dressed in various bits of fur, feather, and horn that identify them with twelve animals.[12] Animal processions and costumed dancing have been tentatively identified with specific myths—for example, the triumph of the Yellow Sovereign (Huangdi) over the demonic Chiyu. The former is associated with the bear, the latter with the serpent. Their function at festivals is well documented in the histories.

What has not been understood in similar costumes and dancing outside of religious events. The *fu* descriptions of Zhang Heng and the appearance of animal costumes on the Sichuan pictorial tiles and tiles from central and northeastern sites make clear that these festival dances or derivative dances were performed with the *baixi*, "hundred shows," and *zaji*, "sundry skills," in a largely secular setting.

So vast was the variety of entertainments during the Han that even the emperor had to go down to the arena to see the full scope of the hundred shows or sundry skills. The range of these entertainments was broad, including conjurer acts, comic and musical skits, concerts, martial arts, and the varied skills of acrobats, jugglers, and costume dancers. Apparently the range of professionalism varied greatly and the performances were often characterized by a strong foreign flavor. The residents of the Han capital obviously had great curiosity about the frontier regions. Descriptions in the Han texts celebrate the exotic qualities, fantastic costuming, and extravagant variety of these performances.

The hundred shows and sundry skills were included in both musical and nonmusical performances. At one extreme is the dance theatrical *Donghai Huanggong* (Master Yellow from the Eastern Sea), in which an aging warrior, once in possession of secret martial powers, dies in battle with a tiger.[13] (To date no pictorial representation has been found of this performance, which is described in the Han texts.) At the other extreme are the jugglers and the table balancers, extensively described and illustrated. Han texts such as Zhang Heng's *fu* on Chang'an lists a rich variety of performances, including wrestling, pole climbing, tightrope walking, weight lifting, monkey dancing, horse shows, sword swallowing, fire spitting, mask acts, sword juggling, ball juggling, table stacking, and several kinds of animal and mythical beast dance.

The Han inherited from archaic China a division between civil (*wen*) and military (*wu*) art, between the feather dance and the sword dance, between music of the strings and bells and music of the horns and drums. Although many cases are not perfectly categorized by this general scheme, it is a guide to understanding the generic trends in Han performances. Many Han tomb tiles show musical performances of a distinctly military nature, on horses, in chariots, and even on camels. Two important genres of military music are described in the Han texts, both depending heavily on wind instruments and both associated with military use. The "Drum and Wing" type *Guchui*, also called *Qichui*, "Mounted Winds," used *paixiao* panpipes and *jia* double reed horns in addition to the side-carried drums, bells, and gongs. *Hengchui*, "Transverse Wind," relied on drums and *jiao* horns. Military music is thought to have originated with the nomadic tribes of the northwest. The *jia* horn is alternately called the *hujia*, "barbarian horn."

One of the most important representations of military music yet discovered is seen in a rubbing from Chengdu showing six mounted musicians (plate 51). The horses appear in full regalia, with plumage and other riggings clearly shown. Tightly reined, high-stepping, they stand in precise formation and appear to move in unison. The musicians in the front row play a clapper drum, a mouth organ, and a panpipe. Those in the back row play a hand-held clapperless bell, a *jia* trumpet, and another panpipe. Among the identifiable instruments in other tiles are bells, gongs, horns, and pole drums, which were used in battle to send signals to the troops; part of the military band performance was a formalization of what was a functional battlefield use of noisemakers.

Textual descriptions emphasize the importance of rhythm making in all dance music, and the pictorial reliefs confirm this. Drums are always depicted in the feast scenes to accompany the dancers. Sometimes the dancers are shown playing hand-held clapper drums, and drums often outnumber other instruments in ensembles. Other percussion instruments, including stone chimes, bronze bells, clappers, and rattles, are frequently represented. In the "sundry show" relief, the dancer moves back and forth on top of rows of flat *pan* disc-drums. Texts describe the dance as a performance in which the dancer actually "plays" the disc-drums with his or her feet, at a remarkably fast pace, with widely varied rhythms, volumes, and articulation. The portrayal of the *pan* dancers in the Han tiles suggests a highly energetic, light, and swift-footed movement.

THE CULTURAL ORIGINS OF HAN MUSIC, INSTRUMENTS, AND ENTERTAINMENTS

In the Han court conservative ideologues sought to reconstruct the ritual music of the halcyon days of the Zhou, and in so doing, they rejected the extravagant and complex melodies and movements of unorthodox forms. Debates centered on technical issues in the ritual music and on the propriety of certain entertainments in the court. But some music lovers objected to the austerity of the orthodox forms, complaining they were boring and soporific. Thus, in spite of the protest of the ritualists, foreign or non-Han music was popular even at the center of Chinese culture. In the world of arts and letters, music proved to be the best medium of cultural exchange.

An interesting story about Liu Bang illustrates how non-Han or non-Chinese dances were brought into the Han court and became mixed with traditional Chinese music and dances. The story records the dance prowess of early non-Han residents of the Sichuan plain and emphasizes that dance was a common entertainment at a feast. Records beginning with the *Hou Han shu* (History of the Later Han) tell of Liu Bang's campaign against the state of Chu, key battles of which were carried out in the old state of Ba, part of present-day Sichuan. Liu Bang was assisted by fierce fighters from Ba's minority tribes, and when he triumphed over Chu, he witnessed the dance of the Ba minority tribes at a victory banquet—a dance referred to as the *Bayu*. As Liu Bang watched the dancers perform, he saw in them the kind of fervor and courage that he associated with the victory of the Zhou founder King Wu over the last Shang king. He was so moved by the martial zeal and virtues of the *Bayu* dance that he decided to make it an official Han court dance.[14]

Dances and music from outlying areas are mentioned here and there in the annals of the Han emperors. Emperor Ling, for example, was said to be particularly fond of *Hu* dances and *Hu* music.[15] The intercultural influences enriched and invigorated Han music and dances. An association with central Asia is borne out by the Sichuan relief of "Drummers on Camel," in which the camel carries a pole drum complete with pennant cap (plate 53). The camel is clearly an import from northwest

China or central Asia, while the pole drum is one of the oldest known indigenous Chinese instruments. The mixing of cultural traditions in Sichuan is well illustrated by this pictorial relief, a unique discovery according to the Chinese archaeologists' reports.

The Han continued and expanded an administrative agency started during the Qin dynasty, the music bureau called *Yuefu*, to organize the court ritual, collect folk music from outside the court, train musicians, and develop entertainment repertories for the aristocracy. The *Yuefu* had as its primary responsibility maintenance of the ritual traditions, but it responded to the interests of the emperors, the tastes of the aristocracy, and the inclinations of its own top leaders. The *Yuefu* encouraged new musical forms, but not necessarily those of the conventional tastes. Shortly before the turn of the millennium the *Yuefu* repertory had become so dominated by unorthodox entertainments that its music was likened to the music of the degenerate states of Zheng and Wei of the Zhou dynasty, and its activities and resources were sharply curtailed.[16]

During the first two hundred years of the Han, before the curtailment of the *Yuefu*, a number of non-Han instruments, primarily from nomadic peoples of the northwest, became very popular in court and in urban settings. Influential Han imports included the *jia* reed trumpet and the *pipa* lute. The *jia*, mentioned previously in connection with the mounted military music, was a wooden or bamboo horn driven by a leaf reed. The *jia* was loud, a suitable battlefield instrument. The *pipa* was one of several fretted string instruments imported during the Han. The vertical harp, called *hu konghou*, "barbarian harp," came into China during the second century A.D. Non-Han influence on more basic instruments, especially the vertical and horizontal flutes, is more difficult to assess. References to both *di*-style horizontal flutes and *xiao*-style vertical flutes predate the Han, but both were probably influenced in size and shape by central Asian instruments. The vertical flute may be seen in the pottery figure of the flute player (plate 43) in the exhibition.

Inasmuch as the Han unified a larger portion of the Chinese continent than any previous administration and maintained power for nearly four hundred years, it provided the communication and transportation to facilitate massive cultural exchange between the court and a variety of non-Han frontier civilizations. In the examples introduced thus far, we have seen that fascination with foreign music and entertainments was shared by both the court and the common people. Conversely, we see from the Sichuan pictorial tomb reliefs that traditional Han instruments and entertainments were well entrenched in the southwest as well; this suggests that in music and entertainment the native and the non-native mixed with ease. Along with the music came an assortment of jugglers, acrobats, and conjurers who practiced their arts inside and outside of court. The multicultural flavor of Han music and entertainments is well documented in the Sichuan archaeological objects.

In the Han court and in public circles ritual music had an identity distinct from secular music and entertainments. Yet ritual and secular interacted in much the same way as Han and non-Han. The emperor and the common people followed an annual calendar of ritual events, many of which had substantial musical content. In the higher echelons of society the ritual music of the emperor is associated with the impressive stone chimes and massive sets of bronze bells sometimes illustrated in Han tomb reliefs and frequently recovered from pre-Han tombs. These are instruments the Han associated with their own archaic ancestry, the instruments of their sage forefathers. They were the embodiment of just and proper musical values and were therefore important moral instruments for the rulers of the state. Festivals surrounding the New Year in particular included extensive music and dance related to year-end exorcistic practices, both at the court and among the populace. Animal dancing was related to Han exorcistic dances among the court performers and common people, even though they were also performed in the entertainment arenas.

The Han burial goods and pictorial reliefs have been indispensable in reconstructing the daily life of the Han Chinese some two thousand years ago. Of all the arts, performance arts—including music and dance—are perhaps the most challenging to reconstruct because these arts are essentially without artifacts and are not well preserved in scores and written descriptions. However, when the pictorial depictions are studied in conjunction with the musical instruments recovered from the tombs, they bring to life those otherwise fleeting moments of pleasure and entertainments enjoyed by the Han in the distant past.

How are we to understand the presence of the sculptured musician figures and the numerous pictorial representations of entertainment in the Han tombs? During the Han the belief prevailed that the human body possessed two souls, a grosser *bo* soul, that was always earthbound, and a lighter *hun* soul, that could flee the grave for higher places.[17] Some scholars therefore argue that figures of entertainers made the tomb a more attractive place for the *hun* soul so as to slow the dissolution of the physical remains. Others suggest that the *bo* soul was kept satisfied with abundant burial goods, thus preventing it from wandering and causing mischief among the living. Still another theory emphasizes the provision of lavish burial goods as an expression of the status needs of the living descendants, the patrons of the tombs. There is no doubt that the burial goods were provided for the needs and comforts of the deceased owner in his afterlife whatever the specific motives for the creation of these objects and reliefs.

The significance of Han burial goods, especially representations of performers, must also be assessed in light of the historical background, especially the evolving practice of substituting sculptured figures made of clay or wood for human sacrificial victims. By the Han, tomb furnishings as well as figurines had evolved from the actual to the representative and symbolic. The figurines, the furnishings, and the pictorial scenes decorating the tomb walls often evoked activities of daily life the deceased owner had enjoyed while alive. In their use of these objects and reliefs as substitutes for the real, the Han reveal a rather optimistic view of death. After all, the tomb was not a silent vault but a chamber in which many of life's sensual pleasures, including the pleasures of music and dance, could continue to be enjoyed.

NOTES

1. John Steele, *The "I'li," or Book of Etiquette and Ceremonial*, 2 vols. (London, 1917; reprint, Taipei, 1966), 150–67; and Walter Kaufman, *Musical References in the Chinese Classics* (Detroit, 1976), 173–92.
2. Kenneth DeWoskin, *A Song for One or Two: Music and the Concept of Art in Early China* (Ann Arbor, 1982), 21–24.
3. *Shiji*, 99; and *Han shu*, 43. References to these dynastic histories are to the Beijing Zhonghua shuju editions.
4. *Shiji*, 7.312–13, in Burton Watson, trans., *Records of the Grand Historian of China*, 2 vols. (New York, 1961), 1:52.
5. Jan Fontein and Wu Tung, *Han and T'ang Murals* (Boston, 1976), 22; Yü Ying-shih, "Han," in *Food in Chinese Culture: Anthropological and Historical Perspectives*, ed. K. C. Chang (New Haven, 1977), 63–67.
6. Yan Kejun, *Quan Shanggu Sandai Qin Han Sanguo Liuchao wen* (Complete writings of High Antiquity, Three Dynasties, Qin, Han, and Six Dynasties), 5 vols. (Beijing, 1958), 705–6, 769.
7. David Knechtges, trans., *Wen xuan or Selections of Refined Literature* (Princeton, 1982), vol. 1, *Rhapsodies on Metropolises and Capitals*, 228–33.
8. An interesting comparative example of a Han banquet is pictured on a Han mural from the Dahuting tomb in Mixian, Henan. For a detailed discussion of the banquet, see Yü Ying-shih, "The Seating Order at the Hong Men Banquet," in *The Translation of Things Past: Chinese History and Historiography*, ed. George Kao (Hong Kong, 1982), 49–61.
9. *Han shu*, 97; Ch'u T'ung-tsu, *Han Social Structures* (Seattle, 1972), 151.
10. The objects and human remains unearthed from the tomb of Marquis Yi of Zeng, interred in 433 B.C., included the remains of twenty-one young women ranging from fifteen to twenty-one years of age, probably dancers and musicians. Elaborate sets of rare musical instruments were also buried with the owner.
11. There exists a considerable body of *qin* lore extolling this feature of the instrument. See DeWoskin, *Song for One or Two*, 101–51.
12. Derk Bodde, *Festivals in Classical China: New Year and Other Annual Observances During the Han Dynasty 206 B.C.–A.D. 220* (Princeton, 1975), 75–138.
13. Zhang Heng, "Western Metropolis Rhapsody," in Knechtges, *Rhapsodies*, 233–34. An expanded description is in *Xijing zaji*.
14. *Hou Han shu*, 116 (references to this dynastic history are to the Beijing Zhonghua shuju edition); and Yang Yinliu, *Zhongguo gudai yinyue shigao* (Draft history of ancient Chinese music), 2 vols. (Beijing, 1980), 120.
15. Fei Bingxun, "*Gudai wudao shihua*" (History of ancient dance), pts. 1 and 2, in *Wudao* (Dance), nos. 3 and 4, 1981.
16. DeWoskin, *A Song for One or Two*, 92–94.
17. For additional discussion of Han concepts of the afterlife, see Anna Seidel, "Tokens of Immortality in Han Graves," *Numen* 29, no. 1 (1982): 79–114.

MYTHS AND LEGENDS IN HAN FUNERARY ART:
Their Pictorial Structure and Symbolic Meanings as Reflected in Carvings on Sichuan Sarcophagi

by
Wu Hung

Engraved on the walls of underground tomb chambers, inside burial caves, and on stone sarcophagi, carvings in low relief vividly depict the ancient myths and legends popular in Sichuan during the Han dynasty. Scholars have studied the sources of these stories and their conclusions have provided invaluable evidence for the history of Chinese literature, religion, and mythology. Rather than restrict myself to literary identifications, I propose to interpret the pictorial and ideological relationships between the stories and to show that, even though the stories were based on divergent sources, they form a coherent pictorial structure. These tomb carvings reveal the distinctive significance of myth and folklore in Sichuan funerary art and the way in which this art reorganizes stories from the literary and oral traditions according to its own demands.

THE BAOZISHAN AND WANG HUI SARCOPHAGI: STRUCTURAL KEYS TO COFFIN CARVINGS

Since Victor Segalen found the first sarcophagus (stone coffin) during his expedition to Sichuan from 1914 to 1917,[1] many coffins have been recovered from excavations, demonstrating the great popularity of coffin burial in Sichuan during the Han. Many of these coffins are made of wood or clay, while others are carved out of a single block of red sandstone, with flat, arched, or roof-shaped lids. The most elaborate ones are engraved with ornaments and narrative scenes. More than twenty-five of these complete pictorial coffins have been discovered, along with many fragments.[2] They may be roughly divided into three stages of development according to their decorative features.

During the first stage, which occurred around the mid-Later Han dynasty, carvings depict decorative motifs without any narrative content.[3] Coffins belonging to the second stage, towards the end of Later Han, show a far more complicated and sophisticated decorative style in their themes and artistic quality. The best works of this period are exemplified by those from Xinjin and attest to the flourishing pictorial art of Sichuan. In their style these carvings substantiate Paul Pelliot's contention that "Han sculpture in Sichuan has quite a different character from what it has in Shandong; it is more spontaneous and more alive."[4] More important to the present study, these carvings also display a large variety of mythological and historical narratives. This style, however, changed dramatically around the end of the Han. Coffins belonging to the third stage show few narrative elements in decoration; instead, they are carved with isolated mythical animals organized into a more abstract symbolic structure. The Baozishan and Wang Hui sarcophagi are excellent examples of the second and third stages of this development.

Unfortunately, all the Xinjin sarcophagi had been cut into pieces and sold by antique merchants before 1949.[5] Today the coffin from Baozishan (which was reconstructed) is the only extant example of a pictorial composition in its entirety. Scenes are carved on the four sides and the top. The front is decorated with a *que* pillar gate through which a rider holding a banner enters (plate 57a). The rear depicts a pair of deities, Fu Xi and Nü Wa, identified by their characteristic iconography: they have human bodies and intertwined serpentine tails and hold up the sun and the moon with their hands (plate 57b). One side of the coffin represents two runners guiding a carriage procession toward a gate (plate 57c). The other side shows two separate scenes, each consisting of two figures. The scene on the left depicts a familiar Sichuan motif: two immortals kneel at a gaming board playing *liubo* with excitement (plate 57d). The scene on the right represents two men, one playing the *qin* zither and the other listening (plate 57e). A vulture-like bird flies towards the two men from the left, and a mythical beast, perhaps a winged dragon, appears on the right, balancing the image of the bird. The scholar Richard Rudolph has identified this scene as the story of the legendary musician Yu Boya.[6] The top of the coffin is decorated with a large, elaborate pictorial composition, dominated by two intertwined tree branches on which a pair of large elaborate birds rest in symmetrical fashion (plate 57c). Smaller birds are scattered throughout the scene. Below the tree branches, an archer draws his bow and aims at one of the birds. As has been suggested by scholars, this represents the story of Yi shooting down the nine false suns.[7]

This description of the pictorial decoration of the Baozi-shan coffin offers identifications of the individual motifs. Several questions arise, however. Why were these motifs especially favored by the Sichuan people during the Han? Did these motifs have any specific meanings in a ritual context? What is the relationship between individual motifs? Art historians have proposed that these questions could be answered only by comprehending the entire pictorial complex—that is, its pictorial program or context. The larger pictorial composition rather than the individual motifs is directly linked with the symbolic context and gives special meaning to the motifs.

As Wilma Fairbank stated forty-five years ago in her pioneering paper, "The Offering Shrines of 'Wu Liang Tz'u'": "The interrelationships and positional significance of the engraved stones is lost when they are studied as scattered slabs or rubbings. A grasp of this positional significance will be shown to illuminate subject matter at present obscure."[8] Here the term *positional significance* means the significance of a given motif, as defined by its position in an entire pictorial composition containing several other motifs and corresponding to the form of a ritual structure. A pictorial motif did not exist independently but was purposefully composed together with other motifs to decorate a funerary object—a coffin—and thus, a symbolic structure underlies its pictorial scheme.

The motif of the *que* pillar gate on the front of the Baozi-shan coffin appears in the same position on many other Sichuan sarcophagi. It represents the pillar gate in Han cemeteries that marked the entrance of the *mingfu*, "the Dark House," and flanked a road called the *shendao*, "the path of the soul." Such pillars were built in both imperial mausoleums and graveyards for some of the wealthy.[9] Historical records tell us that during a royal funerary ceremony a mourning procession carried the coffin of the deceased emperor through this gate, along the *shendao*, and then buried him in the tomb located at the end of the path. During the monthly sacrifices, a procession escorted the crown and clothes of the emperor through this gate to his temple.[10] Thus, the *que* pillar gate scene symbolizes the passage of the soul of the deceased into the spiritual world. This explains why the *que* pillar gate and a "greeting" figure are often carved on the front of a coffin. It also provides an interpretation for the arrangement of the pictorial scenes in Yangzishan Han tomb number one (see Appendix). A pair of double-roofed *que* pillars decorate the walls of the antechamber at the entrance, thus forming a "gate" leading into the tomb itself.

The simple *que* motif may perhaps be viewed as a condensed version of a larger procession or greeting scenes in which carriages proceed toward a door and are welcomed by officials. Such procession scenes are common in Han funerary carvings and have been interpreted by some scholars as representations of journeys taken by the deceased when they were alive. In some cases such interpretations may be accurate, depending on the pictorial context. A newly excavated inscription, however, provides a different interpretation: "[You, the honorable deceased, and your assistants] ride in small chariots. One follows the other, galloping to a rest-house. An officer entitled *youxi* waits there and comforts you. At the end of the procession, the ram-pulled car symbolizes [your] coffin, while divine birds fly above in floating clouds."[11]

While this inscription clearly indicates the symbolic or ritual significance of the procession scene as the journey of the tomb occupant's soul into a spiritual world, the union of Fu Xi and Nü Wa depicted on the rear transforms the coffin into a microcosm of the universe. These two deities read almost like a diagram of *yin* and *yang*, the two universal forces. This is suggested not only by their different genders and joining tails but also by the celestial orbs they hold in their hands. Fu Xi supports the sun with his left hand and Nü Wa supports the moon with her left hand. Inside the moon is a hare, and inside the sun, a bird. According to Han mythology, these creatures inhabit the cosmic symbols of the sun and moon.[12] All these images represent the abstract principle of opposition and are depicted in an almost perfectly symmetrical fashion.

On the top of the Baozishan coffin, the concept of heaven is represented by the legend of the divine archer Yi. According to the story, after a series of victories Yi went east, where he discovered a gigantic *fusang* tree; on the tree were ten golden birds blowing fire to form ten suns whose heat was burning up all living creatures. He shot nine arrows in succession and struck the birds; the nine suns immediately turned into red clouds and melted away.[13] In works of Han art, such as offering shrines, this composition is always depicted as corresponding to the east, because the legend is connected with the sun myth.[14] In the basic framework of Han thinking known as the *yin-yang* and Five Elements theory, this composition belonged to the *yang* side and was the symbol of the sun, the sky, and the east—as opposed to the *yin* side, symbolized by the moon, the earth, and the west. Because of its association with the sun and the sky, the legend of archer Yi is appropriately placed on the top of the coffin to symbolize the celestial world.

In general, the motifs carved on the lids of Sichuan sarcophagi are celestial scenes. These include the flying dragons and a beautiful representation of "The Weaving Maid and the Cowherd" legend found on a coffin from Pixian county (plate 56). The kernel of this famous legend first appeared in the *Book of Odes*.[15] In a Han poem we find a more elaborate version:

> Far away twinkles the Herd-boy star;
> Brightly shines the Lady of the Han River.

> Slender, slender she plies her white fingers;
> Click, click go the wheels of her spinning loom.
> At the end of the day she has not finished her task;
> Her bitter tears fall like streaming rain.
> The Han River runs shallow and clear;
> Set between them, how short a space!
> But the river water will not let them pass,
> Gazing at each other but never able to speak.[16]

During the same period the legend began to be depicted in pictorial scenes such as the one seen on the Pixian coffin. In this scene the weaving maid on the right holds what appears to be a spinning loom in one hand and waves a piece of silk in the other. On the left the herdboy pulls his ox furiously toward the maid, as befits an impetuous young lover. A large empty space stretches between them, intended perhaps to evoke the Han River or the Milky Way, described in the poem as linking, yet mercilessly separating, the two lovers. The literary description has been beautifully transformed into an emblematic visual expression.

The celestial associations of both "Yi Shooting the False Suns" and "The Weaving Maid and the Cowherd" determine their decorative position on the coffins. Following the same logic, the ceilings of Han funerary shrines in other parts of China are also decorated with celestial or mythological scenes.[17] This pictorial scheme strongly suggests that the shrines and coffins symbolically represented the universe of the deceased. For the Han people, as for people of all times and all places, the universe was delineated by heaven above and earth below.

An analysis of the Baozishan sarcophagus provides a structural key to this pictorial program: A gate opens at the front through which a rider guides the soul of the deceased into another world—the world defined by the cosmic symbols of sun and moon, Fu Xi and Nü Wa, and by the celestial scenes on the top. The pictorial program is coherent and clearly comprehensible. The same symbolic structure underlies the decoration of the Wang Hui sarcophagus; the pictorial motifs that the artist employed, however, differ from those displayed on the Baozishan coffin.

The Wang Hui sarcophagus, found in a brick tomb in Lushan county in 1940, is the only known Han sarcophagus inscribed with an epitaph (plate 69a): "The deceased Steward of Accounts, Wang Hui, styled Bozhao, died in the last decade of the ninth month of the sixteenth or *xinmou* year of the *Jian'an* era (A.D. 221). He was buried on the *jiaxu* day of the sixth month of the seventeenth year (A.D. 222). Alas!"[18] During Han times the burial day of the deceased was chosen according to ritual calendars. It was believed that the correct day could bring good fortune to the deceased's family.[19] This is probably why Wang Hui was buried one year after his death.

According to the inscribed date, the Wang Hui sarcophagus was made about a half century later than the Baozishan coffin. The shape of this sarcophagus (plate 70) differs markedly from earlier examples and resembles the fashion of later Chinese coffins, which had heavy lids with a waved surface. Compared to the complicated narrative scenes on the Baozishan coffin, the decoration is considerably simplified, consisting of isolated figures and beasts rendered in round relief against an empty background. Two divine animals, the Blue Dragon and the White Tiger, are depicted in a symmetrical fashion on both sides, with similar lengthened bodies and arched tails (plates 70d and 70e). In Han cosmology these two beasts are symbols of the east and the west respectively. Depicted on the rear is the union of a snake and a tortoise—the symbol of the north (plate 70c). Thus, like the decoration of the Baozishan sarcophagus, the design of the Wang Hui coffin clearly reflects the desire to transform the coffin into a cosmic structure. The coffin was originally placed inside the brick tomb so that the front faced south: the symbolic beasts were thus arranged to correspond with the four cardinal directions.

According to this decorative scheme, the front of the coffin should depict the Red Bird, the symbol of the south. But since this section of the coffin had to represent the entrance through which the soul of the deceased entered the other world, the scheme was altered. On the front of the Wang Hui sarcophagus, a divine maiden emerges from a half-opened door (plate 70a). She holds a leaf of the door and seems to be about to open it for the soul of Wang Hui. The symbolism of this scene, there-

fore, resembles the *que* pillar gate engraved in the same position on the Baozishan coffin. Significantly, a wing is growing from her right shoulder and feather-like patterns striate her leg. These features may mark an attempt to merge this anthropomorphic figure with the Red Bird or to identify her as an immortal welcoming the deceased to the immortal paradise.

THE WORLD OF IMMORTALITY AND EARTHLY DESIRES

People of the Han longed to enter the paradise of immortality after death; nevertheless, death represented a stage beyond their lived experience and was a constant source of fear. The darkness where the deceased would enter might be full of harmful ghosts, spirits, and wild beasts, and the soul might encounter great dangers on its journey to the immortal paradise. Such fears had become the central motivation behind various shamanistic practices aimed to guide or to protect the soul in a world unknown. Before the idea of a transcendent paradise had been fully developed, a happy conclusion might simply have been for the soul to return to its old body. The concrete expression of such a belief is found in "Zhaohun" (Summoning the soul) and "Dazhao" (The great summons) in *Chu Ci* (Elegies of Chu). These two poems, in the form of shamanistic prayers, were written during the Eastern Zhou. The idea of immortality had already emerged at this time but it was assumed that it could be reached only through the arduous self-cultivation of philosophers or through a ruler's costly discovery of an overseas immortal land, such as the Three Islands of the Blessed in the Eastern Sea.

During the Han the idea of summoning the soul and the idea of immortality were amalgamated in popular beliefs dealing with death. People were now convinced that immortality was not the exclusive pursuit of philosophers or emperors who possessed great intelligence or wealth: immortality could also be achieved by an ordinary person, whose soul would enter the realm of Xiwangmu, the "Queen Mother of the West." There it could enjoy happiness greater than in any earthly abode. As this immortality cult rose to an unprecedented height, representations of Xiwangmu and the western paradise came to be found on many Han tombs, offering shrines, and coffins.

Even so, the old belief in summoning the soul was still deeply rooted and the old assumption that the most pleasant dwelling place for the soul was the deceased's homeland continued. This paradox led to a dualism in Sichuan funerary art. On the one hand, this art reflects the desire that the deceased be transported to a transcendent immortal paradise. On the other hand, the world of the deceased was also depicted as an extension of his former life and, more importantly, as an idealized model of the secular world: death would permit the deceased to enjoy that which he had been deprived of during his lifetime. He would live in elaborate halls served by numerous attendants and feast on delicacies while watching colorful performances. An ideal society would be realized in death, a society regulated by the highest social and moral values of Confucian teachings. The elaborate banquet scenes, carriage processions, and Confucian morality tales illustrated in funerary art enact these earthly desires.

Myths and Legends of Immortality

On Sichuan sarcophagi the central figure most frequently depicted in the paradise scenes is Xiwangmu "Queen Mother of the West." The tale of Xiwangmu may have developed from antiquity; some scholars believed that the worship of this goddess can be traced back to the Shang.[20] In the writings of Zhuangzi and Xunzi, the two famous philosophers of the Eastern Zhou, she was described as timeless and deathless. During the Former Han Xiwangmu was further associated with Kunlun, an immortal land to the west. Shortly before the Christian era she became the subject of a religious cult. A mass movement, centered on the worship of the goddess, burst out in 3 B.C.

In the first month of the fourth year of the *Jianping* era, the population was running around in a state of alarm, each holding a stalk of straw or hemp, carrying them on and passing them to one another, saying that they were transporting the wand of the goddess's edict. Large numbers of persons, amounting to thousands, met in this way on the roadsides, some with dishevelled hair or going barefoot. Some of them broke down the barriers of gates by night; some clambered

over walls to make their way into [houses]; some harnessed teams of horses to carriages and rode at full gallop, setting up relay stations so as to convey the tokens. They passed through twenty-six commanderies and kingdoms, until they reached the capital city.

That summer the people came together, meeting in the capital and in the commanderies and kingdoms. In the village settlements, the lanes and paths across the fields, they held services and set up gaming boards; and they sang and danced in worship of Xiwangmu. They also passed round a written message, saying "The Queen Mother tells the people that those who wear this talisman will not die; let those who do not believe her words look down at the pivots on their gates, and there will be white hairs to show that this is true.[21]

Interestingly, we find many elements of this cult in the pictorial representations of Xiwangmu. Wearing a jade crown called a *sheng*, she is seated upon the dragon-and-tiger throne on Kunlun mountain, as if holding court before immortals and divine animals including a nine-tailed fox, an elixir-pounding hare, an immortal toad, and other attendants (plates 61, 62, and 63). Her worshipers hold long-stalked objects, presumably a stalk of straw or hemp—the wand of the goddess. In some reliefs the scene of immortals playing the game *liubo* is depicted (plate 69), reminiscent of the "gaming boards" used in the ceremonies of the Xiwangmu cult. As Xiwangmu's role in the cult of immortality expanded, her tale gradually integrated many other legends.

One of these legends pertains to the divine turtle believed to support on his back immortal mountains in the sea. The final version of this legend is found in *Lie Zi*, a philosophical work dated to the Six Dynasties period.[22] The prototype of the story, however, appeared during the Eastern Zhou in "Tianwen" (Heavenly questions), a poem attributed to Qu Yuan. Among other questions about the universe, we find these:

> When the Great Turtle dances along with an island on his back,
> How does he keep it steady?
> If he leaves the sea and walks over dry land,
> How does he move it?[23]

The legend of the turtle supporting an immortal island may have been based on the ancient belief that this reptile has power over water. Two passages from the same poem shed light on this belief. One states that when Gun, the father of Yu, was trying to regulate the Yellow River, he saw a procession of turtles walking beak to tail. He then built his dike on the path the turtles had indicated.[24] The other passage suggests that, in an effort to prevent flooding, Gun himself was transformed into a "yellow turtle."[25]

In the Han period the turtle legend was connected with the idea of immortality, just as the story of "The Weaving Maid and the Cowherd" had been. The islands borne by the turtle are identified as the three famous immortal mountains in the Eastern Sea. Liu Xiang remarked in his *Lie xian zhuan* (Biographies of immortals), "There is a giant divine turtle who dances and plays in the ocean with the immortal island Penglai on his back."[26] The Later Han poet, Zhang Heng, chanted in a *fu* rhapsody:

> Unworried,
> I step on immortal Penglai.
> The turtle dances,
> But keeps the island steady.[27]

The theme of the divine turtle was expressed in various media—dance, drama, architectural design, and pictorial carving.[28] On a side of the coffin from Pixian that is decorated with the Weaving Maid and the Cowherd on the top, fairies play the game *liubo* and auspicious birds and heavenly animals fly in the sky. A giant turtle walks toward this immortal land with a mountain island sitting on its back. Raising its head and brandishing its claws, the creature seems to be dancing in joy, just as Liu Xiang and Zhang Heng describe him.

Alongside the *liubo* scene on the Baozishan sarcophagus is the story of Yu Boya, the divine musician of ancient China (plate 57e). Boya's portrait, accompanied by an inscription with his name, sometimes decorates Han-type mirrors.[29] The Baozishan carving, however, is the only example of a stone relief depicting this story.

As early as the Eastern Zhou, Boya was considered the world's finest zither player. The philosopher Xunzi once mentioned that when Boya was playing the zither, even

horses raised their heads and laughed with enjoyment.[30] Towards the Qin dynasty, however, another version of the story was told. Boya's audience was no longer the horses but his bosom friend, Zhong Ziqi. Boya's tale of deep friendship and sorrow became one of the most beautiful Chinese legends.

Boya played the zither and Zhong Ziqi was the audience. As soon as Boya started playing he was transported to the Tai Mountains, and Ziqi sighed: "How wonderful is the music! It is as imposing as the Tai Mountains!" In a little while, Boya's mind shifted to the flowing river, and Ziqi was moved: "How graceful is the music! It is as vast as a flowing river!" After Ziqi died, Boya smashed his zither, cut the strings, and never played again in his life. He no longer had a soul mate in this world worthy of his music.[31]

Boya's story continued to develop during the Former Han,[32] and later the story was integrated with the popular idea of immortality. An additional episode relates that Boya's teacher, Cheng Lian, had transported his pupil to the Isles of the Immortals to perfect his technique.[33] The pictorial scene on the Baozishan coffin seems to represent this later version, showing Boya and Ziqi in an immortal paradise, next to the two immortals playing *liubo*.

Legends and Stories of Secular Ideology

As mentioned previously, some of the stories and images carved on the Sichuan coffins embody ideological values and meanings that differ from those related to immortality. These are illustrations of Confucian texts. The best example of a Confucian morality tale is the story of Qiu Hu's wife. This story is depicted on coffins from Xinjing in Sichuan (plate 55)[34] as well as on a carving from the Wu Liang shrine in Shandong (figure 13). Although the Wu Liang carving differs in style, its iconography closely resembles that of the coffin and inscriptions identify the names of the figures.

The story of Qiu Hu's wife, told in the Han text *Lie nü zhuan* (Biographies of outstanding women), was a celebrated exemplary model for women. Legend had it that she had been married only five days when her husband, Qiu Hu, who was from the state of Lu, had to leave home to take up office in the state of Chen. Five years later he returned. On his way home he saw a woman by the roadside picking mulberry leaves and he stopped to flirt with her. She happened to be his wife, but they did not recognize each other because of the long absence.

Qiu Hu was pleased with her and he descended from his carriage and spoke to her, saying, "as it is very hot to pick mulberries and I have come a long journey, I desire you to allow me to eat in the shade of the mulberry tree and to spread out my cloak to rest." The woman went on picking mulberries without stopping and [again] Qiu Hu spoke to her saying, "To labor in the field is not so good as to happen on one good harvest; to pick mulberries is not so good as visiting with the minister of the state. I have money that I desire to give you." The woman said, "Oh no! I use my strength to pick mulberries; I spin and weave in order to supply clothes and food; and I serve my parents-in-law and raise my husband's children. I do not want men's money; I had hoped that the minister would have no ulterior motive; and also I have no intention of giving in to lust. Take up your travelling cloak and your money![135]

In the Xinjin relief the setting is indicated by a mulberry tree on the left. A woman preoccupied with picking the leaves turns her head to respond to a man behind her, who seems to be conversing with her. She rejects his advances. The artist focuses on her virtue and deliberately avoids the tragic ending of the tale. After their meeting Qiu Hu returned home and learned that the woman he had met was his own wife. She upbraided him for being unrighteous and then cast herself into a river. Like many other Confucian tales about virtuous women and filial sons depicted in Han pictorial art, this didactic story treats problems of the secular world rather than the delights of the immortal world.

In Sichuan funerary art such Confucian tales are presented alongside motifs of immortality. This duality is also evident in the pictorial decorations of the Wu Liang shrine, where ancient emperors, sages, filial sons, and virtuous women are carved in orderly fashion on the walls, while images of Xiwangmu and other immortals decorate the gable (figure 17). The arrangement of the pictorial representations on the Wu Liang shrine clearly indicates that the wall scenes were intended to remind people of the figures who embodied the highest level of Confucian morality, the basic code of conduct during the Han. The images of immortals on the gables embodied people's dreams of eternal life or immortality. The

mingling of these two ideals—the worldly and the transcendent, the Confucian and the immortal—is common in Han art and appears in the Sichuan reliefs. The difference, however, is that the Confucian motifs are overwhelming in the Shandong reliefs such as the Wu Liang shrine, while in pictorial scenes from Sichuan, the immortality motif, which was often related to Daoist beliefs, predominates. This is understandable in light of the different religious histories of the two regions: the Shandong area was the heartland of Han Confucianism; Sichuan, on the other hand, was dominated by a form of religious Daoism known as the "Sect of the Five Pecks of Rice."

The distinctive religious and ideological values underlying Sichuan pictorial art explain its modification of "imported" imagery and selection of decorative motifs. For example, a coffin from Xinjin is carved with three groups of images on its side wall (plate 54). To the left are two figures, identified by the inscribed names Shen Nong and Cang Jie. In ancient mythology Shen Nong was venerated as the creator of agriculture and medicine, and Cang Jie, as the creator of writing. A portrait of Shen Nong also appears in the Wu Liang shrine, where this legendary figure is depicted as an emperor, wearing an imperial crown and a ritual costume. He is placed in a group of ancient sovereigns who symbolize the Confucian tradition. In the Sichuan relief, however, Shen Nong and Cang Jie are portrayed together as a pair of immortals or Daoist recluses and seem most interested in the "long-life" plants they have picked. The dramatic and delightful nature of such a "botanical outing" scene differs radically from the solemnity of the Wu Liang carving.

Next to Shen Nong and Cang Jie in the Sichuan scene are two other figures, identified by inscriptions as Confucius and Laozi. The picture represents a historical meeting between these two masters. According to *Shiji* (Historical records), written by the great Han historian Sima Qian, Confucius set out with a disciple to inquire about ritual affairs from Laozi, who at that time was a high dignitary in the Zhou capital of Luo-yang. Confucius obtained an audience with the old sage, who concluded the meeting with the following words of wisdom: "The rich of this world are accustomed to give presents to parting guests; wise men prefer to give them good advice. How many men who call themselves intelligent, close their eyes to their own pitiable state, in order to take pleasure in criticizing others; how many who pretend to be wise, hide from their own defects, and spend their lives haranguing the labors of others."[36]

In this passage Sima Qian, an admirer of Daoism, obviously emphasized the superiority of Laozi, who assumed the role of teacher. The meeting scene in the Xinjin carving clearly reveals the same idea in pictorial language, even though it discloses a conscious choice of a "Confucian" theme. In this scene it is the Confucian master who is represented as bowing and paying respect to Laozi. With both hands in his sleeves, Laozi is deferentially raising his head and watching the visitor.

There was a very different emphasis in Shandong. Portraits of Confucius were extremely popular in Shandong during the Later Han. The master and his seventy-two disciples were frequently portrayed in ritual buildings; his image became almost an icon of state worship. The "Meeting of Confucius and Laozi" carved on a Wu family shrine (figure 12) represents Laozi going out of the capital and greeting Confucius on the road as a token of respect.

These divergences in the same pictorial themes lead us to consider a general tendency regarding the transformation and localization of Han pictorial art. Although the decorative schemes of Sichuan coffins and Shandong funerary shrines share a mixture of Confucian and Daoist ideas on life and death, the pictorial traditions of these two regions emphasized different aspects. A number of pictorial motifs such as "Immortals Playing *Liubo*" and "The Divine Turtle Carrying an Immortal Mountain" occur only in the Han art of Sichuan and may be considered the innovations of Sichuan artists. The finest pictorial representations of stories such as "The Weaving Maid and the Cowherd" and "Bo Ya Playing the *Qin*" are also found in the Sichuan reliefs. These myths and legends are associated with Daoism and immortality. In contrast, the Confucian stories and images on the Sichuan coffins are considerably simplified, the imagery

revised, and the implications altered. These changes show that Sichuan artists followed the prevailing scheme of Han funerary art in their decoration of stone coffins, but they also responded to the special demands of their local patrons and the particular values of their own culture. Judging from the pictorial evidence, Daoist motifs were in greater demand than Confucian themes.

Han tomb reliefs were the anonymous and probably collective work of several artisans and were created for symbolic rather than for purely aesthetic purposes. Certain pictorial motifs were widespread and were duplicated from region to region and from generation to generation. But Han pictorial art also developed in different regions along various lines. The relationship with and the difference between Han narrative art and literature is also worth considering here, for many pictorial motifs depicted on the Sichuan reliefs are found in literature. When a story was transformed from the written or oral tradition into a pictorial representation on a coffin, the narrative content and meaning changed. An individual pictorial scene is meaningful on two levels, the literary and the ritual or symbolic. On one level a scene—such as the meeting between Qiu Hu and his wife or Yi shooting the false suns—tells the story by depicting a specific episode; it was assumed that even without an inscription, the rest of the plot would be reconstructed by the viewer who would have been familiar with the well-known story. An understanding of the plot would lead the viewer to comprehend the symbolic meaning of the picture in its ritual context. He would understand the celestial symbolism of the Yi legend and the Confucian morality embodied in the tale of Qiu Hu's wife. These individual scenes or motifs thus became elements of an overarching symbolic pictorial structure.

The examples discussed in this essay show that the pictorial scenes decorating Later Han coffins follow a structural program. The celestial scenes appear on the top. The entrance scene and cosmic symbols occupy the front and the rear respectively. Various combinations of motifs are depicted on the two sides of the coffins, but they always focus on specific themes such as the protection of the soul,[37] feasting and entertainment,[38] the world of immortality, and Confucian values. The repetition of pictorial scenes in different compositions suggests that sets of pictorial motifs existed and that a specific choice may have reflected the preferences of the artisan or the patron. The motif chosen nevertheless always belongs to one of the above categories and becomes a readily understood symbol. As symbols, the motifs embody certain general ideas and meanings, so that even if they are replaced by other motifs belonging to the same category, the whole structure will remain intact. These images, derived from different literary sources, powerfully create the illusion that the coffin is no longer a simple stone funerary box but a universe, a paradise, a temple, or a banquet hall inhabited by the deceased in the afterlife.

NOTES

1. Victor Segalen, *La sculpture et les monuments funéraires* (Provinces du Chan-si et du Sseu-tchouan, Mission archéologique en Chine 1914–1917) (Paris, 1923), plate LXVII.

Before 1958 scholars debated the function and the proper name of the "stone boxes" found in Sichuan. V. Segalen called them "sarcophagi"; Shang Chengzuo considered them containers of clothes and prized possessions of the deceased; He Changqun argued that their proper name should be *shi-chuang*, "stone bed." The latter opinion was further supported by Wen Yu. In 1958 Chinese archaeologists published the excavation report of the Han tomb in Tianhui Shan, Sichuan. They reported that "remains of a skeleton, as well as other artifacts," were found inside such stone boxes. This report proves that these boxes were used as coffins during the Han and thus seems to clinch the argument. Cf. Richard C. Rudolph, *Han Tomb Art of West China* (Berkeley and Los Angeles, 1951), 8; Wen Yu, *Sichuan Handai huaxiang xuanji* (A selection of Han pictorial carvings from Sichuan) (Beijing, 1955), 1–2; Shang Chengzuo, "Sichuan Xinjin dengdi Han yamu zhuanmu kaolue" (On Han cave tombs and brick tombs at Xinjin and other places in Sichuan), *Jinling xuebao* 10 (1940): 1–18; He Changqun, *Sichuan de Mandong yu Xiangxi de yamu* ("Barbarian caves" in Sichuan and cave tombs in West Hunan) (1940); Liu Zhiyuan, "Chengdu Tianhuishan yamu qingliji" (The excavation of the cave tomb at Tianhuishan in Chengdu), *Kaogu xuebao*, no. 1 (1958): 91.

2. Segalen, *La Sculpture*; Chang Renxia, "Chongqing fujin faxian zhi Han-dai yamu yu shique yanjiu" (A study of cave tombs and stone pillars found near Chongqing), reprinted in *Chang Renxia yishu kaogu lunwen xuanji* (A selection of Chang Renxia's art and archaeological studies) (Beijing, 1984), 9–14; "Chongqing Shapingba chutu zhi shiguan huaxiang yanjiu" (A study of the pictorial carvings on the stone coffin unearthed at Shapingba), reprinted in *Chang Renxia yishu*, 1–8; Shang, "Sichuan Xinjin"; He, *Sichuan de Mandons*; Ren Naiqiang, "Lushan xinchutu Han shi kao" (On the Han stone carvings newly unearthed at Lushan), *Kangdao yuekan* 4, nos. 6 & 7 (1942): 13–32; Ren Naiqiang "Bian Wang Hui shiguan fudiao" (An examination of the bas-reliefs on the Wang Hui stone coffin), *Kangdao*

yuekan 5, no. 1 (1943): 7–17; Liu, "Chengdu Tianhuishan"; Wu Zhongshi, "Sichuan Yibin Han mu qingli henduo chutu wenwu" (Many cultural relics have been unearthed from Han tombs in Yibin, Sichuan), *Wenwu cankao ciliao*, no. 12 (1954): 190; Kuang Yingda, "Sichuan Yibinshi Cuipingcun Hanmu qinglijianbao" (A brief excavation report of the Han tombs at Cuiping village in Yibin, Sichuan), *Kaogu tongxun*, no. 3 (1957): 20–25; Lan Feng, "Sichuan Yibinxian yamu huanxiang shiguan" (The pictorial stone coffins from cave tombs at Yibin, Sichuan), *Wenwu*, no. 7 (1982): 24–27; Xun Bing, *Sichuan Handai diaoso xuanji* (A selection of Han sculptures from Sichuan) (Beijing, 1959); Li Fuhau and Guo Ziyou, "Pixian chutu Donghan huanxiang shiguan lueshuo" (On the Eastern Han pictorial coffins from Pixian county), *Wenwu*, no. 8 (1975): 63–65; The Sichuan Provincial Museum and Pixian Cultural House, "Sichuan Pixian Donghan zhuanmu de shiguan huaxiang" (Pictorial carvings on the stone coffins from an Eastern Han brick tomb at Pixian, Sichuan); Lu Deliang, "Sichuan Neijing Faxian Donghan zhuanmu" (The excavation of an Eastern Han brick tomb in Neijiang, Sichuan), *Kaogu tongxun*, no. 2 (1957): 54–57; T. K. Cheng, *Archaeological Studies in Szechuan* (Cambridge, 1957), 222, plate 24; Gao Wen, "Xunli duocai de huaxiangshi—Sichuan jiefanghou faxian de wuge shiguanguo" (On the five stone coffins found after 1949 in Sichuan), *Sichuan wenwu*, no. 1 (1985): 12–18.

3. Cf. Xin Lixiang, *Han huaxiangshi de fengi he fengu* (A periodization and regionalization of Han pictorial carvings) (Master's thesis, Beijing University, 1982), 65.

4. From a passage quoted in Rudolph, *Han Tomb Art*, 17.

5. According to Wen Yu, all coffins found at Xinjin before 1949 had been cut into pieces by antique merchants who then sold them in Chengdu. Wen, *Sichuan Handai*, interpretation of fig. *ding*.

6. Rudolph, *Han Tomb Art*, 28–29.

7. Ibid., 28; Wen, *Sichuan Handai*, interpretation of fig. 31.

8. W. Fairbank, "The Offering Shrines of 'Wu Liang tz'u'," *Harvard Journal of Asiatic Studies* 6, no. 1: 3. Pat Berger expressed a similar idea in *Rites and Festivities in the Art of Eastern Han China* (Microfilm of Ph.D. diss., University of Michigan, Ann Arbor), 179.

9. Cf. *Gu jin zhu* (Commentaries on antiquity and the present), quoted in Fan Ye's *Hou Han shu* (History of the Later Han) (Beijing, 1965), 3149–3150; Yang Shuda, *Handai hunsang lisu kao* (An examination of marital and funerary ritual customs of the Han dynasty) (Shanghai, 1933), 172–78.

10. Cf. "Biography of Shusun Tong" in Ban Gu's *Han shu* (History of the Former Han) (Beijing, 1962), 2130.

11. Cf. Li Falin, *Shandong Han huaxiangshi yanjiu* (A study of Han pictorial carvings from Shandong) (Jinan, 1982), 97.

12. Cf. T. K. Cheng, "Yin-Yang Wu-Hsing and Han Art," *Harvard Journal of Asiatic Studies* 20, nos. 1&2 (June 1957): 182.

13. The story is recorded in the "Ban Jing Xun" chapter in *Huai Nan Zi* and in the "Zhao Hun" and "Tian Wen" in *Chu Ci*, attributed to Qu Yuan. Cf. Yuan Ke, *Zhongguo gudai shenhua* (The ancient mythology of China) (Shanghai, 1957), 173–86.

14. Cf. Fairbank, "Offering Shrines," 35.

15. Cf. A. Waley, *The Book of Songs* (1937), 319.

16. Translated by A. Waley in *Chinese Poems* (London, 1982), 53–54. Scholars have suggested that a more advanced version of the "Weaving Maid and the Cowherd" legend had existed during the Former

Han. One source in the *Huai Nan zi* states that "Black magpies fill up the Milky Way, and thus enable the Weaving Maid to cross the heavenly river." A passage from the *Fengshu tongyi* says that "The Weaving Maid crosses the Han River at night every July Seventh, and she has magpies construct a bridge." See Li Jianguo, *Tanggian zhiguai xiaoshuo shi* (A History of pre-Tang "Zhiguai" stories) (Tianjin, 1984), 409. However, these two passages are both absent from the present texts and were cited by authors of the Tang dynasty. Their authenticity still remains open to question.

17. Jiang Yingju and Wu Wenqi, "Wu shi ci huaxiangshi jianzhu beizhi kao" (On the architectural restoration of the pictorial stones from the Wu family shrines), *Kaogu xuebao* 2 (1981): 181.

18. Based on Rudolph's translation in *Han Tomb Art*, 32.

19. Cf. Yang, *Handai hunsang*, 145.

20. The development of the Xiwangmu tale has been discussed by many scholars. Two recent discussions can be found in Kominami Ichiro, *Toho Gakuho* 46 (1974): 33–82; M. Loewe, *Ways to Paradise* (Cambridge, 1979), ch. 4, 86–126.

21. Based on Loewe's translation in *Ways to Paradise*, 99.

22. This dating is based on Yang Bojun's opinion in *Lie Zi jishi* (A general commentary on *Lie Zi*) (Shanghai, 1958), 224–43.

23. Based on D. Hawkes's translation in *Ch'u Tz'u, the Songs of the South* (Boston, 1959), 51.

24. Ibid., 48.

25. Ibid., 50.

26. This passage from *Lie xian zhuan* is quoted by Wang Yi in his commentary on *Chu Ci*. Cf. Zhu Xi, *Chu Ci jizhu* (A general commentary on the *Chu Ci*) (Shanghai, 1979), 61–62.

27. Zhang Heng, "Si Xuan Fu" in *Han Wei Liu-chao bai-san jia ji* (An anthology of one hundred and three masters of the Han, Wei, and Six Dynasties), 11: 19a.

28. The "Music" chapter in the *History of the Jin* records two performances, called *shen-gui-pu-wu*, "the divine turtle's dance," and *bei-fu-ling-yue*, "carrying the divine mountain on one's back," which are evidently related to the turtle legend. Cf. Fang Xuanling, *Jin shu* (History of the Jin dynasty) (Beijing, 1974), 718. Ban Gu describes the Shang-lin Garden: "Within it there were: Giant soft-shelled turtles. . . ." Cf. D. R. Knechtges, trans., *Wen Xuan or Selections of Refined Literature* (Princeton, 1982), 211.

29. Cf. Rudolph, *Han Tomb Art*, 28.

30. Cf. Wang Xianqian, *Xun Zi jijie* (A general commentary on *Xun Zi*) (1891), 1: 7a. The interpretation of the text here is based on Gao You's commentary on *Huai Nan zi*. Cf. Liu Wendian, *Huai Nan hong lie jijie* (A general commentary on *Huai Nan zi*) (Shanghai, 1923), 16: 2.

31. Lü Buwei, *Lü Shi chun qiu*, "Ben Wei." Cf. Xu Weiju, *Lü Shi chun qiu jishi* (A general commentary on *Lü Shi chun qiu*) (Beijing, 1954), 14: 6. The same passage also appears in the *Kong Zi jia yu* cited in *Tai ping yu lan* (Beijing, 1960), 577: 2605.

32. Cf. Yang Shuda, *Huai Nan zi zhengwen* (Testimony of *Huai Nan Zi*) (Beijing, 1957), 117. Two versions of Boya's story coexisted during the Former Han. The earlier one was followed by *Huai Nan zi*, while the later version appeared in Liu Xiang's *Shuo yuan*. Cf. Yu Jiaxi, *Shuo yuan buzheng* (Supplementary verification of *Shuo yuan*) (Taipei, 1955), 84–85.

33. The story about Boya and his teacher Cheng Lian first appeared in *Yue fu jie ti* and is cited in *Tai ping yu lan*, 578: 2608.

34. In addition to the scene discussed in the text, another slab from Xijin shows a similar composition that may be also identified as the story of Qiu Hu's wife. See Rudolph, *Han Tomb Art*, no. 38.

35. Based on A. R. O'Hara's translation in *The Position of Woman in Early China* (Westport, 1945), 141–42.

36. Based on H. Dore's translation in *Researches into Chinese Superstitions*, trans. L. F. McGreal (Taipei, 1967), 13:21.

37. I have discussed pictures of Sichuan coffins concerning the motif "warding-off evil" in "The Earliest Pictorial Representations of Ape Tales—An Interdisciplinary Study of Early Chinese Narrative Art and Literature," *T'oung Pao* 73, no. 1–3: 86–112.

38. A great number of Han bas-reliefs represent banquet scenes and musical and dancing performances. An inscription discovered in 1973 in a tomb in Cangshan, Shandong, provides solid evidence to interpret the meaning of these pictorial carvings. Following the passage about the soul's journey, the inscription describes how the deceased, whose image is carved inside the tomb, would be served delicacies by jade maidens and that actresses would amuse him with colorful performances. Cf. Li, *Shandong Han huaxiangshi*, 42. The carvings on stone coffins that represent banquet scenes and various performances, therefore, may be identified as representations of the entertainment of the soul rather than depictions of the deceased's former life.

Pottery Model of Pond with Fish and Lotuses Unearthed
from the Chengdu Vicinity in 1957. (Collection of Sichuan
Provincial Museum)

Rice cultivation was a major agricultural activity in Sichuan during the Han dynasty. The plain of Chengdu is exceptionally rich in water resources; its intersecting rivers and canals not only promoted the growth of rice crops but also the cultivation of lotus and taro plants. (See plates 3, 4, and 5.)

Literary texts document the fertility of the land and the abundance of the harvest. The poet Zuo Si, for instance, described the richness of the land in *Shu Du Fu* with the following words: "Ditches spread out like arteries, criss-crossing everywhere within the borders of the field. The millet crops are as dense as clouds and the rice stalks are as luxuriant."

The scene in "Weeding and Planting" shows two connecting water fields. The right field appears to be a shallow water pond, teeming with domestic fowl, fish, and lotus seedpods. Two farmers work with scythes raised high. The left field shows a lush growth of rice seedlings. Here two farmers lean on long poles and weed with their feet. This method of weeding may still be seen in some farming villages of Sichuan today. —GW

PLATE 1

"Weeding and Planting"
Later Han Dynasty (A.D. 25–220)
Rubbing of Pottery Tomb Relief Unearthed from Xindu County in 1978
33.5×41 cm. (13¼″×16⅛″)
Private Collection

"Sowing" shows another aspect of Sichuan's thriving farming activities. Four men with scythes are clearing the fields, while two farmers behind them scatter the seeds in preparation for planting. The stylized depiction of the figures—especially conveyed by the almost identical rhythmic movement of the four men with scythes—has led some Chinese scholars to speculate that the scene could possibly represent some sort of ritual dance, connected with sacrifices made during the harvesting season. Actual scythes made of iron have been uncovered from the Sichuan Han tombs. Other farming implements excavated have included wooden poles, being tools introduced by the minority peoples of Sichuan that are still used in some farming areas of the province today. An example of the wooden poles is seen in "Weeding and Planting" (plate 1) in which the farmers used them for weeding. —LL

PLATE 2

"Sowing"
Later Han Dynasty (A.D. 25–220)
Rubbing of Pottery Tomb Relief Unearthed in 1955 from Deyang County
24 × 39.5 cm. (9½″ × 15½″)
Sichuan Provincial Museum

PLATE 3

"Digging for Taro"
Later Han Dynasty (A.D. 25–220)
Rubbing of Pottery Tomb Relief Unearthed from Pengshan
County in 1955
30 × 50 cm. (11¾″ × 19¾″)
Sichuan Provincial Museum

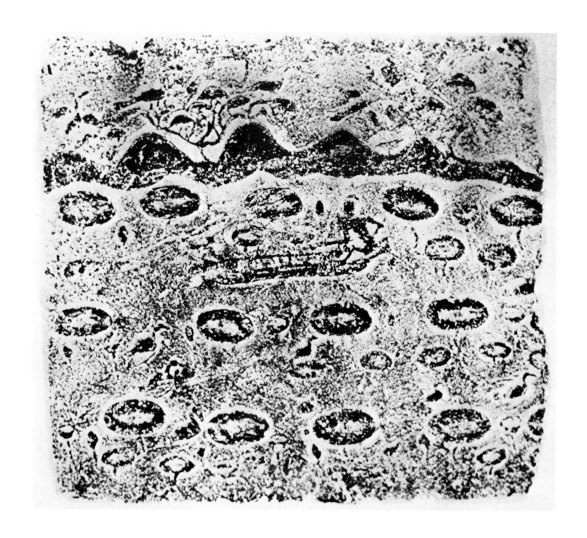

PLATE 4

"Lotus Pond"
Later Han Dynasty (A.D. 25–220)
Rubbing of Pottery Tomb Relief Unearthed from Deyang
County in 1952
32.6 × 29.6 cm. (12¾″ × 11¾″)
Chongqing Museum

PLATE 5

"Picking Lotuses"
Later Han Dynasty (A.D. 25–220)
Rubbing of Pottery Tomb Relief Unearthed from Xindu
County in 1978
34.5 × 40.5 cm. (13½″ × 16″)
Private Collection

"Lotus Pond" and "Picking Lotuses" are among the most beautiful Sichuan Han reliefs. Although they depict scenes and activities common to Sichuan, they are rendered in a highly individual, poetic style quite unlike the more realistic style that characterizes many of the other tiles.

In "Lotus Pond" the artist has created a wonderful sense of abstract rhythm and movement through the repeated use of the circular forms of the lotuses in the pond, in which a solitary boat floats, set against a row of curving hills in the background. The scene is impressionistic in style, imbued with a dreamlike quality. It is unique among the Sichuan Han pictorial reliefs. Unfortunately, the tomb tile from which this rubbing was made was lost some years ago and only rubbings of it remain today.

"Picking Lotuses" is rendered in a much more abstract style, its naiveté and whimsical feeling evocative of the work of the modern master Paul Klee. Indeed, it may be readily appreciated as a modern piece of art. Two figures ride in boats, presumably picking lotuses. One of them gestures with outstretched arms, as if in an ecstatic mood. Stalks of lotuses are portrayed in a sketchy manner, zigzagging this way and that, while water fowls are interspersed in their midst. Three large fish are conspicuously depicted in the upper portion of the tile, their size disproportionate in comparison to the other elements. It is a delightful world of fantasy, more imaginary than real. The pottery tile of "Picking Lotuses" is kept in the collection of the Xindu County Cultural Bureau.

Lotus ponds abound in Sichuan and enhance the beauty of the province's well-known natural landscapes. The theme of the lotus is celebrated by Chinese poets and artists throughout the ages, even to this day. The lotus is a staple food of Sichuan; its buds and seeds are cooked in delicate soups. The artists of these pictorial scenes perhaps found it difficult to portray one of the most celebrated symbols of Chinese art and culture in an ordinary, realistic manner and have instead created scenes that may be considered unconventional, romanticized flights of fancy. These highly original compositions attest to the versatile talents of the Han artists who in general were striving for representational, realistic effects, as is evident in the "Hunting and Harvesting" scene (plate 9). But they were also capable of creating imaginative works that captured the spiritual and poetic feeling of the scene.

In either approach, however, a fondness for depicting simple everyday activities is evident. This inclination is also expressed in "Fishing" (plate 6) and "Rafting" (plate 7)—unpretentious genre-like scenes portrayed with charm and touches of humor. —LL

PLATE 6

"Fishing"
Later Han Dynasty (A.D. 25–220)
Rubbing of Pottery Tomb Relief Unearthed from Xindu
County in 1982
29×49 cm. (11½″×19¼″)
Xindu County Cultural Bureau

PLATE 7

"Rafting"
Later Han Dynasty (A.D. 25–220)
Rubbing of Pottery Tomb Relief Unearthed from Guanghan
County in 1975
26.5 × 45 cm. (10½" × 17¾")
Guanghan County Cultural Institute

PLATE 8

"Hulling and Winnowing Grain"
Later Han Dynasty (A.D. 25–220)
Pottery Tomb Relief Unearthed from Peng County in 1979
28 × 49.5 cm. (11″ × 19¼″)
Xindu County Cultural Bureau

This tile shows four men working in front of a tile-roofed granary supported by tall pilings that probably were intended to protect the contents from dampness and rodents. Two men on the left hull grain by stepping on and off the levers of triphammers that have pestles attached to the opposite ends. The fulcrums of the levers and planks supporting the men rest on heavy stakes. Mortars, which must be made of stone, contain the grain to be hulled and are sunk into the earth.

Two men on the right winnow the hulled grain. From a large basket held over his shoulder, one man pours grain and chaff in front of a device operated by the second. This is a crude, but probably quite efficient, type of winnowing machine. It appears to consist of two narrow bamboo mats or boards mounted on vertical posts set in a base on the ground. Handles at right angles to the posts are used by the operator to rapidly oscillate these fans in an arc of about forty-five degrees to create a strong draft. This device solves the riddle of a puzzling figurine found in a Han tomb in this part of China. It was a standing man holding by his side an object exactly like one of these winnowing fans, but previously its use was not clear.

Traces of color remain on this tile, which indicate that these tiles which decorated the tombs were originally painted.
—RCR

Pottery Model of Granary with Trip-Hammers and Pestles
Dated to the Later Han Dynasty Unearthed from the Chengdu
Vicinity. (Collection of the Chengdu Museum)

The common rural occupations of hunting and harvesting are illustrated in the upper and lower registers of the same tile. Two bowmen, using tree branches as a blind, crouch beside a lotus pond stocked with over-sized fish, aiming their bows at ducks or geese flying overhead. They are using a type of short arrow or dart, called *zeng*, which is attached to a strong, thin cord; this leads to large spools of additional line on spindles set into a stand, originally made of stone for stability, which has a loop handle. This equipment allows easy retrieval of the downed fowl.

In the lower register two men are cutting standing grain with implements resembling scythes which undoubtedly have iron blades. Three stooping figures behind them are gathering the fallen stalks and sheaving them. On the far left a person, probably a woman, holds a carrying-pole loaded with sheaves in her left hand and carries a large, bail-handled container in her right hand. The sheaves are obviously headed away from the field toward the threshing floor, so one may presume that the container is now empty but earlier held the laborers' midday meal. Descriptions of harvesting scenes, including the food being carried to the fields, may be found in the *Book of Songs* (*Shijing*) dating around the eighth to tenth centuries B.C. These rural activities still occur in Sichuan today. —RCR

PLATE 9

"Hunting and Harvesting"
Later Han Dynasty (A.D. 25–220)
Pottery Tomb Relief Unearthed from Chengdu in 1975
39.5×48 cm. (15½″×19″)
Chengdu Museum

DETAIL OF PLATE 9

The Han artist has achieved unusually realistic effects in this scene of "Hunting and Harvesting" which conveys a sense of natural atmosphere. The style is remarkably different from the poetic, whimsical mood evoked in "Lotus Pond" (plate 4) and "Picking Lotuses" (plate 5).

Actual sickles and scythes have been excavated from the Sichuan Han tombs, documenting what is depicted in the relief. Molds for casting iron implements have also been excavated, dated to as early as the Eastern Zhou dynasty (770–221 B.C.). The Chinese used the process of casting iron seventeen centuries earlier than did the West, where forging was long the method. —LL

PLATE 10

"Driving Away the Birds from Eating the Grain"
Later Han Dynasty (A.D. 25–220)
Rubbing of Pottery Tomb Relief Unearthed from Peng
County in 1979
26 × 44 cm. (10¼″ × 17¼″)
Xindu County Cultural Bureau

Several very large stone reliefs were excavated from two Later Han tombs called M1 and M2 (see plate 37, stone relief from Tomb M2) at Zengjiabao near Chengdu in 1975. (The Chinese archaeological report has just recently appeared in *Sichuan Wenwu*, 1981, no. 10.) Both tombs were constructed of bricks and stone slabs, covered by a vaulted ceiling, and divided into several chambers (antechamber, central chamber, and two rear chambers). Their style of construction is similar to that of Yangzishan tomb number one (see Appendix) and the tomb furnishings uncovered are of similar types. They therefore belong to the same period, the end of the Later Han.

One of the most striking pictorial scenes was found on the west rear wall, comprised of a large stone slab divided into three registers portraying a medley of activities. The top shows a hunting scene, with a hunter aiming his arrow at a deer and birds flying above. The second register depicts a weapon rack at the right center. To its left are a monkey on a pole, a horse, and a covered wagon. Two women at the weaving looms are represented on the right and lower left (see plates 11 and 12). The bottom section of the second register and the third register are devoted to scenes of making wine. A man arrives with a cart, presumably bringing the grain (rice, millet, or sorghum) for making wine. Several large wine jars are set in a row. In the third register a woman attends to the stove, while another woman at the left is drawing water from a well. Several animals—dogs and chickens—are scattered throughout the scene, perhaps there to eat the grain that must have fallen to the ground. It is interesting to compare this wine-making scene with that represented in plate 18. —LL

Numerous historical records mention that an advanced textile industry flourished in Sichuan during the Han, and some of its regional specialties were in demand far away. Reliable records frequently mention *Shujin*, or Shu brocade. A report written in 126 B.C. by Zhang Qian, a Han court official, says that he saw *Shubu*, or Shu cloth, in Bactria and that the locals imported it from India. However, pictorial representations of mulberry picking and weaving are rare among the Sichuan reliefs.

In 1975, several large stone reliefs were excavated from a vaulted brick tomb of the Later Han at Zengjiabao near Chengdu, one of which illustrates two weavers at their looms amidst other activities. The looms are of two different types. The simpler one shown at the lower left of the stone relief (plate 11) is said to be used for weaving less complicated textiles. The one at the upper right (plate 12), identified by Chinese archaeologists as a brocade loom, has the weaving frame raised twenty-five degrees or more above its horizontal supports, which greatly increases the efficiency of the weaver. The warp beam at the top of the frame has two hourglass-shaped "locknuts" that keep it from rotating after it is set in the proper position. Parallel warp threads are strung from it to the cloth beam at the lower end of the frame, hidden by the woman seated before it.

At ground level are two foot treadles, an important addition in the evolution and efficiency of the loom. The treadles are connected by cords to heddles supported by the "horse head"—the horizontal rod on uprights below the warp beam. When this apparatus is activated by pressing on a treadle, the horse heads swing back and forth, separating the warp threads into upper and lower layers. The angle formed between them is the shed, or passageway, through which the shuttle containing the weft is thrown. This arrangement makes it possible to produce quickly much more complicated weaves and designs than the simple over-one-and-under-one type and also leaves the weaver's hands free for other tasks.

It appears as if the woman at the brocade loom has pressed one of the treadles and thrown the shuttle through the shed with her right hand. Her upraised left arm suggests that she is pulling the beater toward her to compact the weft, which at first lies loosely woven between the warp. When enough finished cloth lies in front of her, it will be wound around the cloth beam, and more warp will be supplied by the upper or warp beam, thus allowing a continuous length of cloth to be woven.

PLATE 11

"Woman at Weaving Loom (for textile)"
Later Han Dynasty (A.D. 25–220)
Rubbing of Stone Relief Unearthed from the Chengdu Vicinity in 1975
27.5 × 27.5 cm. (10¾" × 10¾")
Chengdu Museum

The treadle loom, invented in China even before Han times, seems to have first appeared in the West in the sixth century but was not in widespread use until about the thirteenth.

The famed brocades of ancient Sichuan, especially those of "Brocade City," as Chengdu was then called, were made on looms like this one depicted in the relief. Well-preserved examples of these brocades have been found in tombs in different parts of China. Sichuan today is still famous for its brocades and silk. —RCR

PLATE 12

"Woman at Weaving Loom (for brocade)"
Later Han Dynasty (A.D. 25–220)
Rubbing of Stone Relief Unearthed from the Chengdu Vicinity in 1975
Chengdu Museum

Rubbing of Stone Relief Depicting Weavers at their Looms amidst other Activities, Unearthed in 1975 from a Vaulted Brick Tomb of the Later Han at Zengjiabao near Chengdu.

A figure (probably a woman) stands near the gate of an estate holding a long pole diagonally over her shoulder and gazing at a grove of trees. Chinese sources are divided over whether they are mulberry trees (*Morus alba*) or wood-oil (*tung*) trees (*Aleurites fordii*). Both are indigenous to southern China and are important items in industry and commerce. Mulberry leaves are the important source of nourishment for silkworms. *Tung* trees bear a fruit whose seeds contain an oil that, when processed, is used for waterproofing things like paper and silk, as a caulking compound for boats, and for insecticides and varnish; it is widely used in the West as a drying agent in paint.

The argument over mulberry and *tung* arises from a lack of clear botanical detail in the tile. In support of the "*tung* trees" interpretation, a pole like that held by the person could be used for knocking the fruit containing the needed seeds from the trees.

The tile from which this rubbing is made is in the collection of the History Museum in Beijing. —RCR

PLATE 13

"Grove of Mulberry of *Tung* Trees"
Later Han Dynasty (A.D. 25–220)
Rubbing of Pottery Tomb Relief Unearthed in Peng County
in the 1950s
24 × 44 cm. (9½″ × 17¼″)
Private Collection

FIGURE 1

Drawing of a Mulberry-picking Scene Cast on a "Pictorial" Bronze Vessel of the Eastern Zhou Warring States Period Unearthed near Chengdu in 1965.

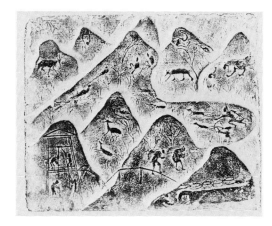

The salt-mining industry flourished in Sichuan during the Han and continues to be one of its major industries today. Several versions of this pictorial scene have been found in tombs whose owners probably engaged in this industry during their lifetimes. It is characteristic of Sichuan artists to depict such everyday activities related to the trade and commerce of the time—themes shunned by the artists of northern Shandong province, where the salt-mining industry also thrived.

In the lower left corner of the tile is a derrick erected over a salt-brine well, with four men standing on two levels of scaffolding and hauling up brine from the well below the pulleys. The brine is poured into a big container to the right of the scaffolding and then conducted by pipes to the evaporating pans seen in the lower right. The pipes were probably made of bamboo, as they are today. Drilling wells in order to obtain salt brine, which was then evaporated, was one of the most ingenious methods the ancient Chinese used to produce large quantities of salt. Chinese literature contains numerous references to these salt mines and their administration. The *Huayang guoji* (*Record of the kingdoms south of Mt. Hua*), compiled around A.D. 347, is among the most useful of the early references. The pictorial reliefs illustrating the salt-mining industry have enabled archaeologists to reconstruct the process the Han used to obtain salt from the wells and also substantiate what was documented in the texts.

The scene is represented in a mountain landscape setting, indicated by silhouetted, overlapping mountain forms. Scattered among the mountains are hunters and animals, and in the foreground are workers drilling the well and two others carrying loads of salt bags. The size of the figures and the animals are disproportionate in scale to the landscape elements, as often occurred in early representational art of this period, even though the Han artist was attempting to convey the feeling of a natural environment. —RCR & LL

PLATE 14

"Salt Mining"
Later Han Dynasty (A.D. 25–220)
Pottery Tomb Relief Unearthed from Chengdu in 1975
39.5×48 cm. (15½″×19″)
Chengdu Museum

CITY SCENES AND SOCIAL PRACTICES

Sichuan was generously blessed with a rich variety of natural products, had a favorable cash flow from its exports, and was the home of some of the wealthiest families known in Han times. All of this is reflected in the reliefs and grave furnishings from this area, as well as in the evocative lines of Zuo Si. Even allowing for some hyperbole in his rhapsodic description of Chengdu's commercial area, his image of its atmosphere, affluence, and metropolitan character seems credible:

> Its shop rows stand a hundred layers deep,
> With thousands of stalls nestled neatly together.
> Goods and wares are heaped in mountainous piles;
> Delicate and lovely crafts are amassed in stellar profusion.
> The men and women of the capital
> Are splendidly attired, gaily painted.
> Merchants hawk and barter, hoard and sell,
> Haggling back and forth, dickering left and right.
> Their unusual products are unique and strange,
> Rarer than anything in the eight directions.

—RCR

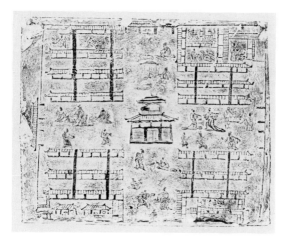

PLATE 15

"City Scene"
Later Han Dynasty (A.D. 25–220)
Pottery Tomb Relief Unearthed from Chengdu in 1975
40.5 × 49 cm. (16″ × 19¼″)
Chengdu Museum

This tile offers a good example of how visual materials can supplement written historical sources. Literary texts imply that the Later Han capital Luoyang was laid out on a grid. Yet there is little direct evidence to verify that the capital was really laid out in a rational, grid-like fashion. This tile would seem to suggest that even a city in Sichuan, perhaps Chengdu, was designed in such a manner, with narrow lanes of merchants' booths adjoining intersecting thoroughfares. In the narrow lanes there are hints of activity, but the details are difficult to make out. On the main streets men in long gowns with voluminous sleeves meet and converse. If these are not officials, then they are men of means. Elsewhere pedestrians stop before seated figures hawking their wares.

At the intersection of the two major thoroughfares sits a prominent, two-story building. Another Sichuan tile of a market scene shows an almost identical building inscribed "the market building" (published by Wen Yu). Within this building a man wearing an official cap confers with a citizen in more ordinary attire, while shopkeepers tend to their business all about them. Presumably this is the government office charged with regulating local commerce. By analogy it seems reasonable to suggest that the building in the center of this tile is, likewise, a government office in charge of the market. What kinds of duties did the officials in the "market building" shoulder? In A.D. 10 the government charged officials with keeping records of the assets of several categories of enterprise for tax purposes. It is easy to imagine that in some districts they may have assumed other duties as well, such as running a post office, posting official notices, and so on.

In the pictorial art of other regions of China we rarely get a glimpse of this world of shopkeepers and traders. In Sichuan, by contrast, local families seem to have been proud of the commercial progress enjoyed in their communities. —MJP

If we could zoom in on one of the side alleys of the market represented in the "City Scene" (plate 15), we might encounter a scene such as this. The artist has successfully captured something of the business and excitement of the market, for in every corner of this composition some kind of exchange is taking place. In the left foreground a merchant behind a small table makes a pitch to a customer. Just off to the right a woman and her child inspect some goods, while several merchant/customer pairs in the center lane seem to be haggling over prices. It is clear that various grades of merchants operate here. Some show their wares in open-front stores such as one can still find in Asia today. A man at left, center, seems to have commanded less capital, for he simply spreads his wares out on a mat. Another at rear, center, displays his goods on a kind of low table. This may be a cut above placing goods on a mat, but it is far less imposing than a permanent shop. Still others are little more than hawkers stopping passersby on the street.

From Han literary sources we may infer that many sorts of activities went on in the markets other than commercial exchange. The government sometimes held executions there so as to impress the greatest number of citizens with the wages of crime. Sometimes intellectually inquisitive young men might read books set out for sale in the market. Public libraries did not exist at the time. And for those who did not wish to read, eloquent scholars could sometimes be heard debating the causes of social ills in the market. As in other societies, the market in Han times was an important public place where people gathered to acquire all manner of goods, services, and information. —MJP

PLATE 16

"City Market"
Later Han Dynasty (A.D. 25–220)
Rubbing of Pottery Tomb Relief Unearthed from Peng
County in 1975
28×49 cm. (11″×19¼″)
Xindu County Cultural Bureau

The Chinese word for wine, *jiu*, refers to a fermented grain beverage usually made from rice, millet, or sorghum. The method of making wine in China was discovered in ancient times, as attested by various ancient texts such as the *Lü Shih chun qiu* and *Zhan Guo ce*, which allude to "ceremonial attendants making wine" and "kings and ladies enjoying wine for their merriment." Inscriptions on the oracle bones used for divination purposes during the Shang dynasty also refer to the popularity of drinking wine, while the bronze artifacts of that period and especially during the subsequent Zhou dynasty include several types of vessels for storing, warming, and drinking wine. The methods of making wine progressed considerably during the Han dynasty, when yeast came into use. Wine making contributed to the economic growth of Sichuan during the Han and today it is still one of the province's famous products. —LL

PLATE 17

"Wine Shop"
Later Han Dynasty (A.D. 25–220)
Rubbing of Pottery Tomb Relief Unearthed from Peng County in 1979
24.5 × 43 cm. (9¾" × 17")
Xindu County Cultural Bureau

PLATE 18

"Making Wine"
Later Han Dynasty (A.D. 25–220)
Rubbing of Pottery Tomb Relief Unearthed from Xindu County
28.4 × 50 cm. (11¼" × 19¾")
Xindu County Cultural Bureau

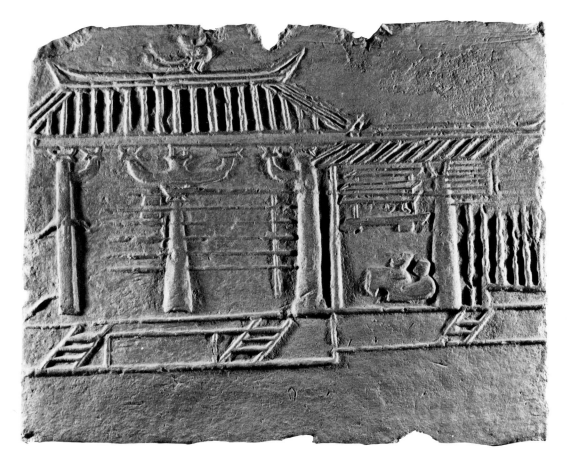

In ancient China, grand and imposing architectural structures were in existence by the Qin and Han dynasties. They are described in the texts and visual evidence is provided by several Sichuan Han tiles. Since the 1950s, tomb tiles representing armories have been found in more than ten locations in Sichuan. During the Former Han, not only the central government constructed armories, but also a few wealthy families possessed armories for their own weaponry. These extremely exalted families were, however, rare. By the Later Han, as a result of the growing power of tyrannical groups, private armies increased rapidly and private armories multiplied as well. Weapon racks are portrayed in this tile, one of the most recent discoveries, and in others found in Chengdu. A pottery model of an armory has been found in Xinjin county. —GW

PLATE 19

"Armory"
Later Han Dynasty (A.D. 25–220)
Pottery Tomb Relief Unearthed from Xindu County in 1978
33.5×41.5 cm. (13¼″×16½″)
Sichuan Provincial Museum

Although arranged a bit like a map with some three-dimensional details, this tile provides a perfectly lucid illustration of the main features of a Han estate. The walls with their tiled eaves are clearly visible around the perimeter. The front gate opens into a barnyard with fowl, while the kitchen, complete with a well, a stove, and racks for provisions and utensils, lies just off to the right. Behind the kitchen is a small courtyard with a tower. Towers must have contributed to the defense of the estate in bad times, but in the literature of the period they are often mentioned in connection with pleasure viewing. In either case they were a mark of a prosperous family. Below the tower a servant attends to the yard while a dog stands guard. Visitors to the estate most likely would not see either the kitchen or the tower, except from a distance, for these parts of the estate are separated from the rest by a roofed wall or corridor. The main gate is situated so that guests may proceed directly to the main building, with its stairway and fluted pillars, at the upper left of the composition. There the host can be seen seated with his guest and being entertained by a pair of dancing cranes.

Dancing phoenixes are part of the imagery of paradise in the literature of the period. Cranes were specifically associated with immortality and longevity. The inclusion of cranes in this scene could be interpreted to refer to the deceased in his new life as an immortal, but it might just as easily be understood as a wish for the happiness of the deceased and long life for his family. —MJP

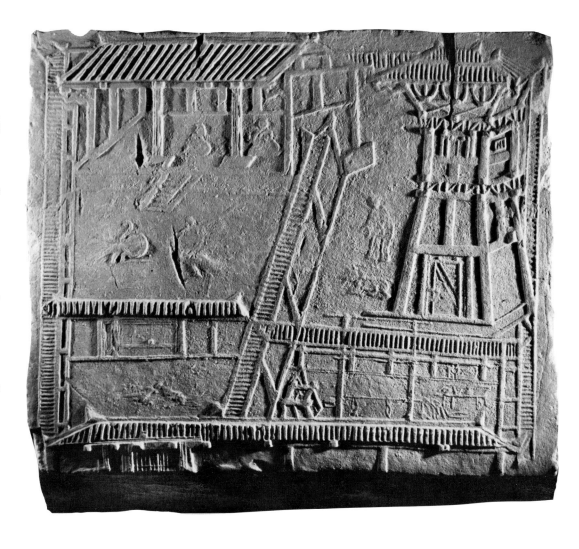

PLATE 20

"Courtyard"
Later Han Dynasty (A.D. 25–220)
Pottery Tomb Relief Unearthed from Chengdu in 1975
39.5 × 47 cm. (15½″ × 18½″)
Chengdu Museum

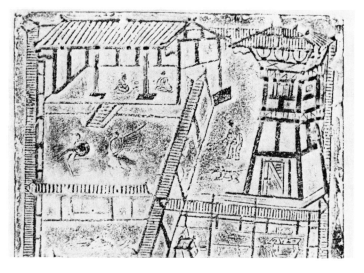

PLATE 21

"*Que* Pillar Gate"
Later Han Dynasty (A.D. 25–220)
Pottery Tomb Relief Unearthed from Chengdu in 1975
39 × 48 cm. (15½″ × 19″)
Chengdu Museum

Que "pillar gate" is often represented in Sichuan Han tomb reliefs. This architectural construction was erected in palaces, city gates, entrance doors, and tomb sites.

Although these two tomb reliefs both represent the *que* pillar gate, some differences in iconography are noticeable. On the relief from Deyang (plate 22) the *que* is relatively simple, consisting of a pair of isolated pillars in elevation. An official appears in the gateway; holding a ceremonial object, he bows submissively. On the relief from Chengdu (plate 21), however, a door with a tile roof is built between the two pillars. It consists of two double leaves; one of these cannot be seen because it has been shoved all the way open. A flying buttress is also attached to each principal pillar on the outer side; during the Han dynasty this type of double *que* belonged to people of high official rank. A large bird with elaborate tail feathers is perched above the doorway. It may be a portrayal of a mythical auspicious bird, but it is also possibly part of the architectural decor. The *Guanzhong Ji* records that a copper phoenix was mounted above the *que* in front of the Jianzhang Hall in the Han imperial palace; this *que* was then known as "the phoenix tower gate."

These two pottery reliefs were originally built into the walls of underground tomb chambers. The decorations of Yangzishan tomb number one sheds light on the symbolism of these reliefs in funerary art. In this tomb a pair of double-roofed *que* pillars appear at the entrance of the antechamber, thus forming a "gate" leading into the tomb itself. Such motifs represent the actual pillar gate in Han cemeteries that marked the entrance of the graveyard and flanked the road known as "the path of the soul." During a funeral a mourning procession carried the coffin of the deceased through this gate, along "the path of the soul," and then the mourners buried him in the tomb located at the end of the path. Whether erected in a cemetery, carved on the front of a sarcophagus, or featured in the antechamber of a tomb, the *que* pillar gate in Sichuan art always symbolizes the passage of the soul of the deceased into the spiritual world.
—WH

PLATE 22

"Figure at the Gate"
Later Han Dynasty (A.D. 25–220)
Rubbing of Pottery Tomb Relief Unearthed from Deyang
County
29 × 47.5 cm. (11½″ × 18¾″)
Sichuan Provincial Museum

Carved from a single block of red sandstone, this two-story house represents an architectural structure known as *ganlan*. Three octagonal columns support the upper floor which is again covered by a heavy tile roof. Large windows are built symmetrically in the front, flanking a door in the center of the upper floor. The door is half open and a woman, perhaps the house owner's wife, is emerging from within. This suggests that the living quarters are located on the second floor. On the ground floor, a man on the left, perhaps the house owner, sits in the traditional kneeling manner and seems to be conversing with two guests. A ladder placed diagonally near the center beckons the way to the living quarters of the household.

The artist of this three-dimensional sculpture has obviously attempted to represent a scene from ordinary life, yet he has still utilized some of the prevailing formulas of Han pictorial art. The motif of a half-opened door revealing a female figure also appears on the Wang Hui's sarcophagus (plate 70a), as well as in stone carvings from Shandong and Jiangsu. A large number of Han carvings represent two-story houses. Without exception, in such a composition the master of the house always appears in the ground hall, receiving an audience of guests. His wife, on the other hand, always remains on the second floor with other female figures. An example may be seen in a rubbing of the Wu Liang reliefs (figure 2). This pattern may reflect the different functions of the two sexes in Han society. —W H

PLATE 23

Stone House
Later Han Dynasty (A.D. 25–220)
Unearthed from Lushan County in 1953
58 cm. (22¾″) ht., 40 cm. (15¾″) w.
Leshan Museum

FIGURE 2

"Two-story House with Host and Hostess among Guests"
Rubbing of Stone Relief from the Wu Liang shrine, Shandong province. Later Han Dynasty (A.D. 25–220)

PLATE 24

"Kitchen Preparations"
Later Han Dynasty (A.D. 25–220)
Rubbing of Pottery Tomb Relief Unearthed from Xindu
County in 1982
25.5×44.5 cm. (10″×17½″)
Xindu County Cultural Bureau

FIGURE 3

Rubbing of Stone Relief Depicting "Kitchen Preparations"
from Tomb Number One at Mixian, Henan Province.

The Sichuan pieces displayed in this exhibition are mostly free of the moral overtones so characteristic of the art of northern Shandong. Although it is known that the scholars who paid for decorated shrines and tombs in Shandong typically collected rent from tenants, unambiguous depictions of such activity are lacking. In the Sichuan pictorial representation the exchange of wealth is portrayed in a natural, genre-like scene. There are inscriptions in Shandong that speak of money, but in terms of the sacrifice suffered by the family rather than income. It was probably the high standard of Confucian morality in Shandong that encouraged imagery alluding to charity rather than trade and industry. In Sichuan, however, the various scenes of trade and industry show that labor and money were not considered cause for embarrassment but were treated in a natural, open manner in tomb decorations. —MJP

PLATE 25

"Charity"
Later Han Dynasty (A.D. 25–220)
Pottery Tomb Relief Unearthed from Peng County in 1984
28 × 48 cm. (11" × 19")
Sichuan Provincial Museum

The gentleman kneeling in the right foreground of this composition carries a staff with a pigeon on the tip. In Han pictorial art this attribute signifies a man of venerable age. Because of this, one might suppose that the tile depicts a young man serving his aged father in a filial manner, but this is certainly not the case. The younger man, after all, sits comfortably on a mat while the old gentleman cringes on the ground before him.

The tile makes sense, however, if we read it as an illustration of charity work by the owner of a large estate, as suggested by the Chinese scholar Xun Bing. The heavy-beamed, double-towered structure that dominates the composition may represent a granary or, more generally, a large estate. The gentleman at the lower left is to be seen as the owner of the estate, for he sits upright on a mat and gestures actively towards the other figures as though issuing orders. The consequence of his wealth and the orders he issues is evident on the right, where one of his stewards pours grain into a sack while the old gentleman bows on the ground in gratitude.

Private charity was by no means the only hope for the poor and destitute of Han times. Throughout the four hundred years of the empire, the Han government sponsored many legal and institutional innovations aimed at alleviating social and economic inequalities. One of the government's solutions to economic problems was to establish public granaries that could provide welfare for the needy and at the same time be used to adjust the supply of grain so as to counter the effects of hoarding and speculation by commodities merchants. Other measures taken to adjust for social inequalities included the appointment of local and provincial officials to review court records for infringements of justice and the appointment of a kind of ombudsman through whom ordinary citizens could appeal directly to the central government. Although Han society was far from egalitarian, these attempts to balance inequalities through intervention by the central government were remarkable for the time.

During the Later Han there seems to have been a greater emphasis on private charity, but the government still set the example. In A.D. 30, for instance, Emperor Guangwu granted government provisions for "the aged, widows, orphans, the seriously ill, those with no family and those who cannot support themselves." Later emperors did likewise. The local government encouraged wealthy landowners, both directly and indirectly, to practice charity. —MJP

PLATE 26

"Collecting Rent"
Later Han Dynasty (A.D. 25–220)
Pottery Tomb Relief Unearthed from Guanghan County in
1974
25.5×44 cm. (10″×17½″)
Guanghan County Cultural Institute

It is noteworthy that this scene, with its granary, differs sharply from the granary scene from Yi'nan in northern Shandong province. The Yi'nan engraving lacks the peasant and, hence, any indication that an exchange of wealth is taking place. The peasant represented in this tile makes the nature of the event explicit, and so Chinese scholars have identified the illustration as collecting rent on a Han estate. The correctness of this view is supported by a more detailed rent-collecting scene in Dahuting tomb number one in Mi county, Henan province, which shares many features with this tomb relief.

A closer look at the pictorial representation of the title also supports the interpretation. A man with official cap sits in front of a building with heavy timbers and tiled roof. He leans forward in a relaxed pose, his voluminous clothing hanging loosely on his shoulders and spreading wide beyond his feet. Presumably he is leaning forward to regard more closely the actions of a farmer with simple headdress who pours grain from his cart into a measure on the ground between them. The man with the cap knows exactly how much grain he should receive, for in his left hand he holds the bamboo tallies that record the amount owed, a detail found at Dahuting as well. The artist made no attempt to disguise the farmer's subordinate status. That his clothing is of coarser material is suggested by its stiffer contours; his skirt, unlike that of the tally holder, stops short at the shins, revealing a pair of spindly legs. To wear a longer skirt would cost more money and would interfere with his work in the fields. Loose, voluminous clothing was for those who did not engage in manual labor. The farmer's social status is further suggested by his stooped back and drooping head. These details, together with the small stature of the farmer in comparison to the tally-holder, tell the whole story with surprising candor, if not compassion.

In the early years of the Han dynasty, large numbers of small farmers tilled their own land, paying taxes directly to the government. Taxes could be paid in measures of grain and bolts of silk. The central government, not wishing to lose its revenues, attempted to adjust tax demands to realistic levels, averaging and taking into account such things as acreage, soil quality, and the number of working members in a family. Still the system was too inflexible, and over the years many farmers, unable to make their tax payments, took refuge in the employ of large estates. By the second century A.D. this process had seriously eroded the empire's tax base while filling the granaries of private landowners. Pictorial records of the time, such as this tile, mark not only shifting patterns in the exchange of wealth but, by their candid display of social realities, highlight the very inequities that had been a major focus of state policy throughout the dynasty. —MJP

PLATE 27

Pottery Horse with Saddle
Later Han Dynasty (A.D. 25–220)
Unearthed from Leshan in 1982
95 cm. (37½″) ht., 78 cm. (30¾″) l.
Leshan Museum

Numerous pottery horses dated to the Han dynasty have been excavated from Sichuan. This one, unearthed in 1982 from a cave tomb in Leshan, is one of the best and the tallest. The horse also has a saddle, indicating its utilitarian purpose. The modelling clearly delineates the vigorous contour of the horse and expressive facial details—in particular, the half-open mouth.

The stubby build of this horse suggests it is of a breed probably indigenous to Sichuan, different from the tall Western breed introduced to China from Sogdiana at the beginning of the first century B.C. and well known by the Later Han. Han sculptural models of horses of the Western breed, sometimes called "celestial horses," were introduced to American audiences through the first archaeological exhibition from China (called "The Chinese Exhibition") that toured Europe and the United States respectively in 1973 and 1975. Included in that mammoth show was a memorable bronze "flying horse" figurine (34.5 centimeters in height) stepping on a swallow, accompanied by numerous models, also made of bronze, of horse carriages and attendants. All were excavated in 1969 from a Later Han tomb in Wuwei county of northwest Gansu province. In ancient China, the horse was believed to possess divine power and the mythical "celestial horse," associated with the immortality cult, could transport the dead to the heavenly or immortal realm. The bronze models excavated from the Wuwei tomb show various types of carriages similar to those seen in the Sichuan reliefs.

The earliest known example of monumental, life-size horse sculpture from the Han is a stone horse trampling on a barbarian Xiungnu invader, found near Xianyang in northern Shaanxi province at a mound believed to be the grave of the Han general Huo Qubing, who died in 117 B.C. in a military campaign.

From 1976 to 1977 huge armies of sculpted life-size terracotta soldiers and horses from the Qin dynasty (221–207 B.C.) were excavated near the city of Xi'an in Shaanxi province, near the mausoleum (yet to be excavated) of China's first unifier, Qin Shih Huangdi. They were created as an imperial entourage to serve the Qin ruler in his life-after-death. (Several examples were displayed in the exhibition "The Great Bronze Age of China," which toured the United States from 1980 to 1981.)
—LL

Later Han Dynasty Bronze Figurine of a "Flying Horse" Standing on a Swallow Excavated in 1969 from Wuwei County, Gansu Province in Northwest China. 34.5 cm. (13¾") ht., 45 cm. (17¾") l.

PLATE 28

"Carriage Crossing Bridge (*zhao che*)"
Later Han Dynasty (A.D. 25–220)
Rubbing of Pottery Tomb Relief Unearthed from Chengdu in 1956
40 × 46 cm. (16¼″ × 18¼″)
Sichuan Provincial Museum

Horses and carriages were the basic means of transportation during the Han, so it is not surprising that they were among the most frequently depicted themes in Han pictorial art. During the Later Han, the rank of an official may be judged by the number of carriages in his cortege, just as during the earlier Warring States Period the power of the state was determined by the number of chariots it possessed. Models of horses and carriages, made of pottery and bronze, were buried with the tomb owner, and images of them were painted on the walls of his tomb. Numerous examples have been uncovered from the Han tombs.

According to the *Hou Han shu* (History of the Later Han), a complicated carriage system took shape about the middle of the second century B.C. Within this system, the shape of the carriage and the scale of a procession were indications of the rank, as opposed to the social status, of the persons using the carriage. A carriage drawn by three horses could only be used by members of the imperial family, for example, while one drawn by two horses was reserved for the highest-ranking officials. The number of horsemen, inspectors, ushers, guards, keepers of accounts, and other members of the processional retinue varied according to the rank of the official involved, who usually rode in the chief carriage towards the middle of the procession. The pomp and splendor of a panoramic processional scene are exemplified by the stone reliefs decorating the walls of the central chamber of Yangzishan tomb number one (see Appendix).

Various types of carriages existed during the Han and several examples are represented in the Sichuan reliefs. "Carriage Crossing Bridge" (plate 28) is of a type called *zhao che* which has an umbrella-shaped canopy over it, with tassels hanging from the four corners. Like the "Ax Carriage (*fu che*)" (plate 29), it was reserved for high-ranking officials. Both the umbrella and the ax signify authority. The drivers of these carriages sat behind a wide dashboard within the simple, open structure of the carriage which allowed the occupants an unobstructed view.

Special types of carriages were used by women, such as "Canopy Carriage (*ping che*)" (plate 30), "Covered Carriage (*rong che*) with Attendants" (plate 31), and another type of "Covered Carriage (*rong che*)" (plate 32) which could also be used for carrying possessions. The "Canopy Carriage," which was smaller and had a more elegant shape, was used by aristocratic women. "Covered Carriage with Attendants" shows a woman rider followed by attendants and a runner with a wheelbarrow presumably carrying her belongings. All of these carriages used by women shared the same feature of having a covered compartment, undoubtedly to protect their privacy. That women enjoyed the privileges of having special carriages made for them indicate they had considerable status in Han times. —LL

PLATE 29

"Ax Carriage (*fu che*)"
Later Han Dynasty (A.D. 25–220)
Rubbing of Pottery Tomb Relief Unearthed from Deyang
County in 1955
28.5×48 cm. (11¼"×19")
Sichuan Provincial Museum

PLATE 30

"Canopy Carriage (*ping che*)"
Later Han Dynasty (A.D. 25–220)
Rubbing of Pottery Tomb Relief Unearthed from Chengdu
40 × 49 cm. (15¾″ × 19¼″)
Chengdu Museum

In the Han empire, as in other ancient societies, women did not enjoy the same privileges as men. If a woman was revered, this was often because of her husband's achievements. But this was not necessarily the case. One of the most famous business persons of Han times (and, incidentally, a resident of Sichuan), was a woman, and one of the dynasty's great literary figures, Ban Biao (A.D. 3–54), was also a woman. Few women could match acts like these, but most enjoyed a position of considerable authority *vis-à-vis* their sons, and so, as with men, funerary monuments could be erected in their honor. One such monument is the decorated shrine at Cangshan, Shandong, dated A.D. 151. Unlike their counterparts in late imperial China, women of the Han were generally free to remarry. Even in the Han legal code there is some suggestion of a level at which men and women shared certain basic rights. Presumably it was on such principles that Emperor Guangwu, while granting the protection of law to slaves in A.D. 35, did not neglect to explicitly mention females as well: "It is the nature of Heaven and Earth that mankind is noble; those who kill male or female slaves shall not have their punishments reduced." Given the historical record in other countries, the inclusion of women under the rubric "mankind" is by no means to be taken for granted.

In Han funerary art women figure in numerous ways. In northern Henan, for instance, beautifully dressed women and sometimes undressed women adorn the walls of several large, lavish tombs, apparently as pretty playthings or as evidence of material success, but this is virtually never the case in the more modest tombs and shrines of Shandong and Sichuan. There women are often to be found in feasting scenes beside their spouses, in covered carriages arriving at the gates of an estate, or in architectural scenes together with maids-in-waiting. They may be seen spinning or weaving and, of course, they are featured in illustrations of exemplary women such as in the relief of Qiu Hu and his wife (plate 55).

In "Covered Carriage with Attendants" (plate 31), the wheelbarrow is of special interest as a rare pictorial record of technical progress. Joseph Needham used this tile, together with the Shandong engravings, to show that wheelbarrows were in use in China as early as the second century A.D. In Europe the contrivance is difficult to document before the twelfth or thirteenth century A.D. —MJP

PLATE 31

"Covered Carriage With Attendants (*rong che*)"
Later Han Dynasty (A.D. 25–220)
Pottery Tomb Relief Unearthed from Chengdu in 1975
40 × 48 cm. (15½″ × 19″)
Chengdu Museum

PLATE 32

"Covered Carriage (*rong che*)"
Later Han Dynasty (A.D. 25–220)
Rubbing of Pottery Tomb Relief Unearthed from Guanghan
County in 1984
26×44 cm. (10¼″×17¼″)
Guanghan County Cultural Institute

LIFE OF THE OFFICIALS

Pictorial funerary decor did not flourish evenly through-out the Han empire. Large numbers of tomb reliefs have been found in the modern-day provinces of Shandong, Jiangsu, Henan, Shaanxi, and Sichuan. These areas had both enough material and sufficient number of prosper-ous citizens to support the production of tomb decora-tions. In their style and content, however, the various regions differed widely. While the Shandong artists gen-erally were more conservative and depicted themes related to the prevailing Confucian ideology, the Sichuan artists were more innovative in many ways and favored the ordinary aspects of life. Nevertheless, the Sichuan artists were not indifferent to learning and to traditional practices associated with the Confucian bureaucracy. A number of the Sichuan reliefs show the Confucian offi-cials and their way of life.

—MJP

PLATE 33

"Archery"
Later Han Dynasty (A.D. 25–220)
Rubbing of Pottery Tomb Relief Unearthed from Deyang
County in 1955
24.5×39.5 cm. (9¾″×15½″)
Sichuan Provincial Museum

This representation shows archers engaged in a ritual archery contest. Archery served not only as a useful skill in hunting and warfare, but it was also part of the highly ritualized train-ing of the Confucian gentleman. It was practiced along with other arts as part of a program in self-cultivation and social rites. The ritual archery contest is described in archaic books from the Confucian canon—for example, the I'li (Book of Ceremonial). The contest brought together a number of par-ticipants, formally attired, into an almost theatrical program of pacing, turning, bowing, feasting, and shooting, all accompa-nied with music. In many ways the archery contest was the ultimate rite of civilization, for it brought the acts and tools of warfare into a highly stylized, peaceful, and friendly social event. The long robes and full sleeves, the caps, the modest bows of the archers, and, most importantly, their unaggressive postures distinguish their social status and background. —KJD

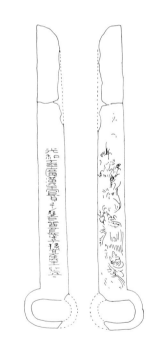

PLATE 34

"Lecture Scene"
Later Han Dynasty (A.D. 25–220)
Pottery Tomb Relief Unearthed from the Chengdu vicinity in
1953
40×46 cm. (15½×17¾")
Chongqing Museum

FIGURE 4

Book knives with inlaid designs and inscriptions bearing date
of Guanghe seventh year (A.D. 184).

A man, presumably a teacher, sits on a low *dais* table and six male students of varying sizes and ages are seated in a half-circle before him. They are sitting in the traditional kneeling manner still common in Japan, called *seiza*, on what appear to be thick, padded mats because of the double lines used to delineate them. Their attitudes suggest that of the utmost respect and attention, and their formal headdress and long gowns with wide sleeves add to this impression. All six hold bamboo or wooden books, or the individual tablets from which they are made, in front of them, and the figure in the lower right corner has a book knife hanging from his belt. The lattice-like structure above the teacher is not clear enough to identify with certainty, but it appears to function as some sort of protection, probably a screen or awning, suggesting that the class is being held adjacent to or inside a building. Well before this tile was made, Confucianism had been officially adopted as the state philosophy, which makes it reasonable to assume that the subject being taught is one of the Confucian classics.

Around 150 B.C. the people of Sichuan were fortunate to have the enlightened Wen Weng appointed as their governor. Coming from Anhui, a more "civilized" area to the east, he perceived this southwestern area as a rather backward place, short of schools and properly educated officials. For these reasons he sought out promising junior civil servants and intelligent youths and sent them to the capital—modern Xi'an, about four hundred miles northeast of Chengdu—to study under the great masters there. In order to conserve public funds and help pay for their tuition, he sent with them a quantity of two famous export products, book knives and textiles. Wen Weng himself established a school in Chengdu. After completing their studies in the capital, those young men returned home to open schools and enter officialdom. Schools proliferated in Sichuan and it later became renowned for its productive scholars, all due to Wen Weng's wisdom and foresight. He was so venerated that a temple was built to him in Chengdu and annual festivals were observed to keep his memory alive. The scene on this tile may have been inspired by his introduction of formal education into Sichuan.

FIGURE 5

Part of the bamboo slips of Sun Pin's *Art of War* lost more than 1,700 years ago and recovered from a Former Han tomb in Linyi, Shandong Province, in 1974.

The bamboo slips or tablets depicted in this tile were used for writing as early as the Shang dynasty, and wooden ones were used later, as was silk, before the invention of paper. This great contribution to world culture is traditionally ascribed to one Cai Lun, who described its manufacture in a memorial presented to the throne in 105 A.D. But archaeological evidence indicates that a serviceable paper made from hemp was used in the reign of Han Wudi (140–87 B.C.), who was so encouraged by Wen Weng's success that he opened schools throughout the empire. The book knife (figure 4) was used to scrape off errors in writing or, in some cases, to clean the entire tablet for reuse. Whole volumes were made from the tablets by tying them together in proper order with cords in the middle or at both ends. Silk volumes naturally were in the form of scrolls and could be of any length. Examples of such books, still in good condition, have been unearthed in various parts of China (figure 5). —RCR

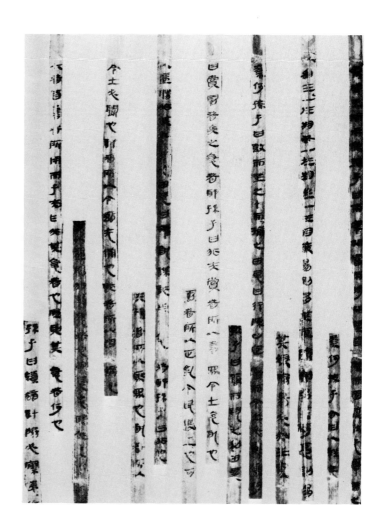

The scene shows the formal greeting ritual associated with the arrival of important officials. The central figure in official costume bows in politeness, while two figures in front of him appear to be kneeling. Two guards behind him hold flags, signifying the arrival of important guests. —LL

PLATE 35

"Greeting Scene"
Later Han Dynasty (A.D. 25–220)
Rubbing of Pottery Tomb Relief Unearthed from Peng County in 1959
28.5 × 48 cm. (11¼″ × 19″)
Guanghan County Cultural Institute

Liubo was a very popular board game in Han times. People playing the game are represented on reliefs and decorated mirrors and also in three-dimensional pottery figurines. Although the method of playing the game has long been lost, from textual records and pictorial representations we know that the game was played by two people or two teams; a player first threw six strips, called *zhu*, on a mat, and then moved draughtsmen, called *qi*, on a patterned gaming board according to his throw.

In this tile from Chengdu the two figures kneeling in the foreground are drinking and chatting, while two other figures behind them enjoy the spirited game. The figure kneeling on the left sits bolt upright, excitedly waving his arms in the air. He has obviously just made a successful throw, and his opponent stares blankly at the strips on the mat. Beside the mat is the gaming board with "TLV" patterns, which are standard for a *liubo* board.

This relief not only provides information about the lost game but it also demonstrates the high achievement of Sichuan pictorial art. The curtain hanging from the ceiling indicates the indoor setting of the scene, and the diagonal placement of mats, the gameboard, and the low table create a convincing three-dimensional space. The artist uses the thin, raised, relief lines to portray the figures and the drapery; they are analogous to the "silk-thread" lines seen in Han paintings. —WH

PLATE 36

"Playing *Liubo*"
Later Han Dynasty (A.D. 25–220)
Rubbing of Pottery Tomb Relief Unearthed from Chengdu in
1975
38×47 cm. (15″×18½″)
Chengdu Museum

Pottery Figurines Playing *Liubo* Unearthed from a Later Han Tomb at Lingbao, Henan Province, in 1972.

These two large stone doors decorated with greeting figures rendered in relief formed the entrance to Tomb M2 excavated from Zengjiabao near Chengdu in 1975. A woman holding a mirror and a kneeling scholar or official with a book in his hand are depicted on the left door, while a man holding a mirror and another man in official robe beside him are represented on the right door. Auspicious deers are depicted at the upper portion of the stone doors. It is common to find greeting figures decorating the entrance to the tomb or the front of stone coffins, such as may be seen in plate 23 and plate 38. It is not clear, however, whether there is any special symbolic meaning attached to the male and female figures holding mirrors (compare plate 45). —LL

PLATE 37

"Greeting Scene"
Later Han Dynasty (A.D. 25–220)
Stone Slab Doors Decorated with Pictorial Scenes Unearthed from the Chengdu Vicinity in 1975
Approximately 1.63 meters (64") high and 1.55 meters (61") wide
Chengdu Museum

SCENES OF INTIMACY

Some of the most surprising finds among the Sichuan archaeological materials are representations of intimate scenes in which a man and woman are embracing and kissing. Such frank and vivid portrayals of intimacy between the sexes are rarely seen in Chinese pictorial art of this early period or even in later periods. (Erotic paintings were done by Ming artists but they are unlike the warm and affectionate depictions seen in these Sichuan Han reliefs.) These unusual Han reliefs seem to epitomize the Sichuan artists' open and honest acceptance of life in its various aspects and the joy they took in human relationships.

"Embracing Couple in Architectural Setting" (plate 38) shows an intimate couple on the left, while a frontal, seated figure—perhaps the owner of the house—occupies the right side of the picture. A woman opens the door at the center, flanked by auspicious motifs of two phoenixes. The woman resembles the emerging figures depicted in the sculpted stone house (plate 23) and on the front of Wang Hui's stone sarcophagus (plate 70a) but, like the secular figure in the stone house, she does not have wings. Architectural brackets typical of Han times define the setting. The rubbing is made from a pictorial relief decorating one side of a stone coffin unearthed from Rongjing county in 1972 and reported (without much information) in *Sichuan wenwu* 1985 no. 1. The other side of the coffin depicts a horse and two figures. The context of the pictorial representation is ambiguous.

The rubbing of "Scene of Intimacy" (plate 39), even though its details are somewhat unclear, shows a man and woman with two attendants. The man is stroking the chin of the woman and has one arm around her waist. The attendants are fanning them, and one of them appears to be holding a musical instrument. Chinese archaeologists call this scene "Entertaining at a Banquet." It is conceivable that the couple are sharing a moment of intimacy during a feasting occasion. Their garments and the fact that two attendants are at their service suggest they are of the aristocratic class.

Several stone sculptural reliefs depicting explicit scenes of couples embracing and kissing have been found in cave tombs at Leshan (plate 40) and at Pengshan county (plate 41), which are unique examples of Chinese representational art. —LL

PLATE 38

"Embracing Couple in Architectural Setting"
Later Han Dynasty (A.D. 25–220)
Rubbing of Stone Relief Unearthed from Rongjing County in
1972
81.5 × 310 cm. (32″ × 91″)
Rongjing County Cultural Institute

PLATE 39

"Scene of Intimacy"
Later Han Dynasty (A.D. 25–220)
Rubbing of Pottery Tomb Relief Unearthed from Fayang
County in 1953
24×39.5 cm. (9½″× 15½″)
Sichuan Provincial Museum

PLATE 40

Stone Sculptural Relief Depicting a Couple Embracing and
Kissing, of the Later Han Dynasty, *in situ* at Leshan.

PLATE 41

Stone Sculptural Relief Depicting a Man and a Woman
Embracing and Kissing, his Hand Caressing her Breast.
Unearthed from Pengshan County in 1942 and Dated to the
Later Han Dynasty. 49 cm. ht. (This sculptural relief is now
kept in the Beijing Palace Museum.)

MUSIC, DANCE, AND ENTERTAINMENT

Han culture inherited a legacy of ritual music from its archaic predecessors and labored hard to reconstruct it by replicating the accurate instruments and recovering the proper pitches. But as the Han unfolded, what became most characteristic of Han music and entertainments was their eclectic nature. The Han empire expanded the boundaries of a central administration beyond what it had ever been previously. The silk route was open for traffic. A network of administrative, military, and trade links to several frontier areas facilitated the transmission of culture to the court and throughout the empire. As a result, musicians with their instruments, conjurers and jugglers with their props, and dancers with their costumes circulated from region to region and had relatively easy access to the emperor's court, the palaces of the nobility, and the entertainment areas that sprang up in Han urban centers. —KJD

Of all the objects recovered from the Sichuan Han tombs, the burial figures popularly called "storytellers" (*shuochang yong*) are the most engaging and have inspired the widest interest. (So far, these figures dating to the Han have been found only in Sichuan, although much later examples have appeared in Tang and Song tombs.) To call them storytellers is a bit of a misnomer, since if they told stories at all, they probably sang them and acted out key parts while beating their drums. In many respects they are similar to court jesters, being versatile entertainers kept at the court to perform a variety of amusing acts. They were especially popular during the Qin dynasty. Literary records mention that thousands of them were kept at the Qin court. Later, because of the changes in Han social structure, they also served at the residences of the officials and the landowners and even performed among the common people.

The standing storyteller figure in this exhibition is a striking and dramatic example, found in Pixian (Pi county) in 1964. Fashioned of gray clay and standing about twenty-six inches tall, he is a rather large-sized tomb figure whose portrayal evokes a theatrical atmosphere combining the real and imaginary. His stomach shoves forward while his shoulders are thrown back and upward. His hair is tied in a top knot and he wears a bangle on his upper arm. The baggy pants he wears appear to be falling off; his grimacing face, bordering on the grotesque, is the most expressive of all the storyteller figures found to date. His open mouth and protruding tongue further enhance the dramatic impact of this comic, caricature-like character, who must have delighted many audiences with his acts during the Han.

PLATE 42

Pottery Figure of Storyteller/Entertainer
Later Han Dynasty (A.D. 25–220)
Unearthed from Pi County in 1963
67 cm. (26¼″) ht., 26 cm. (10″) w.
Sichuan Provincial Museum

More than ten pottery storyteller figures, both seated and standing, have been discovered in the Sichuan Later Han tombs (figure 6). The earliest example, a seated figure with grimacing features wearing a cap and holding a stick and drum, was found in 1957 near Chengdu and is kept in the History Museum in Beijing. A similar piece—almost identical—was found near Xindu county in 1982 and is now in the collection of Sichuan Provincial Museum (figure 7). The other storyteller figures were found between 1974 and 1979, mostly rather crudely made. Whether standing or seated, the storyteller figures from Sichuan are depicted as dwarf-like figures with comic, exaggerated features; half-naked and wearing baggy pants, they are characterized by contorted bodies, protruding buttocks, heads that thrust forward, and grimacing faces. These lively figures appear to be caught in their act, with stick in one hand, about to strike a drum clamped under the other arm.

Han writers link the dwarfish storytellers with actors and singers and suggest that they sometimes performed in the hundred shows and the sundry acts popular during the Han. Although they are considered to be of low status among Han entertainers, the storytellers have been praised in the texts for their ability to act, to provide comic entertainment, and to sing to their own drum accompaniment. The Han writer Cai Yong wrote a *Fu on Dwarfs* describing their various postures and animal imitations. That several of these figures have been found in the Sichuan Han tombs attests to their popularity in the regional culture of Sichuan. —KJD & LL

FIGURE 6

Pottery Figure of Storyteller/Entertainer
Later Han Dynasty (A.D. 25–220)
Unearthed from Xindu County in 1982
51 cm. (20″) ht.
Sichuan Provincial Museum

FIGURE 7

Examples of Pottery Storytellers/Entertainers Unearthed
from Sichuan of the Later Han Dynasty.

The pottery figure of the flute player is an elegant and tranquil piece of sculpture. The flutist is a male figure, wearing an official cap and a long gown, sitting on his knees with his hands resting on the flute. Crouched on his knees, he is nearly two feet tall. The flute is rather large, stretching to ten times the width of his hands. Its bottom is supported in a ladle-shaped device that anchors to the player's belt. Most of the other Han tomb representations, whether three-dimensional or in low relief, capture a climactic moment; this figure sits motionless with a knowing smile on his face.

His flute is a vertical *di*-style flute, also called a *xiao*. By the Han both vertical and transverse flutes were in use. Some scholars believe the vertical flute was brought to China by western nomadic tribes. In earlier classics, many flute-like pipe instruments are mentioned, but their identity is uncertain, and they cannot be fully identified with the instrument held by this figure. It is clear that in antiquity there were open-ended pipes, held vertically and sounded by blowing across one end hole.

Pipes had a special place in Chinese musical theory. They channeled the *qi* energy that connected heaven and earth and were the key to the pitch standards that brought man's music into harmony with nature, with what the Daoist philosopher Zhuangzi called the "music of heaven." The skillfully crafted face of this flutist bears an enlightened smile suggesting that harmony. —KJD

PLATE 43

Pottery Flute Player
Later Han Dynasty (A.D. 25–220)
Unearthed from Leshan in 1982
60 cm. (23½″) ht., 35 cm. (13¾″) w.
Leshan Museum

136

This figure, sculpted from stone, is unusual for its medium and its highly expressive style. It is from a rare group of about ten stone sculptures of humans and animals discovered in 1977 in Emei county, in a brick tomb of the Later Han. Most Han tomb figures, from Sichuan as well as other locations, are made of pottery or wood (figure 8).

The figure is simply carved with minimal detail, but it conveys a sense of serenity appropriate for a player of the *qin* zither. The *qin*, a short seven-stringed zither, is China's most noble instrument. Examples of well-preserved *qin* have been found from as early as the fifth century B.C. By the Han dynasty, the instrument had become largely standardized, with seven strings and a compact size that made it easy to carry and easy to hold in the lap. The *qin* is a true zither, having no frets and being capable of an infinite number of pitches. One hand strums the strings; the other presses them against the long wooden finger board to produce a subtle variety of pitches, timbres, and vibrati.

The *qin* was thought of as the constant companion of the gentleman, and it was associated with the likes of Confucius as an instrument of self-cultivation more than public performance. It is often seen in the hands of sage figures in Chinese landscape paintings. This representation emphasizes the tranquility that *qin* practice brought the player. Its deep and quiet voice, resonating with the inner self, induced a feeling of harmony between the self and the outside world. Ideal *qin* music bordered on the inaudible, and it could induce in the player a meditative state. The *qin* occurs in a number of tomb tiles as part of ensembles, especially those that appear in the tiles to be playing to the accompaniment of long-sleeved dancers and pennant dancers. —KJD & LL

PLATE 44

Stone Figure of Musician Playing *Qin* Zither
Later Han Dynasty (A.D. 25–220)
Unearthed from Emei County in 1977
57 cm. (22½″) ht., 40 cm. (15¾″) w.
Sichuan Provincial Museum

FIGURE 8

Wooden Tomb Figurine Excavated from a Former Han Tomb at Mawangdui near Changsha, Hunan Province, in 1972.
78 cm. (30¾″) ht.

This charming female figure is made in two sections, allowing the head to be removed. She is wearing an elaborate costume with triangular decorations and scalloped sleeves. Her headband is intertwined with four rosettes. She is seated in the traditional kneeling manner (*seiza*).

In her left hand she holds a mirror decorated with an unidentified symbol, while her right hand rests on her knee. Han inscriptions attribute various symbolic and religious meanings to mirrors, and this one, with its unidentified marking, has led to speculation that this piece may possibly represent a cult figure or some sort of Daoist worshipper.

However, similar costumes and headdresses have been found on Sichuan pottery female figures that are clearly identified as entertainers (for example, figure 9). Also, her smiling expression is typical of that seen on Sichuan entertainer figures, such as the pottery flute player (plate 43). Her worldly appearance further suggests that she represents a secular figure, portraying an entertainer or an attendant in a noble household. It is not clear whether there is any symbolic significance attached to the fact that she is holding a mirror in a prominent, rigid position.

This figure, unearthed from a brick tomb of the Later Han period at Baihuadan village near Chengdu, is of an exceptionally high quality. —LL

PLATE 45

Pottery Figure of Female Holding Mirror
Later Han Dynasty (A.D. 25–220)
Unearthed from the Chengdu Vicinity in 1978
65 cm. (25½″) ht., 35 cm. (13¾″) w.
Chengdu Museum

FIGURE 9

Pottery Figurines of Female Dancers in the Collection of the Sichuan Provincial Museum.

Their costumes are of the same type as that seen on the female pottery figure holding the mirror.

This pottery model of a two-story house has tiled roofs, eaves, and bracket—all characteristic of Han architecture. It is constructed in two sections; the upper roof may be removed. Two musician figurines occupy the upper story, while a dwarfish storyteller figurine stands on the lower floor. (See details.)

A number of literary sources, including the dynastic history, describe ritual dances performed at the court and the elegance of feasts and entertainments held by the nobles and the officials. But the written records do not provide much information about popular dance and entertainment. However, according to a Han *fu* prose-poem written by Zhang Heng, performances were held in a popular milieu. In the large entertainment arenas, all sorts of dancing, singing, acrobatics, and magical acts were performed and watched by the emperor as well as the general public.

Archaeological discoveries from the tombs have enriched our knowledge of Han music and entertainments, complementing and clarifying the textual sources. This pottery house with entertainer figurines inside may very well represent the type of house, perhaps a teahouse, used for informal entertainments during the Han. —KJD & LL

PLATE 46

Pottery House
Later Han Dynasty (A.D. 25–220)
Unearthed from Suining County in 1971
62 cm. (24½″) ht., 47 cm. (18½″) w.
Sichuan Provincial Museum

FIGURE 10

Lacquer Vessels of the Later Han Dynasty from Sichuan.
(Replicas)

Sichuan was famous for its lacquerwares during the Han
which were exported to various parts of China and have been
discovered in tombs as far away as Korea and in Anhui
province.

The pictorial scene on this rubbing shows a feast accompanied by music and dance performances. Literary references to such social occasions may be found in contemporaneous texts. The Han dynastic history *Han Shu*, for example, describes a feast held at the home of an official that accords well with what is depicted in this scene.

In the upper right, the host and the guest are seated in a kneeling posture on mats; in front of them are low *dais* tables on which foods are served. A pair of musician figures occupy the upper left corner. The man in front strums the long *se* zither, an instrument without frets that has as many as twenty-five strings. Behind him is a woman, probably a singer, wearing the elaborate hairdo typical of the time. At the lower left the drum player, in the lively act of beating the drums, lifts his stick high. Close to him, at the lower right, a woman dances, striking a graceful pose with arms extended and waving. She wears a typical Han costume, a draped gown with long billowing sleeves that accentuate the languid movement of her dance.

This simple scene has provided important visual information on the Han such as social customs and the types of musical instruments that were used and are described in the texts. Actual examples of low *dais* table and lacquer food vessels often used on festive occasions have been unearthed from the Han tombs, being part of the mortuary furnishings (*mingqi*) intended to provide for the comforts of the tomb owner in his life-after-death. (See figure 10.)

In its composition the scene reveals how the Han artist strove to convey a realistic sense of three-dimensional space. A "space-cell" unit is formed by the figures seated at the rear and those at the front, the latter serving as a repoussoir for the foreground. Tables, food vessels, and musical instruments are scattered throughout to define areas of space. The diagonal (represented by the zither) and the overlapping forms (of the figures) are innovative devices employed by the Han artist to achieve recession and perspective. —KJD & LL

PLATE 47

"Feasting and Entertainment"
Later Han Dynasty (A.D. 25–220)
Rubbing of Pottery Tomb Relief Unearthed from Chengdu in 1975
40 × 48.5 cm. (15¾″ × 19¼″)
Chengdu Museum

FIGURE II

"Entertainer with Animal Costume"
Rubbing of Stone Relief from Yi'nan, Shandong Province
Later Han Dynasty (A.D. 25–220)

The Han histories describe costumed animal dancers and
processions as part of an annual, scheduled festival cycle.
Strange animal-like figures appear in many Han pictorial tomb
tiles. The most important examples are from Yi'nan in northeast Shandong province. A figure resembling an animal dancer
appears on the Sichuan relief "Feasting and Entertainment"
(plate 48). —KJD

PLATE 48

"Feasting and Entertainment"
Later Han Dynasty (A.D. 25–220)
Pottery Tomb Relief Unearthed from Chengdu in 1975
39.5×48 cm. (15½″×19″)
Chengdu Museum

During the Han, dancers and entertainers often performed several different shows simultaneously, in something of an informal three-ring-circus style. In this relief from Pengxian a juggler, a table-balancing acrobat, and a *pan* dancer are all on stage. The *pan* dance is pictured in a number of reliefs from several parts of China, so it was apparently a popular and widespread entertainment by the Han. Dancers, both male and female, moved at a brisk pace, with sleeves swirling, across rows of large and small drums. From literary accounts we know that the *pan* dance was performed with great agility, the dancers beating out complex rhythms with their steps, varying the rhythm and the volume as they moved.

In this tile, a female dancer sports a tall headdress and holds streaming pennants in her hands to accentuate her arm movements. The dynamics of the dance are carefully captured by the tile sculptor, who freezes the motion of the dancer exactly between the two *pan* drums.

To the left of the dancer a table balancer does a handstand atop a pile of twelve tables, an acrobatic feat still popular in China today. The tables are similar to the serving tables pictured in other tiles, and we can imagine that the stack of twelve would be quite wobbly. To the right of the *pan* dancer is a juggler, keeping three balls in the air. With his head cocked and his buttocks thrust backwards, he strikes a posture that resembles the dwarfish jesters found in Sichuan's Han tombs. —KJD

PLATE 49

"Sundry Show"
Later Han Dynasty (A.D. 25–220)
Pottery Tomb Relief Unearthed from Peng County in 1956
28.5×47.5 cm. (11¼″×18¾″)
Sichuan Provincial Museum

PLATE 50

"Jugglers"
Later Han Dynasty (A.D. 25–220)
Unearthed from Guanghan County
Guanghan County Cultural Institute

Military music was an important part of Han musical life. Among the most important representations of military music yet discovered is this tile of six mounted musicians. A matched set of horses in full regalia and plumage steps rhythmically to the pacing bell and strident pipes. The musicians in the front row play a clapper drum, a mouth organ, and a panpipe. The clapper drum is a small, post-mounted, double-headed barrel drum, with two sets of free-swinging clappers that swing into the drum heads as the post is twisted. Those in the back row play a hand-held clapperless bell, a *jia* trumpet, and another panpipe. The *jia* trumpet is a double-reed instrument with a very large voice. Among the identifiable instruments in other tiles are bells, gongs, horns, and pole drums. All of these are arguably battlefield instruments, which were used in fighting to send signals to the troops. —KJD

PLATE 51

"Mounted Musicians"
Later Han Dynasty (A.D. 25–220)
Rubbing of Pottery Tomb Relief Unearthed from Chengdu in 1952
43 × 47 cm. (17″ × 18½″)
Chongqing Museum

This mounted band, like that in the previous tile, shows musicians, with fully dressed, tightly reined horses stepping high in near unison. The most striking instrument is a pole-mounted drum with flaring pennants, clearly marking the drum master of the troupe. —KJD

PLATE 52

"Mounted Musicians"
Later Han Dynasty (A.D. 25–220)
Rubbing of Pottery Tomb Relief Unearthed near Chengdu,
Yangzishan Tomb Number One, in 1954
40×48 cm. (15¾" × 19")

Pipe and drum music occupied a major place in Han official musical genres, emphasizing the military nature of much musical performance. Instruments that were probably once used as battlefield signals were civilized and adapted to parade performance use. There are several kinds of mobile music pictured in Han tomb tiles, including instruments carried on chariots and hand-held pipes and drums carried on horseback.

This rubbing shows an unusual camel-back drum scene, the earliest example of its kind found in China. Horseback musicians usually carry a hand drum. Here the pole drum, typically mounted on a chariot, is perched on the camel's back while two musicians (one now effaced) vigorously beat it with long sticks. Pennants fly from the top of the drum-mounting pole, and the camel is portrayed with lively footwork, almost as if dancing to the rhythm.

The camel suggests the influence of frontier non-Han cultures, especially those of the northwestern desert regions, where the camel was widely used for transportation across the vast barren stretches of central Asia. We know from both pictorial and literary sources that music of the frontier, especially of the Sichuan area, was prized by the Han rulers, intentionally brought to court, and introduced into the entertainment repertoire enjoyed by Han aristocracy.

The pole drum itself is typical of stationary pole drums, frequently seen in Archaic, Han, and later art. A central post supports the horizontal, two-headed barrel drum. The long, tasseled pennants are attached to a cross beam at the top of the axial pole. The drum is struck on both sides—in this example by two players who ride on the camel's back beside the drum-mounting fixture. —KJD

PLATE 53

"Drummers on Camel"
Later Han Dynasty (A.D. 25–220)
Pottery Tomb Relief Unearthed from Xindu County in 1979
33.5×41.5 cm. (13½″×16½″)
Xindu County Cultural Bureau

HISTORICAL NARRATIVES AND LEGENDS

Han tomb reliefs were the anonymous and probably collective work of several artisans and were created for symbolic rather than for purely aesthetic purposes. Certain pictorial motifs were widespread and were duplicated from region to region and from generation to generation. But Han pictorial art also developed in different regions along various lines. The relationship with and the difference between Han narrative art and literature are also worth considering, for many pictorial motifs depicted on the Sichuan reliefs derived from literature. When a story was transformed from the written or oral tradition into a pictorial representation on a coffin, however, the narrative content and meaning changed: an individual pictorial scene became meaningful on two levels, the literary and the ritual or symbolic. —WH

See plate 55.

The Xinjin relief from Sichuan represents a historical meeting between the two masters, Confucius and Laozi. According to the historical text, *Shiji*, written by the great Han historian Sima Qian, Confucius set out with a disciple to inquire about ritual affairs from Laozi, who at that time was a high dignitary in the Zhou capital of Luoyang.

The text by Sima Qian, an admirer of Daoism, emphasized the superiority of Laozi, who assumed the role of teacher. The meeting scene in the Xinjin carving clearly reveals the same idea in pictorial language, even though it discloses a conscious choice of a "Confucian" theme. In this scene it is the Confucian master who is represented as bowing and paying respect to Laozi. With both hands in his sleeves, Laozi is deferentially raising his head and watching the visitor. —WH

PLATE 54

"Meeting of Confucius and Laozi" (at left center)
Later Han Dynasty (A.D. 25–220)
Rubbing of Stone Relief Unearthed from Xinjin County
66 × 217 cm. (26″ × 85½″)

FIGURE 12

Rubbing of Stone Relief Depicting Scene of "Confucius Meeting Laozi" (at center) from the Wu Liang Shrine, Shandong Province, of the Later Han Dynasty.

There was a very different emphasis in Shandong. Portraits of Confucius were extremely popular in Shandong during the Later Han. The master and his seventy-two disciples were frequently portrayed in ritual buildings; his image became almost an icon of state worship. The "Meeting of Confucius and Laozi" carved on the Wu family shrine represents Laozi going out of the capital and greeting Confucius on the road as a token of respect. —WH

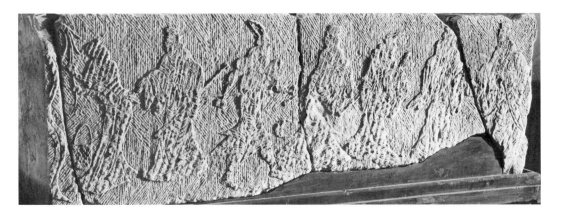

The Confucian morality story of Qiu Hu's wife, told in the Han text *Lie nü zhuan* (Biographies of outstanding women), was a celebrated exemplary model for women. Legend had it that she had been married only five days when her husband, Qiu Hu, who was from the state of Lu, had to leave home to take up office in the state of Chen. Five years later he returned. On his way home he saw a woman by the roadside picking mulberry leaves and he stopped to flirt with her. She happened to be his wife, but they did not recognize each other because of the long absence.

In the relief the setting is indicated by a mulberry tree on the left. A woman preoccupied with picking the leaves turns her head to respond to a man behind her, who seems to be conversing with her. She rejects his advances. The artist focuses on her virtue and deliberately avoids the tragic ending of the tale. After their meeting Qiu Hu returned home and learned that the woman he had met was his own wife. She upbraided him as being unrighteous and then cast herself into a river.
—WH

PLATE 55

"Qui Hu and His Wife"
Later Han Dynasty (A.D. 25–220)
Pottery Tomb Relief Unearthed from Xinjin County
74.5 × 213 cm. (29¼″ × 84″)
Sichuan University Museum

Detail of "Qui and His Wife"
Later Han Dynasty (A.D. 25–220)
Pottery Tomb Relief Unearthed from Xinjin County
74.5 × 213 cm. (29¼″ × 84″)
Sichuan University Museum

The stone relief of "Qiu Hu and his Wife" shows the sophisticated use of pictorial devices that were developed by the Later Han artists. The turning and twisting of the figures, in three-quarter views and contraposto poses, create a sense of depth and three-dimensional space. They are interrelated by their psychological rapport as well as by their postures. The traditional linear style of drawing, called the "silk-thread" line because of its fine, sinuous quality, appears to be used here.

Tʰˑ se stylistic devices have precedents in the art of the Former
        ʰey are visible in a rare painting depicting a banquet
         ʒure 14) that decorates Tomb M61 near Luoyang,
             vince, and in a tile painting of conversing figures
              ᵃt belongs to the collection of the Museum of
               ᵢston. Both are dated to around the end of the
                  or the early first century A.D. The Boston tile
                   ᵈ sophisticated, is one of the most beauti-
                    ᵎ Han period that has been preserved

ERRATA:
Plate 55 of "Qiu Hu and his Wife" is a stone tomb relief,
as mentioned in the caption text on page 153, not a pottery
tomb relief.

FIGURE 13

Detail of Rubbing of Stone Relief Depicting "Qiu Hu and His Wife" from the Wu Liang Shrine, Shandong Province, of the Later Han Dynasty.

FIGURE 14

Detail of "Banquet Scene (perhaps the Hong Men Banquet)"
Depicted on the Tile Architrave on the Rear Wall of Tomb
M61 near Luoyang, Henan Province. Dated to the Former
Han Dynasty, Around the End of the First Century B.C. or
Early First Century A.D.

FIGURE 15

Tile Painting of Conversing Figures in the Collection of the
Museum of Fine Arts, Boston, and Dated to Probably
Around the End of the First Century B.C. or Early First Cen-
tury A.D. (Photograph courtesy of Museum of Fine Arts,
Boston)

PLATE 56

"The Cowherd and the Weaving Maid"
Later Han Dynasty (A.D. 25–220)
Rubbing of Pictorial Scene Decorating Pixian Stone Coffin
Number One

The kernel of this famous legend first appeared in the *Book of Odes*. In a Han poem we find a more elaborate version:

> Far away twinkles the Herd-boy star;
> Brightly shines the Lady of the Han River.
> Slender, slender she plies her white fingers;
> Click, click go the wheels of her spinning loom.
> At the end of the day she has not finished her task;
> Her bitter tears fall like streaming rain.
> The Han River runs shallow and clear;
> Set between them, how short a space!
> But the river water will not let them pass,
> Gazing at each other but never able to speak.

In this scene the Weaving Maid on the right holds what appears to be a spinning loom in one hand and waves a piece of silk in the other. On the left the herdboy pulls his ox furiously toward the maid, as befits an impetuous young lover. A large empty space stretches between them, intended perhaps to evoke the Han River or the Milky Way, described in the poem as linking, yet mercilessly separating, the two lovers. The literary description has been beautifully transformed into an emblematic visual expression. —WH

PLATE 57A

Front: "Rider Entering through *Que* Pillar Gate"

PLATE 57B

Rear: "Fu Xi and Nü Wa"

PLATES 57A–E

Pictorial Scenes Depicted on the Baozishan Stone Sarcophagus
of the Later Han Dynasty: (Please refer to Wu Hung's essay for
the symbolic pictorial structure of these scenes.)

PLATE 57C

Top: "Legend of Yi, the Divine Archer"

On the top of the Baozishan coffin, the concept of heaven is represented by the legend of the divine archer Yi. According to the story, after a series of victories Yi went east, where he discovered a gigantic *fusang* tree; on the tree were ten golden birds blowing fire to form ten suns whose heat was burning up all living creatures. He shot nine arrows in succession and struck the birds; the nine suns immediately turned into red clouds and melted away. In works of Han art, such as offering shrines, this composition is always depicted as corresponding to the east, because the legend is connected with the sun myths. In the basic framework of Han thinking known as the *yin-yang* and Five Elements theory, this composition belonged to the *yang* side and was the symbol of the sun, the sky, and the east—as opposed to the *yin* side, symbolized by the moon, the earth, and the west. Because of its association with the sun and the sky, the legend of archer Yi is appropriately placed on the top of the coffin to symbolize the celestial world. —WH

PLATE 57D

Side: (left) "Immortals Playing *Liubo*; (right) Story of the Legendary Musician Yu Boya" 72 × 220 cm.

Side (right): "Story of the Legendary Musician Yu Boya"

As early as the Eastern Zhou, Boya was considered the world's finest zither player. The philosopher Xunzi once mentioned that when Boya was playing the zither, even horses raised their heads and laughed with enjoyment. Towards the Qin dynasty, however, another version of the story was told. Boya's audience was no longer the horses but his bosom friend, Zhong Ziqi. Boya's tale of deep friendship and sorrow became one of the most beautiful Chinese legends.

> Boya played the zither and Zhong Ziqi was the audience. As soon as Boya started playing he was transported to the Tai Mountains, and Ziqi sighed: "How wonderful is the music! It is as imposing as the Tai Mountains!" In a little while, Boya's mind shifted to the flowing river, and Ziqi was moved: "How graceful is the music! It is as vast as a flowing river!" After Ziqi died, Boya smashed his zither, cut the strings, and never played again in his life. He no longer had a soul mate in this world worthy of his music.

Boya's story continued to develop during the Former Han, and later the story was integrated with the popular idea of immortality. —WH

PLATE 57E

Side: "Carriage Procession Arriving at the Gate"

THEMES OF IMMORTALITY

People of the Han longed to enter the paradise of immortality after death; nevertheless, death represented a stage beyond their lived experience and was a constant source of fear. The darkness where the deceased would enter might be full of harmful ghosts, spirits, and wild beasts, and the soul might encounter great dangers on its journey to the immortal paradise. Such fears had become the central motivation behind various shamanistic practices aimed to guide or to protect the soul in a world unknown.

During the Han the idea of summoning the soul and the idea of immortality were amalgamated in popular beliefs dealing with death. People were now convinced that immortality was not the exclusive pursuit of philosophers or emperors who possessed great intelligence or wealth: immortality could also be achieved by an ordinary person, whose soul would enter the realm of Xiwangmu, the "Queen Mother of the West." There it could enjoy happiness greater than any earthly abode. As this immortality cult rose to an unprecedented height, representations of Xiwangmu and the western paradise came to be found on many Han tombs, offering shrines, and coffins. —WH

"Queen Mother of the West" flanked by "Sun Deity" (left) and "Moon Deity" (right).

PLATE 58

Bronze "Money Tree" (*yaoqianshu*) with a Pottery Base
Later Han Dynasty (A.D. 25–220)
Unearthed from Guanghan County in 1983
153 cm. (60¼") ht.
Guanghan County Cultural Institute

The "money tree" is unique to southwestern China during the Later Han dynasty. It consists of two principal sections: a pottery or stone base and a bronze tree whose branches are densely decorated with "coin" motifs and other mythological images. Because of their extraordinarily fine openwork design, very few Later Han "money trees" have survived intact. The "money tree" shown in the exhibition is not only the best preserved but also the largest and most elaborate, although some sections have been restored and repaired.

Perched on top of the tree is a large bird with an elegant swan neck and an elaborate peacock tail. This design derives from the Chinese sun myth. In the Eastern Sea grows a gigantic *fusang* tree; every morning, the golden sun-bird perches on the top of this tree and presents the world with light and warmth.

Underneath the bird motif are six layers of branches; each consists of four identical branches pointing to the four directions (north, south, east, and west). The top layer differs from others in decoration. Xiwangmu, "Queen Mother of the West," the ruler of the immortal land, sits on her dragon-and-tiger throne on each branch, while figures flanking the goddess perform acrobatics and play chess. Five coins hang down in a row from each branch. Embossed with leaf and stamen patterns, these coins are represented as flowers or fruit growing from the tree.

The branches in the five lower layers are completely identical.
—WH

DETAIL OF PLATE 58

Branches of the Bronze "Money Tree" with Openwork Designs Depicting Xiwangmu "Queen Mother of the West," hunters, musicians, *wuzhu* coins, and other motifs.

The bronze "money tree" with pottery base (plate 58) is unique to Sichuan Han art and only two complete examples have been preserved, both being quite spectacular for their openwork designs of symbolic motifs that hint at the wishes and aspirations of the people of Sichuan during the Han. A number of pottery bases mostly decorated with mythical animals intended to ward off evil have been excavated but without the tall and striking bronze "money tree" and its proliferation of branches.

Nevertheless, a most unusual and strange-looking pottery base for "money tree" was unearthed from the Chengdu vicinity in 1978, from a vaulted brick tomb of the Later Han dynasty located at Baihuadan village. (This is the same site where the pottery female figure holding mirror, plate 45, was excavated.) The base is composed of contorted mountain forms presided over by the cult figure of Xiwangmu at the top, symbolizing the wish for immortality. Figures are scattered in the midst of the mountain landscape; they are perhaps her followers seeking immortality, for they do not look like her attendants such as portrayed in several Sichuan Han reliefs (plates 61, 62, and 63). The concept of this landscape representation is akin to that embodied in the stone sculptural base for "money tree" (plate 60), but the rendering of this base is idealized and surrealistic when compared to the more realistic setting attempted by the artist who made the stone base. These two "money tree" bases are without doubt among the most unusual archaeological objects to have been uncovered from Sichuan. —LL

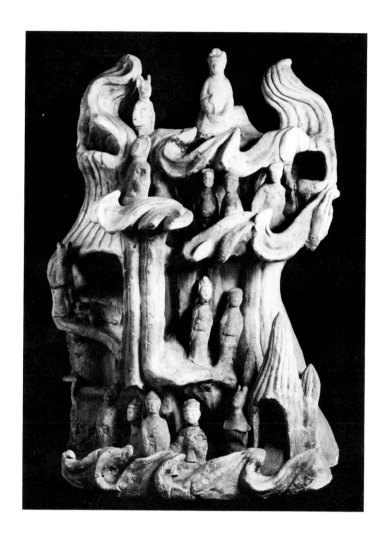

PLATE 59

Pottery Base for "Money Tree"
Later Han Dynasty (A.D. 25–220)
Unearthed from the Chengdu Vicinity in 1978
60.5 cm. (23¾") ht., 42 cm. (16½") w.
Chengdu Museum

PLATE 60

Stone Sculptural Base for "Money Tree"
Later Han Dynasty (A.D. 25–220)
Unearthed from Lushan County in 1971
46 cm. (18″) ht., 102 cm. (40″) diameter
Lushan County Museum

Although a large number of pottery "money tree" bases with different decorations have been excavated, the stone material and representation of a landscape make this base from Lushan distinctive.

This base is decorated with three prominent motifs of the Sichuan "money tree" bases: the single-horned auspicious beast—the *Bixie*—on the top, the goddess Xiwangmu, and the immortal mountain Kunlun. Kunlun was usually believed to consist of three peaks. As the Han book *Huainanzi* records: "He who climbs onto the Chilly Wind peak of Kunlun will achieve deathlessness; he who climbs twice as high onto the Hanging Garden will become a spirit and will be able to make wind and rain; he who climbs twice as high again will reach Heaven and will become a god." Images of Xiwangmu residing on this three-peaked immortal mountain are frequently seen on Han "money tree" bases or stone bas-reliefs.

On the Lushan base, however, neither Xiwangmu nor Kunlun are represented in the schematic fashion we often find in other works of Han art. It is evident that the artist tried to flesh out the supernatural tale with a realistic setting. The mountain is formed by layers of rocks of different shapes, while Xiwangmu appears as a hermit on a terrace in their midst. Surrounding the mountain are carved trees, animals, and other human figures. Some of the figures hold musical instruments or play them; they are probably the "music people" who, the *Huainanzi* tells us, also resided on Kunlun. These figures are represented in various poses and gestures, behind rocks or inside caves. Their vivid and overlapping images demonstrate a serious attempt to incorporate naturalism into decorative art.
—WH

FIGURE 16

Drawings of the Decorations on Stone Sculptural Base for "Money Tree" (plate 60)

PLATE 61

"Queen Mother of the West (Xiwangmu)"
Later Han Dynasty (A.D. 25–220)
Rubbing of Pottery Tomb Relief Unearthed from Xindu
County in 1982
29.5 × 50.5 cm. (11⅝″ × 20″)
Xindu County Cultural Bureau

PLATE 62

"Queen Mother of the West (Xiwangmu)"
Later Han Dynasty (A.D. 25–220)
Rubbing of Pottery Tomb Relief Unearthed from Pengshan
County in 1984
46×38 cm. (18¼"×15")
Pengshan County Cultural Bureau

FIGURE 17

Rubbing of Stone Relief from the Wu Liang Shrine, Shandong
Province. Later Han dynasty.

Depiction of Xiwangmu at the top gable

Representation of historical personages in the second register
from the top

PLATE 63

"Queen Mother of the West (Xiwangmu)"
Later Han Dynasty (A.D. 25–220)
Pottery Tomb Relief Unearthed from the Chengdu Vicinity in
1965
40×46.5 cm. (15¾″×18¼″)
Sichuan Provincial Museum

Xiwangmu, the "Queen Mother of the West," was the most prominent figure in Han mythology. The roots of her legend may go back to antiquity. The name Ximu, "Mother of the West," appears in Shang oracle bone inscriptions; this has led some scholars to believe that the worship of this goddess already existed before the tenth century B.C. In the writings of two famous Eastern Zhou philosophers, Zhuangzi and Xunzi, Xiwangmu is described as timeless and deathless. During the Former Han she was further linked with the concept of a western immortal land. Shortly before the Christian era she was worshiped both at imperial court and among the masses. Stone temples for the goddess were erected by the government in different provinces; her image was also standard decoration for tombs and funerary shrines.

The popularity of the Xiwangmu cult derived from the search for immortality, which rose to an unprecedented height during the Han. In popular belief Xiwangmu was the deity who controlled the secret of immortality. She was omnipotent, able to bless people with wealth and children, and especially efficacious in helping people escape from worldly troubles. She was said to live on the summit of the immortal mountain Kunlun, where trees of deathlessness grew and the water of deathlessness flowed. There she was seated on her dragon-and-tiger throne and accompanied by fairies and divine animals.

Many of these iconographic attributes are found on the two pictorial representations from Chengdu and Pengshan. On the Chengdu relief a canopy appears above the goddess and may represent an offering chamber. Similar images also decorate the bronze "money tree" from Guanghan (plate 58). In front of Xiwangmu is a dancing toad, symbol of the moon; beside the toad stands a three-legged crow, symbol of the sun. To the right of the goddess are an auspicious nine-tailed fox and a hare holding the elixir known as the "tree of three pearls." In the lower left corner, a figure called *Dazongbo* stands guard holding a halberd. A man kowtows and two women walk in the foreground; their costumes suggest that they are lay worshipers who have come to Xiwangmu's court to seek eternal happiness.

These iconographic elements are represented less rigidly in the Pengshan scene. Here the artist has emphasized the delights of the immortal world: animals play musical instruments while a spirit dances with excitement. The goddess wears the *sheng* headdress, which is usually represented in Han art as a bar connecting two discs. On this relief, however, the discs are square. This change is related to the unusual emphasis on geometric forms in this carving.

In Sichuan art Xiwangmu always appears individually in the center of a composition; sometimes she is flanked by sun and moon deities symbolizing the two cosmic forces, yin and yang. In the Wu Liang shrine carvings from Shandong in north China, however, Xiwangmu is paired with a male deity called Dongwanggong, the "King Father of the East." These two deities, symbols of immortality, have also become the embodiment of the two cosmic forces. —WH

The sun and the moon deities are represented on these two rubbings as a pair of hybrid figures; each has a human head and feathered wings and a tail. Wings outspread, these two deities seem to be soaring on high. Variations in hairstyle and headdress indicate their gender: the sun-bird is a male who wears a cap, while the moon-bird is a female with her hair worn in a coil. The body of each deity is depicted as a circular form representing the sun or the moon; the identity of each heavenly orb is indicated by additional images. Inside the sun a smaller flying bird appears as a miniature of the large hybrid deity. Inside the moon there is a toad under a tree, which, according to Chinese legend, can be identified as an auspicious Osmanthus tree.

The ancient Chinese believed that a crow with three legs abided in the sun. According to legend, in the remote past ten suns appeared in the sky and their heat burned up all living creatures. A hero named Yi located the suns in the east coast, where he discovered that on a gigantic tree ten golden birds were blowing fire. He shot nine arrows in succession and struck the birds; the nine additional suns immediately turned into red clouds and melted away. After this victory Yi went to the west and obtained the elixir of deathlessness from Xiwangmu, the "Queen Mother of the West." However, his beautiful wife Chang'E secretly ate the elixir. Her body became weightless. She fled to the moon, where she metamorphosed into a toad and was never able to return to earth.

PLATE 64

"Sun Deity"
Later Han Dynasty (A.D. 25–220)
Rubbing of Pottery Tomb Relief Unearthed from the
Chengdu Vicinity in 1965
28.5×48.5 cm. (11¼"×19")
Sichuan Provincial Museum

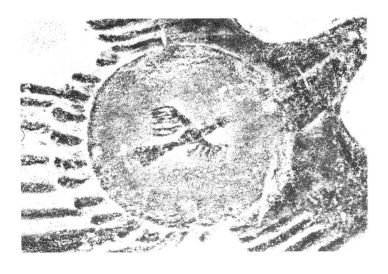

The ancient origin of the sun myth is supported by works of art. Jade and ivory artifacts from the Hemudu and Dawenkou cultures in east China (4000–3000 B.C.) are decorated with compositions of sun and bird motifs. The famous Eastern Zhou poet, Qu Yuan, mentioned this myth in his poem "Heavenly Questions," which, according to the Han scholar Wang Yi, was written in response to the mural painted inside a temple. The toad as the symbol of the moon, however, may have appeared later; the earliest example of this image is found on the silk painting from Mawangdui tomb number one (figure 18), which is dated to the first century B.C. The sun and moon with their distinctive animal symbols appear in juxtaposition in the upper corners of this painting, which is thus a close prototype of the Sichuan examples.

Images of the sun and moon are frequently found in Later Han tombs from Sichuan. People may have hoped that these two celestial orbs would light up the dark underground world. They were sometimes juxtaposed with Xiwangmu, the ruler of the immortal paradise. While Xiwangmu is represented as the supreme god in the center, the sun and moon symbolized *yin* and *yang*, the vital forces of the universe. This symbolism may be understood even more clearly in another scene in this exhibition where the sun and the moon are supported by the god Fu Xi and the goddess Nü Wa (plate 66). —WH

PLATE 65

"Moon Deity"
Later Han Dynasty (A.D. 25–220)
Pottery Tomb Relief Unearthed from the Chengdu vicinity in 1965
28.5 × 48 cm. (11¼" × 18¾")
Sichuan Provincial Museum

FIGURE 18

Drawing of the Pictorial Scenes Depicted in the T-shaped Silk Banner Painting found in Tomb Number One at Mawangdui near Changsha, Hunan Province, Dated to the Former Han Dynasty (206 B.C.–A.D. 8). (The scenes are divided into three registers representing the celestial world, the human world, and the nether world.)

Detail of Mawangdui Tomb Number One's Silk Banner Painting (Figure 18), Which Shows the Human World with the Matron of the Tomb and her Attendants.

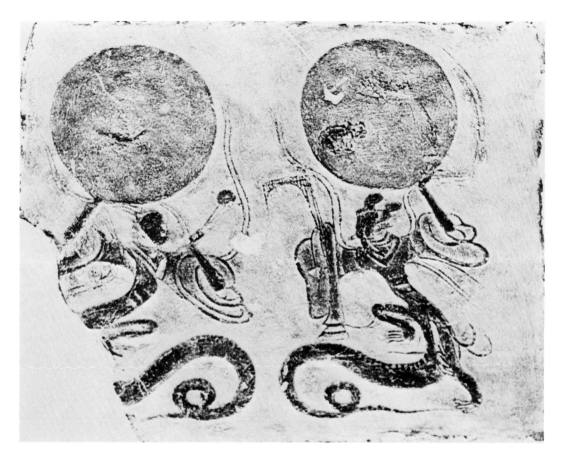

The union of Fu Xi and Nü Wa is one of the most popular motifs in Han art. With human bodies and serpentine tails, these two deities are almost a diagram of the two universal forces, *yin* and *yang*. The *yin-yang* symbolism of Fu Xi and Nü Wa is suggested not only by their different genders, perfect symmetry, and sometimes intertwining tails but also by the celestial orbs they hold in their hands. Fu Xi supports the sun with his right hand while Nü Wa supports the moon with her left hand. Inside the moon is a toad under a cassia tree, and inside the sun, a bird. According to Han mythology, these creatures inhabited the sun and moon.

Fu Xi and Nü Wa are both creation deities in Chinese mythology. After the separation of heaven and earth, Nü Wa fashioned clay figurines of human beings and the myriad creatures that came to life. Afterwards disaster struck. The sky collapsed; earthquakes shook the land; violent waves destroyed people's houses; and hungry beasts menaced people's lives. Nü Wa repaired the broken sky with melted five-colored stones and thus saved the human race from extinction. Fu Xi, on the other hand, is the creator of the sacred Eight Diagrams, which allowed people to decipher the secrets of nature and to communicate with heaven. He is also the god of music and inventor of the institution of marriage, the foundation of human society.

Following the rise of *yin-yang* theory, these two deities were coupled during the Han dynasty. The tight united form of this rubbing, however, appeared only after the first century A.D. The Former Han painting (figure 19) in the Pu Qianqiu tomb in Luoyang and the first-century carving on the Xiaotangshan shrine in Shandong both contain images of Fu Xi and Nü Wa. But there the two figures are depicted separately, on the two ends of a composition or on the two side walls of a building.

During the second century A.D. the united form of Fu Xi and Nü Wa prevailed, but variations in iconography and symbolism are also evident. For example, these two deities are usually represented holding a compass and a carpenter's square, symbolizing their ability to regulate heaven and earth. On the tile from Chongqing, however, these objects are replaced by musical instruments—Fu Xi holds a small drum and Nü Wa holds a kind of panpipe called a *paixiao*. This change may be related to their creation of music.

The symbolism of Fu Xi and Nü Wa in Sichuan art also differs from that in other regions. On the Wu Liang shrine in Shandong these two deities head a series of ancient sovereigns and usher in the onset of human history. In Sichuan art, however, Fu Xi and Nü Wa always form an independent unit, either inside a tomb chamber or on the rear of a sarcophagus. These images of Fu Xi and Nü Wa transformed a plain funerary structure into a microcosm of the universe, generated by the twin forces yin and yang. —WH

PLATE 66

"Fu Xi and Nü Wa"
Later Han Dynasty (A.D. 25–220)
Rubbing of Pottery Tomb Relief Unearthed in 1951 from Chongqing County
39.5 × 48 cm. (15½″ × 19″)
Sichuan Provincial Museum

FIGURE 19

Painted Figures of "Fu Xi" (left) and Nü Wa" (right) from the
Tomb of Pu Qianqiu of the Former Han Dynasty Discovered
in 1976 near Luoyang, Henan Province.

This relief recounts a well-known tale. The deer suddenly stops short and the man on his back sees a woman approaching him. Her clothes are fine and elaborate, with ribbons flying in the soft breeze. She wears flowers in her hair and holds strange plants in both hands. Offering him a *lingzhi* mushroom, she says that this will bring him longevity. This tale was described by the famous poet Cao Zhi in a song:

> As I traveled over Qin Mountain one morning,
> Clouds and mist were swirling.
> All of sudden I met two fairies,
> Both of brightness and beauty.
> Riding on a white deer,
> They were holding divine *lingzhi*.
> I realized they were immortals,
> And kneeled and begged for the Dao.
> "Go west and climb the Jade Terrace,
> There are gold pavilions and corridors."
> They gave me an immortal elixir,
> The Divine Sovereign had made it.
> They taught me how to take it,
> To replace my lost energy.
> "Your longevity will match that of gold and jade,
> And you will never reach senility."

Like this poem, the Pengxian relief expresses the desire of Han people for longevity and immortality. —WH

PLATE 67

"Ascending to Heaven"
Later Han Dynasty (A.D. 25–220)
Rubbing of Pottery Tomb Relief Unearthed from Peng County in 1979
26 × 45 cm. (10¼″ × 17¾″)
Xindu County Cultural Bureau

FIGURE 20

Rubbing of Stone Tomb Relief Depicting "Ascending to Heaven in Deer Chariot" from Nanyang, Henan Province. Later Han Dynasty.

A woman, her hair worn in a coil, sits in a carriage being driven by a male driver. Although the images of these two figures are naturalistic, the scene represents a supernatural or fantastic motif. The chariot is being pulled by three dragons. These divine beasts, their bodies elongated into an S-shape and their legs outstretched, gallop through the sky. Stars shine around the chariot, indicating that this is a heavenly journey. A snake, coiled into concentric circles, forms the wheels of the chariot. (Chariots with similar wheels are also depicted on stone bas-reliefs from Xuzhou in east China.)

A more complex but comparable scene (figure 21) decorates a ceiling stone that originally belonged to one of the Wu family shrines in Shandong. There a chariot is also being pulled by three dragons and also carries a female figure. The celestial setting, however, is suggested by fairies and heavenly animals flying through floating clouds. The chariot on the left proceeds towards the right, where a welcoming figure stands. Both this scene and the Sichuan scene recall the Eastern Zhou poet Qu Yuan's description of his own imaginary heavenly journey and a passage from the Han text *Yi Lin*: "Driving dragons and riding on a tiger, I will travel around heaven and earth and become a messenger of the gods. I will go west to see Xiwangmu, and I will never worry about danger." —WH

PLATE 68

"Dragon Chariot"
Later Han Dynasty (A.D. 25–220)
Pottery Tomb Relief Unearthed from Peng County in 1982
24.5 × 13.5 cm. (10″ × 17¼″)
Xindu County Cultural Bureau

FIGURE 21

"Dragon Chariot"
Rubbing of Stone Relief from the Wu Liang Shrine, Shandong Province. Later Han Dynasty.

PLATE 69

"Immortals Playing *Liubo*"
Later Han Dynasty (A.D. 25–220)
Rubbing of Tomb Relief
26×9 cm. (10¼″ × 3½″)
Sichuan Provincial Museum

This scene depicting *xien* immortals playing *liubo*, a motif popular in Han funerary art, has been interpreted as a performance of magic or divination. It differs from the more realistic rendering that characterizes human figures playing the *liubo* board game (plate 36). While this scene is simply rendered without any indication of setting, other scenes depicting immortals playing *liubo* often show them on mountain tops or in supernatural surroundings. —LL

FIGURE 22

Detail of Lacquer Painted Basket from Xutai, Jiangsu Province, depicting Animal and Cloud Patterns
Former Han Dynasty (206 B.C.–A.D. 8)

FIGURE 23

Detail of Rubbing of Tomb Relief from Mixian, Henan Province, Depicting Immortal and Animal Amidst Stylized Cloud Scrolls
Later Han Dynasty (A.D. 25–220)

FIGURE 24

Rubbing of Stone Relief from Nanyang, Henan Province,
Depicting Animals, Immortal, and Cloud Patterns.
Later Han Dynasty (A.D. 25–220)

Depictions of immortals and animals amidst cloud scrolls, pictorial motifs derived from the art of the Former Han, appear in
the Later Han pictorial reliefs from other regions of China but
are not seen among the Sichuan reliefs.

THE DIRECTIONAL ANIMALS

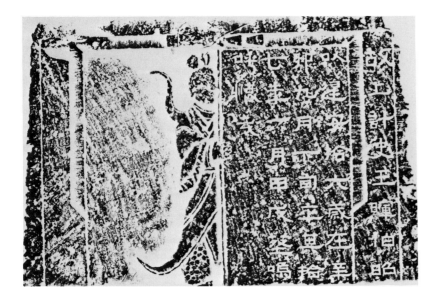

PLATE 70A

Front (entrance scene):
"Epitaph/Winged Figure"
55 × 83 cm. (21¾" × 32¾")

PLATES 70A–E

Rubbings of the Pictorial Motifs Decorating the Wang Hui's Stone Sarcophagus Dated A.D. 221 Excavated from Lushan County in 1940:
Collection of the Lushan County Museum

The Wang Hui sarcophagus is the only dated example among the many engraved sarcophagi from Sichuan. It was found in an arched brick tomb, with its rear end close to the back wall of the rear chamber. Scattered around the coffin were pottery figurines, miniature houses, and offering vessels.

The sarcophagus consists of two parts: a heavy lid with a waved surface and a stone box carved from a single block of sandstone. Animal images appear in round relief on both sides and on the rear of the coffin. On the side walls, the Blue Dragon and the White Tiger are depicted symmetrically, with similar lengthened bodies and arched tails. In Han cosmology these two mythical beasts were symbols of the east and west; they also had the ability to ward off evil forces. On the rear of the stone box is the Black Warrior—the union of a snake and a tortoise—the symbol of the north. The coffin was originally placed in the tomb facing south, and so the directional animals were arranged to correspond exactly with the cardinal directions. The design clearly reflects a cosmic structure; the plain funerary box was purposefully tranformed into a microcosm of the universe.

In the place of the Red Bird, the symbol of the south, a divine maiden is engraved on the front of the sarcophagus. She is emerging from a half-open door, holding a leaf of the door as if to open it. Carved on the front of many Sichuan pictorial sarcophagi, the motif of a *que* pillar gate represents the entrance for the soul. The "entrance" scene on the Wang Hui sarcophagus possesses the same symbolic meaning. The female figure holding the door has a wing sprouting from her right shoulder and her leg is decorated with feather-like patterns. These avian features may denote an attempt to identify her as an immortal welcoming the deceased Wang Hui to the immortal paradise or an attempt to merge this anthropomorphic figure with the Red Bird. Another animal appears above the "entrance" scene in frontal view. The animal has winged shoulders and is holding a ring in its hands and in its mouth. This animal may be the *Bixie*—"the exorciser of evil spirits"—whose image often decorates Han funerary objects.

The epigraph inscribed on the front of the sarcophagus records the name and official title of the deceased, as well as the dates of his death and burial: "The deceased Steward of Accounts, Wang Hui, styled Bozhao, died in the last decade of the ninth month of the sixteenth or *xinmou* year of the *Jianan* era [A.D. 221]. He was buried on the *jiaxu* day of the sixth month of the seventeenth year [A.D. 222]. Alas!" During Han times a burial day was chosen according to a ritual calendar. People believed that the correct day would bring good fortune to the deceased's family. This is why Wang Hui was buried a full year after his death. —WH

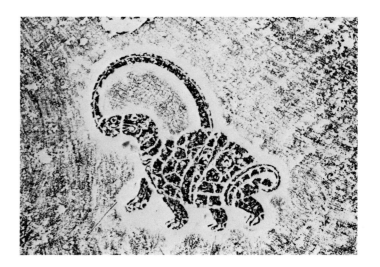

PLATE 70B

Front (above entrance scene):
"Animal Mask"
38 × 52 cm. (15″ × 20½″)

PLATE 70C

Rear:
"Tortoise"
54 × 83 cm. (21¼″ × 32¾″)

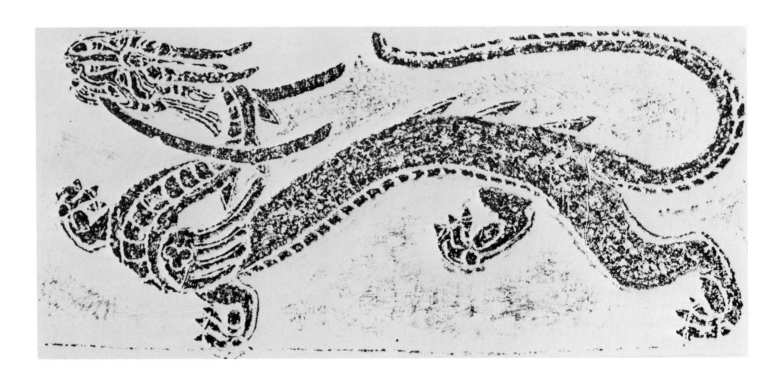

PLATE 70D

East Side Wall:
"Dragon"
58.5 × 122 cm. (23″ × 48″)

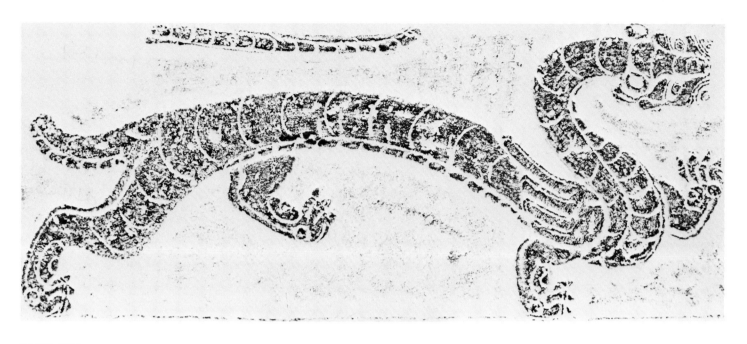

PLATE 70E

West Side Wall:
"Tiger"
61 × 134.5 cm. (24″ × 53″)

Chinese Archaeologists Excavating Yangzishan Tomb Number One Near Chengdu in the 1950s.

YANGZISHAN TOMB NUMBER ONE:
A VAULTED BRICK TOMB

Between 1953 and 1956 Chinese archaeologists excavated a large burial site at Yangzishan (Yangzi Hill), about 2.5 miles north of Chengdu, the capital of Sichuan province. More than two hundred tombs were uncovered at the site; among them, Yangzishan tomb number one is the most outstanding, both because of its large size and the rich variety of techniques and styles displayed in its pictorial decorations.

The tomb, 45.4 feet long, consists of three underground chambers connected by passageways. Although this tomb had been looted four times, some burial objects were recovered that, together with the interior carvings, suggest the different functions of the chambers. Remains of coffins, two skulls, and hairpins were found in the rear chamber, showing that this small, flat-ceilinged hall was the "bedroom" of a deceased couple. The middle chamber, 23.2 feet long, 11.5 feet high, and 8.8 feet wide, is the largest. Its vaulted roof and upper walls are built of clay bricks, while the lower sections of the walls are constructed of large stone panels. This chamber was probably a "reception hall," or "sacrificial hall," where the deceased's family and friends placed offerings and held mortuary ceremonies before the tomb was sealed. In front of this main hall is a small vaulted antechamber that functioned as the entrance.

by
Yu Dezhang
(Translated by Wu Hung)

Four different types of Han tomb structures have been found in Sichuan: (1) simple pit tombs, (2) cave tombs carved into cliffs, (3) multichambered stone tombs, and (4) multichambered tombs built of both stone and brick. Yangzishan tomb number one belongs to the last type, which enjoyed popularity at the end of the Later Han dynasty.

Various methods were used to decorate the tomb. The pottery bricks of the walls are all stamped with decorative designs such as phoenixes, auspicious plants, *wuzhu* coins, and linked *bi* discs. These felicitous motifs are intended to convey wishes for peace, happiness, and prosperity.

The walls of the tomb chambers are decorated with various pictorial scenes carved on the tomb tiles and stones. In the antechamber, a double-roofed *que* pillar flanked by two officials is represented near the entrance in the first scene on the left and right walls. These pillars are often erected at the entrances of Han cemeteries, symbolizing the separation of the world of the dead from that of the living. Other scenes in the antechamber include officials in carriages, mounted musicians, hunting and harvesting, salt-mining, and the sun deity. Most impressively, the long stone reliefs in the central chamber portray panoramic views of carriage processions and a banquet/entertainment scene. The procession scenes are among the most elaborate examples of such pictorial carvings, depicting twelve carriages, fifty-six horses, and eighty-three horsemen. Following the guiding team are official carriages, each surrounded by horsemen and walking attendants. Six riders playing different musical instruments, including a drum, a horn, and different pipes, comprise an orchestra. It has been suggested that a carriage depicted on the left wall belongs to the master of the whole procession, since this carriage is pulled by four horses and is of a type representing high official rank.

The master carriage is racing towards a banquet hall that is divided by a curtain into two sections. On the left is a kitchen, where servants are preparing and delivering food; on the right, guests are seated on mats in the traditional manner, drinking and chatting as they watch lively sword dances and acrobatic performances. A female dancer performs the scarf dance while an actor is doing the *pan* dance.

Yangzishan tomb number one is one of the most important archaeological discoveries to have been made in Sichuan. The lavish decorations exemplify exquisite technique and adhere to a coherent pictorial structure; they also provide vivid glimpses into an affluent way of life that existed in Sichuan during the Han. The pictorial reliefs are now kept in the collection of the Chongqing Museum.

Wall of Yangzishan Tomb Number One Decorated with Stone
Reliefs Depicting "Kitchen Preparations." (Photograph taken
in situ during the excavation in the 1950s.)

Wall of Yangzishan Tomb Number One Decorated with Stone
Reliefs Depicting "Procession of Carriages." (Photograph
taken *in situ* during the excavation in the 1950s.)

Rubbing of Pictorial Relief Depicting Procession of Carriages
45×251.5 cm. (17¾″×99″)

Rubbing of Pictorial Relief Depicting Procession of Carriages
25×232 cm. (17¾″×91½″)

Detail of procession of carriages

Rubbing of Pictorial Relief Depicting Procession of Carriages
45 × 223.5 cm. (17¾″ × 88″)

*Yangzishan
Tomb*

Detail of procession of carriages

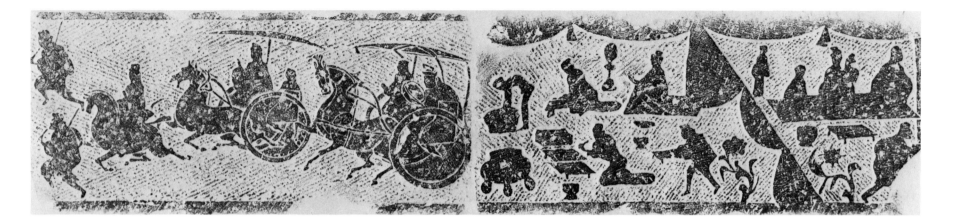

Rubbing of Pictorial Relief Depicting Procession of Carriages
and Kitchen Preparations 45 × 99 cm. (17¾″ × 78¼″)

Detail of kitchen preparations

Rubbing of Pictorial Relief Depicting Feasting and Entertainment 43 × 217 cm. (17″ × 85½″)

Yangzishan Tomb

Detail of entertainment scene

View of Antechamber Decorated with Pictorial Reliefs (reconstructed model)

View of Central Chamber Decorated with Long Pictorial Reliefs Depicting Procession of Carriages (reconstructed model)

Six-foot-Long Reconstructed Model of Yangzishan Han Tomb Number One.

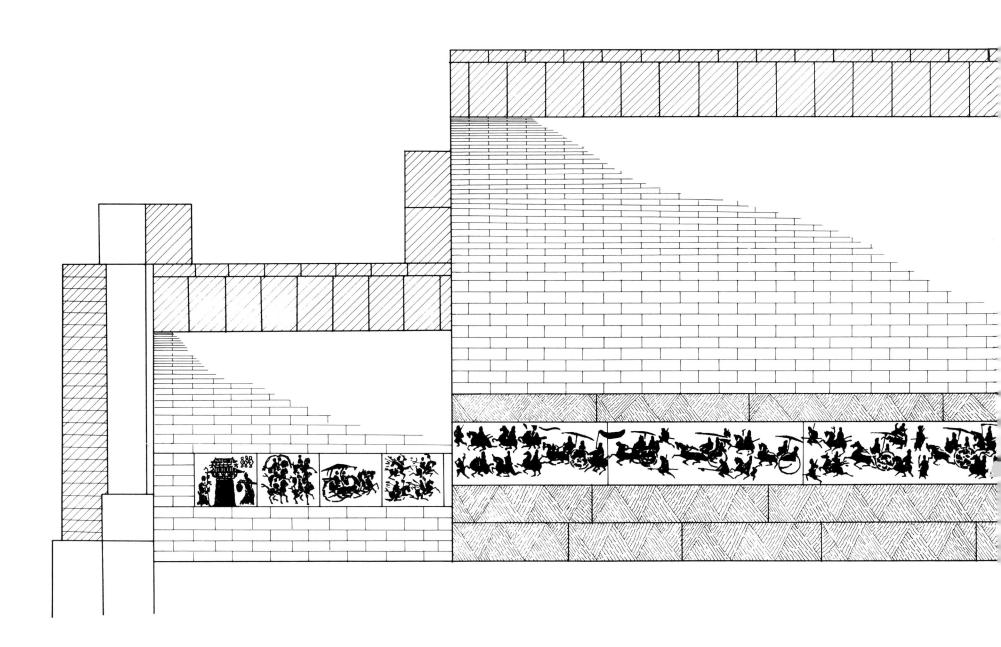

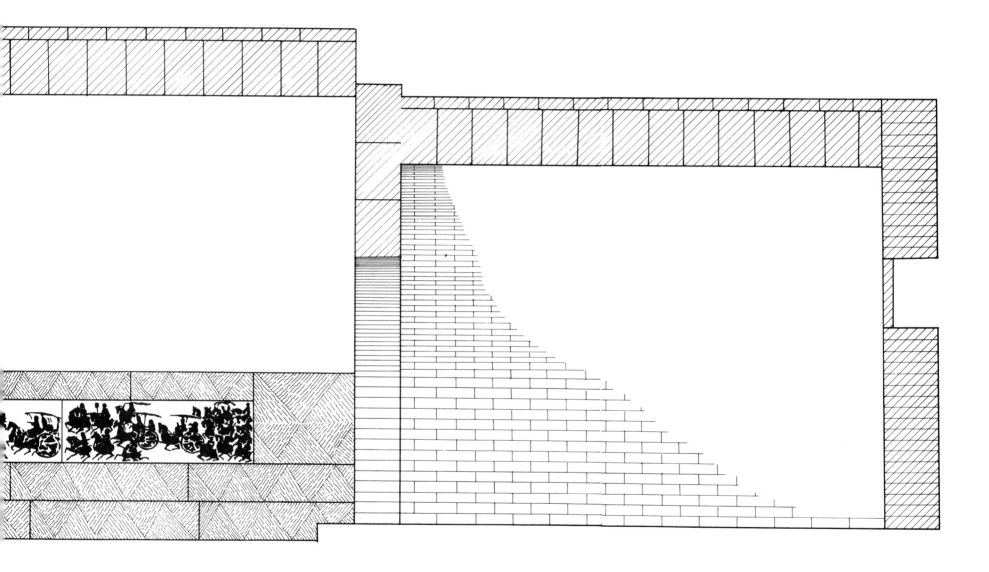

THE MAHAO CAVE TOMB AT LESHAN

The Mahao cave tomb represents a major type of tomb construction in Sichuan during the Later Han: an artificial cave carved into the red sandstone cliff. Although hundreds of small, simple pit tombs dot the mountain cliffs along the Min and Chialing River, the Mahao cave tomb is much larger, comprised of an irregularly shaped front chamber (2.8 meters high, 11 meters wide, and 29 meters long) connected by passageways to three small rear chambers. (See Ground Plan of the tomb.) The tomb entrance is formed by pillars cut out of living rock, in the same manner as the fifth-century Northern Wei Buddhist caves at Yunkang in north China. This gives the tomb the appearance of a shrine.

The pictorial reliefs for which the tomb is well known decorate the front chamber. Many of them are now badly eroded and barely visible, but the two important reliefs of the Buddha image and the attempted assassination of the King of Qin (who later became China's first unifier Qin Shih Huangdi) are relatively well preserved.

The Buddha image is depicted in a dominant position on the lintel of the front chamber, just above the passageways leading to the rear chambers. One immediately sees it upon entering the tomb. The seated figure wears a draped robe; its right hand is raised in the "*abhaya*" ("have no fear") gesture, and its head surrounded by a halo. Most scholars identify it as a representation of the Buddha because of these attributes, making it one of the earliest-known representations of the Buddha image in China.

How were this image and the Buddhist religion introduced into Sichuan in southwest China during this early period? This issue is controversial since Buddhism is known to have penetrated China through the northwest, from India across central Asia into Gansu province. One possibility is that a portable Buddhist icon might have been brought to Sichuan from the northwest region. The unusual discovery of the Sichuan tomb relief "Drummers on Camel" (plate 53) suggests that there were contacts between the two regions—the northwest and the southwest—during the Han. According to the archaeologists in Sichuan, several similar seated Buddha images have been found recently in other Han cave tombs but have not yet been properly studied. (Other examples of early Buddha images include those depicted on a Han "money tree" base and a bronze sculptural piece mentioned in Gao Wen's essay.) Whether there was a southern route for the introduction of Buddhism into south China during the Han remains a puzzling issue.

The pictorial scene of the attempted assassination of the King of Qin in 227 B.C., a historical event described in the Grand Historian Sima Qian's *Shiji* (Historical records) of the first century B.C., is depicted with much liveliness and movement on the left (east) wall of the front chamber. The drama of this event, represented also at the Wu Liang shrine, has been best captured in this Sichuan relief which vividly shows the fleeing figures with unusually realistic effects.

Carvings of architectural ornaments simulating eaves and brackets adorn the walls of the front chamber. They are designed to create the illusion of an actual house which the deceased tomb owner would inhabit in his life-after-death. There is however no unified pictorial scheme in the decorative motifs, most of which seem to have been selected at random. Scattered on the walls of the front chamber are carvings of a fisherman with rod, a farmer pulling a cart, guardian figures, a ram, a fish, and an animal mask. Burial objects such as daily utensils, animal and human figurines, and pottery houses as well as the coffin are placed within the rear chambers.

Unlike most Han tombs that face south, the Mahao cave tomb is oriented at an angle of 258 degrees towards the northern direction. This may be attributed to the fact that such an orientation enables the tomb to look out to the beautiful wide expanse of the Min River. The lush scenery of Leshan undoubtedly stimulated the construction of many cave tombs and pit tombs in this region

by
Lucy Lim

during the Han. Most of the pit tombs are buried under the trees and bushes and do not possess any significant grave goods.

According to Richard C. Rudolph, these cave tombs were once called "tombs of the barbarians" by the local inhabitants, who believed that they were made for dwelling purposes. It was later proven that they were constructed for burial, and subsequent excavations have yielded numerous archaeological objects from the Leshan region. However, these tombs were used at various times by refugees and the homeless, especially during times of war. Many Chinese retreated to remote Sichuan province during the Sino-Japanese War and the cave tombs were used as air-raid shelters. (Other Western scholars who have studied the Sichuan cave tombs include Professor Richard Edwards and Wolfgang Franke, the latter a German scholar who wrote the first article on the subject in 1948.)

Today, the Mahao cave tomb has been preserved in its original site, incorporated within the newly constructed Leshan Museum, not far from the famous "Big Buddha" of Leshan dated to the Later Tang dynasty.

The Tomb Entrance

(Photographs of the Mahao cave tomb by Lucy Lim.)

Left (East) Wall of the Front Chamber Depicting the Attempted Assassination of the King of Qin

Detail of the Left Wall and the Assassination Scene

The Buddha Image Depicted on the Lintel of the Front Chamber

Detail of the Buddha Image

View of the Rear Chamber with Burial Objects

GLOSSARY OF CHINESE NAMES AND TERMS (partial list)

An Guo	安國	Dahuting	打虎亭
Baihuadan	百花潭	Dano	大儺
baixi	百戲	Dawenkou	大汶口
Ban Biao	班彪	Dazhao	大招
Ban Gu	班固	Dazongbo	大宗伯
Bayu	巴渝	Deyang	德陽
Baozishan	寶子山	di	笛
bixie	辟邪	Dong Xian	董賢
bo	魄	*Dongdu fu*	東都賦
bozhao	伯昭	*Donghai Huanggong*	東海黃公
Cai Yong	蔡邕	Dongwanggong	東王公
Cang Jie	蒼頡	dui	碓
Cangshan	蒼山	Emei	峨眉
Cao Zhi	曹植	fu	賦
Chang'E	嫦娥	fu che	斧車
Chen	陳	fusang	扶桑
Cheng Lian	成廉	Fu Xi	伏羲
Chu	楚	ganlan	干欄
Chu Ci	楚辭	Gaoping	高平
Chuyu	蚩尤	Guangwu	光武

guchui	鼓吹	hu jia	胡笳
Gu Kaiji	顧愷之	hu konghou	胡箜篌
Han Aidi	漢哀帝	*Huainanzi*	淮南子
Han Chengdi	漢成帝	*Huayang guozhi*	華陽國志
Han Feizi	韓非子	Huan Tan	桓譚
Han Gaozu	漢高祖	Huangdi	黃帝
Han Jingdi	漢景帝	hun	魂
Han Mingdi	漢明帝	Huo Qubing	何去病
Han shu	漢書	*I'li*	儀禮
Han Wudi	漢武帝	*Ji Jiu Pien*	急就篇
Han Wendi	漢文帝	jia	笳
Han Xuandi	漢宣帝	Jianan	建安
Han Zhangdi	漢章帝	Jiang Hu	江胡
He Bo	河伯	Jianglan	江覽
Hemudu	河姆渡	Jianping	建平
Henan	河南	jiao	角
hengchui	橫吹	jiaomen	譙門
Hongmen	鴻門	jiaxu	甲戌
Hou Han shu	後漢書	jin	巾
hu	胡	jiu	酒

jun zi	君子	Mingguang	明光
Kang Wang	康王	mingqi	明器
Kunlun	崑崙	mingzhai	冥宅
la	臘	Mixian	密縣
Le Song	樂松	*Nan chao lu*	南詔錄
Li Bai	李白	Nangong yundai	南宮雲台
Li luan pien	禮亂篇	Nanyang	南陽
Lidai minghuazi	歷代名畫記	Nü Wa	女媧
Lie nu zhuan	列女傳	paixiao	排簫
Lie xian zhuan	列仙傳	pan	盤
Liezi	列子	Pengxian	彭縣
lingzhi	靈芝	Penglai	蓬萊
Liu Bang	劉邦	Pengshan	彭山
liubo	六博	ping che	軿車
Liu Xiang	劉向	pipa	琵琶
Lu	魯	Pixian	郫縣
Lu Shi chun qiu	呂氏春秋	Pu Qianqiu	卜千秋
Lun heng	論衡	qichui	騎吹
Luoyang	洛陽	qin	琴
Mahao	麻浩	Qin	秦
Mawangdui	馬王堆	Qiu Hu	秋胡
mingfu	冥府	Qu Yuan	屈原

rong che	容車	Wang Hui	王暉
Shan hai jing	山海經	Wang Jian	王堅
shangfang	尚方	Wang Shu	王叔
Shen Nong	神農	Wang Yi	王逸
shendao	神道	Wen Weng	文翁
sheng	繩	*Wen xuan*	文選
sheng tung	生動	wu	武
Shiji	史記	Wuliang tzu	武梁祠
Shijing	詩經	Wuwei	武威
Shubu	蜀布	wuzhu	五珠
Shu du fu	蜀都賦	Xialushan	夏蘆山
Shujin	蜀錦	Xi'an	西安
shuochang yong	說唱俑	Xiang Yu	項羽
Sima Qian	司馬遷	Xianyang	咸陽
Sou shen ji	搜神記	xiao	蕭
Suining	遂寧	Xiaotangshan	孝堂山
taichao	太朝	*Xijing zaji*	西京雜記
tianfu chih guo	天府之國	Xinjin	新津
Tian wen	天問	xinmou	辛卯
tung	桐	Ximu	西母
Wang Chong	王充	Xiwangmu	西王母
Wang Fu	王符	Xunzi	荀子

Xuzhou	徐州	zhao che	軺車
Yan tie lun	鹽鐵論	Zhaohun	招魂
yangzhai	陽宅	zhi	蟱
Yangzishan	羊子山	Zhiyang	資陽縣
yaoqianshu	搖錢樹	Zhong Ziqi	鍾子期
Yi	羿	Zhuangzi	莊子
Yi Lin	易林	Zuo si	左思
Yi'nan	沂南	*Zuo zhuan*	左傳
ying	嬰		
Yongyuan	永元		
youxi	遊徼		
Yü	禹		
Yu Boya	俞伯牙		
Yuefu	樂府		
zaji	雜技		
zeng	矰		
Zengjiabao	曾家包		
zhan che	棧車		
Zhan guo ce	戰國策		
Zhang Heng	張衡		
Zhang Yanyuan	張彥遠		
Zhang Qian	張騫		

SELECTED BIBLIOGRAPHY

Chinese archaeological journals most frequently cited in the bibliography:

Chengdu wenwu 成都文物
Kaogu 考古
Kaogu xuebao 考古學報
Sichuan wenwu 四川文物
Wenwu 文物

An Jinhuai 安金槐 and Wang Yugang 王興剛. "Mixian dahuting Handai huaxing shimu he bihua mu" 密縣打虎亭漢代畫像石墓和壁畫墓 (Han dynasty tombs with stone reliefs and mural paintings at Dahuting in Mixian). *Wenwu*, no. 2 (1972): 49–62.

Ao Tianzhao 敖天照. "Guanghanxian chutu yipi Han huaxiangzhuan" 廣漢縣出土一批漢畫像磚 (Han dynasty tiles unearthed from Guanghan county). *Sichuan wenwu*, no. 4 (1985): 12.

Ban Gu 班固 (A.D. 32–92) et al. *Han shu* 漢書 (History of the Former Han). Beijing, 1962.

Bielensten, Hans. *The Bureaucracy of Han Times.* Cambridge, 1980.

Bielensten, Hans. "Lo-yang in Later Han Times." *Bulletin of the Museum of Far Eastern Antiquities* 48 (1976): 1–149.

Bodde, Derk. *Festivals in Classical China: New Year and Other Annual Observances During the Han Dynasty 206 B.C.– A.D. 220.* Princeton, 1975.

Chang Renxia 常任俠. *Chang Renxia yishu kaogu lunwen xuanji* 常任俠藝術考古論文選集 (Collection of essays on art and archaeology by Chang Renxia). Beijing, 1984.

Chang Renxia 常任俠. *Han hua yishu yanjiu* 漢畫藝術研究 (Studies on Han pictorial art). Shanghai, 1955.

Chavannes, Edouard. *Mission archéologique dans la Chine septentrionale.* Paris, 1913.

Chavannes, Edouard. *La sculpture sur pierre en Chine au temps des deux dynasties Han.* Paris, 1893.

Chaves, Jonathan. "Han Painted Tomb at Loyang." *Artibus Asiae* 30, no. 1 (1968): 5–27.

Chen Fan 陳凡. "Fushanxian faxian Handai shiguan" 富順縣發現漢代石棺 (The discovery of Han dynasty stone coffin in Fuxun county). *Sichuan wenwu*, no. 3 (1985): 35.

Cheng Te-k'un. *Archaeological Studies in Szechuan.* Cambridge, 1957.

Chengdu Cultural Bureau. "Sichuan Chengdu Zengjiabao Donghan huaxiang zhuan shimu" 四川成都曾家包東漢畫像磚石墓 (A Later Han tomb with pictorial reliefs at Zengjiabao near Chengdu, Sichuan). *Wenwu*, no. 10 (1981): 25–32.

Chongqing Museum. *Chongqingshi bowuguan cang Sichuan Han huaxiangzhuan xuanji* 重慶市博物館藏四川漢畫像磚選集 (A selection of Sichuan Han dynasty pictorial tiles in the collection of the Chongqing Museum). Chongqing, 1957.

Chongqing Museum. "Hechuan Donghan huaxiang shimu" 合川東漢畫像石墓 (Pictorial stone reliefs in a Later Han tomb in Hechuan). *Wenwu*, no. 2 (1977): 63–69.

Chongqing Museum. *Lishi kaogu wenji* 歷史考古文集 (Collection of essays on history and archaeology). Chongqing, 1984.

Ch'u T'ung-tsu. *Han Social Structures.* Seattle, 1972.

DeBary, Theodore, Wing-tsit Chan, and Burton Watson. *Sources of Chinese Traditions.* New York, 1959.

DeWoskin, Kenneth. *A Song for One or Two: Music and the Concept of Art in Early China.* Ann Arbor, 1982.

Dien, Albert, and Jeffrey Riegel, eds. *A Decade of Chinese Archaeology: Abstracts from Chinese Archaeological Journals Published between 1972 and 1981.* Los Angeles, 1985.

Dong Qixiang 董其祥. "Bayu wu yuanliu kao" 巴渝舞源流考 (Studies on the origins of dance in Sichuan). In *Lishi Kaogu wenji,* edited by Chongqing Museum, 28–37. Chongqing, 1984.

Dore, H. *Researches into Chinese Superstitions.* Taipei, 1967.

Drake, F. S. "Sculptured Stones of the Han Dynasty." *Monumenta Serica* 8 (1943): 296–318.

Duan Shi. 段拭. *Han hua* 漢畫 (Han painting). Beijing, 1958.

Edwards, Richard. "The Cave Reliefs at Mahao." *Artibus Asiae* 17/1 and 17/2 (1954): 5–28 and 103–29.

Fairbank, Wilma. "The Offering Shrines of 'Wu Liang Tz'u'." *Harvard Journal of Asiatic Studies* 6 (1941): 1–36.

Fairbank, Wilma. *Adventures in Retrieval.* Cambridge, Mass., 1972.

Fan Ye 范曄 (A.D. 398–445). *Hou Han shu* 後漢書 (History of the Later Han). Beijing, 1965.

Fei Bingxun 費秉勛. "Gudai wudao shihua" 古代舞蹈史話 (History of ancient dance). Parts 1, 2. *Wudao* 舞蹈 (Dance), nos. 3, 4 (1981).

Feng Hanji 馮漢驥. Sichuan de huaxiang zhuanmu ji huaxiang zhuan" 四川的畫像磚墓及畫像磚 (Pictorial tiles and tombstones of Sichuan). *Wenwu*, no. 11 (1961): 35–42.

Feng Yixia 馮一下. "Sichuan Han que de jiazhi" 四川漢闕的價值 (An assessment of the Sichuan Han dynasty *que* pillars). *Sichuan wenwu*, no. 4 (1984): 58–59.

Finsterbusch, Kate. *Verzeichnia und Motivindex der Han Darstellungen.* 2 vols. Wiesbaden, 1971.

Fitzgerald, C. P. *China: A Short Cultural History*. London, 1961.

Fontein, Jan, and Wu Tung. *Han and T'ang Murals*. Boston Museum of Fine Arts exhibition catalogue. Boston, 1976.

Franke, Wolfgang. "Die Han'zeitlchen Felsengraber bei Chiating (West Ssu-chuan)." *Studia Serica* 7 (1948): 19–39.

Franke, Wolfgang. "Graber aus dem I. jahr-hundert n. chr, in Ssu-chuan." *Sinological Review of Chinese Culture and Science* 2 (1949–1950): 294–98.

Fung Yu-lan. *A Short History of Chinese Philosophy*. Edited by Derk Bodde. New York, 1948.

Gao Wen 高文 . "Sichuan Handai huanxiangshi chutan" 四川漢代畫像石初探 (Preliminary study on Han dynasty pictorial stone reliefs from Sichuan). *Sichuan wenwu*, no. 4 (1985): 4–8, 68.

Gao Wen 高文 . "Xunli duocai de Sichuan Handai huaxiangshi—Sichuan jiefanghou faxian de wuge shiguanguo" 絢麗多采的四川漢代畫像石棺 (On pictorial stone reliefs and five stone coffins found in Sichuan after the Liberation). *Sichuan wenwu*, no. 1 (1985): 12–18.

Graham, D. C. "The Ancient Caves of Szechwan Province." *Proceedings of the United States National Museum* 80 (1932): 1–13.

Graham, D. C. "Han Dynasty Tombs in Szechwan." *Asia* 42 (1942): 59–63.

He Haotian 何浩天 . *Hanhua yu Handai shehui shenghuo* 漢畫與漢代社會生活 (Han pictorial art and Han society). Taipei, 1969.

Hou Wailu 侯外廬 . *Handai shehui yu Handai sixiang* 漢代社會與漢代思想 (Han society and Han thoughts). Hong Kong, 1978.

Hsu Cho-yun. *Han Agriculture*. Seattle and London, 1980.

James, Jean H. "Interpreting Han Funerary Art: The Importance of Context." *Oriental Art* 31.3 (Autumn 1985): 283–92.

Karlgren, Bernhard. "Legends and Cults in Ancient China." *Bulletin of the Museum of Far Eastern Antiquities* 18: 199–365.

Kaufmann, Walter. *Musical References in the Chinese Classics*. Detroit, 1976.

Knechtges, David. *The Han Rhapsody—a Study of the Fu of Yang Hsiung (53 B.C.–A.D. 18)*. Cambridge, 1976.

Knechtges, David, trans. *Wen Xuan or Selections of Refined Literature*. Vol. 1, *Rhapsodies on Metropolises and Capitals*. Princeton, 1982.

Kuang Yingda 鄺盈達 . "Sichuan Yibinshi Cuipingcun Hanmu qinglijianbae' 四川宜賓翠屏村漢墓清理簡報 (Brief excavation report of the Han tombs at Cuiping village in Yibin, Sichuan). *Kaogu tongxun* 考古通訊 , no. 3 (1957): 20–25.

Lam, Peter, ed. *Archaeological Finds from Han Tombs at Guangzhou and Hong Kong*. Exhibition catalogue of the Art Gallery, University of Hong Kong. Hong Kong, 1984.

Lan Fong 蘭峯 . "Sichuan Yibin xian yamu huaxiangshiguan" 宜賓縣崖墓畫像石棺 (Pictorial stone coffins from cave tombs at Yibin county, Sichuan). *Wenwu*, no. 7 (1982): 24–27.

Laufer, Bertold. *Chinese Grave Sculptures of the Han Period*. London, 1911.

Laufer, Bertold. *Chinese Pottery of the Han Dynasty*. London, 1909.

Li Chunyi 李純一 . "Zhongguo gudai zaji he yinyue" 中國古代雜技和音樂 (Sundry entertainments and music in ancient China). *Yinyue yanjiu* 音樂研究 (Studies on music), no. 1 (1982): 46–52.

Li Falin 李發林 . *Shandong Han huaxiangshi yanjiu* 山東漢畫像石研究 (Studies on the Han pictorial carvings of Shandong). Jinan, 1982.

Li Fuhua 李復華 , and Ziyou Guo 郭子游 . "Pixian chutu Donghan huaxiang shiguan tuxiang lueshuo" 郫縣出土東漢畫像石棺圖像略說 (The pictorial representations of the Later Han stone sarcophagus unearthed from Pi county [Sichuan]).

Li Yanle 李彥休 . "Xindu Donghan yamuchu de jijian wenwu shangxi" 新都東漢崖墓出的幾件文物賞析 (An analysis of some cultural objects unearthed from the Later Han cave tombs at Xindu). *Chengdu wenwu*, no. 3 (1985): 44–46.

Liu Guangyi 劉光義 . "Qin Han shidai de baijizaxi" 秦漢時代的百技雜戲 (Sundry entertainments of the Qin and Han). *Dalu zazhi* 大陸雜誌 (Taipei) 22.6 (1971): 24–26.

Liu Wenjie 劉文杰 . "Handai de taogou yo Zhongguo gudai de yanggou fengxi" 漢代的陶狗與中國古代的養狗風習 (Han pottery models of dogs and the practice of raising dogs in ancient China). *Sichuan wenwu*, no. 3 (1986): 7–10.

Liu Wenjie 劉文杰 . "Handai de zhongyu huaxiang shiwu yu gudai zhongyu luekao" 漢代的種芋畫像實物與古代種芋略考 (On the Han pictorial reliefs of planting taro and the method of its planting in ancient times). *Sichuan wenwu*, no. 4 (1985): 9–11, 56.

Liu Zhiyuan 劉志遠 . *Sichuan sheng buowuguan yanjiu tulu* 四川省博物館研究圖錄 (Collection of the Sichuan Provincial Museum). Beijing, 1958.

Liu Zhiyuan 劉志遠 . "Chengdu Zhaojiaoshi Han huaxiangzhuan mu" 成都昭覺寺漢畫像磚墓 (A Han tomb with pictorial reliefs at the Zhaojiao temple in Chengdu, Sichuan). *Kaogu*, no. 1 (1984): 63–68.

Liu Zhiyuan 劉志遠 . "Chengdu Tianhuishan yamu qingliji" 成都天迴山崖墓清理記 (Excavation report on the cave tomb at Tianhuishan near Chengdu). *Kaogu xuebao*, no. 1 (1958): 87–103.

Liu Zhiyuan 劉志遠 . "Sichuan Handai huaxiangzhuan fanying de shehui shenghuo" 四川漢代畫像磚反映的社會生活 (Social life as reflected in Sichuan Han pictorial reliefs). *Wenwu*, no. 4 (1975): 45–55.

Selected Bibliography

Liu Zhiyuan 劉志遠 , Yu Dezhang 余德章 , and Liu Wen-jie 劉文杰 . *Sichuan Handai huaxiangzhuan yu Handai shehui* 四川漢代畫像磚與漢代社會 (Sichuan Han pictorial tomb tiles and Han society). Beijing, 1983.

Loewe, Michael. *Chinese Ideas of Life and Death*. London, 1982.

Loewe, Michael. *Everyday Life in Early Imperial China*. New York, 1968.

Loewe, Michael. *Ways to Paradise: The Chinese Quest for Immortality*. London, 1979.

Lu Deliang 陸德亮 . "Sichuan Neijiang Faxian Donghan zhuanmu" 四川內江發現東漢磚墓 (The discovery of a Later Han brick tomb in Neijiang, Sichuan). *Kaogu tongxun* 考古通訊 , no. 2 (1957): 54–57.

Maspero, Henri. "La vie privée en Chine à l'époque des Han." *Revue des arts Asiatiques* 7 (1932): 185–201.

Nagahiro Toshio 長廣敏雄 . *Kandai gazō no kenkyu*, 漢代画像 の研究 (The representational art of the Han dynasty). Tokyo, 1965.

Needham, Joseph. *Science and Civilization in China*. Cambridge, 1954.

Pirazzoli-t'serstevens, Michele. *The Han Dynasty*. New York, 1982.

Powers, Martin J. "A Late Western Han Tomb near Yangzhou and Related Problems." *Oriental Art* 29, no. 3 (Autumn 1983): 275–90.

Powers, Martin J. "Pictorial Art and its Public in Early Imperial China." *Art History* 7, no. 2 (June 1984): 146–49.

Ren Naiqiang 任乃强 . "Lushan xinchutu Hanshi kao" 蘆山新出土漢石考 (On the Han stone carvings recently unearthed from Lushan [Sichuan]). *Kangdao yuekan* 康導月刊 nos. 6 & 7 (1942): 19–25.

Ren Naiqiang 任乃强 . "Bian Wang Hui shiguan fudiao" 辨王暉石棺浮雕 (An examination of the reliefs on the Wang Hui stone sarcophagus). *Kangdao yuekan* 5, no. 1 (1943): 7–17.

Riegel, Jeffrey K. "A Summary of the Excavation of Han Tombs Two and Three at Mawangdui, Changsha." Translated from *Wenwu*, no. 7 (1974). *Chinese Sociology and Anthropology* 10.2 (1977–78): 51–103.

Rudolph, Richard C., ed. *Chinese Archaeological Abstracts: Monumenta Archaeologica* 6. Los Angeles, 1978.

Rudolph, Richard C. "Early Bas Reliefs from West China." *Archaeology* 6 (1953): 24–29.

Rudolph, Richard C. "The Enjoyment of Life in the Han Reliefs of Nanyang." In *Ancient China: Studies in Early Civilization*, edited by David T. Roy and Tsuen-hsuin Tsien, 269–82. Hong Kong, 1978.

Rudolph, Richard C. "Han Dynasty Reliefs from Nanyang." *Oriental Art*, n.s. 24 (1978): 179–84.

Rudolph, Richard C., and Wen Yu. *Han Tomb Art of West China*. Berkeley, 1951.

Rudolph, Richard C. "A Second-Century Chinese Illustration of Salt Mining." *Isis* 43 (1952): 39–41. Reprinted in *Science and Technology in East Asia*, edited by Nathan Sivin, 171–73. New York, 1977.

Rudolph, Richard C. "Two Recently Discovered Han Tombs." *Archaeology* 26 (1973): 106–115.

Rudolph, Richard C. "A Wealth Motif on a Han Dynasty Tomb Brick." *Palaeologia* (Japan) 2 (1953): 214–17.

Schloss, Ezekiel. *Art of the Han*. Exhibition catalogue of China Institute in America. New York, 1979.

Segalen, Victor. *La sculpture et les monuments funéraires (provinces du Chan-si et du Sseu-tchouan, mission archéologique en Chine 1914–1917)*. Paris, 1923.

Seidel, Anna. "Tokens of Immortality in Han Graves." *Numen* 39, no. 1 (1982): 79–114.

Shang Chengzuo 商承祚 . "Sichuan Xinjin dengdi Han yamu zhuanmu kaolue" 四川新津等地漢崖墓磚墓考略 (On Han cave tombs and brick tombs at Xinjing and other places in Sichuan). *Jinling xuebao* 金陵學報 10 (1940): 1–18.

Shen Zhongchang 沈仲常 . "Jieshao Chongqingshi bowuguan cang Sichuan huaxiang zhuan xuanji" 介紹重慶市博物館藏四川漢畫像磚選集 (Introduction to the Chongqing Museum's collection of Sichuan pictorial tiles). *Kaogu*, no. 8 (1959): 452.

Shen Zhongchang 沈仲常 . *Sichuan gu taoci yanjiu* 四川古陶瓷研究 (Studies on the antique ceramics of Sichuan). Vols. 1 and 2. Chengdu, 1984.

Shen Zhongchang 沈仲常 , and Li Xianwen 李顯文 "Pengshan chutu de tongyao qianshu" 彭山出土的東漢銅搖錢樹 (Bronze "money tree" unearthed from Pengshan [Sichuan]). *Chengdu wenwu*, no. 1 (1986): 17–18.

Shi Yen 史岩 , ed. *Zhongguo diaososhi tu lu* 中國彫塑史圖錄 (Pictorial history of Chinese sculpture). Shanghai, 1983.

Shih Hsio-yen. "I-nan and Related Tombs." *Artibus Asiae* 22 (1959): 277–312.

Shuai Xipeng 帥希彭 . "Pengshanxian yanmu faxian de huaxiangzhuan" 彭山縣岩墓發現的畫像磚 (Pictorial tiles discovered in the cave tombs of Pengshan county [Sichuan]). *Sichuan wenwu*, no. 4 (1985): 11, 56.

Sichuan Cultural Bureau. "Zai Sichuan Deyangxian shonji de Han huaxiangzhuan" 在四川德陽縣收集的漢畫像磚 (A collection of Han dynasty pictorial tombs tiles from Deyang county [Sichuan]). *Wenwu cankao ziliao*, no. 7 (1956): 43–44.

Sichuan Cultural Bureau. "Sichuan Pengxian Yihegongshe chutu Handai huaxiangzhuan jianjie" 四川彭縣義和公社出土漢代畫像磚簡介 (An introduction to Han dynasty pictorial reliefs unearthed from the Yihe community in Peng county [Sichuan]). *Kaogu*, no. 10 (1983): 897–902.

Sichuan Provincial Bureau of Culture and Education. "Dujiangyan Chutu Donghan libingxiang" 都江堰出土東漢李冰像 (The Han sculpture figure of Libing unearthed from Dujianguan [Sichuan]). *Wenwu*, no. 7 (1974): 27–28.

Sichuan Provincial Museum. "Dujiangyan you chutu yiqu Handai Shixiang" 都江堰又出土一軀漢代岩像 (More Han dynasty stone reliefs unearthed from Dujiangyai [Sichuan]). *Wenwu*, no. 8 (1975): 89–90.

Sichuan Provincial Museum. *Sichuansheng Bowuguan gudai wenwu ziliao xuanji* 四川省博物館古代文物資料選輯 (Selected essays on ancient cultural objects). Chengdu, 1983.

Sichuan Provincial Museum. *Sichuan Handai huaxiangzhuan tapian* 四川漢代畫像磚拓片 (Rubbings of Han pictorial tiles from Sichuan). Shanghai, 1961.

Sichuan Provincial Museum. "Sichuan Xindu huaxiang hanzhuan" 四川新都畫像漢磚 (Han dynasty pictorial tiles from Xindu [Sichuan]). Sichuan, 1981.

Sichuan Provincial Museum. "Sichuan Xinduxian faxianyipi huaxiangzhuan" 四川新都縣發現一批畫像磚 (Some pictorial tiles discovered in Xindu County [Sichuan]). *Wenwu*, no. 2 (1980): 56–57.

Sichuan Provincial Museum and Pixian Cultural Bureau. "Sichuan Pixian Donghan zhuanmu de shiguan huaxiang" 四川郫縣東漢磚墓的石棺畫像 (Pictorial carvings on the stone coffin from a Later Han brick tomb in Pi County [Sichuan]). *Kaogu*, no. 6 (1979): 495–503.

Soper, Alexander. "Early Chinese Landscape Painting." *Art Bulletin* 23 (1941): 141–64.

Soper, Alexander. "Life-motion and the Sense of Space in Early Chinese Representational Art." *Art Bulletin* 30 (1948): 167–86.

Sun Hua 孫華 . "Gudai chejia zashuo" 古代車駕雜說 (On ancient carriages). *Sichuan wenwu* 2 (1986): 9–14.

Sun Wenqing 孫文清 . *Nanyang Han huaxiang huicun* 南陽漢畫像彙存 (A collection of Han dynasty pictorial reliefs from Nanyang). Nanyang, 1936.

Swann, Nancy Lee. *Food and Money in Ancient China*. Princeton, 1950.

Tang Changshou 唐長壽 . "Wo guo zuizao de pipa tuxiang" 我國最早的琵琶圖像 (The earliest representation of the *pipa* in our country [China]). *Sichuan wenwu*, no. 4 (1985): 69–70.

Tang Yujiu 湯玉玖 . "Zai xinjinxian de Han yanmu" 東新津縣的漢岩墓 (A Han dynasty tomb in Xinjin county). *Chengdu wenwu*, no. 2 (1985): 51–52.

Tsien, T. H. "A Study of the Book Knife in Han China (206 B.C.–22 A.D.)." Translated by John H. Winkelman. *Chinese Culture* 12 (1971): 87–101.

University of Paris Institute for Sinological Studies. *Handai huaxiang quanji* 漢代畫像全集 (A comprehensive collection of Han dynasty pictorial reliefs). Beijing, 1951.

Wang Jianwei 王建緯 . "Qinglong, baihu, zhuque, xuanwu" 青龍，白虎，朱雀，玄武 (Dragon, tiger, bird and tortoise [four directional animals]). *Sichuan wenwu*, no. 1 (1985): 72.

Wang Kaijian 王開建 . "Hejiangxian chutu Donghan shiguan" 合江縣出土東漢石棺 (Stone sarcophagi of the Later Han dynasty unearthed from Hejiang county [Sichuan]). *Sichuan wenwu*, no. 3 (1985): 67.

Wang Kefen 王克芬 . *Zhongguo gudai wudao shihua* 中國古代舞蹈史話 (History of ancient Chinese dance). Beijing, 1980.

Wang Zhongshu 王仲殊 *Han Civilization*. Translated by Chang Kwang-chih. New Haven and London, 1982.

Wang Zhongshu 王仲殊 . "Zhongquo gudai muzang kaishuo" 中國古代墓葬概說 (On ancient Chinese tomb burials). *Kaogu*, no. 5 (1981): 449–58.

Watson, Burton. *Early Chinese Literature*. New York, 1962.

Watson, Burton, trans. *Records of the Grand Historian of China*. 2 vols. New York, 1961.

Wen Yu 聞闈 . *Sichuan Handai huaxiang xuanji* 四川漢代畫像選集 (Selections of Han pictorial reliefs from Sichuan). Beijing, 1955.

Wright, Arthur. *The Civilization of Imperial China: Traditional Culture, Religion and Rule*. New Haven, 1979.

Wu Hung. "The Earliest Pictorial Representations of Ape Tales—an Interdisciplinary Study of Early Chinese Narrative Art and Literature." *T'oung Pao* 73, nos. 1–3: 86–112.

Wu Hung. "Buddhist Elements in Early Chinese Art (2nd and 3rd centuries A.D.)." *Artibus Asiae* 47, nos. 3/4 (1985): 263–352.

Wu Hung. "Bird Motifs in Eastern Yi Art." *Orientations* 16, no. 10: 30–41.

Wu Zhongshi 吳仲實 . "Sichuan Yibin Hanmu qingli hen duo chutu wenwu" 四川宜賓縣漢墓清理很多出土文物 (Cultural objects unearthed from the Han tombs in Yibin, Sichuan). *Wenwu cankao ziliao* 文物參考資料 , no. 12 (1954): 190.

Xindu County Cultural Institute. "Xinduxian wenwu kaogu do xin shouhuo' 新都縣文物考古的新收穫 (New archaeological discoveries from Xindu county [Sichuan]). *Chengdu wenwu*, no. 3 (1985): 47–51.

Xu Zhongshu 徐中舒 , and Tang Jiahong 唐嘉弓 . "Gudai Chu Shu de guanxi" 古代楚蜀的關係 (The relationship between Chu and Shu in ancient times). *Wenwu*, no. 6 (1981): 17–25.

Xun Bing 迅冰 . *Sichuan Handai diaoso xuanji* 四川漢代雕塑選集 (A selection of Han sculptures from Sichuan). Beijing, 1959.

Yan Kejun 嚴可均 . *Quan Shanggu Sandai Qin Han Sanguo Liuchao wen* 全上古三代秦漢三國六朝文 (Complete writings of High Antiquity, Three Dynasties, Qin, Han, and Six Dynasties). 5 vols. Beijing, 1958.

Yang, Lien-sheng. "A Note on the So-called TLV Mirrors and the Game of Liupo." *Harvard Journal of Asiatic Studies* 9 (1947): 202–7.

Yang, Lien-sheng. "Great Families of Eastern Han." In *Chinese Social History*. Translated and edited by Sun Zen E-tu and John De Francis. Washington, D.C., 1956.

Yu Dagang 俞大綱 . "Zhongguo baixizaji fazhan xiaoshi" 中國百戲雜技發展小史 Brief history of hundred theatricals and sundry entertainments in China). *Zhongguo xueshu yu xiandai wenhua* 中國學術與現代文化 (1981): 402–34.

Yu Dezhang 余德章 . "Fuxi, Nuwa, shuang long huaxiang-zhuan shishi" 伏羲女媧・雙龍畫像磚試釋 (Pictorial tiles representing Fuxi, Nuwa, and double dragons). *Sichuan wenwu*, no. 3 (1984): 46–48.

Yu Dezhang 余德章 , and Gong, Tingwan 龔廷萬 . "Yangzishan yihao Donghan mu de huaxiang shike" 羊子山一號東漢的畫像石刻 (Pictorial stone reliefs from the Later Han tomb number one at Yangzishan). *Chengdu wenwu*, no. 3 (1984): 35–41, 109.

Yu Dezhang 余德章 . "Cong Handai jifang 'nangjiu' huax-iangzhuan shi kan shudi de nangjiu lishi" 從漢代幾方"釀酒"畫像磚石看蜀地的釀酒歷史 (The history of making wine in Sichuan as reflected in the Han pictorial reliefs). *Chengdu wenwu*, no. 2 (1985): 1–3.

Yu Haoliang 于豪亮 . "Ji Chengdu Yangzishan yihao mu" 記成都揚子山一號墓 (Report on Yangzishan tomb number one near Chengdu). *Wenwu cankao ziliao* 文物參考資料 , no. 9 (1955): 70–78.

Yu Haoliang 于豪亮 . "Sichuan Deyang jisi lingxing de wudao de huaxiang zhuan shuoming" 四川德陽祭祀靈星的舞蹈的畫像磚說明 , (On the pictorial tile 'Lingxing sac-rificial dance' from Deyang, Sichuan). *Kaogu tongxun*, no. 6 (1958): 63–64.

Yu Weichao 余偉超 . "Donghan tongzhi taozuo yaoqian-shu" 東漢銅枝陶座搖錢樹 . (On the bronze "money-tree" with pottery base from the Later Han dynasty). In *Sichuansheng Bowuguan gudai wenwu ziliao xuanji*, 45–46. Chengdu, 1983.

Yu Weichao 俞偉超 "Donghan fojiao tuxiang kao" 東漢佛教圖像考 (Study on the Later Han Buddhist imagery). *Wenwu*, no. 5 (1980): 68–77.

Yu Weichao 俞偉超 and Li Jiahao 李家浩 . "Mawangdui yihao Hanmu chutu qipin zhidi zhu wenti" 馬王堆一號漢墓出土漆品制地諸問題 (Some questions on the prove-nance of the lacquers excavated from Mawangdui tomb number one). *Kaogu*, no. 6 (1975): 344–48.

Yü, Ying-shih. "Han." In *Food in Chinese Culture: Anthropolog-ical and Historical Perspectives*, edited by K. C. Chang. New Haven, 1977.

Yü, Ying-shih. "Life and Immortality in the Mind of Han China." In *Harvard Journal of Asiatic Studies* 25 (1964–65): 80–122.

Yü Ying-shih. "The Seating Order at the Hung Men Ban-quet." In *The Translation of Things Past: Chinese History and Historiography*, edited by George Kao, 49–61. Hong Kong, 1982.

Yuan Ke 袁珂 : *Zhongguo gudai shenhu* 中國古代神話 (The ancient mythology of China). Shanghai, 1957.

Zeng Zhaoyu 曾昭燏 et al. *Yi'nan gu huaxiang shi mu fajue bao-gao* 沂南古畫像石墓發掘報告 (Archaeological report on the Yi'nan tomb reliefs). Shanghai, 1956.

Zhang Songhe 張松鶴 . "Fengfu duocai de Sichuan gudai shike yishu" 豐富多彩的四川古代石刻藝術 (The diverse art of ancient stone carvings from Sichuan). *Meishu*, no. 6 (1957): 42–44.

Zhang Wanfu 張萬夫 . *Han hua xuan* 漢畫選 (Selected pic-torial art of the Han dynasty). Tianjin, 1982.

CHINESE CULTURE FOUNDATION OF SAN FRANCISCO

BOARD OF DIRECTORS

CHAIRPERSONS
Paul Hertelendy
Rolland C. Lowe

PRESIDENT
Emory M. Lee

EXECUTIVE VICE PRESIDENT
Norman Lew

VICE PRESIDENTS
Roderick K. MacLeod
Wilma Wong
Mae C. Woo
Thomas Yee

SECRETARY
Sallie T. Wong

TREASURER
Beatrice Wong

Nancy Donnell
James R. Frolik
Bernice Hemphill
Peter Hertzmann
Robert Holstrom
Helen Y. Hui
Thomas J. Klitgaard
Kam Hong Kwong
Sau-wing Lam
George Lau
Mary Lee
Tatwina Lee
Sally Yu Leung
Stephen Lin
Paul Lum
Donald J. MacIntyre
Charles Nip
Jack T. Quan
Mayre J. Rasmussen
Julie Reinganum
David Strand
Stanley Tom
Eileen Tong
Leland Whitney
Edwin Wong
Barbara Yee
Alon Yu

ADMINISTRATION

EXECUTIVE DIRECTOR/CURATOR
Lucy Lim

ADMINISTRATOR
Vivian Chiang

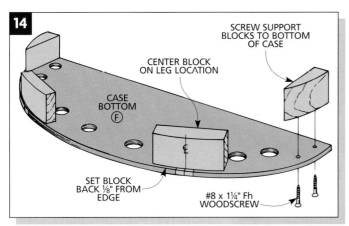

14
SCREW SUPPORT
BLOCKS TO BOTTOM
OF CASE

CENTER BLOCK
ON LEG LOCATION

CASE
BOTTOM
(F)

SET BLOCK
BACK ⅛" FROM
EDGE

#8 x 1¼" Fh
WOODSCREW

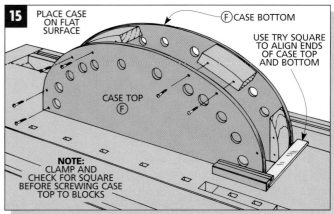

15
PLACE CASE
ON FLAT
SURFACE

(F) CASE BOTTOM

USE TRY SQUARE
TO ALIGN ENDS
OF CASE TOP
AND BOTTOM

CASE TOP
(F)

NOTE:
CLAMP AND
CHECK FOR SQUARE
BEFORE SCREWING CASE
TOP TO BLOCKS

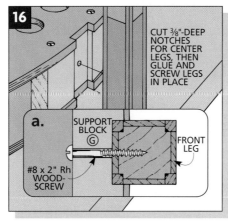

16
CUT ⅜"-DEEP
NOTCHES
FOR CENTER
LEGS, THEN
GLUE AND
SCREW LEGS
IN PLACE

a.
SUPPORT
BLOCK
(G)

FRONT
LEG

#8 x 2" Rh
WOOD-
SCREW

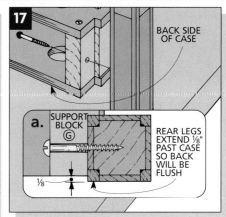

17
BACK SIDE
OF CASE

a.
SUPPORT
BLOCK
(G)

REAR LEGS
EXTEND ⅛"
PAST CASE
SO BACK
WILL BE
FLUSH

⅛

edge with the back edge resting on a flat surface *(Fig. 15)*. Then, use a try square to align one end of the case top with the bottom. Once the top and bottom are aligned, clamp them together. Then, slide the square around the curved case slowly, checking to make sure the two pieces are square with each other.

If they're not square at each support block, you can shift the top or the bottom of the case to bring them into square. Once the case pieces are aligned properly, screw the case top to the support blocks.

Note: Countersink the screws into the plywood so the table top (added later) will sit flat on the case top.

CUT NOTCHES. After the case is screwed together, the notches can be cut ⅜" deep and to fit the legs *(Fig. 12)*.

I cut these notches on the band saw by cutting the sides of the notch first and then removing the waste with a series of cuts. You could also use a hand saw to cut the sides and a chisel to remove the waste.

Whichever method you use, it's very important that the back of each notch (from top to bottom and from side to side) be parallel to the front edge of the case. If they aren't, this can cause a couple of problems.

First, the legs can twist and won't be parallel to each other. Second, the aprons that are added later won't butt up against the legs squarely. So, check the notches as you cut them.

ATTACH LEGS. Once all four notches are cut, the next step is to screw the legs to the case. To do this, start by drilling a ³⁄₁₆"-dia. shank hole through each support block *(Figs. 16 and 17)*. Center the hole in the notch.

The next step is to locate a pilot hole in each leg. To make it easier to do this,

turn the case upside down and place it on a flat surface. Then insert a leg in a notch and hold it in place. Next, push an awl or brad-point bit through the shank hole so it leaves a mark on the leg.

After drilling the pilot holes in the back of each leg, spread glue in the notches and on the back of each leg. Then screw the legs in place, making sure they're perpendicular to the case.

SHOP INFO .... *Flush Trim Bit*

Flush trim bits are used with a template to produce an exact copy of the template.

A flush trim bit is a straight bit with a bearing on the end that aligns with the cutting edges of the bit (see drawing below).

By running the bearing along a template, a workpiece can be cut to

the same shape as the template.

To use a flush trim bit, first trace the outline of the template onto the workpiece. Then you can cut the work-piece to rough shape, staying ⅛" outside the line.

Next, fasten the template to the workpiece with double-sided carpet tape or screws. Then adjust the height of the bit so that the bearing rides on the edge of the template (see drawing). Now you can rout the workpiece to final shape.

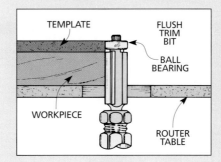

TEMPLATE

FLUSH
TRIM
BIT

BALL
BEARING

WORKPIECE

ROUTER
TABLE

The next step is to make the apron that wraps around the front of the case.

CUT BLANK. The apron (H) starts as a strip of $3/4$"-thick plywood, 4" wide and 48" long *(Fig. 18)*. This blank will be cut into three sections later.

Note: The face grain of the plywood should run the length of the strip.

Before cutting the apron into sections, I added a walnut inlay (I) strip. To do this, rout a $1/4$"-wide rabbet along the bottom edge *(Fig. 18a)*. Then cut the inlay strip to fit the rabbet. After it's glued in place, sand the inlay flush.

CUT SECTIONS. Now the apron can be cut into three sections. To determine the rough length of each section, measure between the legs along the curved case. Then, to allow for the thickness of the plywood and for trimming later, add $1\frac{1}{2}$" to each measurement. (I cut the two end sections 14" long and the middle section 18" long.)

KERFS. The next step is to kerf the aprons so they will follow the curve of the case (refer to the opposite page). I spaced the kerfs $1/4$" apart *(Fig. 18b)*.

To make it easier to get a tight fit where the aprons meet the legs, cut a

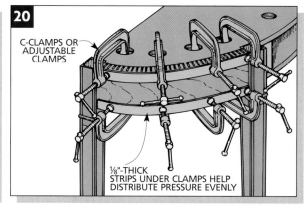

18

H APRON

I APRON INLAY

4

48

$1/4$

GLUE INLAY INTO RABBET BEFORE CUTTING APRONS TO ROUGH LENGTH. THEN KERF EACH SECTION.

a. CUT RABBET FOR INLAY
$1/4$
$1/16$

b. $1/4$ $1/8$
LEAVE $1/8$" UNKERFED

10° bevel on one end of each apron *(Fig. 19a)*. Then to get an idea of the final length, curl the apron around the edge of the case and make a mark where the unbeveled end meets the leg *(Fig. 19)*. Sneak up on the final length by taking light, 10° bevel cuts until the apron just fits between the legs.

After fitting all three apron sections between the legs, they can be glued and clamped to the case *(Fig. 20)*. I added clamping strips to protect the apron and distribute the pressure evenly.

BACK. The next step is to add the back. To determine the length of the back, measure the inside distance between the rear legs *(Fig. 21)*. Then measure the height (thickness) of the case to determine the width of the back. Finally, cut the back (J) to size.

RABBETS. Since the legs protrude $1/8$" from the back of the case, you need to cut rabbets that leave $1/8$"-thick tongues on the edges of the back (J). Cut the rabbets on the ends to match the width of the rear support blocks *(Fig. 21a)*.

The rabbets along the top and bottom edges of the back (J) match the thickness of the plywood in the case ($1/2$"). Finally, glue the back to the case.

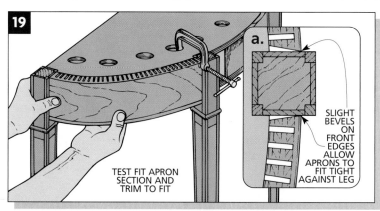

19

a.

SLIGHT BEVELS ON FRONT EDGES ALLOW APRONS TO FIT TIGHT AGAINST LEG

TEST FIT APRON SECTION AND TRIM TO FIT

20

C-CLAMPS OR ADJUSTABLE CLAMPS

$1/8$"-THICK STRIPS UNDER CLAMPS HELP DISTRIBUTE PRESSURE EVENLY

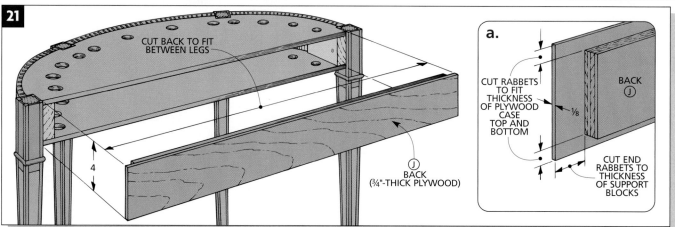

21

CUT BACK TO FIT BETWEEN LEGS

4

J BACK ($3/4$"-THICK PLYWOOD)

a.

CUT RABBETS TO FIT THICKNESS OF PLYWOOD CASE TOP AND BOTTOM

$1/8$

BACK **J**

CUT END RABBETS TO THICKNESS OF SUPPORT BLOCKS

TECHNIQUE .... Kerf Bending

Kerf bending is an easy way to bend wood. It's just a matter of cutting a series of grooves (kerfs) to relieve the back of the workpiece so that it will flex.

KERF DEPTH

When you cut kerfs for bending, you cut almost all the way through the workpiece (see photo and *Fig. 1*).

PLYWOOD. Kerf bending works on solid wood and even hardboard (which can then be covered with veneer). But

to save money and the trouble of veneering, I chose cherry plywood for the Curved-Front Table.

One reason plywood works well has to do with the ply just beneath the face veneer *(Fig. 1)*. When kerfing plywood, you barely score this second ply. The web that remains consists of the thicker second ply and the thin face veneer.

By kerfing plywood *across* the face grain, the kerf runs with the grain of the second ply *(Fig. 2)*. The face veneer holds it together and allows it to flex.

Once it's kerfed, hardwood plywood typically bends more easily than softwood (fir) plywood. The main reason is that the face veneer on hardwood plywood is thinner, so it's more flexible.

SPACING

The spacing between kerfs not only will affect the radius that you can bend, but also how smooth the bent piece will look. The reason is the "flats" that form over the ribs between the kerfs *(Fig. 3)*.

As a general rule, the closer the kerfs are together, the tighter the radius you can bend. But more important, closely spaced kerfs provide a smooth curve. In most cases, I space the kerfs about $1/4$" to $3/8$" apart.

If you cut the kerfs close together, you may still experience flats to some degree — even if you can't see them easily. But they may become noticeable when you apply a finish.

SANDING. Small flats can be removed easily by sanding. But the wider the flat is, the more sanding you'll have to do. To allow the most control, I use a hardwood sanding block (not a power sander). Take smooth, gradual strokes following the contour, and constantly check the surface of the work. Stop

sanding as soon as all the flats disappear — don't over-sand. Since face veneers on hardwood plywood may be $1/32$" thick or less, it's very easy to sand right through it *(Fig. 3)*.

FINISHING

Any remaining flat areas will become apparent when you apply a finish. So first, I apply a light coat of sealer to the kerf-bent piece and examine it closely. To do this, I use a light at a low angle to the surface of the piece, checking once more for flats before applying the final coats.

I also recommend a satin finish rather than a high gloss. The reason for this is if there are any flats (even small ones), they'll show up more with a gloss finish than with a satin or matte finish.

KERFING JIG

A simple indexing jig will help you cut uniformly spaced kerfs.

To make the jig, drive a No. 4 screw near the bottom edge of an auxiliary fence fastened to your saw's miter gauge. Then cut off the head *(Fig. 4)*. As each kerf is cut, just lift the board and place the kerf over the screw.

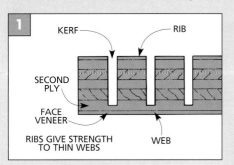

1 KERF — RIB — SECOND PLY — FACE VENEER — WEB — RIBS GIVE STRENGTH TO THIN WEBS

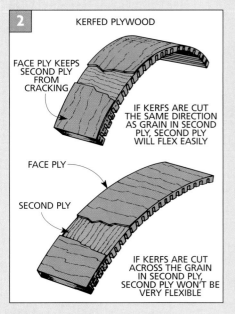

2 KERFED PLYWOOD

FACE PLY KEEPS SECOND PLY FROM CRACKING

IF KERFS ARE CUT THE SAME DIRECTION AS GRAIN IN SECOND PLY, SECOND PLY WILL FLEX EASILY

FACE PLY — SECOND PLY

IF KERFS ARE CUT ACROSS THE GRAIN IN SECOND PLY, SECOND PLY WON'T BE VERY FLEXIBLE

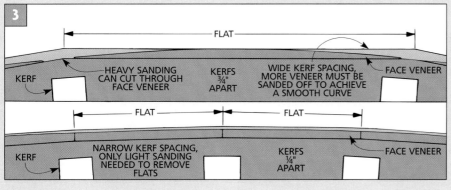

3 FLAT

KERF — HEAVY SANDING CAN CUT THROUGH FACE VENEER — KERFS $3/4$" APART — WIDE KERF SPACING, MORE VENEER MUST BE SANDED OFF TO ACHIEVE A SMOOTH CURVE — FACE VENEER

FLAT — FLAT

KERF — NARROW KERF SPACING, ONLY LIGHT SANDING NEEDED TO REMOVE FLATS — KERFS $1/4$" APART — FACE VENEER

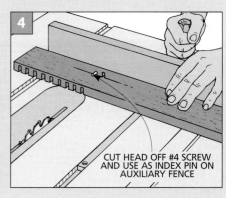

4 CUT HEAD OFF #4 SCREW AND USE AS INDEX PIN ON AUXILIARY FENCE

The last step is to add the table top. I made the top out of cherry plywood and covered the edges with strips of walnut. For an accent, I also added an inlay strip of walnut just inside the perimeter of the top.

TOP BLANK. Start work on the table top (K) by cutting a blank of $^3/_4$"-thick plywood to rough size (mine was about 15" x 38") *(Fig. 22)*. This blank is then cut into a half-oval shape so it will overhang the case by $1^1/_2$" on each side and along the front edge.

To do this, you could make a new template that's $1^1/_2$" larger than the one used for making the case. But there's an easier way — just enlarge the size of the original template onto the plywood blank by using a compass *(Fig. 22)*. Once the layout lines are drawn, rough cut the top $^1/_8$" outside of the pencil line.

That's great for getting the top to rough shape. But how do you use a router to trim the top to final shape without a new template? Simple. Use a pilot strip to position the bit the correct distance from the template *(Fig. 22a)*. (For more on this, see the Shop Tip at the bottom of page 17.)

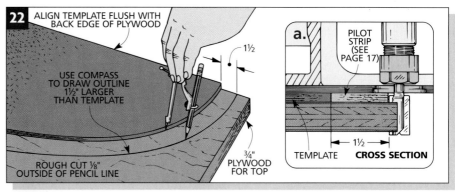

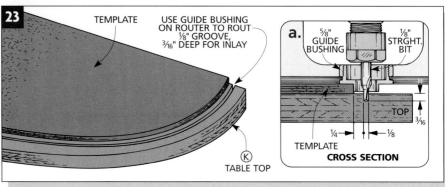

CUT GROOVE FOR INLAY. Once you've trimmed the top, the next step is to cut a groove for a top inlay strip *(Fig. 23)*. To do this, leave the template fastened to the top (K). But this time, mount a $^5/_8$"

guide bushing and a $^1/_8$" straight bit in the router to rout a $^3/_{16}$"-deep groove in the top *(Fig. 23a)*.

INLAY. After routing the groove, an inlay strip (L) of walnut can be cut to fit.

SHOP TIP . . . . *Drawing a Partial Ellipse*

Drawing a partial ellipse onto a hardboard template isn't difficult. All it takes to lay it out is a pencil, a piece of thin wire and a couple of nails.

Start by drawing a line $1^3/_8$" from one edge of the hardboard, and as long as the length of the table top template (33") *(Fig. 1)*. Mark one end of the line A, and the other end C. Now find the centerpoint and mark it B.

Now, draw a perpendicular line from the centerpoint (B). Make it the same length as the width of the table top (11"). Mark the top end of this line D.

Next, locate two nail points. To do this, use a ruler or compass to find the distance from A to B (or B to C, which should be the same). Then measure this distance from point D to line AB, and also to line BC *(Fig. 2)*. These are your nail points. Mark them N1 and N2.

So much for the hard part. The next step is to drive a nail or brad into N1,

N2, and D. Then loop a piece of thin wire (I used 32 gauge) tightly around all three nails and twist the ends together. (Don't use string — it stretches too much.)

Finally, to draw the ellipse, remove the nail at D and replace it with a pencil point. Keeping the wire taut, draw an arc from D to A and from D to C *(Fig. 3)*.

Note: To keep the wire from sliding, notch the pencil tip about $^1/_2$" from the end *(Fig. 3a)*.

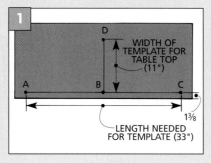

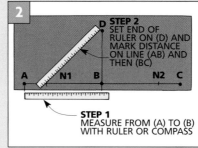

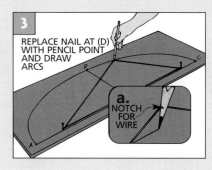

SHOP TIP

Trimming Inlay Flush

STRAIGHT BIT

INLAY STRIP

PAD

To trim inlay without chipout, fasten a pair of pads onto the router base with carpet tape so the bit straddles the inlay. Then adjust a straight bit so it *almost* contacts the table top. After routing, sand the inlay flush.

At the same time, I cut the strips for the back trim (M) and front trim (N) since they're all the same thickness (1/8").

Rip the top inlay to 1/4" wide and glue it into the groove *(Fig. 24)*.

Note: To make it easier to glue the inlay in place, you may want to plane a slight bevel on each face of the inlay.

When the glue dries, trim the inlay flush with the top. The Shop Tip above shows a trick for trimming most of the waste using a router.

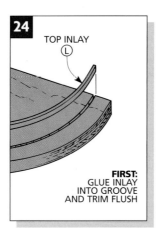

24 TOP INLAY (L)

FIRST: GLUE INLAY INTO GROOVE AND TRIM FLUSH

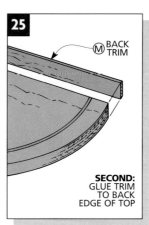

25 BACK TRIM (M)

SECOND: GLUE TRIM TO BACK EDGE OF TOP

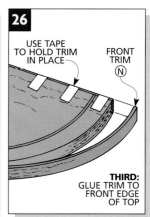

26 USE TAPE TO HOLD TRIM IN PLACE — FRONT TRIM (N)

THIRD: GLUE TRIM TO FRONT EDGE OF TOP

TRIM. The next step is to glue on the trim strips that hide the plies on the edges of the top. I glued on the back trim (M) first *(Fig. 25)*. A few strips of tape will help hold the strip in place *(Fig. 26)*. When the glue is dry, cut the trim flush with the ends of the top. Then, the front trim (N) can be glued on to overlap the ends of the back trim *(Figs. 26 and 27)*. Again, trim it flush after the glue dries.

ATTACH TOP. Now the top can be attached to the case. Since both the top and the case are made from plywood (which won't expand or contract with changes in humidity), I simply glued the top to the case.

When doing this, position the top so the back trim (M) is flush with the back (J), and so that the top (K) overhangs an equal amount on both ends *(Fig. 27)*. Then clamp the top in place.

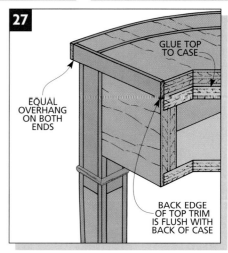

27

GLUE TOP TO CASE

EQUAL OVERHANG ON BOTH ENDS

BACK EDGE OF TOP TRIM IS FLUSH WITH BACK OF CASE

FINISH. After attaching the top, I sanded the entire table and then wiped on one coat of an oil/urethane finish. I added two coats of a satin top coat once the oil had dried. ■

SHOP TIP .... *Router Pilot Strip*

When it came time to make the top for the Curved-Front Table, there was a problem. I wanted the top to have the exact same elliptical shape as the case — only larger.

The best solution was to find a way to use the same template that I made for the case parts.

The technique I came up with is to tape a strip of wood to the base of the router (see drawing). This pilot strip keeps the router bit a uniform distance from the edge of the tem-

plate. And that makes the top the same shape as the template, but larger.

To make the pilot strip, cut a small scrap of stock 1 1/2 " wide and 5 " long. The strip should be the same thickness as the template (1/4 " in my case).

Then fasten the strip to the router base using double-sided carpet tape. Position the strip so it just touches the edge of the straight bit you use for trimming (see drawing).

Now, to use the pilot strip, start by taping the

template in place and cutting the workpiece slightly oversize (refer to *Fig. 22* on opposite page). Then set the router on the workpiece so the edge of the pilot strip rides against the edge of the template

(see drawing). Try not to "rock" the router along the template as you trim. Rocking will increase the distance between the table top and the bit. Clean up any unevenness with a final pass.

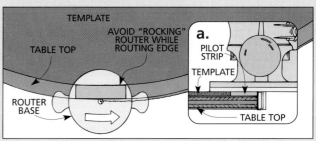

TEMPLATE

TABLE TOP

AVOID "ROCKING" ROUTER WHILE ROUTING EDGE

ROUTER BASE

a.

PILOT STRIP

TEMPLATE

TABLE TOP

DESIGNER'S NOTEBOOK

Even though this table is built without inlays, it still has plenty of details. The tapered legs have cove accents, beads are added below the aprons, and the solid wood top features a classic edge profile.

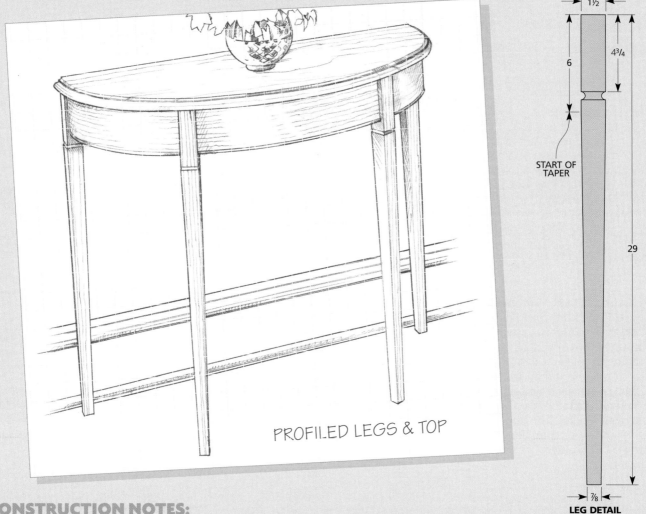

PROFILED LEGS & TOP

LEG DETAIL

1½

4¾

6

29

⅞

START OF TAPER

CONSTRUCTION NOTES:

■ Construction of this table is largely the same as that for the regular Curved-Front Table. Begin by cutting the legs to width and length (see Leg Detail above). Then taper all four sides.

MATERIALS LIST

CHANGED PART
K Table Top (1)   ¾ x 14⅛ - 36¼
NEW PARTS
O End Apron Beads (2) ¼ x 3½ - 14 rgh.
P Front Apron Bead (1) ¼ x 3½ - 20 rgh.

Note: Do not need parts B, C, D, E, I, L, M, N.

HARDWARE SUPPLIES
(6) No. 8 x 1" Fh woodscrews

■ Instead of cutting rabbets or dadoes in the legs, a ½" cove is routed around each one (*Fig. 1* and Leg Detail above).

■ With the legs completed, the case pieces can be cut to size and the case assembled the same way as the regular table. Then the legs can be attached.

■ Next, cut the aprons to width and kerf them to wrap around the table's front.

Note: Since they don't receive an inlay, don't rabbet the edges of the aprons.

■ Glue the aprons in place, then cut the back (J) to size and glue it to the case.

BEADING

■ This table has beading (O, P) below the aprons. Start by cutting two blanks from ¼" stock (*Fig. 2*).

■ Then attach a blank to the top of the case with carpet tape so that the back edge of the blank is aligned with the back inside corners of two legs (*Fig. 3*).

■ Turn the table upside down. Then transfer the locations of the edges of the legs onto the blank (*Fig. 4*).

■ Next, use a compass to scribe the curve of the top onto the blank (*Fig. 5*). Repeat this process with the two remaining bead blanks.

■ Now the beading can be cut to shape. I used a bevel gauge to transfer the angle of the layout line from the blank to my table saw's miter gauge. Then I trimmed the ends of each blank.

Note: I cut the blanks a little wide of the marks so I could sneak up to the final width, testing the fit between the legs until I had a uniform, $\frac{1}{4}$" reveal along the front of the table.

■ The curved fronts can be trimmed to rough shape on the band saw. Then sand up to the lines.

■ The curved edge of each apron bead (O, P) is rounded over using a $\frac{1}{8}$" roundover bit mounted in the router table *(Fig. 6)*. Routing the first side is simple. But when making the pass on the opposite face, there isn't a flat edge for the bearing to ride on. To remedy this, align the router table fence with the bearing on the bit.

■ Before gluing the beading in place, the bottom of the case needs to be cut away so you can reach in later to screw the top on *(Fig. 7)*. I used a jig saw to saw between the clamp holes, then sanded the edges smooth. To keep the back (J) rigid, leave a 1"-wide strip of the case bottom along the back edge.

■ Now you can glue the beading (O, P) in place below the aprons *(Fig. 8)*. The ends of the beads should fit snug against the legs.

TABLE TOP

■ With the case completed, work can begin on the table top (K). Start by gluing up a solid wood blank to a rough size of $14\frac{1}{2}$" x $36\frac{1}{2}$".

■ Once the blank is dry, the template used to shape the case top and bottom is needed to lay out the shape of the table top (K) (refer to *Fig. 22* on page 16).

■ Before cutting the top to shape, fasten a piece of $\frac{1}{4}$" hardboard to the bottom edge using double-sided carpet tape. (After this assembly is cut to shape, the hardboard will provide a wider surface for the router bit bearing when a profile is cut on the top edge of the table top.)

■ Now you can cut the table top and the hardboard to shape on the band saw.

■ Next, a profile is routed on the curved edge of the table top *(Fig. 8)*. (The back edge is left square.) To avoid chipout where the end grain transitions into edge grain, refer to the "PROFILE" section and the Shop Tip on page 25.

■ Once the profile is completed, the top can be fastened to the case. Remove the hardboard, then place the table top on the case. There should be an equal amount of overhang on each side and the back of the top should be flush with the back of the case *(Fig. 8)*. To allow the top to expand and contract, drill oversized shank holes through the case, then screw the top in place.

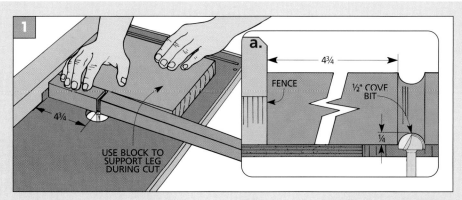

1

USE BLOCK TO SUPPORT LEG DURING CUT

$4\frac{3}{4}$

a.

$4\frac{3}{4}$

FENCE

$\frac{1}{2}$" COVE BIT

$\frac{1}{4}$

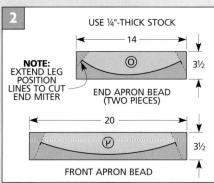

2

USE $\frac{1}{4}$"-THICK STOCK

14

○

$3\frac{1}{2}$

NOTE: EXTEND LEG POSITION LINES TO CUT END MITER

END APRON BEAD (TWO PIECES)

20

(P)

$3\frac{1}{2}$

FRONT APRON BEAD

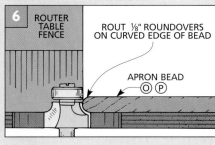

3

ALIGN BACK EDGE OF BLANK WITH CORNERS OF LEGS

FASTEN BEAD BLANK TO CASE WITH DOUBLE-SIDED CARPET TAPE

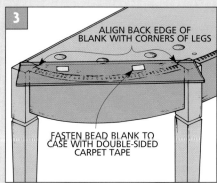

5

SET COMPASS TO $\frac{1}{4}$" WIDTH, THEN TRANSFER CURVE TO BEAD BLANK

4

FIRST: MARK EDGE OF LEG ONTO BLANK

END APRON BEAD BLANK

SECOND: EXTEND LINE TO EDGE OF BLANK

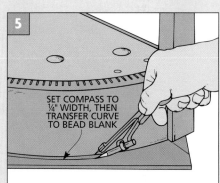

6

ROUTER TABLE FENCE

ROUT $\frac{1}{8}$" ROUNDOVERS ON CURVED EDGE OF BEAD

APRON BEAD ○ (P)

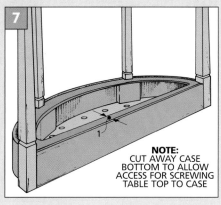

7

1

NOTE: CUT AWAY CASE BOTTOM TO ALLOW ACCESS FOR SCREWING TABLE TOP TO CASE

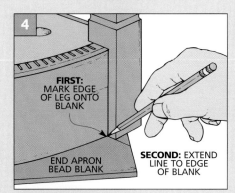

8

ATTACH TABLE TOP TO CASE TOP WITH #8 x 1" Fh WOODSCREWS

REFER TO PAGE 25 TO ROUT TABLE TOP PROFILE

SUPPORT BLOCK

APRON

CASE TOP

CROSS SECTION

APRON BEAD

CASE BOTTOM WITH CENTER SECTION CUT OUT

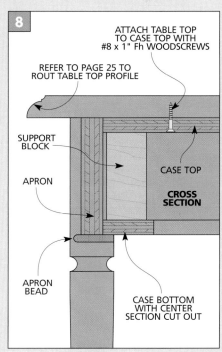

Coffee Table

Simply elegant and easier to build than you might think, this table is sure to become an heirloom. You can make the cabriole legs with just a band saw and some hand tools, or buy them ready-made.

This mahogany Coffee Table is in the elegant Queen Anne style. It features graceful cabriole legs, scalloped aprons around the base, and an oval top with a hand-rubbed finish. But don't assume that any of those features demand a lot of highly specialized skills or tools. They don't.

CABRIOLE LEGS. The legs are the most involved part of this table. But even so, it takes only three cuts on the band saw to give you a roughed-out leg. Then, with some handwork, you can bring it to final shape easily. To walk you through making them, there's a step-by-step article on page 106.

APRONS. The aprons that tie the legs together each have a scallop along the bottom edge. One template is all you need to lay out the profiles on both the front and side aprons before cutting them on the band saw.

PRE-MADE LEGS. If you'd rather buy legs than build them, a variety of pre-made legs are available (see page 126 for sources). They allow you to change the look of the table easily, plus it speeds up construction considerably. In fact, the Designer's Notebook on page 28 offers a set of three tables with a simpler look. By using pre-made legs, the entire set can be built in just a few days.

JOINERY. Whichever version you choose to build, the aprons are fastened to the legs with traditional mortise and tenon joints. And since the table top is a solid wood panel, Z-shaped fasteners secure it to the aprons while allowing the top to expand and contract.

FINISH. Even if you purchased legs for the table, you can still show off a bit of handwork. The high gloss finish on the table top is the result of hand rubbing. Here again, no special skills are needed to handle this job. You can easily buff a mirror-like finish on the table top by following the steps in the Finishing article on page 42.

EXPLODED VIEW

OVERALL DIMENSIONS:
30W x 48L x 18H

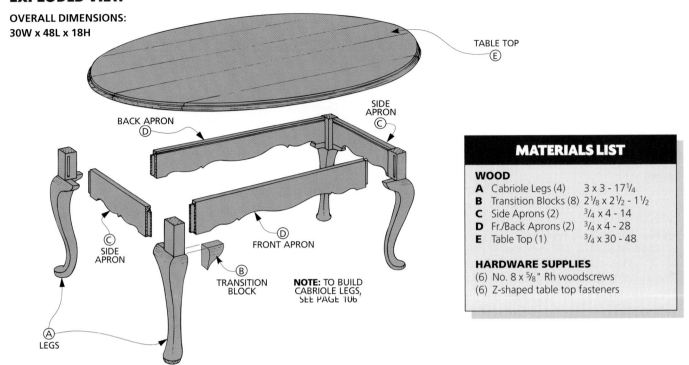

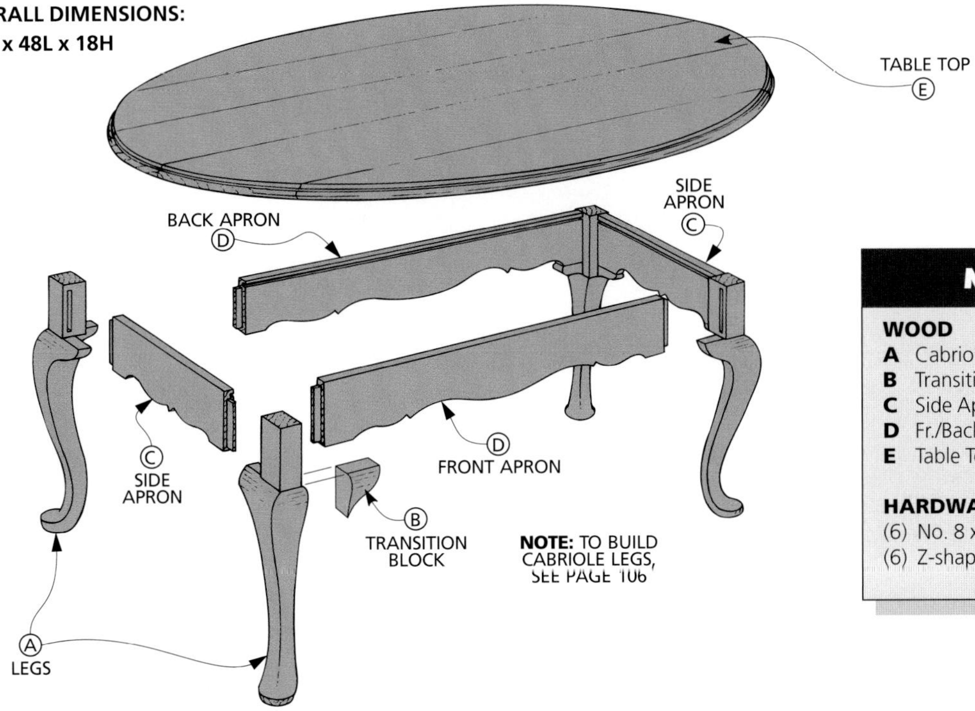
TABLE TOP
E
SIDE APRON
C
BACK APRON
D
C
SIDE APRON
D
FRONT APRON
B
TRANSITION BLOCK
NOTE: TO BUILD CABRIOLE LEGS, SEE PAGE 106
A
LEGS

MATERIALS LIST		
WOOD		
A	Cabriole Legs (4)	3 x 3 - 17¼
B	Transition Blocks (8)	2⅛ x 2½ - 1½
C	Side Aprons (2)	¾ x 4 - 14
D	Fr./Back Aprons (2)	¾ x 4 - 28
E	Table Top (1)	¾ x 30 - 48

HARDWARE SUPPLIES
(6) No. 8 x ⅝" Rh woodscrews
(6) Z-shaped table top fasteners

CUTTING DIAGRAM

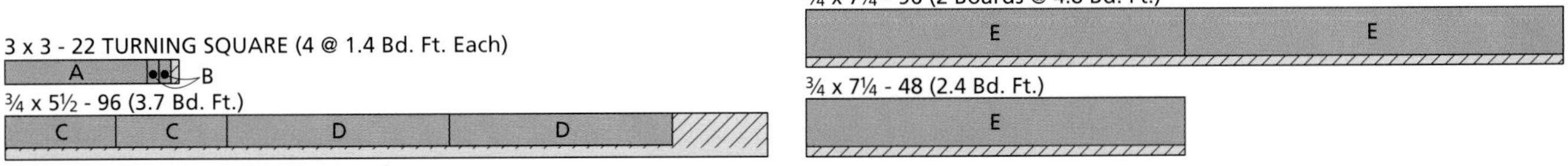
3 x 3 - 22 TURNING SQUARE (4 @ 1.4 Bd. Ft. Each)
A
B
¾ x 5½ - 96 (3.7 Bd. Ft.)
C
C
D
D
¾ x 7¼ - 96 (2 Boards @ 4.8 Bd. Ft.)
E
E
¾ x 7¼ - 48 (2.4 Bd. Ft.)
E

SHOP JIG . . . . Leg Clamping Jig

After cutting cabriole legs to rough shape on the band saw, they still need to be filed and sanded to their final shape. To do this, you need a way to hold the leg steady that leaves room to work around it. My solution was a jig that attaches to a pipe clamp.

The jig pieces are 8" lengths of 2x4 stock with a hole bored through one end of each piece for the pipe *(Fig. 1)*.

To keep the tailstock from swiveling, I cut a kerf along the bottom edge using a band saw *(Fig. 2)*. Then I added a carriage bolt and wing nut. Once the jaw is set where you need it, tighten the wing nut to keep the tailstock from turning.

Keeping the headstock from moving is even easier. Just cut a notch in one edge to fit the jaw of the clamp *(Fig. 1)*.

As the clamp is tightened, both the headstock and tailstock tend to tilt back. To compensate for this, I planed a slight taper on the inside edge of each piece. Finally, I added a piece of self-adhesive sandpaper to the inside face of each jaw to give it a better grip.

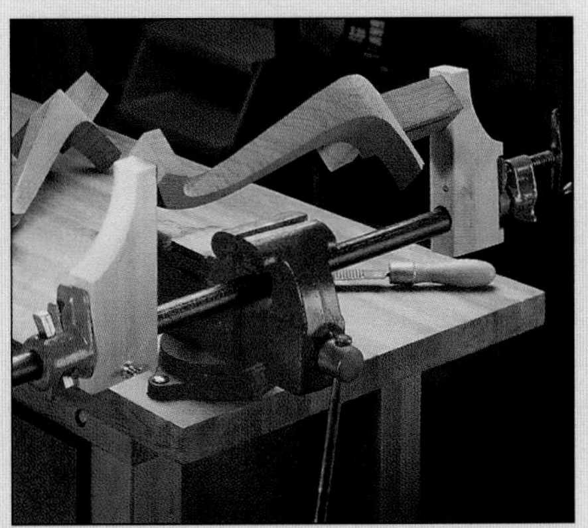

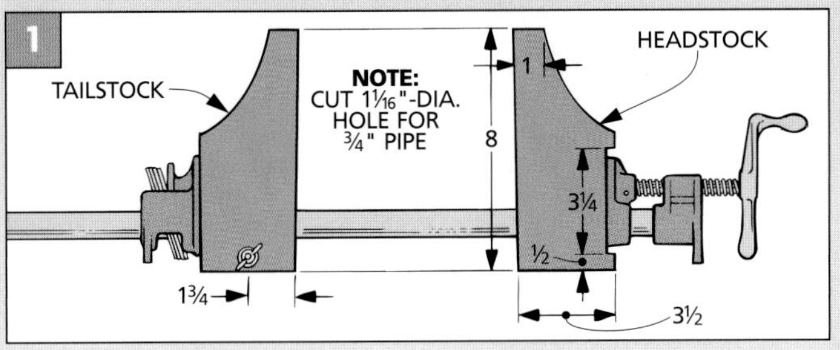
1
TAILSTOCK
NOTE: CUT 1¹⁄₁₆"-DIA. HOLE FOR ¾" PIPE
HEADSTOCK
1
8
3¼
½
1¾
3½

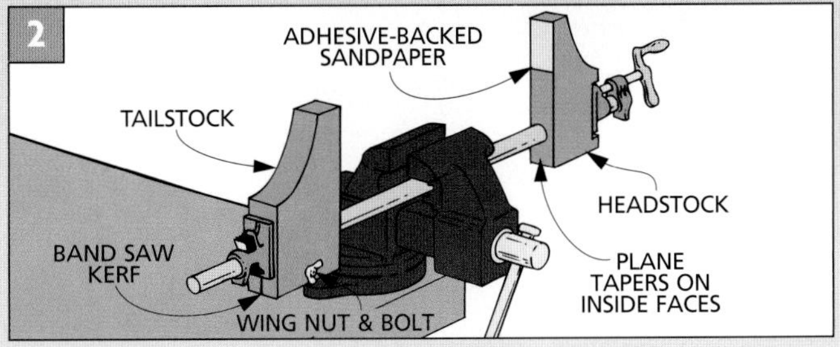
2
ADHESIVE-BACKED SANDPAPER
TAILSTOCK
HEADSTOCK
BAND SAW KERF
WING NUT & BOLT
PLANE TAPERS ON INSIDE FACES

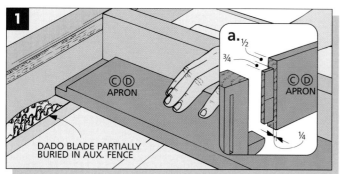

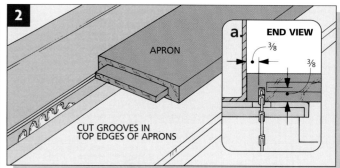

BASE

The base of the table consists of the cabriole legs at each corner and the aprons that tie them together.

CABRIOLE LEGS. The first thing you need to do is to make the legs (A). To do this, refer to the Technique article on page 106. Or you can buy legs already made (see page 126 for sources). If you prefer to use pre-made legs, see the Woodworker's Notebook below.

APRONS. When the legs are complete, the next step is to connect them with ³/₄"-thick side aprons (C) and front

and back aprons (D). These pieces are all the same width and each will have a scalloped profile cut on its bottom edge later (refer to *Fig. 3*).

Before cutting the decorative profiles, I cut the tenons on the aprons to fit the mortises in the legs (*Fig. 1*).

To do this, I secured a plywood auxiliary fence to my table saw's rip fence. Then I used a dado blade to cut the tenons, centering each one on the thickness of the apron (*Fig. 1a*).

Then, after the tenons had been cut, I cut a groove on the top inside face of each apron (*Fig. 2*). These grooves

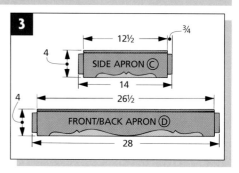

hold the Z-shaped fasteners used later to secure the table top to the base. This groove is simply a ³/₈"-deep saw kerf that runs the length of the apron.

WOODWORKER'S NOTEBOOK

Ready-made legs save you time and effort, especially with this simple block to help drill the mortises.

DRILLING FACTORY-MADE LEGS

One option that will make the Coffee Table and the Jewelry Cabinet (pages 96-109) easier to build is to purchase the legs instead of making them (see photo at right). (For sources, see page 126.) But even pre-made legs will need mortises drilled in the corner posts to hold the stretchers and rails.

The shape of a cabriole leg will not allow the post to sit flat on the drill press table when drilling mortise holes. So to

keep the leg square, I made a spacer block to cradle it.

It's made from two pieces of 1¹/₂"-thick stock glued together to form an L-shaped block (see drawing). It holds the cabriole leg up off the table and out from the fence (see photo below).

This way, the block keeps the face of the corner post square to the bit. And it also keeps the leg and fence aligned so the mortises are drilled in a straight line.

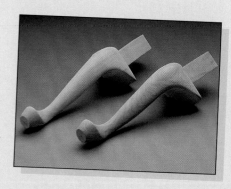

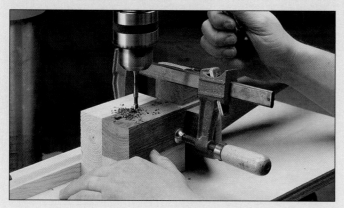

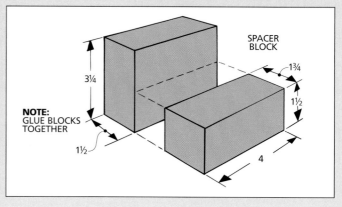

SCALLOPED PROFILES. Now the aprons are ready for their decorative profiles. The nice thing is, the profile is the same on both the side aprons and the front/back aprons, so only one template is needed to lay out both.

To create this template, you can lay it out on a sheet of paper using the simple grid and pattern shown below. Or to make things easier, you can buy a set of full-sized patterns from *Woodsmith Project Supplies*. This includes patterns for the cabriole legs, aprons, and top (see page 126 for information).

With the template complete, I began laying out the profile on the front and back aprons *(Fig. 4)*. To do this, the base will need to be dry-assembled first. That's because the curve on the apron must start where the transition block on the leg ends *(Fig. 4a)*. (It's also important to keep the top edges of the template and apron flush.)

Draw the profile onto the apron, then flip the template over and draw it again, starting from the other end. The lines should meet in a shallow curve at the center of the apron *(Fig. 3)*.

The profile on the side aprons duplicates part of the profile on the front/back aprons *(Fig. 5)*. So I simply trimmed off the template. As with the front/back aprons, the curve starts at the transition block, so you may need to adjust the centerpoint of the profile.

After the profiles are laid out, the scalloped edges can be cut. The important thing here is to get a clean, sharp corner at the "point" of the profile. To do this, I started by cutting the point of each profile *(Fig. 6a)*. Then I cut from the ends along the curves to the point to remove the waste *(Fig. 6)*. A narrow (1/8") blade in the band saw makes it easy to cut clean curves.

Finally, I glued and clamped the base together. After the glue dried, I sanded the scalloped edges smooth, making sure the joint lines between the transition blocks on the legs and the aprons were flush *(Fig. 7)*. A dowel wrapped with sandpaper makes a good sanding block for this curved surface.

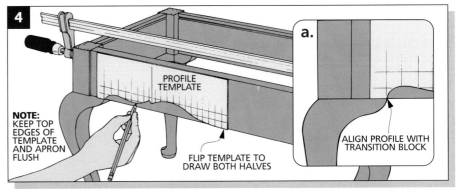

4

PROFILE TEMPLATE

NOTE: KEEP TOP EDGES OF TEMPLATE AND APRON FLUSH

FLIP TEMPLATE TO DRAW BOTH HALVES

a.

ALIGN PROFILE WITH TRANSITION BLOCK

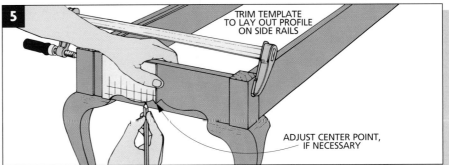

5

TRIM TEMPLATE TO LAY OUT PROFILE ON SIDE RAILS

ADJUST CENTER POINT, IF NECESSARY

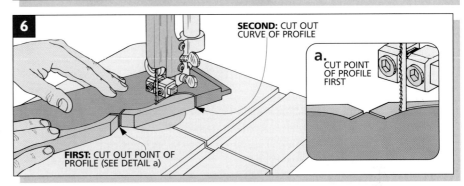

6

SECOND: CUT OUT CURVE OF PROFILE

a. CUT POINT OF PROFILE FIRST

FIRST: CUT OUT POINT OF PROFILE (SEE DETAIL a)

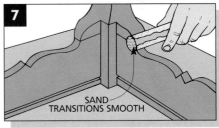

7

SAND TRANSITIONS SMOOTH

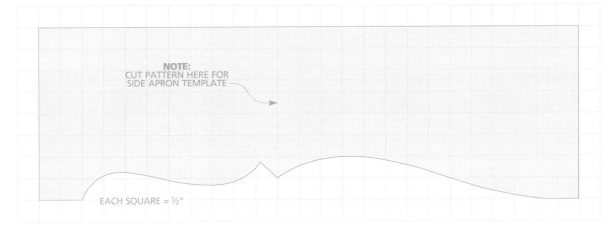

NOTE: CUT PATTERN HERE FOR SIDE APRON TEMPLATE

EACH SQUARE = 1/2"

With the base complete, I set about to build the top. This is pretty simple, really. The top is just a glued-up mahogany panel cut in an oval shape.

PAPER PATTERN. The first thing to do is to create a paper pattern for the top (see pattern at right). Then I created a hardboard template from this pattern and used the template as a guide when cutting and routing.

The oval shape of this table isn't a true ellipse. So it has to be drawn "freehand." The Shop Tip below shows you a way to do this.

Note: There's no need to make a full pattern; a quarter pattern will do. And if you don't want to make your own, a full-sized quarter pattern is available. See page 126 for information.

HARDBOARD TEMPLATE. With the paper quarter pattern complete, I used it to make a full-sized template out of ¼"-thick hardboard *(Fig. 8)*. There are a couple of advantages to creating a hardboard template for this project.

For one thing, if you happen to make a mistake when cutting or sanding the template, it's no big deal. Hardboard is cheap compared to mahogany. And it's much easier to shape and sand a ¼"-thick hardboard template than a panel made from ¾"-thick solid wood.

Also, I was able to use the template to guide the router bits as I shaped the edge (refer to *Figs. 10 and 11*).

To make the template, I started by cutting an oversized blank (30" x 48")

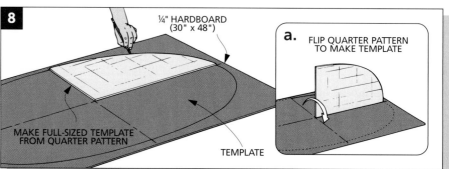

EACH SQUARE = 2"

TABLE TOP QUARTER PATTERN

NOTE:
TO LAY OUT GRID,
SEE SHOP TIP BELOW

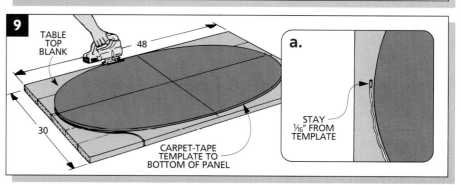

8 ¼" HARDBOARD
(30" x 48")

MAKE FULL-SIZED TEMPLATE
FROM QUARTER PATTERN

TEMPLATE

a. FLIP QUARTER PATTERN
TO MAKE TEMPLATE

9 TABLE
TOP
BLANK   48

30

CARPET-TAPE
TEMPLATE TO
BOTTOM OF PANEL

a. STAY
1⁄16" FROM
TEMPLATE

SHOP TIP . . . . *Quick and Easy Grid*

Here's a quick way to draw freehand curves by first creating a rough grid.
  To make the grid, just hold a tape measure firmly with one hand and

"hook" a pencil on the end of the tape (left and center photos). A finger serves as a guide along the edges of the bench.

With the grid drawn, plot the points of the desired curve on the grid. Then just connect the dots with a smooth line (right photo).

and drawing centerlines on the top to create "cross hairs" *(Fig. 8)*. Next, I drew the pattern on the blank, flipping it around the centerlines until the layout was complete *(Fig. 8a)*.

When cutting out the template, I used a jig saw with a fine-tooth blade, staying $1/16$" from the line. Then I sanded up to the line.

OVERSIZED PANEL. Now that the template is complete, the next step is to glue up a $3/4$"-thick blank for the top (E). This blank starts out the same size as the template blank (30" x 48").

When the glue is dry, plane and sand the panel flat. Then use carpet tape to attach the hardboard template to the bottom face of the panel *(Fig. 9)*.

TRIM FLUSH. Like the template, I cut the panel to rough size using the jig saw. But this time, to get the panel flush with the template, I used a flush trim bit in the router *(Figs. 10 and 10a)*.

However, when routing the edge of the table top, you're likely to run into some chipout on the end grain. The solution is to backrout the edge. This means taking a number of *light* passes moving the router clockwise around the table top (see the Shop Tip below).

Safety Note: When backrouting, have the workpiece clamped securely to the bench, take *very light* cuts and keep your arms tucked into your body for better control of the router.

PROFILE. Next, I routed a profile along the top edge of the table *(Figs. 11 and 11a)*. I chose a special bit designed specially for table top edges. (For sources of this bit, see page 126.)

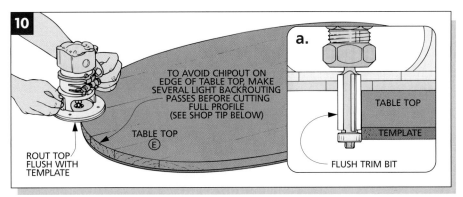
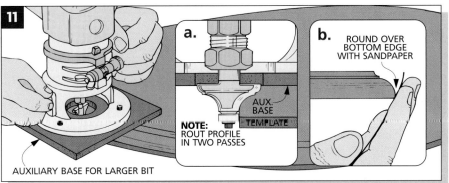

10 TO AVOID CHIPOUT ON EDGE OF TABLE TOP, MAKE SEVERAL LIGHT BACKROUTING PASSES BEFORE CUTTING FULL PROFILE (SEE SHOP TIP BELOW)

TABLE TOP (E)

ROUT TOP FLUSH WITH TEMPLATE

a. TABLE TOP / TEMPLATE / FLUSH TRIM BIT

11 a. AUX. BASE / TEMPLATE / NOTE: ROUT PROFILE IN TWO PASSES

b. ROUND OVER BOTTOM EDGE WITH SANDPAPER

AUXILIARY BASE FOR LARGER BIT

Note: This bit didn't fit the opening in my router base, so I made an auxiliary base from hardboard *(Fig. 11)*.

This profile also requires backrouting. In this case, the router will be easier to control if you start with only a small portion of the bit exposed and then lower it slightly between passes.

Once the profile was complete, I hand sanded the bottom lightly to remove the sharp edge *(Fig. 11b)*.

Before attaching the table top to the base, I applied the stain to everything. (For some tips on staining end grain, see the Finishing article on pages 26-27.) Then I applied a couple of coats of varnish to all the pieces. The table top received a third coat. This way, there's a thicker film of finish so you can "rub out" the table top to a high gloss. (Refer to the Finishing article on page 42.)

When the finish is done, attach the table top to the base *(Fig. 12)*. ■

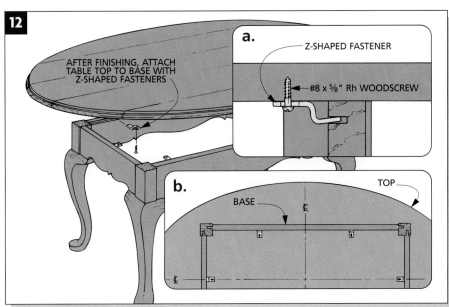

12 AFTER FINISHING, ATTACH TABLE TOP TO BASE WITH Z-SHAPED FASTENERS

a. Z-SHAPED FASTENER / #8 x $5/8$" Rh WOODSCREW

b. BASE / TOP

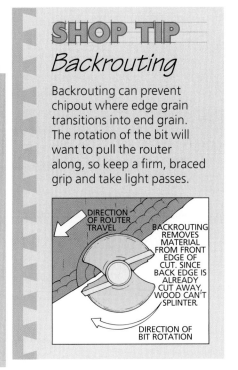

SHOP TIP
Backrouting

Backrouting can prevent chipout where edge grain transitions into end grain. The rotation of the bit will want to pull the router along, so keep a firm, braced grip and take light passes.

DIRECTION OF ROUTER TRAVEL

BACKROUTING REMOVES MATERIAL FROM FRONT EDGE OF CUT. SINCE BACK EDGE IS ALREADY CUT AWAY, WOOD CAN'T SPLINTER.

DIRECTION OF BIT ROTATION

There's one finishing problem that doesn't get a whole lot of attention: end grain. Often after staining, the end grain on a workpiece will look much darker than the face grain.

Maybe the reason why this problem doesn't get much attention is that woodworkers have just learned to "live with it." Still, there are a few steps you can take that will prevent this from happening. But it helps to know why it happens in the first place.

OPEN PORES. End grain naturally looks a little different than face grain, and it also acts differently. The reason for this is that the end of a board is made up of open pores that work like a bunch of drinking straws. Whatever is put on the surface of the board won't penetrate very quickly. But any liquid substance (like glue or stain) applied to the pores of the end grain will be pulled deeper into the wood.

STAIN. Applying a stain to a hardwood panel presents special problems.

Because the open pores exposed on the end grain absorb more stain than the face grain on the surface or sides of the panel, the color at the end of the panel often appears darker — not what you want in a piece like the Coffee Table.

Getting the end grain to match the rest of the project is a matter of stopping the stain from penetrating so deeply. That way, all surfaces end up with about the same amount of stain. Fortunately, there are a number of ways to do this.

GEL STAINS

When you're staining a project with a lot of exposed end grain, the easiest way to get a consistent color is to use a gel stain. A gel stain is applied like any other stain — it's just a little thicker. So instead of spreading over the surface of a workpiece, a gel stain will just sit there, like a glob of pudding.

LIMITED PENETRATION. Because a gel stain is thick, it won't penetrate very deep into the wood, whether it's face grain or end grain (see photos below). The result is that the end grain and the face grain end up with an even, consistent color.

You might think that gel stains are all alike; a magic formula that some finishing expert concocted. But while all gel stains are definitely thicker than regular liquid stains, they're not all the same. When it comes to end grain, the biggest difference is their thickness.

I've used some stains that were the consistency of a thick cream. Others were closer to being a paste.

Remember, what you want is a stain that's not going to seep into the end grain. So when choosing a gel stain, just keep in mind that a thick stain will tend to penetrate less and give you a more even color.

DRAWBACKS. Of course, gel stains aren't the answer in every situation. There are times when I want the stain to penetrate as deeply as possible. When I have a piece of figured wood, like bird's eye maple, I'm not going to use a gel stain because I want to highlight the contrasting figures of the wood. The gel stain isn't necessarily going to "hide" the grain. But it will even out the color more than I want it to.

The other time I don't use a gel stain is when I can't find the exact color I want. Here, I usually end up choosing a traditional (liquid) oil or water-base stain. As you can guess, this presents a challenge with the little "straws" in the end grain. But there are a couple of ways to address this problem (see the opposite page).

Apply gel with a brush. *A gel stain is just a thick stain. Its thickness limits the amount it penetrates, so I usually work it into the pores with a brush.*

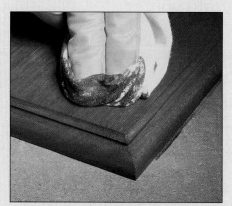

Wipe off excess. *After it's wiped off, you can see that the limited penetration of a gel stain means the end grain is the same color as the face grain.*

LIQUID STAINS

When I work with a traditional liquid stain, I usually get a more even color if I do a little extra sanding on the end grain — to 600 grit instead of 220 (see photos at right). This works because you're burnishing the end grain. The pore openings are being polished so they're smaller and don't soak in as much stain.

CURVED SURFACES. With the Coffee Table on page 20, the stain with the color I liked happened to be a traditional oil-based liquid stain. The problem was the table was curved. In fact, this table threw me more than one curve.

For one thing, the cabriole legs have end grain at the top of the knees and the feet. So there's no "hard" corner where the end grain starts and the edge grain stops. So in this case, instead of sanding finer, and trying to blend the end grain

Sanded to same grit. *When staining end grain, a regular stain will soak deep into the pores of the wood, darkening the ends much more than the face.*

Sanded to finer grit. *One solution to evening out the end grain is to sand it finer than the rest of the board. Here, I sanded the end grain to 600-grit.*

with the face grain, I'd use a wood conditioner (see below).

But the oval top was a different matter. A conditioner applied to just the end grain on the narrow molded edge would seep into the face grain from the

ends. Even with conditioner applied to the face grain, this seepage would cause uneven staining. I didn't want light streaks around the edge of the table, so I went back to the sanding solution and sanded the whole edge to 600 grit.

CONDITIONERS & SEALERS

What can be a little confusing about end grain is that it isn't just limited to the ends of a board. It can show up on the faces of some boards, too.

This is especially true of woods like pine, cherry, and maple that tend to have knots or wild, wavy grain. When these boards are surfaced, you often end up with a small patch of end grain on the face of the board (see drawing).

BLOTCHING. When you apply a stain, these areas of end grain can turn into

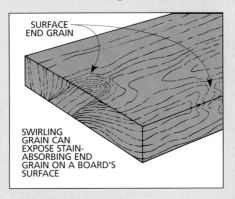

SURFACE END GRAIN

SWIRLING GRAIN CAN EXPOSE STAIN-ABSORBING END GRAIN ON A BOARD'S SURFACE

dark blotches on the face of the board (see the left half of the board in the photo). But there are steps you can take before applying a stain to avoid this.

CONDITIONERS. One solution is to brush on a wood conditioner. This is an oil-based product applied immediately before the stain. It is used mainly to even out stain absorption on the surfaces of softwoods that tend to blotch, like pine or fir. The result is a more even color on the piece (see the right half of the board above).

In some cases, wood conditioner can also be used before staining the end grain of hardwood. This is especially helpful in getting an even color on the cabriole legs, since there is no sharp corner on these pieces to separate end grain from face grain. The end grain will

wick up more conditioner, allowing less stain to penetrate. The face grain areas absorb less conditioner so about the same amount of stain as usual is absorbed there.

Just brush a heavy coat of conditioner on the entire leg. After letting it set a few minutes, wipe off any excess and apply the stain.

SEALERS. Another way to prevent the end grain from soaking up too much stain is to apply a sealer (or a wash coat) before staining. This can be a thinned-down coat of finish or a one-pound cut of shellac. It is brushed on and allowed to dry before applying the stain.

TOP COATS

When it's time to apply a clear top coat (such as an oil or varnish) over the stain, end grain isn't nearly as much of a problem. The top coat penetrates just as deep, and in fact, you may notice that the end grain gets slightly darker. That's because oil and varnish tend to

add an amber tint to the wood anyway. But I've never thought this was objectionable, so I haven't gone to the trouble of sanding any finer.

EXTRA COAT. About the only thing you will notice about putting a clear finish on end grain is that it dries out a

lot quicker. That's because the pores in the end grain are wicking the finish away from the surface. Since the idea is to get an even coat of finish on the top surface of the workpiece, I sometimes end up applying an extra coat or two to build up the finish on the ends.

DESIGNER'S NOTEBOOK

By buying pre-made legs, you can put together an entire set of classic tables in a weekend. The simplified lines make it easy to cut the pieces and assemble this handsome set in very little time.

CONSTRUCTION NOTES:

■ This set of tables uses pre-made cabriole legs *(Fig. 1)*. These legs are available from a number of mail-order sources (see page 126). The lengths of the legs I used for each table are given in the Materials List below. Depending on the supplier, the lengths may be slightly different, but you should be able to find legs that are close to the lengths listed.

■ Once you have the legs, construction of a complete set of tables can move along quickly since the aprons are all the same width (4") and don't need scalloped edges. Once you're set up, rip the aprons needed for each table.

■ Each apron has a $\frac{1}{8}$"-wide groove cut in its inside face to accept the Z-shaped table top fasteners *(Figs. 1 and 5)*.

■ The joinery is identical on the legs and aprons for all the tables *(Fig. 1)*. So once you're set up, you can drill out the mortises in all of the legs (refer to the Woodworker's Notebook on page 22).

■ Next, use the table saw to cut a test tenon on a piece of scrap. Once it fits the mortise in a leg, you can cut all the tenons on the aprons.

■ The edge treatment on each of the table tops is the same as that on the oval Coffee Table *(Fig. 5)*. Since these table tops have 90° corners, chipout isn't as much of a problem as it is on the edge of

THREE TABLE SET

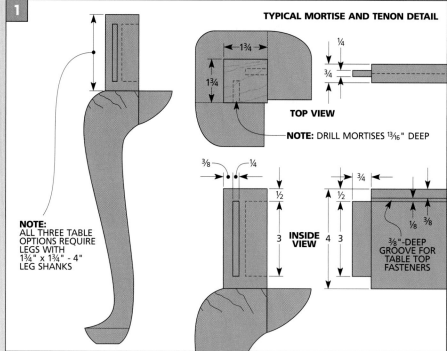

1

NOTE: ALL THREE TABLE OPTIONS REQUIRE LEGS WITH $1\frac{3}{4}$" x $1\frac{3}{4}$" - 4" LEG SHANKS

TYPICAL MORTISE AND TENON DETAIL

$1\frac{3}{4}$

$1\frac{3}{4}$

$\frac{1}{4}$

$\frac{3}{4}$

TOP VIEW

NOTE: DRILL MORTISES $\frac{13}{16}$" DEEP

$\frac{3}{8}$ $\frac{1}{4}$

$\frac{1}{2}$

3

INSIDE VIEW

$\frac{3}{4}$

$\frac{1}{2}$

4   3

$\frac{1}{8}$ $\frac{3}{8}$

$\frac{3}{8}$"-DEEP GROOVE FOR TABLE TOP FASTENERS

MATERIALS LIST

CHANGED PARTS FOR COFFEE TABLE
A	Legs (4)	$17\frac{1}{4}$ long
E	Table Top (1)	$\frac{3}{4}$ x 21 - 36

NEW PARTS FOR END TABLE
F	Legs (4)	$21\frac{1}{4}$ long
G	Side Aprons (2)	$\frac{3}{4}$ x 4 - 13
H	Frt./Bk. Aprons (2)	$\frac{3}{4}$ x 4 - 19
I	Table Top (1)	$\frac{3}{4}$ x 20 - 26

NEW PARTS FOR SOFA TABLE
J	Legs (4)	$28\frac{1}{2}$ long
K	Side Aprons (2)	$\frac{3}{4}$ x 4 - $10\frac{1}{2}$
L	Frt./Bk. Aprons (2)	$\frac{3}{4}$ x 4 - 46
M	Table Top (1)	$\frac{3}{4}$ x 16 - 54

Note: Tables use pre-made legs.

an oval table. So you can rout in the normal direction (left to right). The ends of the panels are still prone to some chipout at the corners, so rout across the ends first. Then rout the sides to clean up any ragged corners.

RECTANGULAR COFFEE TABLE

■ The base of the Rectangular Coffee Table has the same dimensions as the oval Coffee Table. So the end and front aprons are cut to the same lengths as those for the oval table *(Fig. 2)*.
■ To make the rectangular table top,

glue up a blank and — after the glue has dried — trim it to 21" x 36".
■ Next, rout the edge profile on the top.
■ After applying finish to all pieces, center the top on the base and secure it with Z-shaped fasteners *(Fig. 5)*.

END TABLE

■ The End Table uses legs that are slightly taller than those on the Coffee Table *(Fig. 3)*. (Mine were 21¼" long.)
■ The front aprons for the End Table are each cut to a length of 19". The end aprons are cut to a length of 13" *(Fig. 3)*.

■ For this version, the table top measures 20" wide and 26" long.

SOFA TABLE

■ The Sofa Table is the tallest piece in the set. The legs I found for this table were 28½" long *(Fig. 4)*.
■ On this version, the front aprons are 46" long. Cut the end aprons to a length of 10½" *(Fig. 4)*.
■ The top panel for the Sofa Table is 16" wide and 54" long. After gluing up a panel this long, take extra care to make sure the surface is absolutely flat.

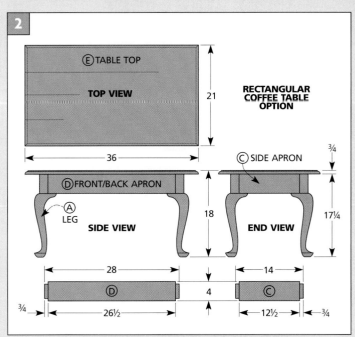

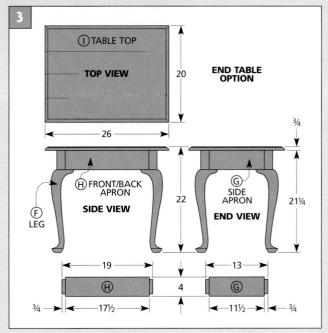

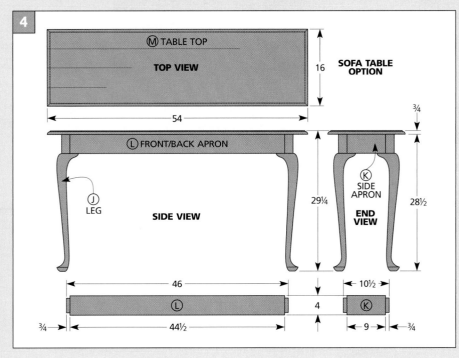

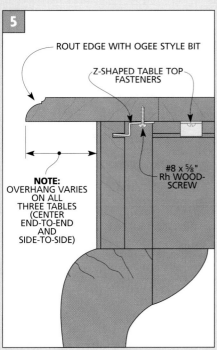

Bow-Front End Table

From the high-gloss, hand-polished finish to the bow-front drawers, the details in this piece are a reflection of your craftsmanship. The secret to the curved drawers is to build them square first.

Here's a little challenge. Set this end table in a room with a bunch of woodworkers and see what they look at first. I'll bet you nine times out of ten, the bow-front drawers will be opened first and given a close inspection. And frankly, I'd do the same thing.

The drawers are one of the most intriguing features of this project. So it's natural to be curious about how they're built. Are they bent to this shape or cut from a thick block? And how do you join the bowed front to the straight sides?

For these drawers, I used a procedure that was a little unusual, but it allowed me to build them without any special jigs or materials. The secret is to start building an ordinary drawer with ½"-thick stock and machine-cut dovetails. But before assembling the drawer, I glued a thick block to the front piece and cut the curves. For a closer look at this process, there's a Technique article that starts on page 40.

FLUTED LEGS. There are a few other design details you'll want to look at a little closer. Take the legs, for instance. They look like square columns with flutes on the outside faces and chamfers on the corners. Here, consistency is everything. The three flutes on each face must be spaced evenly and stop the

same distance from the top and bottom of every leg. But there's nothing complicated about the procedure. All you need is a careful setup on the router table with a common core box bit.

DETAILS AND FINISH. This end table has plenty of other details to attract your eye: the bead profiles on the sides, the curved edging, and the ogee profile around the top. But there's one detail you won't be able to resist *touching* — the finish. Making the top of this table glass-smooth requires a few extra coats of finish and a little elbow grease, but it's well worth it. The article on page 42 shows you how.

EXPLODED VIEW

OVERALL DIMENSIONS:
19W x 24³/₄D x 24¹/₂H

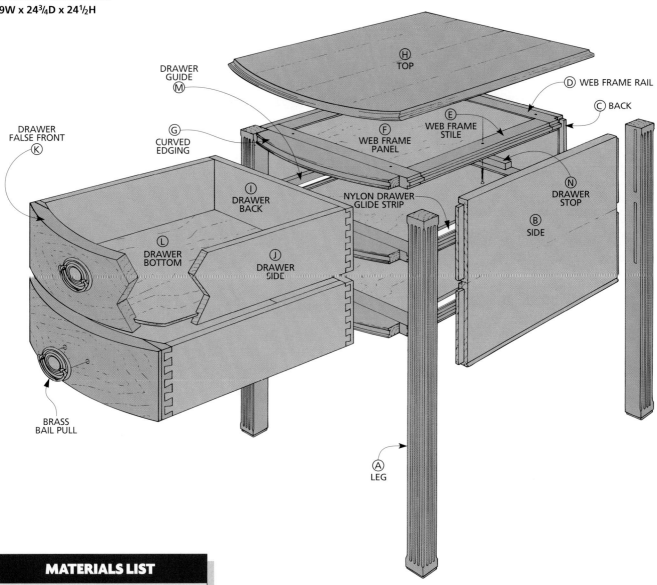

DRAWER GUIDE Ⓜ

Ⓓ WEB FRAME RAIL

Ⓒ BACK

Ⓖ

CURVED EDGING

Ⓔ WEB FRAME STILE

Ⓕ WEB FRAME PANEL

DRAWER FALSE FRONT Ⓚ

Ⓘ DRAWER BACK

NYLON DRAWER GLIDE STRIP

Ⓝ DRAWER STOP

Ⓑ SIDE

Ⓛ DRAWER BOTTOM

Ⓙ DRAWER SIDE

Ⓐ LEG

BRASS BAIL PULL

MATERIALS LIST

WOOD

A	Legs (4)	1¹/₂ x 1¹/₂ - 23³/₄
B	Sides (2)	³/₄ x 11¹/₄ - 19¹/₂
C	Back (1)	³/₄ x 11¹/₄ - 15¹/₂
D	Web Frame Rails (6)	³/₄ x 1¹/₂ - 16
E	Web Frame Stiles (6)	³/₄ x 1³/₄ - 16¹/₂
F	Web Frame Pnls. (3)	¹/₄ ply - 13 x 16¹/₂
G	Curved Edging (3)	³/₄ x 2¹/₂ - 14¹/₂
H	Top (1)	³/₄ x 19 - 25¹/₂ rgh.
I	Drawer Fr./Back (4)	¹/₂ x 4³/₈ - 14³/₈
J	Drawer Sides (4)	¹/₂ x 4³/₈ - 19
K	Drawer False Fr. (2)	1³/₄ x 4³/₈ - 14³/₈
L	Drawer Bottoms (2)	¹/₂ ply - 13⁷/₈ x 19⁷/₈
M	Drawer Guides (4)	³/₄ x ⁹/₁₆ - 18¹/₂
N	Drawer Stops (2)	³/₄ x ⁵/₈ - 4

HARDWARE SUPPLIES

(6) No. 8 x 1¹/₄ " Fh woodscrews
(4) Nylon glide strips
(2) Bail pulls (2 " bore)

CUTTING DIAGRAM

³/₄ x 6 - 96 WALNUT (Two Boards @ 4 Bd. Ft. Each)

| H | H | B | B |

³/₄ x 6¹/₂ - 72 WALNUT (Two Boards @ 3.25 Bd. Ft. Each)

NOTE: ALSO NEED A 48" x 48" PIECE OF ¹/₄"-THICK MAPLE PLYWOOD

| C | E E E | D D | G G |

M   N

1³/₄ x 5 - 96 WALNUT (6.6 Bd. Ft.)

| K | K | A A | A A |

¹/₂ x 5 - 60 MAPLE (Two Boards @ 2.1 Sq. Ft. Each)

| J | J | I |

¹/₂ x 5 - 30 WALNUT (1 Sq. Ft.)

| I | I |

Though the bow-front drawers attract the most attention, construction of the table begins with the fluted legs.

CUT TO SIZE. To make the legs (A), I started with 8/4 stock that's cut 1½" square *(Fig. 1)*. Then the legs can be cut to final length. (I used walnut to build this table, but mahogany or cherry would also look nice for a formal project like this.)

CREATE MORTISES. The legs will be joined by a back and two side panels. This U-shaped case is held together with mortise and tenon joints. However, since the panels will be over 11" wide, I wanted to keep the leg mortises as strong as possible. So instead of a single mortise on each face, I cut two shorter ones ³⁄₄" apart *(Fig. 1a)*.

But before carrying the legs over to the drill press, I took the time to lay out the mortise locations carefully. There's nothing more frustrating than drilling a mortise in the wrong place. Plus, the legs on this table aren't identical *(Fig. 1b)*. The back legs are mortised on two adjacent faces; the front legs on only one face each.

To create mortises, I like to drill overlapping holes and clean up each mortise with a chisel *(Fig. 2)*. And I typically drill them ¹⁄₁₆" deeper than the length of the tenons. This way, there will be room for excess glue.

ROUT FLUTES. With the mortises cut, work can begin on the narrow flutes. The goal with the flutes is to get them spaced evenly and to get them to line up at the top and bottom. This is easy enough to do on the router table with a core box bit. All you need is a long fence and a couple of stop blocks. For more on this, see the opposite page.

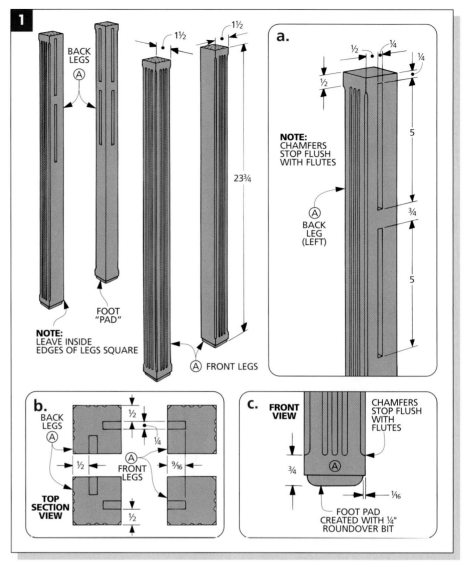

CHAMFER EDGES. I also chamfered the outside edges of the legs. This is the same basic procedure used for the flutes. But you'll need to use a chamfer bit and readjust the fence and stop blocks so the chamfers end up even with the flutes *(Fig. 3)*.

FOOT PADS. There's one last detail to add before the legs are complete. I cut a "foot pad" on the bottom of each leg *(Fig. 1c)*. This pad is routed on the router table using a ¼" roundover bit *(Fig. 4)*. (To back up the cut, I used a miter gauge with an auxiliary fence.)

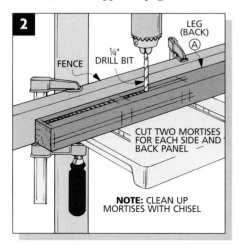

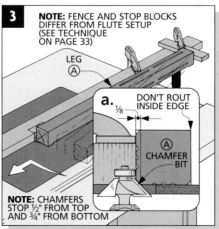

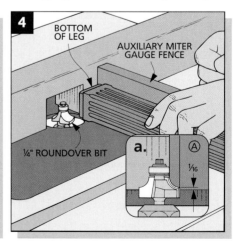

TECHNIQUE .... *Routing Flutes*

Many table legs are pretty basic and don't attract a lot of attention. But the legs on this table are "dressed up" with narrow, half-round flutes.

I routed the $^{1}/_{16}$"-deep flutes on the router table, using a $^{1}/_{8}$" core box bit. Since the flutes are stopped at each end, this is a plunge cut — at both ends. You have to set the leg onto the spinning bit at the beginning of the cut and lift it off at the end. This isn't difficult though. A stop block at each end makes the starting and stopping automatic.

SETTING FENCE. Normally, routing three flutes on a face would require three fence settings. But to keep the spacing even, I set the fence once and then used $^{1}/_{4}$"-thick spacers to shift the piece (*Steps 1-3* below).

Your normal router fence probably won't work though. In order to clamp a stop block at each end, you'll need a fence at least twice as long as the legs. I made mine out of $^{3}/_{4}$" solid wood and clamped it to the table face down so it was only $^{3}/_{4}$" tall (see drawing). This low profile allowed me to hold the legs and spacers together when routing.

There's one more thing to keep in mind when setting the fence. The spacers take care of the spacing, but the flutes should also be centered on the width of the legs. The easiest way to do this is to set the fence to cut the middle flute (routed with one spacer as shown in *Step 1*). If this flute is centered, then the others will be in the correct positions too.

SETTING STOP BLOCKS. With the fence set, the stop blocks can be added.

The trick is that the flutes are different distances from each end (there's an extra $^{1}/_{4}$" on the bottom for a foot pad). So when setting the blocks, make sure the grooves stop $^{3}/_{4}$" from the bottom of the leg and $^{1}/_{2}$" from the top (refer to *Figs. 1a and 1c* on page 32).

Note: To help me remember which end of the leg went against which stop block, I drew an "X" on the bottom of each leg and on the stop block that they butted against (see drawing).

Once the stop blocks are clamped in place, things go pretty quickly. When using the spacers, I simply held them to the legs as I ran them across the core box router bit (*Steps 1 and 2*).

After all the flutes have been routed, you may see some burn marks at the ends. If so, a drill bit wrapped in sandpaper will help remove them (*Step 4*).

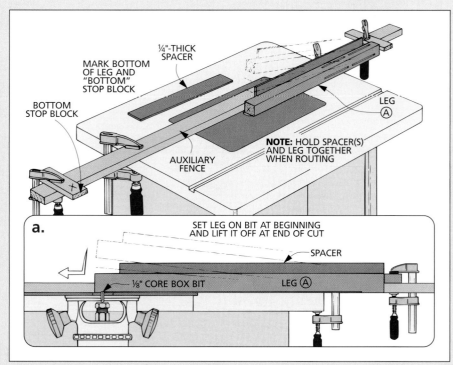

MARK BOTTOM OF LEG AND "BOTTOM" STOP BLOCK
$^{1}/_{4}$"-THICK SPACER
BOTTOM STOP BLOCK
AUXILIARY FENCE
LEG (A)
NOTE: HOLD SPACER(S) AND LEG TOGETHER WHEN ROUTING

a. SET LEG ON BIT AT BEGINNING AND LIFT IT OFF AT END OF CUT
SPACER
$^{1}/_{8}$" CORE BOX BIT
LEG (A)

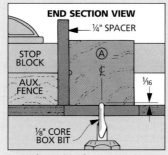

END SECTION VIEW
$^{1}/_{4}$" SPACER
STOP BLOCK
AUX. FENCE
(A)
$^{1}/_{16}$
$^{1}/_{8}$" CORE BOX BIT

1 After the fence and stop blocks have been set, rout the middle flutes, using a single $^{1}/_{4}$"-thick spacer.

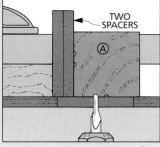

TWO SPACERS
(A)

2 Next, place another $^{1}/_{4}$"-thick spacer between the fence and leg and rout the second set of flutes.

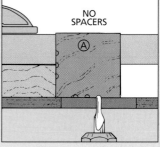

NO SPACERS
(A)

3 Finally, remove both hardboard spacers and rout the last set of flutes on the two outside faces of the legs.

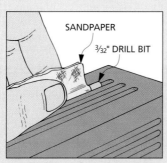

SANDPAPER
$^{3}/_{32}$" DRILL BIT

4 If there has been any burning, wrap sandpaper around a $^{3}/_{32}$"-dia. drill bit and carefully sand the flutes.

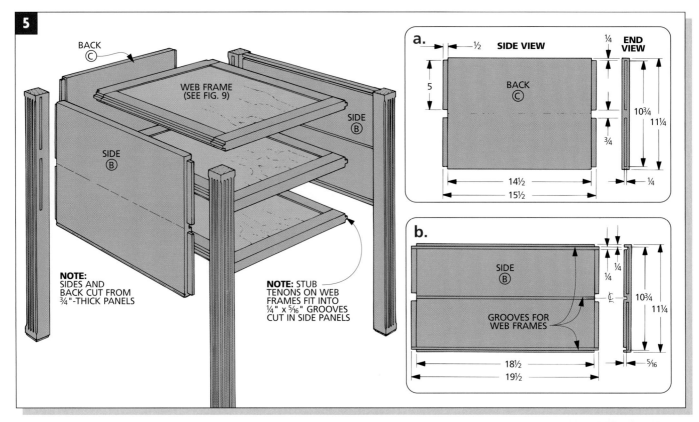

SIDE & BACK PANELS

Once the legs are complete, three wide panels can be made that will connect the legs into a U-shaped case *(Fig. 5)*. After that, three horizontal web frames are added to form the drawer openings.

MAKE PANELS. The first thing to do is to glue up blanks for the side (B) and back panels (C) from ³⁄₄"-thick pieces of stock *(Fig. 5)*. Then the panels can be cut to size *(Figs. 5a and 5b)*.

CUT TENONS. Next, two tenons can be cut on each end of the panels to fit into the mortises you cut in the legs. This is easier than it sounds. I simply cut one long tenon with ¹⁄₄" shoulders on the top and bottom. I did this just like I normally would, placing the pieces face down on the table saw and using a dado blade buried in an auxiliary fence.

To create two shorter tenons out of this one long tenon, I cut a ³⁄₄"-wide notch in its center *(Figs. 6 and 6a)*. Again, I used my dado blade to do this, standing the pieces on end and removing the waste in multiple passes. But I didn't raise the blade up all the way to the shoulder. That could cause score marks on the shoulders that would be visible later. Instead, I cut the notch a bit short and used a chisel to complete the notch.

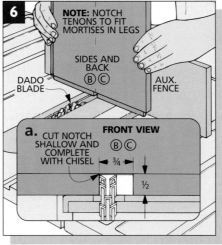

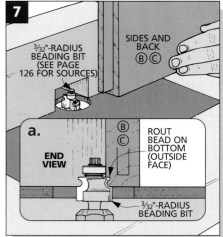

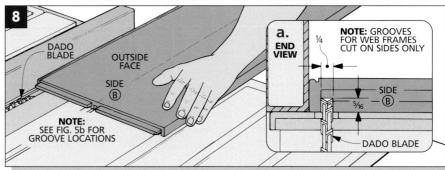

ROUT BEADS. At this point, I added a small decorative bead on the bottom edge of each panel (B, C) *(Fig. 7)*. (These beads will also be cut on the curved edging pieces that divide the drawers later.) To do this, I used a ³⁄₃₂"-radius beading bit. It's simply raised to cut a full bead with no shoulder *(Fig. 7a)*.

CUT GROOVES. Once the bead is cut, the back panel (C) is complete. The sides (B), on the other hand, still need three ¼"-wide grooves that will hold the web frames *(Fig. 8)*. The grooves at the top and bottom are located ¼" from the edges, and the groove in the middle is centered *(Fig. 5b)*.

ASSEMBLE LEGS AND SIDES. After the grooves were cut, I glued the side panels between the front and back legs. (When doing this, just be sure the beads end up on the outside.) As for the back, it'll be glued between the side assemblies a little later.

WEB FRAMES

While the side assemblies were drying, I started on the web frames *(Fig. 9)*. The frames strengthen the front of the case, create the drawer openings, and support the drawers.

RAILS AND STILES. To determine the final size of the frames accurately, I dry-assembled the side assemblies and back panel. Then I could begin cutting the rails and stiles to size *(Fig. 9)*.

The rails (D) are cut to fit between the grooves in the sides, so add ½" to the interior side-to-side dimension of the case. And to find the length of the stiles (E), measure from the inside face of the front legs to the back panel (C). Then subtract the width of the two rails and add ½" for the stub tenons.

GROOVES AND STUB TENONS. To hold the ¼" plywood panels, I cut a groove centered on the inside edge of each rail and stile *(Fig. 10)*. Then cut mating stub tenons on the ends of the stiles to fit into the grooves that were just cut *(Fig. 11)*.

PANELS. Now the ¼"-thick plywood web panels (F) can be cut to fit into the grooves in the frame pieces. Then each of the frame and panel assemblies can be glued together.

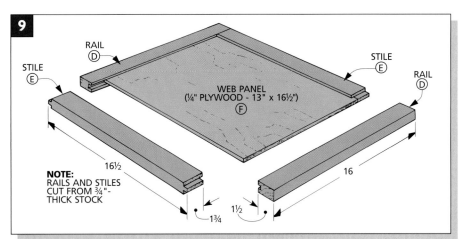

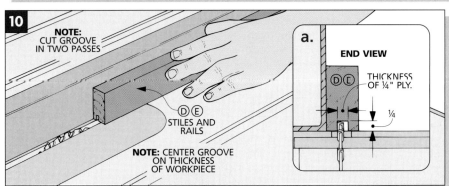

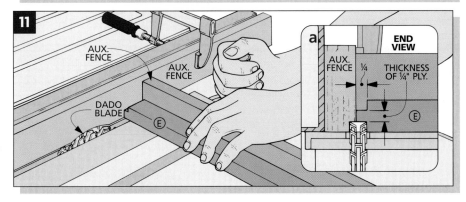

TONGUES AND NOTCHES. There are still a couple of things to do to the frames. First, centered tongues need to be created on both sides of each frame *(Fig. 12)*. These tongues are sized to fit the grooves in the side pieces.

And finally, I cut a notch in each back corner of each web frame *(Fig. 13)*. These allow the frames to fit around the back legs inside the case. You don't need an air-tight fit. I simply laid out the notches, then cut them with a hand saw.

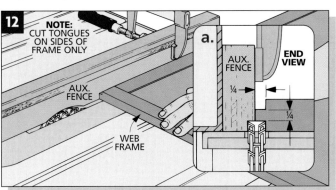

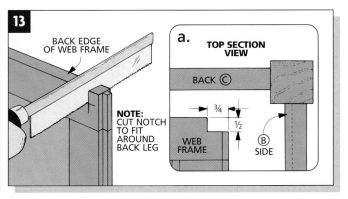

EACH SQUARE = ½"

CURVE PATTERN

The most distinctive feature of this table is obvious — the curves on the front.

But at first glance, you might miss the bead profile on the edging pieces above and below each drawer opening (*Fig. 14a* and photo at left). You can create this curved profile through an innovative process on the router table before the edging pieces are fastened to the web frames.

CUT TO SIZE. The first thing to do is to dry-assemble the case — without the back (*Fig. 14*). (You'll need access to the back later.) Then with the case clamped together, you can cut three ¾"-thick curved edging (G) pieces to fit between the front legs. But keep the edging wide at this point. It's easier to cut a smooth curve on an extra-wide blank. (I cut mine 3" wide.)

CUT CURVES. With the blanks roughed out, you can begin to lay out the curves. These are the same as the curves that will be cut on the drawers, so I took a little extra time to make a reusable ¼" hardboard template (see the pattern above).

Now the template can be used to draw the curves on the three blanks. I roughed out the curves with a band saw, saving one of the "cutoff" pieces for later. Then I sanded to the lines with a drum sander on the drill press.

CREATE PROFILE. With the curves cut, I routed bead profiles on the top and bottom edges (*Fig. 14a*). This is done on the router table with the same bit used on the side panels earlier.

Routing the beads is just the first step. I also removed the material between the beads so they would stand out (*Fig. 14a*). To do this, I used a straight bit and a cradle made from one of the curved waste pieces (see the Technique on the opposite page).

GLUE EDGING TO FRAMES. The curved trim pieces are now complete and can be glued to the front edges of the web frames. To do this, leave the case dry-assembled. This way, the legs

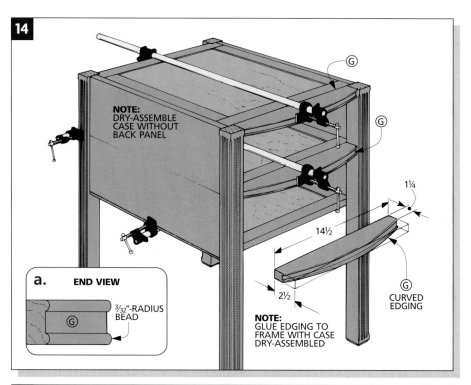

14

NOTE:
DRY-ASSEMBLE
CASE WITHOUT
BACK PANEL

G

G

1¼

14½

2½

G
CURVED
EDGING

a. END VIEW

G

3/32"-RADIUS
BEAD

NOTE:
GLUE EDGING TO
FRAME WITH CASE
DRY-ASSEMBLED

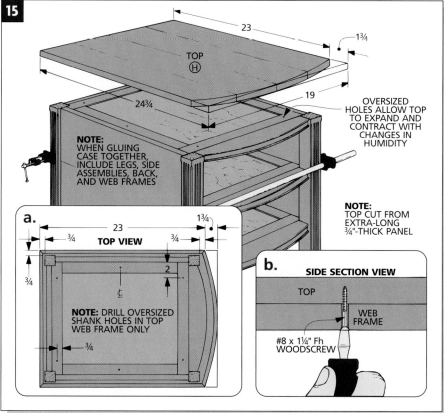

15

23

1¾

TOP
(H)

24¾

19

OVERSIZED
HOLES ALLOW TOP
TO EXPAND AND
CONTRACT WITH
CHANGES IN
HUMIDITY

NOTE:
WHEN GLUING
CASE TOGETHER,
INCLUDE LEGS, SIDE
ASSEMBLIES, BACK,
AND WEB FRAMES

NOTE:
TOP CUT FROM
EXTRA-LONG
¾"-THICK PANEL

a.

23

1¾

¾

TOP VIEW

¾

¾

2

℄

¾

NOTE: DRILL OVERSIZED
SHANK HOLES IN TOP
WEB FRAME ONLY

b. SIDE SECTION VIEW

TOP

WEB
FRAME

#8 x 1¼" Fh
WOODSCREW

The Bow-Front End Table has curved edging pieces that dress up the drawer openings in the case. What's special about these pieces (besides the curves) are the bead profiles that are routed on both the top and bottom edges.

Creating the beads is no problem. I used a 3/32"-radius beading bit in the router table to cut the profile along the top and bottom edge of each edging piece *(Fig. 1a)*. With a face flat on the table, the curve of the workpiece rides against the bearing of the bit *(Fig. 1)*.

However, I wanted to make the two beads "stand proud," so I had to come up with some way to remove the material between the beads (see photo).

Had the pieces been straight, this wouldn't have been any trouble. But how do you guide a curved piece over a straight bit safely and consistently?

The solution was to use one of the waste pieces left from cutting the curves on the edging pieces. I sanded this waste piece and drilled a 1/2"-dia. clearance hole in the center. This hole fits over a 1/4"-dia. straight bit in the router table. And to provide support for the side of the edging piece, I screwed the waste piece to a scrap 2x4. Then I clamped the fence assembly to the router table *(Fig. 2)*.

When routing, you'll want to sneak up on the height of the bit until it's flush with the bottom of the beads *(Fig. 2a)*. And since the 1/4" bit is a hair narrower than the space between the beads, I made two passes at each height setting, flipping the edging piece end for end between passes.

Since the bit will exit the back end of the workpiece, move your hands to the front as the cut progresses *(Fig. 2b)*.

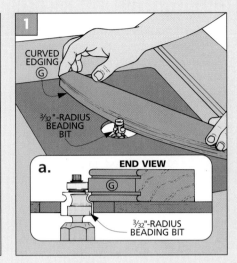

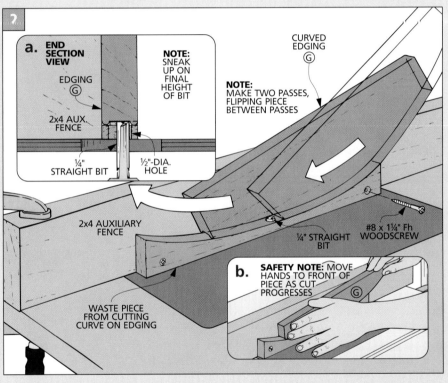

on the sides will automatically position the edging *(Fig. 14)*. (Just be careful that you don't glue the edging to the legs at this point.)

MOUNTING HOLES. With the curved edging glued to the frames, there's one last thing to do before the case can be glued together. The top web frame needs some countersunk shank holes drilled in it so you can mount the top panel later *(Figs. 15a and 15b)*.

Note: Drill the holes slightly oversize so the panel can expand and contract freely with changes in humidity.

ASSEMBLY. Finally, the entire case is ready for final assembly. This means gluing the back panel and the three web frames between the two side assemblies *(Fig. 15)*.

TABLE TOP

Like the legs and drawers, the top of this table should also have a few nice details. The front edge is curved to match the curved edging pieces, and I routed the edges with an ogee fillet bit to give it a classic profile.

GLUE UP PANEL. The first thing to do is glue up a panel from 3/4"-thick stock *(Fig. 15)*. Since the top is the most visible surface on the table, I took extra care to choose and match some nice-looking walnut boards.

After the glue is dry, the top (H) can be cut to finished width *(Fig. 15)*. I simply sized the panel to overhang the legs 3/4" on the sides *(Fig. 15a)*. And though I cut the panel to its final width, I left it a little long. The panel is cut to its final length after the curve is formed on the front edge.

CREATE CURVE. The curve on the front edge of the top (H) is a couple of inches wider than the curved edging (G), so I couldn't use the same template. Instead I simply bent a flexible straightedge against a couple of blocks and drew the curve directly on the top *(Fig. 16)*. Then it's cut out and sanded smooth with a disk or drum sander. Once the curve is formed on the front edge, cut the top to finished length (refer to *Fig. 15a* on page 36).

ROUT PROFILE. Next, to give the top a traditional profile, I routed around the edges with an ogee fillet bit *(Fig. 17)*. This is a two-step process, but you can use the same bit in both steps.

The first pass is made with the router riding on the top face of the top panel (H) *(Fig. 17a)*. (To avoid chipout, rout the ends first, moving the router left-to-right.) For the second pass, you'll need to flip the top over and adjust the depth of the bit so the bearing rides along the flat edge *(Fig. 17b)*. This means there will be a little sanding left to do to round the edge completely.

At this point, the top can be screwed to the case. But before doing this, I applied a coat of finish to the bottom face of the top so the panel would be less likely to cup.

BOW-FRONT DRAWERS

With this table, the best feature is saved for last — the bow-front drawers are both the main attraction and a great woodworking challenge.

BUILD DRAWERS. To build each drawer, you start by making a rectanular drawer with 1/2"-thick stock joined with machine-cut dovetails *(Figs. 18 and 18b)*. (The Technique article on page 40 takes you through this step by step.) I sized the fronts (I) and backs (I) so the completed drawer would have 1/16" gaps at the top, bottom, and sides. And the sides (J) were cut 19" long. This allows for the false front (added next), plus a bit of "breathing room." (My drawer ended up 5/8" short of the back of the case.)

But before assembling the drawer, a thick false front (K) is glued to the front piece. Now the front can be cut to shape

and sanded smooth. Finally, a drawer bottom (L) can be added, and the drawers glued together.

GUIDES. There's still some work left to do before the drawers will slide smoothly in and out of the case.

The first thing I did was add pieces to guide the drawers and center them side-to-side. The 3/4"-thick guides (M) are cut to length to fit between the front and back legs, and they're ripped just wide enough to guide the drawer in and

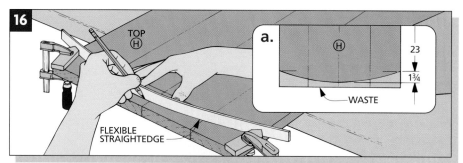

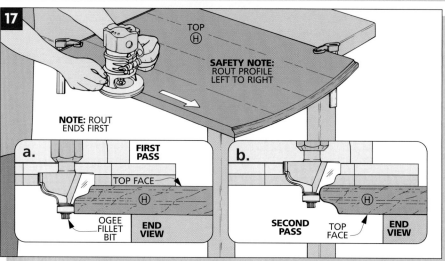

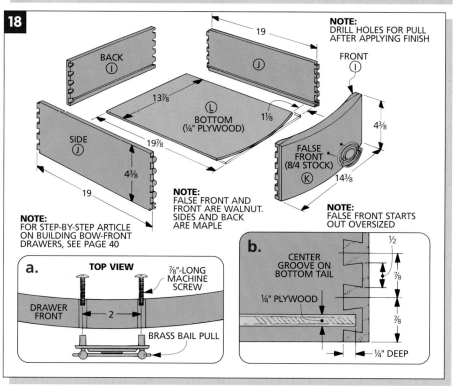

out without binding *(Figs. 19 and 19a)*. (Mine were $9/16$" wide.)

GUIDE STRIPS. Though the guides direct the drawer, you don't want the drawer to rest directly on the web frame. Eventually the drawer sides would rub through the finish and wear a visible groove in the curved edging. So to avoid this, I placed nylon glide strips inside the cabinet for each drawer to ride on *(Fig. 19b)*. These self-adhesive glide strips were roughly $1/16$" thick, so they also established the proper gap at the bottom of the drawer. I cut the strips so they stopped at the joint line between the web frame and the edging strips *(Fig. 19b)*. (See page 126 for sources of nylon glide strips.)

STOPS. The next task is to get each drawer to shut so that its front face is set just behind the bead on the curved edging *(Fig. 19c)*. To do this, I added a short block at the back of the case to act as a drawer stop *(Fig. 19)*. Sneak up on the final width of this stop (N) until the drawer is properly positioned. (My block was $5/8$" wide.) Then glue the block to the back of the case.

DRAWER PULLS. To complete the drawers, all that's left are the bail pulls.

Note: I waited to mount the pulls until after the finish had been applied and rubbed out (refer to page 42).

The Shop Tip at right shows how to lay out the locations of the mounting holes without marring the finish. Once the locations were marked, I drilled the holes for the machine screws that came with the pulls *(Fig. 18a)*. I drilled these holes slightly oversize since the bail back plate will have to "bend" slightly around the drawer. Now all that's left is to remove the tape carefully and screw the pulls in place. ■

SHOP TIP
Pull Layout

Before laying out the locations of the pilot holes for the drawer pulls, I applied several strips of masking tape to the fronts of the drawers to protect the finish. This made it easier to see the lines and provided a no-slip surface for my awl.

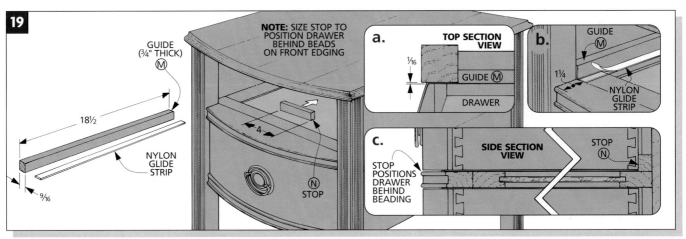

19

NOTE: SIZE STOP TO POSITION DRAWER BEHIND BEADS ON FRONT EDGING

GUIDE ($3/4$" THICK) M

$18\frac{1}{2}$

NYLON GLIDE STRIP

$9/16$

4

N STOP

a. **TOP SECTION VIEW**
$1/16$
GUIDE M
DRAWER
b. GUIDE M
$1\frac{1}{4}$
NYLON GLIDE STRIP

c. STOP POSITIONS DRAWER BEHIND BEADING
SIDE SECTION VIEW
STOP N

SHOP JIG . . . . Rub Arm

For most drawers, I cut the grooves for the bottom panel on the table saw. But the curve on each drawer front on the end table makes that impossible. So I used a slot cutter bit in the router table (see photo).

However, my slot cutter routs a $1/2$"-deep slot — too deep for the $1/2$"-thick drawer pieces. And I didn't have a larger bearing that would reduce the depth of the slot. So I made a rub arm that fits over the bearing (see drawing).

My rub arm looks like a big tongue depressor cut from $1/4$" hardboard. The round end has a clearance hole sized to fit over the bearing on the bit. This hole should be drilled so that only $1/4$" of the cutter is exposed (refer to *Fig. 6a* on page 41).

To position the arm at the right height above the cutter, I screwed it to a support block that can be clamped to the router table.

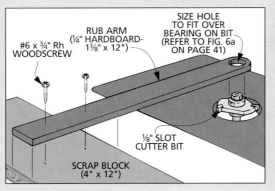

#6 x $3/4$" Rh WOODSCREW

RUB ARM ($1/4$" HARDBOARD— $1\frac{3}{8}$" x 12")

SIZE HOLE TO FIT OVER BEARING ON BIT (REFER TO FIG. 6a ON PAGE 41)

$1/8$" SLOT CUTTER BIT

SCRAP BLOCK (4" x 12")

TECHNIQUE . . . . . Bow-Front Drawers

Though it may sound difficult, there isn't any trick to "bowing" a drawer front. Simply start with a thick blank, cut the curves on a band saw, and sand them smooth. It's that simple.

However, the curved front has to be connected with two straight sides. And the traditional way to do this is with half-blind dovetails.

So how do you go about cutting dovetails on a curved piece? You don't. For the end table, I built "square" drawers with dovetails first and then "bowed" the front pieces later.

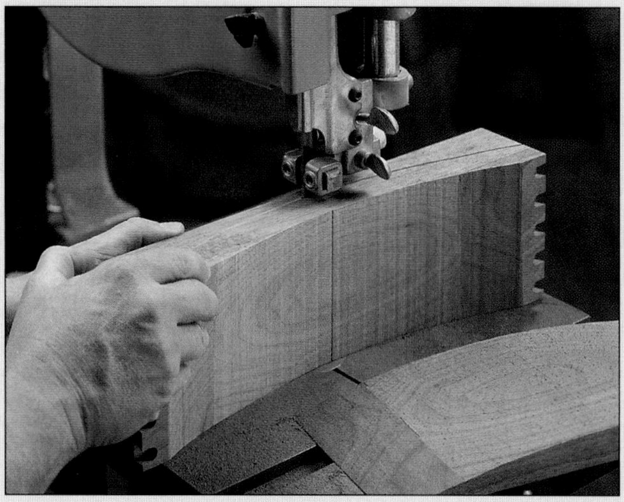

BUILD DRAWER. This drawer starts out like most — the 1/2"-thick pieces are cut to size *(Fig. 1)*. To highlight the dovetails, I used maple for the drawer sides (see photo below).

Note: When cutting the sides to length, you want to make sure the drawer doesn't end up too deep. Take into account that a thick blank glued to the front later will add 1½" to the depth of the drawer. (I cut my sides 19" long, which left about 5/8" between the back of the drawer and the case.)

To connect these pieces, I routed 1/2" dovetails with a hand-held router and a dovetail jig *(Figs. 2 and 2a)*. Then I set the sides and back out of the way. It's time now to work on the drawer front.

OVERSIZED BLANK. To build up the thickness of the drawer front, I added a 1¾"-thick false front made from 8/4 walnut (see photos at right). And to accentuate the curves cut later, I chose a board with a grain pattern shaped like a "bulls-eye" (photo at left). I cut this blank slightly oversize and then glued it to the front of the front piece. (The false front will be trimmed flush later.)

At this point, the front looks massive. But don't worry. The curve gets cut on both the inside and outside faces, so the final thickness of the drawer front will only be about 7/8".

TRIM OVERSIZED BLANK. After the glue is dry, the oversized blank can be trimmed to match the 1/2"-thick piece. I did this on the table saw, but the problem is that the oversized piece gets in the way. The solution is to use a thin auxiliary fence that the 1/2"-thick piece can ride against *(Fig. 3)*.

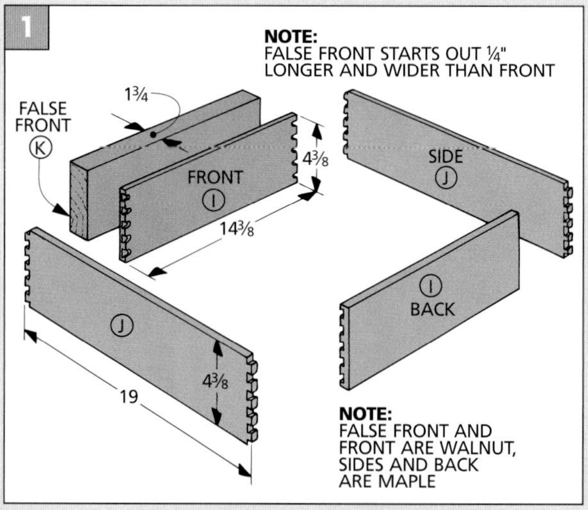
1
NOTE:
FALSE FRONT STARTS OUT ¼" LONGER AND WIDER THAN FRONT
FALSE FRONT
K
1¾
FRONT
I
4⅜
14⅜
SIDE
J
J
4⅜
19
I
BACK
NOTE:
FALSE FRONT AND FRONT ARE WALNUT, SIDES AND BACK ARE MAPLE

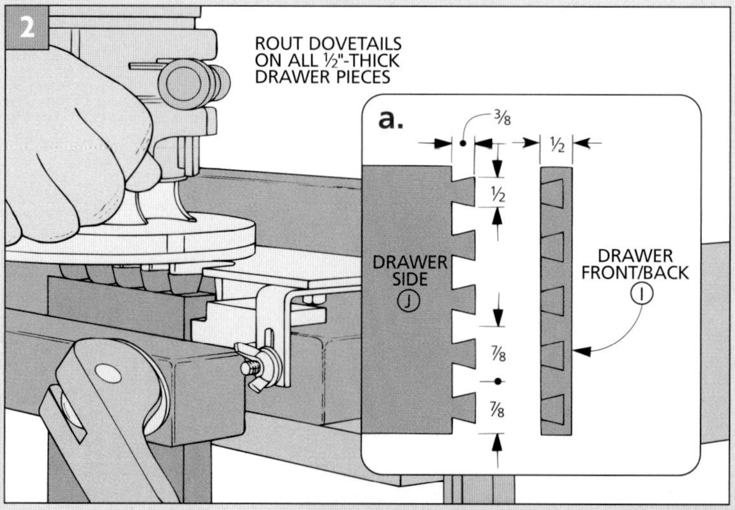
2
ROUT DOVETAILS ON ALL ½"-THICK DRAWER PIECES
a.
⅜
½
½
DRAWER SIDE
J
DRAWER FRONT/BACK
I
⅞
⅞

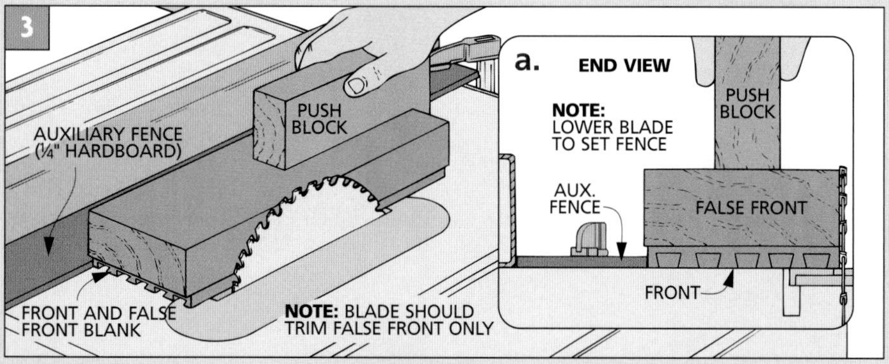
3
AUXILIARY FENCE (¼" HARDBOARD)
PUSH BLOCK
FRONT AND FALSE FRONT BLANK
NOTE: BLADE SHOULD TRIM FALSE FRONT ONLY
a. END VIEW
NOTE:
LOWER BLADE TO SET FENCE
PUSH BLOCK
AUX. FENCE
FALSE FRONT
FRONT

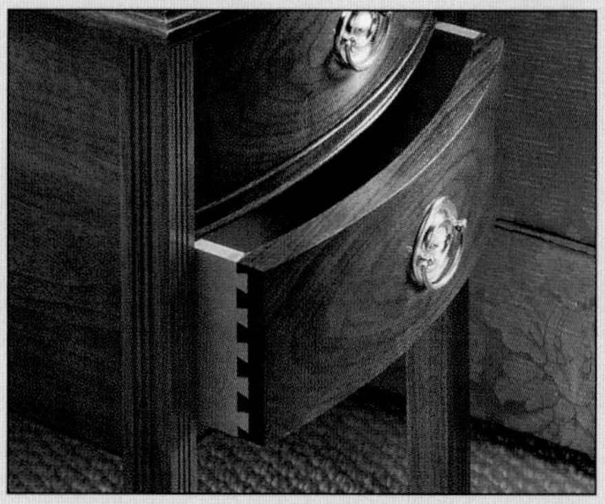

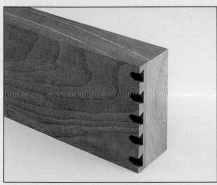

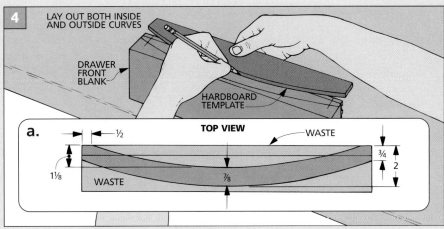

4 LAY OUT BOTH INSIDE AND OUTSIDE CURVES

DRAWER FRONT BLANK

HARDBOARD TEMPLATE

a. TOP VIEW

½

1⅛

WASTE

WASTE

⅞

¾

2

5 NOTE: CUT TO WASTE SIDE OF LINES

WASTE

Built-up Drawer Front. *The secret to cutting dovetails in the curved drawer front is to cut them in a ½"-thick blank first (top photo). Then glue a thick false front to the blank before cutting the curves (bottom photo).*

To trim the oversized blank, lower the blade and position the rip fence and auxiliary fence so the edge of the ½"-thick piece is flush with the blade. Then clamp the auxiliary fence down, raise the blade, and trim the oversized blank *(Figs. 3 and 3a).*

With the long edges of the blank flush, you can trim the ends of the drawer front quickly using the miter gauge and an auxiliary fence.

CUT CURVES. Now that the front has been trimmed, it's time to create the curves on the inside and outside faces by cutting away most of the blank.

Laying out the curves was easy. I used the same template that I used to make the curved edging *(Fig. 4).* Lay out the starting points on the ends and inside face of the blank *(Fig. 4a).* Then simply line up the template with the marks and draw the curves.

To cut the curves, I used the band saw, feeding the blank as smoothly as possible *(Fig. 5).* Just be sure to stay to the waste side of the lines because you'll need to do some sanding later.

SAND CURVES. To smooth the curves, I used a little elbow grease, sanding the pieces by hand. But I did find a simple way to make a curved sanding block that made the job easier (see the Shop Tip at right).

GROOVE FOR BOTTOM. With the drawer front smooth, grooves can be cut on all the pieces for the ¼" plywood bottom. And to do this on the curved fronts, I used a slot cutter bit.

Note: I had to outfit my bit with a rub arm so it would cut a ¼"-deep groove *(Fig. 6).* Refer to the Shop Jig on page 39 for details about this rub arm.

With the grooves routed, I cut out the drawer bottom *(Fig. 7).* Here again, I used the curved template to lay out the front edge before cutting it to shape. Then the pieces can be glued together just as you would with an ordinary square drawer.

Refer to the Shop Jig on page 39 for details about this rub arm.

SHOP TIP

Sanding Block

The waste piece from the drawer front makes a perfect sanding block. Just add adhesive-backed sandpaper.

NOTE: MAKE SANDING BLOCKS FROM CURVED WASTE PIECES

DRAWER FRONT

ADHESIVE-BACKED SANDPAPER

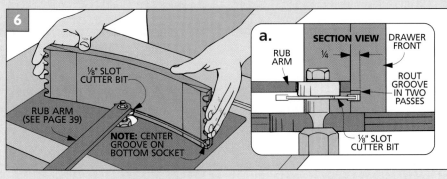

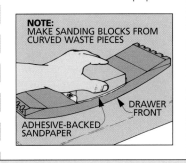

6

⅛" SLOT CUTTER BIT

RUB ARM (SEE PAGE 39)

NOTE: CENTER GROOVE ON BOTTOM SOCKET

a. SECTION VIEW

RUB ARM

¼

DRAWER FRONT

ROUT GROOVE IN TWO PASSES

⅛" SLOT CUTTER BIT

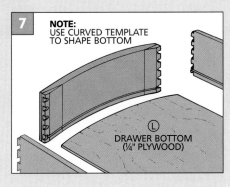

7 NOTE: USE CURVED TEMPLATE TO SHAPE BOTTOM

DRAWER BOTTOM (¼" PLYWOOD)

Choosing a finish for the Bow-Front End Table was easy. I knew I wanted a finish that would attract as much attention as the table without hiding the beauty of the wood. Plus, it had to be durable. That's why I settled on varnish.

An oil-based varnish gives me the best results I can get without expensive spray equipment. By brushing on several coats and then rubbing out the top coat, you can achieve a smooth, glossy finish. It also adds a warm, reddish tint to the walnut without any special stain. And it provides a lot of protection too.

PREPARE SURFACE. I began by sanding the entire end table to 180-grit. (Refer to page 26 for tips about preparing the end grain on the front and back of the table top.)

CLEAN SHOP. Next, I take some time to clean my shop thoroughly with a vacuum cleaner. Because varnish takes a long time to dry, your worst enemy is dust. It settles on the wet finish and creates a rough surface. But be aware that cleaning can also kick dust into the air. So when I'm done, I wait until the next day to start varnishing. This allows the dust to settle.

APPLY VARNISH

With the shop clean, you can begin applying coats of varnish. For the first coat, you may want to thin down the varnish so it flows out a little better, but the technique is the same.

CROSS-GRAIN. I brushed the varnish across the grain first to get the finish on the wood. Then I smoothed out the coat using a light brush stroke with the grain. You'll want to apply thin coats, or the finish will run and sag. (If it does, wipe it off immediately with mineral spirits. Otherwise you'll have to sand or scrape it away after it dries.)

SANDING. After the first coat dries (overnight), you'll want to smooth out the surface and remove any dust nibs with 400-grit wet-dry sandpaper and a sanding block. Then you can add more coats, sanding between coats.

STEEL WOOL. For polishing moldings, curved surfaces, carvings, and all the nooks and crannies that are difficult to sand, steel wool is a good choice. However, steel wool shouldn't be used on flat surfaces since it forms around

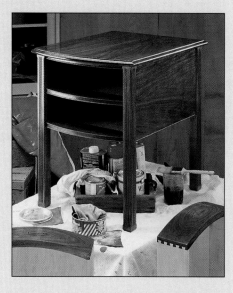

the contours of the imperfections you're trying to remove. You'll get a much better (flatter and smoother) finish if you use sandpaper and a sanding block to sand between coats on flat surfaces.

RUBBING OUT THE TOP

After you've built up several coats of finish, you might want to consider "rubbing out" the top. This requires more time and elbow grease, but you'll end up with a glass-smooth surface.

Basically, "rubbing out" means using finer and finer abrasives to polish the surface. Depending on how fine an abrasive you use, you can have a satin finish or a high-gloss finish.

Before you can begin polishing, the finish needs to be "built up" so it's thicker. (I applied four additional coats to the top.) That way, you won't "cut" through the finish to bare wood.

SATIN FINISH

The difference between a satin finish and a glossy finish is simply in the amount of rubbing and the types of abrasives used.

BUFFING. For a satin finish, I'll buff the surface lightly with 0000 steel wool. But don't use it right out of the package. To create a consistent sheen without cutting through the finish, you need to use a lubricant.

One product made specifically for use with steel wool has a consistency

that's somewhere between axle grease and petroleum jelly. After saturating a steel wool pad with the lubricant and applying some more to the surface of the workpiece, you can quickly create a hand-rubbed satin finish.

PASTE WAX. Another very popular approach is to use paste wax to lubricate the steel wool. It cuts a bit slower than the steel wool lubricant, but leaves a glossier surface when it's buffed out.

HIGH GLOSS

With just a few more steps using finer abrasives, you can achieve a high-gloss finish. Pumice and rottenstone are commonly used in these steps.

POWDER. Pumice is a white-gray material that comes from volcanic ash. It's graded from FF (coarsest) to FFFF (finest). Rottenstone is an even finer, black-gray powder. It's made from ground-up limestone and gets its name from the odor that's released when the raw material is being processed. (Fortunately, the odor is gone by the time you open the bag.)

RUBBING FELT. Pumice and rottenstone can be worked with a clean, soft cloth. But I prefer a block of rubbing felt. It works just like a sanding block to provide a flat surface.

USING POWDERS. Pumice and rottenstone are used the same way. (Be prepared. It gets a bit messy.) First, a thin coat of rubbing oil is spread on the work surface. Then the powder is sprinkled around. Take long, even strokes with the rubbing felt, working with the grain.

Before long, the powder and oil will mix together into a creamy paste. If there's too much oil, you won't feel any cutting taking place. If there's too much powder, the felt will tend to catch rather than glide over the surface.

As you work, check the progress by wiping the paste from different sections of the surface. Try to rub all parts evenly. (One trick is to count off the same number of strokes over each area.) Once the finish is uniform, clean off the residue and move on to the next finer abrasive until you get the sheen you like.

Once I had my table buffed the way I wanted it, I added a coat of wax to give the table a little more shine.

DESIGNER'S NOTEBOOK

With just a single drawer, this version of the Bow-Front End Table has a lighter look. Since there are fewer pieces to make and fewer joints to cut, construction goes more quickly, too.

CONSTRUCTION NOTES:

■ This Single Drawer Table is built with the same techniques used for the Bow-Front End Table.

■ Start by cutting the legs to size. However, you only need to cut one $5\frac{1}{2}$"-long mortise on each face where two are cut for the regular table *(Fig. 1)*. (Refer to *Fig. 1b* on page 32 for locations of mortises on each leg.)

■ All other leg details (flutes, chamfers, and foot pads) are the same as for the two-drawer Bow-Front End Table.

■ The sides (B) and back (C) are cut to a width of 6" *(Fig. 2)*.

■ Next, tenons are cut on the ends of the sides (B) and back (C) to fit the mortises in the legs.

■ After that, the grooves that accept the tongues on the web frames are cut on the inside faces of the sides (B) *(Fig. 2)*.

■ From here, construction is the same as for the two-drawer version of the table. The only differences are that you only need to make two web frames, two curved edging pieces, and one drawer.

SINGLE DRAWER

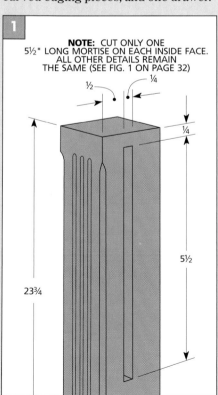

1

NOTE: CUT ONLY ONE $5\frac{1}{2}$" LONG MORTISE ON EACH INSIDE FACE. ALL OTHER DETAILS REMAIN THE SAME (SEE FIG. 1 ON PAGE 32)

$\frac{1}{2}$ $\frac{1}{4}$

$\frac{1}{4}$

$5\frac{1}{2}$

$23\frac{3}{4}$

MATERIALS LIST

CHANGED PARTS

B	Sides (2)	$\frac{3}{4}$ x 6 - $19\frac{1}{2}$
C	Back (1)	$\frac{3}{4}$ x 6 - $15\frac{1}{2}$
D	Web Frame Rails (4)	$\frac{3}{4}$ x $1\frac{1}{2}$ - 16
E	Web Frame Stiles (4)	$\frac{3}{4}$ x $1\frac{3}{4}$ - $16\frac{1}{2}$
F	Web Frame Pnls. (2)	$\frac{1}{4}$ ply - 13 x $16\frac{1}{2}$
G	Curved Edging (2)	$\frac{3}{4}$ x $2\frac{1}{2}$ - $14\frac{1}{2}$
I	Drawer Frt./Bk. (2)	$\frac{1}{2}$ x $4\frac{3}{8}$ - $14\frac{3}{8}$
J	Drawer Sides (2)	$\frac{1}{2}$ x $4\frac{3}{8}$ - 19

K	Drawer False Frt. (1)	$1\frac{3}{4}$ x $4\frac{3}{8}$ - $14\frac{3}{8}$
L	Drawer Bottom (1)	$\frac{1}{2}$ ply - $13\frac{7}{8}$ x $19\frac{7}{8}$
M	Drawer Guides (2)	$\frac{3}{4}$ x $\frac{9}{16}$ - $18\frac{1}{2}$
N	Drawer Stop (1)	$\frac{3}{4}$ x $\frac{5}{8}$ - 4

HARDWARE SUPPLIES

(2) Nylon glide strips
(1) Bail pull (2 " bore)

2

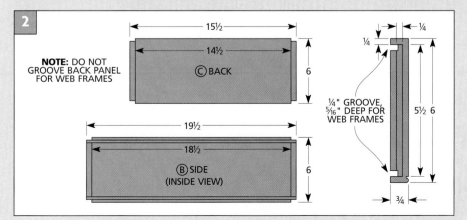

$15\frac{1}{2}$

$14\frac{1}{2}$

NOTE: DO NOT GROOVE BACK PANEL FOR WEB FRAMES

© BACK

6

$\frac{1}{4}$ $\frac{1}{4}$

$19\frac{1}{2}$

$18\frac{1}{2}$

B SIDE
(INSIDE VIEW)

6

$\frac{1}{4}$" GROOVE, $\frac{5}{16}$" DEEP FOR WEB FRAMES

$5\frac{1}{2}$ 6

$\frac{3}{4}$

ACCESSORIES

Chances are if you like the way a home is decorated, it has a lot to do with the accessories. The projects in this section add the warmth of wood to your home's decor. Plus, each one can be customized to suit your tastes. The molded edges of the oval mirror and the classic frames can be modified in numerous ways. The mantel clock is designed to work with either a traditional mechanical movement or a contemporary quartz movement. And the book stand is perfect for a library or den, or even a hallway.

Oval Mirror

This mirror will be a pleasing addition to your foyer or front hallway. It's simple to make by cutting a number of short pieces, gluing them together to form an octagon, and then routing it into an oval.

The idea of building an Oval Mirror has always intrigued me. But without some kind of jig to cut the oval-shaped frame and rout the complex profiles, it's virtually impossible to make a consistent oval. So after a lot of thought (there's more to cutting an oval than a circle), I came up with a jig that made it possible. For more about how this works, see the Shop Jig on page 52.

PROFILE. The most interesting aspects of this project are how the profile is created and how the frame is cut to size.

To cut a profile like this normally requires a shaper and an expensive cutter. But I molded this profile and cut the oval to size with a router (mounted in the jig) and three router bits.

To rout the profile shown here and cut the frame, you'll need a $1/4$" roundover bit (without the bearing), a $3/4$" core box bit, and a $1/4$" straight bit.

JOINERY. The frame is made from eight pieces joined together with splined miter joints. But don't worry, even with sixteen miters, I've come up with a simple way to make sure you end up with nice tight joints. Plus, I used $1/8$"-thick hardboard for the splines because it's very stable and less likely to cause the joints to move during changes in humidity. This can be a real concern in a project like this.

WOOD AND FINISH. To allow enough thickness for the profile, you'll need 5/4 stock ($1^1/_{16}$" actual thickness). I used cherry for my mirror, but another good choice would be walnut.

For the finish I applied two coats of a satin polyurethane finish.

MIRROR. The mirror itself is a standard $1/8$"-thick mirror. And unless you're good at cutting glass, you'll probably have to pay a little extra to have the oval shape cut.

HARDWARE. I used a heavy braided wire and hinged hangers to hang the mirror. See the Technique on page 51 for ideas on hanging heavy frames.

Finally, for more information on how to find the hardware needed to build (and then hang) the frame, see Sources and project supplies on page 126. It also lists sources for the various router bits used in cutting the molding profiles.

EXPLODED VIEW

OVERALL DIMENSIONS:
25W x 1¹⁄₁₆D x 37H

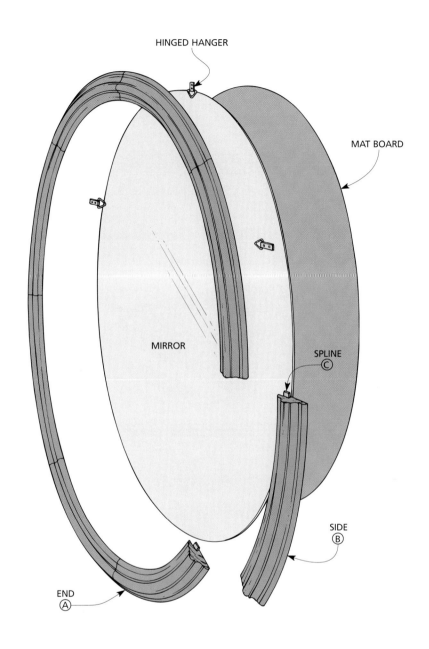

HINGED HANGER

MAT BOARD

MIRROR

SPLINE
Ⓒ

SIDE
Ⓑ

END
Ⓐ

MATERIALS LIST

WOOD

A	Ends (4)	1¹⁄₁₆ x 5 - 12½
B	Sides (4)	1¹⁄₁₆ x 5 - 15
C	Splines (8)	⅛ hdbd. - ⅝ x 2½

HARDWARE SUPPLIES
(1) Oval mirror (cut to shape)
(1) ¹⁄₁₆" - 32" x 40" standard mat board
(16) No. 7 glazing push points
(4) 1⅞" hangers
(8) No. 5 x ½" Fh woodscrews
10' (rough) 20# braided wire
(4) ½" rubber bumpers

CUTTING DIAGRAM

1¹⁄₁₆ x 5 - 60 (2.6 Bd. Ft.)

1¹⁄₁₆ x 5 - 60 (2.6 Bd. Ft.)

NOTE: ALSO NEED ⅛" HARDBOARD FOR SPLINES

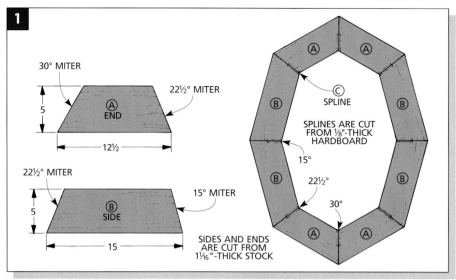

The oval frame actually starts out as an octagonal blank *(Fig. 1)*. Four of the pieces are identical ends (A), and the other four are identical sides (B). To cut all eight pieces, you'll need to set the saw for three different angles.

ENDS AND SIDES. To cut the ends (A) and sides (B), first rip all eight pieces from 5/4 stock (1$\frac{1}{16}$" actual thickness) to a finished width of 5" *(Fig. 1)*. Now miter one end of each piece at 22$\frac{1}{2}$°.

Then cut each end (A) to final length with a 30° miter at the opposite end *(Fig. 1)*. The sides (B) are cut to length by mitering the opposite end at 15°.

Once all the pieces are cut to size, the next step is to rout grooves for splines.

ORGANIZING PIECES. It's important with spline and groove joinery to make sure the grooves align. So before routing the workpieces, first organize them as they're going to appear in the blank *(Fig. 1)*. Then draw an "X" on the top face of each piece so they'll be oriented the same way.

ROUTING GROOVES. Normally, a spline is centered on the thickness of a board. But for this project, a centered spline would be exposed once the profile is routed. So to avoid this, place the splines off-center ($\frac{1}{8}$" from the back) on the thickness of the frame pieces *(Fig. 2)*.

The grooves also have to be stopped short so they won't be seen on the outside of the frame. So first rout one end of each workpiece in the normal, right to left manner stopping at a centerline drawn on both the router table and on one edge of the workpiece *(Fig. 3)*.

Note: Face the "X" *away* from the router table fence.

Then to rout the other end of each piece so the stopped grooves are on the same side, be sure to keep the "X" side of the workpiece facing out and plunge the workpiece onto the bit at the centerline and rout in the normal direction *(Fig. 4)*.

GLUING AN OCTAGON. When cutting miters of an eight-sided frame, there's always a good chance for error.

Each of the pieces requires two miters (one for each end) for a total of sixteen cuts. If the miter gauge is off just $\frac{1}{4}$°, the combined gap would be about $\frac{1}{4}$" when the pieces are assembled *(Fig. 5)*.

HALF FRAMES. The trick to creating tight joints at each miter involves assembling two "half frames," then cutting the ends of each to fit together tightly.

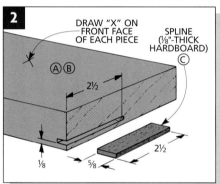

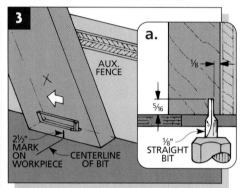

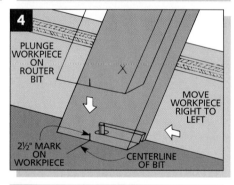

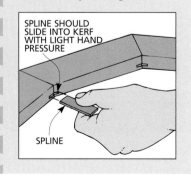

SHOP TIP

Sizing Splines

How tight should a spline be? When dry-assembling the joint, if you can't push the spline in easily with your finger, it will be too tight when there's glue in the joint. So the spline needs to be thinner. But, if the spline falls out when the workpiece is turned over, it's too loose to hold the joint together.

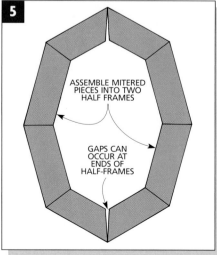

SPLINE SHOULD SLIDE INTO KERF WITH LIGHT HAND PRESSURE

SPLINE

So first, cut the splines from hardboard and glue up four of the pieces (half the frame). See the Shop Tip on the opposite page for how to size the splines.

PLYWOOD CARRIER. After the pieces are dry, I use a piece of plywood as a cut-off table for the half frames *(Fig. 6)*.

To cut the plywood, set up the fence on the saw a little wider than the glued-up half frame, ripping the plywood so the edges are parallel. Now fasten the half frame to the plywood with carpet tape.

Then, if the miters are off, position the half frame so the two long corners extend beyond the edge of the plywood and the two short corners are flush to the edge *(Fig. 6a)*.

MAKING THE CUTS. Next, run the plywood carrier through the table saw, trimming off the long corners of the half frame. Repeat the procedure on the other half frame. Now the two halves can be glued together without a gap.

MOUNTING BLANK TO JIG

Now that the frame blank is complete, you'll need an easy way to rout the profile. To do this, I designed an oval-cutting jig. (For more on the jig, see page 52.) To ensure the profile is routed in the center of the blank, the blank must be positioned correctly on the jig.

To do this, first drill pilot holes for woodscrews that hold the blank to the large plywood base *(Fig. 7)*. I drilled the holes into every other frame piece.

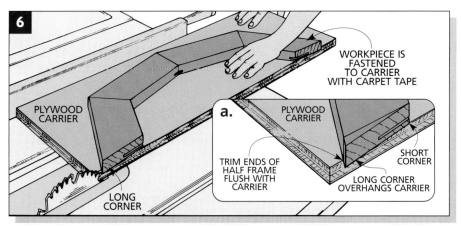

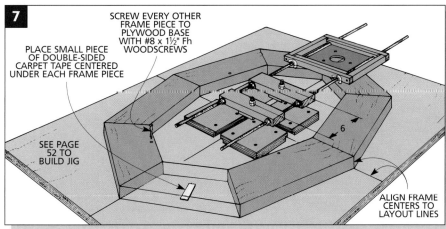

Note: To ensure the router bits clear the screws, place the holes at the center of each piece within ¼" of the inside edge.

Then center double-sided carpet tape on the bottom of each frame piece *(Fig. 7)*. The tape holds the frame to the plywood once it's cut from the blanks.

MOUNT BLANK. Now all that's left is to slip the frame blank onto the oval-cutting jig, aligning the center to the layout lines *(Fig. 7)*. Then screw the blank to the plywood base.

SHOP TIP .... Modifying a Bit

I needed a roundover bit without a pilot bearing to rout the bead in the center of the Oval Mirror.

To do this, I bought a high speed steel bit and arbor set. This bit has a removable rub pilot, but there's a problem. Since the end of this bit isn't made to cut wood, I had to modify it to use it on this project.

To prevent burning, I ground a concave shape on the bit using a grinding wheel (see drawing). Hold the bit with locking pliers and use the corner of the wheel. Grind from the center outwards, being careful not to nick the cutting edge of the router bit.

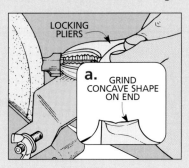

BEFORE: The bit with the flat end is difficult to push through the workpiece, and the friction it produces burns the wood.

AFTER: With the end of the bit hollowed out, the cut is much smoother, and the workpiece shows no signs of burning.

ROUTING THE PROFILE

With the blank mounted on the oval-cutting jig, you're ready to rout the frame's profile and the oval shape.

ROUTER BITS. A shaper cutter can mold the profile shown in the photo. But it also can be routed with three router bits: a $1/4$" roundover bit without a bearing (see the Shop Tip on page 49), a $3/4$" core box bit, and a $1/4$" straight bit.

FIRST PASS. The profile is routed in nine separate steps. In each step the router bit is positioned at a different location on the blank. To determine where the first pass will begin, locate the center of one of the end pieces (A) and then draw a centerline (Fig. 8).

Next, mount the $1/4$" roundover bit in the router. And then set the depth of the bit to rout $1/4$" deep. Now adjust the router carriage so the outside edge of the bit is on the inside of the centerline (Step 1).

After the router carriage is adjusted, follow the steps below (changing the bits and adjusting the carriage as you go).

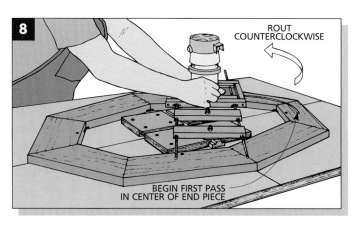

Note: When performing this step by step procedure, always remember to start a little wide from where you want to end up, then sneak up on the final measurement of the profile.

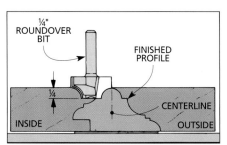

1 With a $1/4$" roundover bit in the router, position the router carriage so the outside edge of the bit is on the centerline. Now rout inside half of $1/2$"-wide bead.

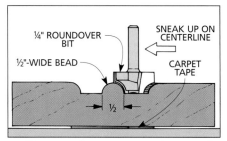

2 Next, readjust router carriage so the inside edge of bit is approximately $1/8$" away from the centerline. Then sneak up on centerline to complete $1/2$"-wide bead.

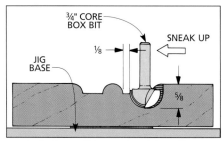

3 Switch to a $3/4$" core box bit. Adjust carriage so inside edge of bit is $1/4$" away from the outside edge of bead. Sneak up on the bead to create a $1/8$"-wide shoulder.

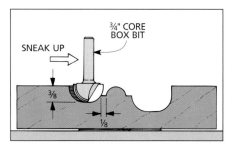

4 Next, reposition carriage so outside edge of bit is about $1/4$" away from inside edge of the bead. Then, sneak up on the bead to create a $1/8$"-wide shoulder.

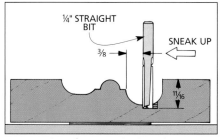

5 Switch to $1/4$" straight bit. Then adjust carriage so the inside edge of the bit is about $7/8$" away from the centerline. Next, sneak up to leave a $3/8$"-wide cove.

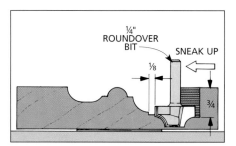

6 Reinstall roundover bit. Reposition carriage so inside edge of bit is about $1/4$" away from outside edge of the cove. Sneak up to leave $1/8$"-wide shoulder.

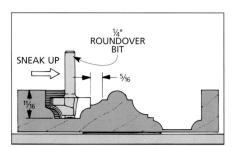

7 Reposition carriage so the outside edge of the roundover bit is approximately $9/16$" away from inside edge of the bead. Sneak up to leave $5/16$"-wide cove.

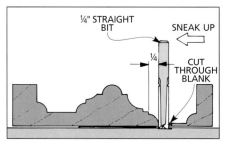

8 Reinstall the straight bit. Then adjust the carriage so the bit is $1/16$" from the outside roundover. Sneak up on the roundover to cut the outside of the oval.

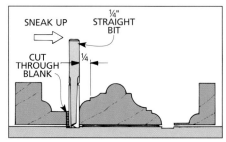

9 Now, readjust carriage so the straight bit is about $1/16$" away from the inside roundover. Sneak up on the roundover and cut through the blank.

INSTALLING THE MIRROR

After the profile has been routed, gently remove the frame from the plywood base. If the double-sided carpet tape won't release the frame, a good way to dissolve the adhesive on the tape is by flowing a small amount of denatured alcohol under the frame.

ROUTING RABBET. The final step in making the frame is to rout a ³⁄₈"-wide rabbet along the back inside edge for the mirror and mat board.

To do this, I used a hand-held router with a rabbet bit *(Fig. 9)*. But, because the back of the frame isn't really very wide, I decided to use carpet tape to fasten a small block of wood to the base of the router for additional support. Then when you rout the rabbet, move the router in a clockwise direction.

FINISH. With the frame complete, the next step is to lightly sand the profile and then apply the finish.

BACKING BOARD AND MIRROR. To protect the silver coating on the back of the mirror from being damaged, I cut a standard mat board to use as a backing board *(Figs. 10 and 10a)*.

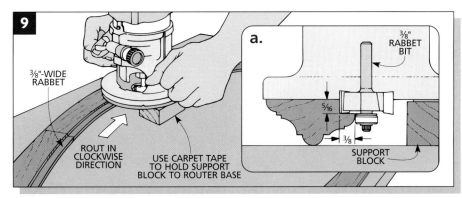

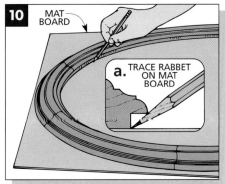

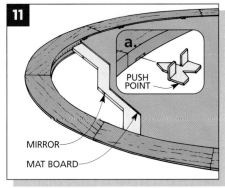

Note: I also brought the mat board to the glass shop so they could use it as a template when cutting the mirror.

Then, install the mirror and mat board with push points spaced evenly around the frame's inside edge *(Fig. 11a)*. ■

TECHNIQUE .... *Hanging Heavy Frames*

The braided wire used to hang this mirror is strung in such a way that it pulls the frame in towards the center of the mirror. This relieves some of the pressure from the weight of the mirror. And it works for both horizontal and vertical mountings *(Figs. 1 and 2)*.

STRINGING WIRE. The first step to installing the hanging system is to screw four hinged hangers to the back of the frame *(Figs. 1 and 2)*. Then string braided wire through the hangers, starting with the bottom one *(Fig. 1a)*.

Now thread the wire through the top, left, and right hangers. Then terminate the wire back through the top hanger, and tie it off just as you did at the bottom hanger *(Fig. 1a)*.

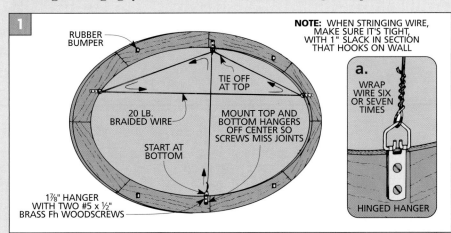

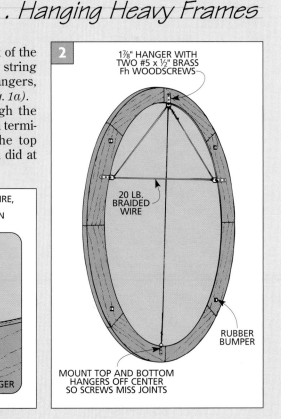

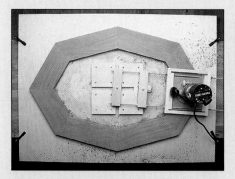

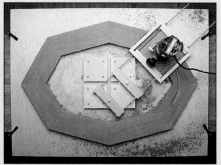

Routing a glued-up blank into a perfect oval (ellipse) requires a trammel. But not the type you might expect. Most trammels swing on one anchor point, allowing you to rout a circle. But to rout an oval, you need a trammel that swings on two anchor points.

This oval-cutting jig does just that. It consists of a trammel platform that supports a large trammel arm. At the end of the arm is a frame that holds a router in place *(Fig. 1)*.

As the arm rotates around the platform, the two anchor points are working together to control the orbit of the router. One anchor point controls the length of the oval (the longer distance across the oval), the other anchor point controls the width of the oval (the shorter distance).

HOW THE JIG WORKS. As the router orbits the platform, the two anchor points chase each other in a circular path. And while this is going on, they're also sliding back and forth in separate tracks that are perpendicular to each other (see photos above).

OVAL FRAMES. This jig allows you to do two things. You can rout the inside and outside edges of an oval frame with the width of the frame being equal all the way around. It's also good for routing a complex profile on the face of the frame (such as that shown on page 50).

JIG FEATURES. If you've ever routed a molding that has an ornate profile, you know that you have to change bits frequently. To make that easy with this jig, the router is mounted on a base plate

that swings up and down to allow easier access to the router's collet. It also lets you gradually lower the bit into the workpiece at the start of each pass.

MATERIALS. Because many of the pieces on the jig either rotate or slide, I used hard maple for most of the parts. The exceptions are the base and trammel platform (3/4"-thick plywood) and some 1/4" hardboard for the tilting base plate and a pair of shims (for routing pieces of different thickness). The hardware should be available at most hardware stores or home centers.

TRAMMEL PLATFORM

When designing this jig, a major consideration was the size of the frame.

The trammel platform has to be small enough to fit inside a glued-up blank. But it also has to be large enough so there will be plenty of track for the guide blocks (C) to travel in *(Fig. 1)*.

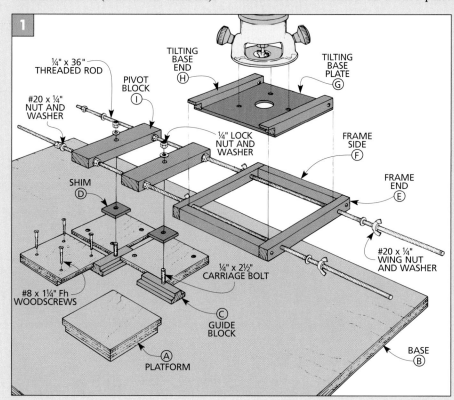

1

1/4" x 36" THREADED ROD

#20 x 1/4" NUT AND WASHER

PIVOT BLOCK (I)

TILTING BASE END (H)

TILTING BASE PLATE (G)

1/4" LOCK NUT AND WASHER

FRAME SIDE (F)

FRAME END (E)

SHIM (D)

#20 x 1/4" WING NUT AND WASHER

#8 x 1 1/4" Fh WOODSCREWS

1/4" x 2 1/2" CARRIAGE BOLT

GUIDE BLOCK (C)

PLATFORM (A)

BASE (B)

MATERIALS LIST

TRAMMEL

A	Platform (1)	3/4 ply - 11 3/8 x 11 3/8
B	Base (1)	3/4 ply - 36 x 48
C	Guide Blocks (2)	3/4 ply - 1 1/2 x 4
D	Shims (2)	1/4 x 2 - 2

TRAMMEL ARM

E	Frame Ends (2)	3/4 x 3/4 - 10 1/2
F	Frame Sides (2)	3/4 x 3/4 - 8 3/4
G	Tilting Base Plt. (1)	1/4 hdbd. - 8 3/4 x 8 1/2
H	Tilting Base Ends (2)	5/8 x 3/4 - 8 1/2
I	Pivot Blocks (2)	3/4 x 2 - 8 1/2

HARDWARE SUPPLIES

(20) No. 8 x 1 1/4" Fh woodscrews
(2) 1/4" x 36" threaded rods
(4) No. 20 x 1/4" wing nuts
(8) No. 20 x 1/4" nuts
(14) 1/4" washers
(2) 1/4" x 2 1/2" carriage bolts
(2) 1/4" lock nuts

Note: The following measurements work for the Oval Mirror beginning on page 46. But they will also work for similar-sized frames.

PLATFORM. The trammel platform (A) is cut from a piece of ¾"-thick plywood *(Fig. 2)*. After the blank is cut to size, the next step is to cut the track for the guide blocks.

Here, I took a slightly different approach. Instead of cutting the track in a large "X" across the blank, I first cut ⅜" rabbets on all four edges of the blank *(Fig. 2a)*. Then I cut the blank into four equally sized squares *(Fig. 3)*.

Now comes the different approach. I turned the four squares so the rabbets faced *in*. The rabbeted edges then create the tracks.

ALIGNMENT BLOCKS. To help align the squares on a base (B), first you cut a 12"-long rabbeted blank *(Fig. 4)*. (Later, this blank becomes the guide blocks.) Then cut the blank into two separate alignment blocks *(Fig. 4)*.

MOUNTING. To mount the platform, first cut a base (B) from ¾"-thick plywood and draw alignment marks on the base *(Fig. 5)*. Now position the first square on the alignment marks and screw it in place *(Fig. 6)*.

Butt the shorter of the two alignment blocks up against the square and screw another square to the base with the block snug between the squares *(Fig. 6)*.

To complete the platform, screw down each of the last squares in the same manner *(Fig. 7)*.

GUIDE BLOCKS AND SHIMS. To make the guide blocks (C), cut the alignment block into two 4"-long pieces *(Fig. 8)*.

Then drill a centered and counterbored hole through each of these guide blocks for a carriage bolt *(Fig. 8a)*. Now you can just slide the guide blocks into the track.

Note: If the guide blocks are too tight in the track, you can lightly sand them as needed for smooth operation.

When routing a frame that will be thicker than ¾", you'll need to shim up the trammel arm so that it rides flat on the surface of the workpiece being routed. For the Oval Mirror, I needed to place ¼"-thick shims (D) on the guide blocks *(Figs. 8 and 9)*.

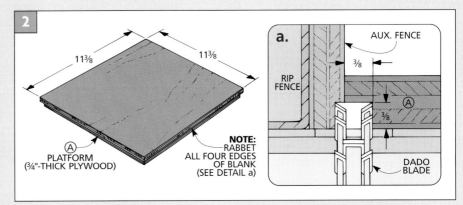

2
11⅜
11⅜
Ⓐ
PLATFORM
(¾"-THICK PLYWOOD)
NOTE: RABBET ALL FOUR EDGES OF BLANK (SEE DETAIL a)

a.
AUX. FENCE
RIP FENCE
⅜
Ⓐ
⅜
DADO BLADE

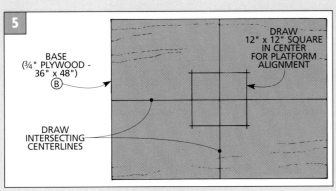

3
5⅝
5⅝
Ⓐ
Ⓐ
Ⓐ
Ⓐ
CUT BLANK INTO FOUR EQUAL SQUARES

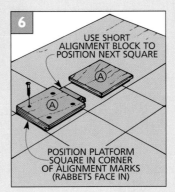

4
SAVE FOR GUIDE BLOCKS
Ⓒ
12
¾
SAVE
9
1½
a.
⅜
⅜
Ⓐ
Ⓒ
1½
BOTH PIECES NEEDED FOR POSITIONING PLATFORM SQUARES (SEE FIGS. 5 AND 6)

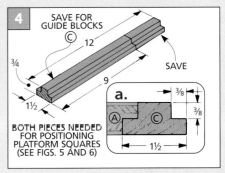

5
BASE (¾" PLYWOOD - 36" x 48")
Ⓑ
DRAW INTERSECTING CENTERLINES
DRAW 12" x 12" SQUARE IN CENTER FOR PLATFORM ALIGNMENT

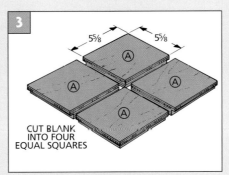

6
USE SHORT ALIGNMENT BLOCK TO POSITION NEXT SQUARE
Ⓐ
Ⓐ
POSITION PLATFORM SQUARE IN CORNER OF ALIGNMENT MARKS (RABBETS FACE IN)

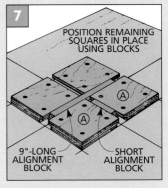

7
POSITION REMAINING SQUARES IN PLACE USING BLOCKS
Ⓐ
Ⓐ
9"-LONG ALIGNMENT BLOCK
SHORT ALIGNMENT BLOCK

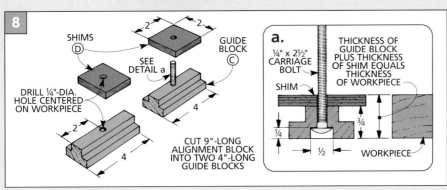

8
SHIMS
Ⓓ
2
2
SEE DETAIL a
GUIDE BLOCK
Ⓒ
DRILL ¼"-DIA. HOLE CENTERED ON WORKPIECE
2
4
4
CUT 9"-LONG ALIGNMENT BLOCK INTO TWO 4"-LONG GUIDE BLOCKS
a.
¼" x 2½" CARRIAGE BOLT
SHIM
THICKNESS OF GUIDE BLOCK PLUS THICKNESS OF SHIM EQUALS THICKNESS OF WORKPIECE
¼
½
¾
WORKPIECE

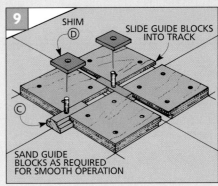

9
SHIM
Ⓓ
SLIDE GUIDE BLOCKS INTO TRACK
Ⓒ
SAND GUIDE BLOCKS AS REQUIRED FOR SMOOTH OPERATION

After the platform is complete, the next part to start working on is the trammel arm. This arm consists of a router carriage and two pivot blocks connected by threaded rods (refer to *Fig. 14*). The carriage supports the router and the pivot blocks determine the shape of the oval. I started on the carriage.

CARRIAGE. When routing an oval frame with a detailed profile, router bits need to be changed frequently. To make this a quick process, the carriage is designed so that it can be tilted up — making it a lot easier to get to the collet.

The carriage is actually a frame with a tilting base to hold the router. To build it, start by cutting two ends (E) and two sides (F) from ³/₄"-thick stock *(Fig. 10)*.

Next, to accept the threaded rods, drill ¹/₄" holes near the ends of each frame end (E). Also drill countersunk holes for the screws that hold the frame together.

TILTING BASE. After the frame is screwed together, a tilting base plate (G) can be cut to size from ¹/₄"-thick hardboard *(Fig. 11)*.

To support the base plate within the frame, cut two tilting base ends (H) to size *(Fig. 11)*. Drill a ¹/₄"-dia. hole for a threaded rod near one end of each piece.

Note: The hole is located ¹/₈" up from the bottom of the base end — it's not centered on the thickness.

Finally, the base ends can be glued to the plate. But first, to keep the bottom of the plate flush with the bottom of the carriage frame, rout rabbets along two edges of the plate *(Fig. 11)*. Then glue the base ends to the plate.

BIT AND MOUNTING HOLES. Now remove the plastic base from your router, and use it as a template to locate the bit and screw holes for mounting your router to the jig *(Fig. 12)*.

NOTCH THE BASE. After the holes are drilled in the base plate, there's one last step on the tilting base before it's complete. To allow it to sit down on the threaded rod *(Fig. 14)*, a notch has to be cut at one end of each base end (H).

To do this, I cut a rabbet on the edge opposite the ¹/₄" hole *(Fig. 13)*.

Note: You'll remove some of the hardboard base plate when doing this.

PIVOT BLOCKS. The last parts to make for the trammel arm are the pivot blocks (I) *(Figs. 10 and 14)*.

After cutting the blocks to size, drill a hole in the center and two holes through the side of each block *(Fig. 10)*.

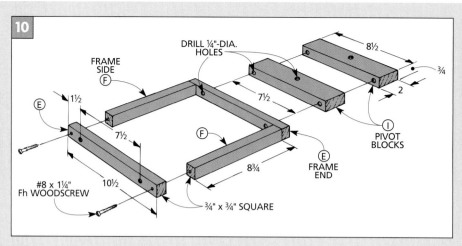

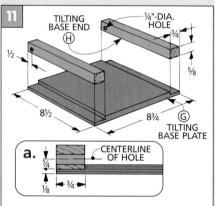

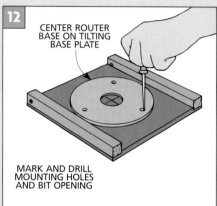

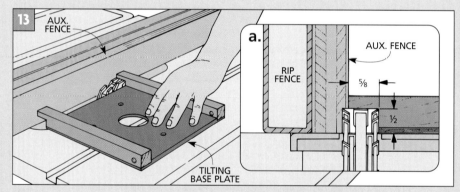

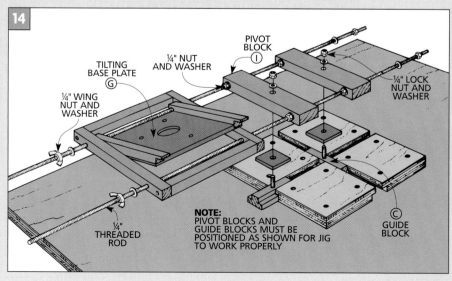

Note: The holes in the sides must align with the holes in the frame ends (E).

ASSEMBLY. Finally, assemble all the wood parts, hardware, and threaded rods for the trammel arm *(Fig. 14)*. Once the arm is completely assembled, attach the pivot blocks to the guide blocks with washers and lock nuts.

SETTING UP THE JIG

One thing I like about this oval-cutting jig is that it can be used to cut ovals of different shapes and sizes. The same jig can be used to cut several combinations of tall, short, wide, or narrow ovals. It all depends on how you set it up.

When setting up the jig for a particular shape, the distance between the front pivot block and the router bit (shown as $12\frac{1}{2}$" in *Fig. 15*) determines the *width* across the oval. And the distance between the back pivot block and the bit (shown as $18\frac{1}{2}$" in *Fig. 15*) determines the *length* across the oval.

AN EXAMPLE. The key setup measurements for the jig are obtained from the dimensions of the oval frame you want to make. With the Oval Mirror, the overall dimensions of the frame are 25" wide and 37" long.

The first step is to calculate the *shape* of the oval. To do this, first divide both the width and length by two. This gives you the minor and major radii of the oval. (The minor radius is $12\frac{1}{2}$" and the major radius is $18\frac{1}{2}$" for the Mirror.) Then subtract the smaller number from the larger number to come up with the *radius differential*. (In this case, it's 6".)

Now adjust the pivot blocks so they're the same distance apart as the radius differential (6") (see *Fig. 15* and Adjusting The Trammel below).

The last step is to adjust the jig for the *size* of the oval. To do this, move the router carriage so the distance between the inside edge of the router bit and the center of the front pivot block equals the radius of the width ($12\frac{1}{2}$"). (Measure from the center of the carriage bolt in the front pivot block.)

DIFFERENT FRAMES. If you're designing an oval frame that's significantly different from the Oval Mirror, keep in mind the limitations of a jig built with the dimensions shown here. It can only cut a certain shape and size frame.

The shape of the oval is limited to a radius differential of 4" to 6" *(Fig. 15)*.

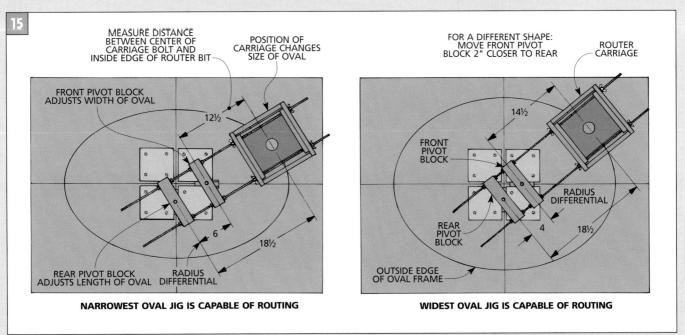

15

MEASURE DISTANCE BETWEEN CENTER OF CARRIAGE BOLT AND INSIDE EDGE OF ROUTER BIT

POSITION OF CARRIAGE CHANGES SIZE OF OVAL

FRONT PIVOT BLOCK ADJUSTS WIDTH OF OVAL

$12\frac{1}{2}$

6

$18\frac{1}{2}$

REAR PIVOT BLOCK ADJUSTS LENGTH OF OVAL

RADIUS DIFFERENTIAL

NARROWEST OVAL JIG IS CAPABLE OF ROUTING

FOR A DIFFERENT SHAPE: MOVE FRONT PIVOT BLOCK 2" CLOSER TO REAR

ROUTER CARRIAGE

$14\frac{1}{2}$

FRONT PIVOT BLOCK

REAR PIVOT BLOCK

RADIUS DIFFERENTIAL

4

$18\frac{1}{2}$

OUTSIDE EDGE OF OVAL FRAME

WIDEST OVAL JIG IS CAPABLE OF ROUTING

ADJUSTING THE TRAMMEL

1 *When setting the radius differential, make sure to use the distance between the centers of the carriage bolts.*

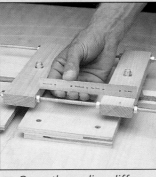

2 *Once the radius differential is set, measure distance between the pivot blocks to make sure they're parallel.*

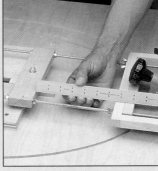

3 *To rout frames with complex profiles, the carriage must be moved back and forth along the threaded rods.*

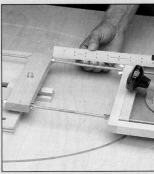

4 *So if the carriage and pivot block are not parallel to each other, you'll need to adjust the trammel again.*

Mantel Clock

At first, your eye will be drawn to the handsome, molded top of this clock. But the sound of the chimes tells you there's much more. A look through the glass sides reveals an intricate brass clock movement.

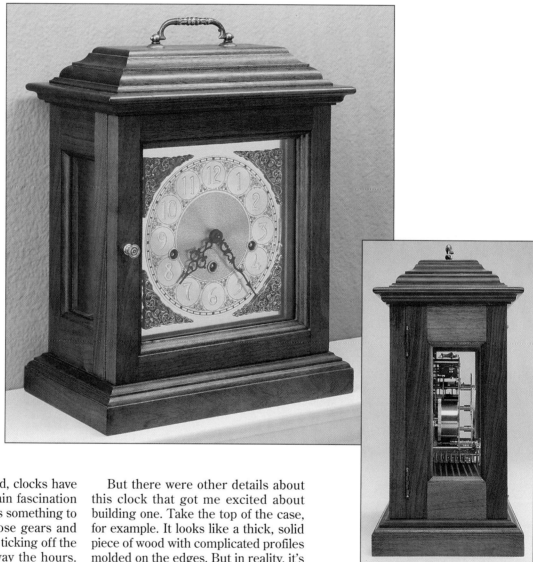

Ever since I was a kid, clocks have always held a certain fascination for me. I think it has something to do with watching all those gears and levers move in harmony, ticking off the seconds and striking away the hours. The problem is that with most clocks, the mechanism is hidden inside a case. To me, that's like looking at an automobile without being able to open the hood.

That's why I like this clock. The sides are glass so you can see right in to the brass clock movement inside. And a glass door at the front of the clock protects the dial but still opens, allowing you to wind the clock and adjust the hands.

But there were other details about this clock that got me excited about building one. Take the top of the case, for example. It looks like a thick, solid piece of wood with complicated profiles molded on the edges. But in reality, it's made up of three pieces. And the profile is created with just a router table and some commonly available router bits.

TRADITIONAL STYLE. And since the top isn't one solid piece, it's easy to customize the Mantel Clock for a simpler, more traditional look. See the Designer's Notebook on page 65 for more on this.

QUARTZ MOVEMENT. Another option is to build the clock with a battery-powered quartz movement. It's less expensive and you don't ever have to worry about winding it. And because there isn't much to look at, walnut plywood panels are substituted for the glass in the sides (see the Designer's Notebook on page 61).

HARDWARE. For sources of clock works and hardware, see page 126.

EXPLODED VIEW

OVERALL DIMENSIONS:
11½"W x 7⅛"D x 14H

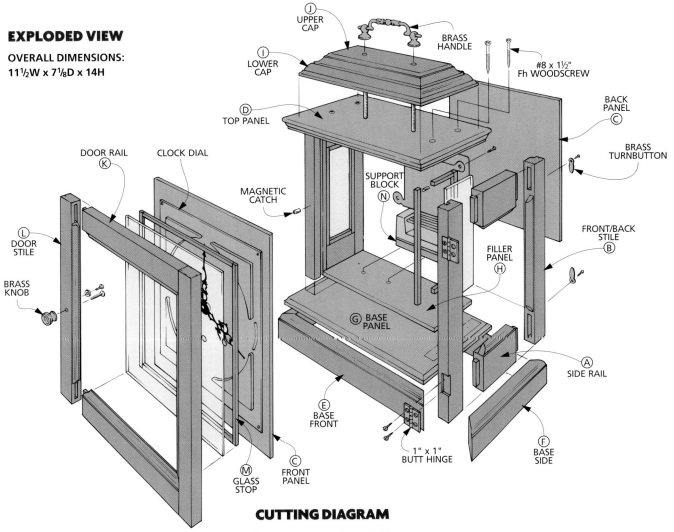

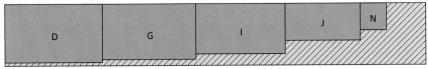

CUTTING DIAGRAM

¾ x 7 - 48 WALNUT (2.33 Bd. Ft)

¾ x 7 - 48 WALNUT (2.33 Bd. Ft.)

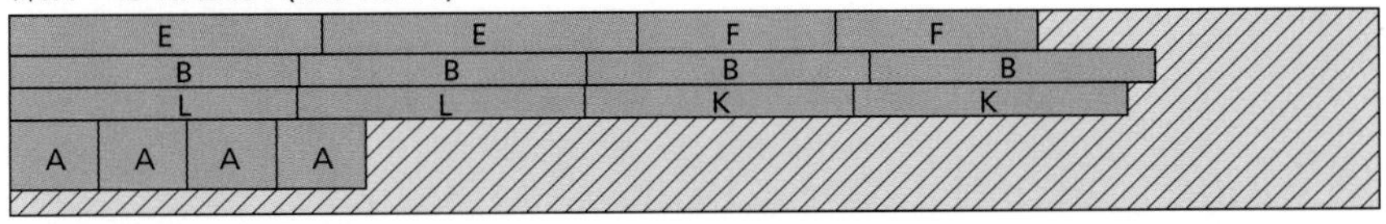

NOTE: CUT PARTS M FROM WASTE. ALSO NEED ONE 2' x 2' SHEET OF ¼" WALNUT PLYWOOD FOR FRONT, AND FILLER PANELS.

MATERIALS LIST

WOOD
A	Side Rails (4)	¾ x 2 - 3¼
B	Front/Back Stiles (4)	¾ x 1¼ - 9⅞
C	Front/Bk. Panels (2)	¼ ply - 8⅞ x 9⅞
D	Top Panel (1)	¾ x 6⅞ - 11¼
E	Base Front/Back (2)	¾ x 1½ - 11½
F	Base Sides (2)	¾ x 1½ - 7⅛
G	Base Panel (1)	¾ x 6⅜ - 10¾
H	Filler Panels (2)	¼ ply - cut to fit
I	Lower Cap (1)	¾ x 5¾ - 10⅛
J	Upper Cap (1)	¾ x 4 - 8⅜
K	Door Rails (2)	¾ x 1¼ - 9
L	Door Stiles (2)	¾ x 1¼ - 9⅞
M	Glass Stop (1)	9/32 x 5/32 - 56
N	Support Block (1)	½ x 3 - 3

HARDWARE SUPPLIES
(4) No. 2 x ¼" Rh brass woodscrews
(4) No. 4 x ⅝" Rh brass woodscrews
(4) No. 8 x 1¼" Fh woodscrews
(8) No. 8 x 1½" Fh woodscrews
(32) No. 18 x ⅝" wire brads

(1) Triple-chime movement
(1) 7⅞"-dia. punched dial
(1 pr.) 3"-long serpentine hands
(1) 4½" ant. br. hdl. w/ thrd. studs & nuts
(1) ½"-dia. antique brass knob
(1) Mini brass knob
(1 pr.) 1" x 1" antique brass hinges
(1) 5/16"-dia. magnetic catch
(4) ⅝" brass turnbuttons
(2) ⅛" glass panels (sides) - 2⅝" x 6¼"
(1) ⅛" glass panel (front) - 7⅞" x 7⅞"

I thought the beautiful brass movement of this Mantel Clock shouldn't be hidden. So to focus attention on the mechanical workings of the clock, I added glass panels to the sides of the case. This gives a clear view inside.

I built the clock from the center out. In other words, I started with the side assemblies, then added the front and back panels, and sandwiched all of this between the top and bottom panels.

The sides of the clock are made up of rails and stiles joined by ordinary mortise and tenon joints. At first glance, it really doesn't look very fancy.

But, since each of the workpieces that make up the sides are small, I decided to add molded edges around the rails and stiles. This way, the inside edges of the rails and stiles create a "frame" around the glass.

Because of the way the molding is made, this also means that you'll have to do a little trimming and fitting to get the pieces to fit together. Plus you'll need to add stops on the inside to hold the glass. But all of that comes later.

RAILS AND STILES. To start, I cut the blanks for the rails (A) and the stiles (B) to width from $3/4$"-thick stock *(Figs. 1 and 1a)*. I left the blanks slightly longer than needed for the time being.

Then the molded edge is created on the router table *(Figs. 2 and 2a)*. Set the fence so that it aligns with the outside edge of the pilot bearing of a $1/4$" roundover bit, raising it enough to leave a $1/16$" shoulder on the workpiece.

To make the rabbet that holds the glass, I switched to the table saw. Using a $3/8$" dado blade buried slightly in an auxiliary fence, I was able to cut a nice, clean rabbet to the back edge of the molding *(Figs. 3 and 3a)*.

TRIM MOLDING. Now that all the roundovers and rabbets have been completed, you can trim the rails and stiles to finished length *(Figs. 1 and 1a)*.

Before you can start working on the mortise and tenon joints, however, there's another detail to tend to.

In order to allow the rails to fit tightly against the stiles, you'll have to trim off part of the molded edges at the ends of each stile. (Later on, some more trimming will be done to the molding edges, so I left just enough extra here to create a small miter.)

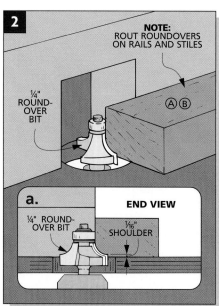

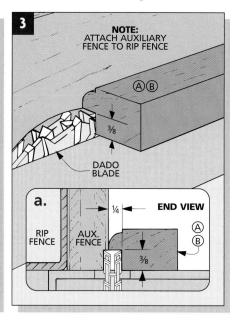

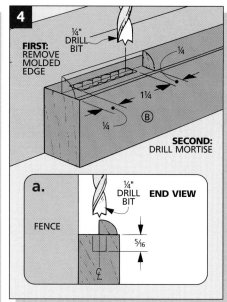

Trimming the built-in molding can be done with a table saw by making several passes over a dado blade. But I wanted a shoulder that wouldn't take a lot of time to clean up, so I used the table saw and a simple jig that holds the workpiece upright while making the cut. For more on how to do this, see the Shop Jig below.

MORTISES. After the molding on the stiles has been trimmed, I went to the drill press and removed the bulk of the waste for the mortises. Then I used a sharp chisel to square the ends and clean up the sides of each of the mortises *(Figs. 4 and 4a)*.

TENONS. With the mortises made, you can now cut the tenons on the rails to fit *(Figs. 5 and 5a)*. Again, I used a dado blade — partially buried in an auxiliary fence on my table saw — to make these cuts.

Note: I used a scrap piece of plywood as a push block while cutting the tenons. The push block supports the small workpieces when cutting the tenons, and also helps prevent tearout on the back side of the cut.

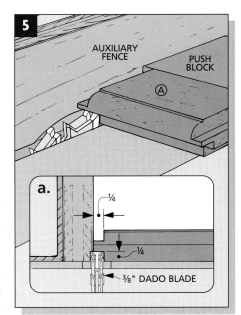

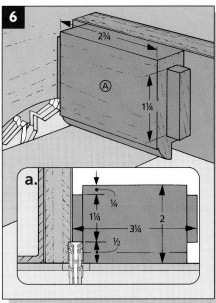

One other thing — on these pieces you don't have to worry about trimming back the molded edges on the rails, since they will be removed when you cut the tenon shoulders *(Figs. 6 and 6a)*.

Finally, there is some trimming to be done before the mortise and tenon joints can actually be fitted together. As I mentioned earlier, the ends of the molded edges must be mitered at 45° to allow the rails and stiles to fit together. To miter these edges, I made a simple jig. (For more on this jig, see the Shop Jig on page 60).

SHOP JIG .... Tenon Jig

Both the side and door frames on the Mantel Clock feature mortise and tenon construction with built-in moldings (see the photo on page 56). But before you can cut the mortises, part of the built-in molding has to be removed.

I could've done this by making multiple passes with a dado blade, but this would've left score lines. So to get a clean shoulder, I used a tenon jig, standing the pieces on end (see photo below).

The tenon jig used here consists of two face pieces and two crosspieces. (I used medium-density fiberboard, also known as MDF.) The crosspieces are sized so the jig slides easily along the fence without any slop (see drawing). (I cut dadoes in the face pieces to make it easy to assemble the jig.) Then I added a vertical stop along the back edge to support the workpiece and keep it square to the table.

Usually when cutting tenons, I place the face of the workpiece against the face of the jig. But to cut away the built-in molding, you'll need to set the outside *edge* of the piece against the face of the jig. It's also a good idea to sneak up on the cut so you don't leave any saw marks on the workpiece.

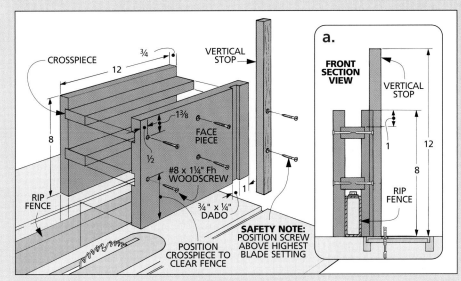

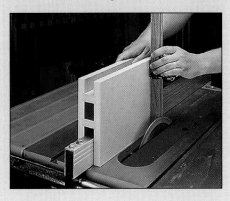

Even after you've cut the mortises and tenons for the Mantel Clock sides (and door), these pieces still won't fit together. That's because the built-in molding along the inside edge needs to be mitered *(Fig. 1)*.

The secret to doing this without marring the workpiece is a simple, shop-made jig *(Fig. 2)*. It fits over the pieces and guides your chisel as you miter the ends of the molding.

The jig is easy to make using ³/₄" MDF — there are only three parts *(Fig. 2a)*. First, a spacer is glued between two guide rails. This forms a pocket for your pieces to fit into. Then the jig is mitered on one end. About the only thing critical for the jig is that the spacer matches the thickness of the pieces you're trimming.

To use the jig to miter the molded edges, simply set it over a frame piece

and clamp it in place *(Fig. 2)*. Then secure the workpiece into a bench vise.

Now you can carefully pare the molding with a sharp chisel. To do this, hold the chisel flat against the mitered center portion of the jig, then slice down until you have cut away a small piece of the molding. The goal is for the rails and stiles to fit together tight. So it's a good idea to sneak up on the cut so you don't end up with a gap.

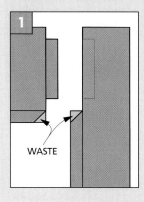
1
WASTE

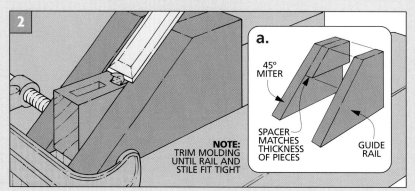
2
a.
45° MITER
SPACER MATCHES THICKNESS OF PIECES
GUIDE RAIL
NOTE: TRIM MOLDING UNTIL RAIL AND STILE FIT TIGHT

GROOVES FOR PANELS. The time you spend fitting the mortise and tenon joints will pay off in the next step — gluing the side pieces up to create two "frames." Once this is done, you can start making the grooves for the front and back panels that will connect the two sides.

Setup for these grooves is very simple. Start by mounting a ¹/₄" dado blade in the table saw and adding a groove near the front edge of each frame to hold the ¹/₄"-thick plywood front panel *(Fig. 7a)*.

Then change to a ³/₈" dado blade, and once again use an auxiliary fence to hide a portion of the blade. Now a

rabbet can be cut along the back edge of each frame to hold the ¹/₄"-thick plywood back *(Fig. 7)*.

HINGE MORTISES. Once that is complete, the next step will be to cut the mortises for the hinges *(Fig. 8)*. It's true that the door will be one of the last parts added to the clock, but it's a lot easier to cut the mortises for the door hinges at this stage, before the sides are sandwiched between the top and bottom assemblies.

To do this, I clamped one of the sides in a woodworking vise and used one of the hinges as a template for laying out the mortises. Then I carefully chiseled out each mortise.

The two side frames are connected by two ¹/₄" plywood panels (C) *(Fig. 8)*. Both panels are identical in size, but the front panel has several holes drilled in it to accommodate the hand shaft and winding arbor for the clock movement.

Note: My clock works had a stem for the hands, stems to adjust the time, and a key hole for winding the spring. There is also a slot for a lever used to select one of three different chimes.

I used a pre-punched dial face to lay out the holes in the front panel. (For sources of dials that are pre-punched, see page 126.) Laying out the holes in the front panel is just a matter of centering the clock dial on the plywood panel, screwing it in place, and then marking out the hole locations *(Fig. 8a)*. Then with the dial removed, drill the holes slightly oversize. (This allows for some adjustment later on.)

To make the slot on the right side of the dial for the chime selector lever, I simply drilled a series of overlapping holes and then used a small file to clean up the edges *(Fig. 8)*.

If you have difficulty locating a dial that is pre-punched, you'll need to use

7
SECOND: CUT RABBET FOR BACK PANEL
AUXILIARY FENCE
9⁷/₈
4³/₄
a.
NOTE: CUT GROOVE AND RABBET TO MATCH THICKNESS OF ¹/₄" PLYWOOD
4³/₄
⁷/₁₆
END VIEW
¹/₄
FIRST: CUT GROOVE TO FIT ¹/₄" PLYWOOD

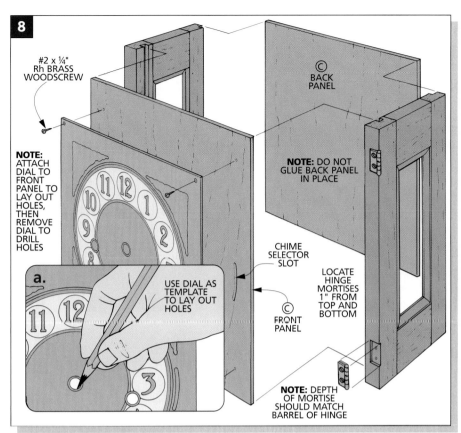

8

#2 x ¼"
Rh BRASS
WOODSCREW

NOTE:
ATTACH
DIAL TO
FRONT
PANEL TO
LAY OUT
HOLES,
THEN
REMOVE
DIAL TO
DRILL
HOLES

a.

USE DIAL AS
TEMPLATE
TO LAY OUT
HOLES

11 12

© BACK
PANEL

NOTE: DO NOT
GLUE BACK PANEL
IN PLACE

CHIME
SELECTOR
SLOT

LOCATE
HINGE
MORTISES
1" FROM
TOP AND
BOTTOM

© FRONT
PANEL

NOTE: DEPTH
OF MORTISE
SHOULD MATCH
BARREL OF HINGE

Using the mechanical movement with your clock, requires a key, pre-punched dial, and chime rods. Also needed are clock hands and hardware.

the actual clock works as a template to lay out the holes and slot on the back of the dial first. (Sources for clock works can be found on page 126.) Then carefully drill and file the holes in the dial.

ASSEMBLY. To assemble these pieces, glue the front panel into the grooves cut on the side frames. The back panel doesn't get glued to the sides, but I did set it in place just to keep everything square. A couple of band clamps will hold the pieces while the glue dries.

DESIGNER'S NOTEBOOK

A quartz movement and plywood panels make this version of the clock much more affordable.

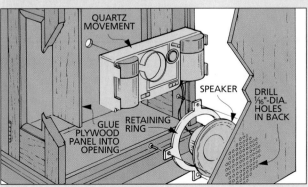

QUARTZ
MOVEMENT

SPEAKER

DRILL
1/16"-DIA.
HOLES
IN BACK

GLUE
PLYWOOD
PANEL INTO
OPENING

RETAINING
RING

CONSTRUCTION NOTES:

■ Should you plan on using a quartz movement in your clock, there are a couple of things you need to know before you start building.

■ For one thing, since quartz movements don't need winding, you'll only need to make one hole in the front panel (for the hand shaft). It will also be much easier to find a clock face for this movement, since only one hole is necessary.

■ Since there won't be very much to look at inside the clock once the quartz movement is installed, the glass panels on the sides of the clock case can easily be replaced with plywood panels. These two ¼"-thick panels are glued into the openings on either side, where the glass goes in the regular clock design.

■ The quartz movement that I used has a separate electronic chip and speaker for the "chimes." In order to allow the sound from the speaker to "escape," I drilled a number of small (1/16"-dia.) holes in the back panel of the clock (see drawing). Then I mounted the speaker to the back panel using the screws and retaining ring supplied with the quartz clock movement.

Quartz Clock. The quartz movement shown has a speaker for authentic-sounding chimes. A dial face, clock hands, and mounting hardware are also needed to complete the project.

The sides, front, and back panels make up the "middle" of the clock. This assembly is then sandwiched between a base and a top.

TOP. The top of the clock looks like it might have been made on a shaper using a massive molding cutter. But it's actually built up out of three separate layers — a wide top panel and a two-piece cap. And the profile is made with a series of router bits (five in all). To start, I made the top panel and base assembly, since they're attached to the sides of the clock. Later, I added the cap.

The top panel (D) is just a piece of $3/4$"-thick stock with $5/32$" ogees routed on all four edges *(Figs. 9 and 9b)*. The challenge here is to rout the edges without any chipout. And to help with this, it's best to start by routing the ends of the panel first.

I also used a router to create the rounded lip above the ogee that was added to the top panel. But instead of routing the workpiece, I used a $1/4$"-dia. core box bit to make a sanding block. Then I simply rounded over the lip with sandpaper *(Figs. 10 and 10a)*. Once that was done, I screwed the top panel to the sides of the clock *(Fig. 9a)*.

BASE. Like the top panel, the base panel is also a piece of $3/4$"-thick stock. But this panel is supported by a frame made up of four pieces. Together, the frame and base panel create a raised "platform" for the clock.

I started by making the base frame. The base front/back (E) and base sides (F) are cut from a single long blank. The blank is ripped to width and then one edge is rounded over, leaving a small $1/16$" shoulder *(Fig. 9c)*.

Next, the individual base pieces are mitered to length and glued up to make a base frame *(Fig. 9)*.

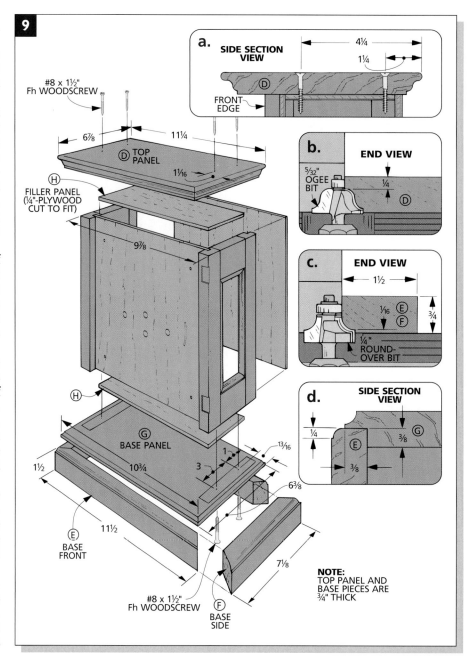

To lock the base panel (G) into the base frame, rabbets are cut on all four bottom edges *(Fig. 9d)*. Then a $1/4$" cove is routed on the top edge *(Figs. 11 and 11a)*. After the panel is glued to the frame, the base is screwed to the sides.

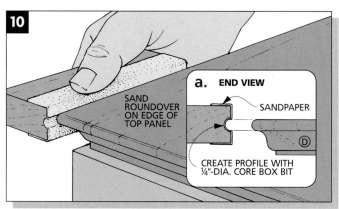

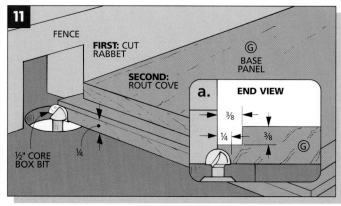

FILLER PANELS. Before moving on to making the top caps, I glued a couple of filler panels (H) to the inside of the clock at the top and bottom *(Fig. 9)*. These panels are cut to fit the inside of the clock. They serve as stops for the back panel.

CAP. All that remains to complete the case of the clock is to add the cap to the top of the clock. The cap is made up of two ³/₄"-thick pieces, each with a different profile routed on its edge. The profiles look a bit complex, but again, a couple of router bits will do the job.

I made the lower cap (I) first *(Fig. 12)*. The profile on this piece consists of a ¹/₂" roundover above a shallow cove. To make this profile, I cut the roundover first *(Figs. 13 and 13a)*. In order to do this, you'll have to stand the workpiece on edge on the router table. To provide a little more support and to prevent the workpiece from tilting, I used the fence, even though the bit has a bearing.

After cutting the roundover, rout the cove using a ¹/₄" core box bit *(Figs. 14 and 14a)*. This time you can place the workpiece down flat. But you'll still need to use the fence as a bearing surface.

UPPER CAP. The steps for routing the profile on the upper cap (J) are similar, but the bits are different sizes. A ³/₈" cove is routed along each edge *(Figs. 15 and 15a)*. Then a ¹/₄" roundover is routed on the top edge, again holding the workpiece on edge *(Figs. 16 and 16a)*.

The overall thickness of the top of the clock is nearly 2¹/₂" (longer than most drill bits). Because of this, I decided to drill the holes for the handle of the clock before gluing the cap in place. I drilled a pair of holes in the upper cap, then transferred the hole locations to the lower cap and then to the top of the clock *(Fig. 12)*.

ASSEMBLY. Assembling the caps is simply a matter of gluing them to the top of the clock, then centering them

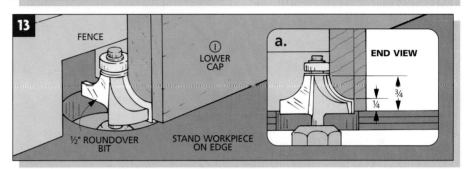

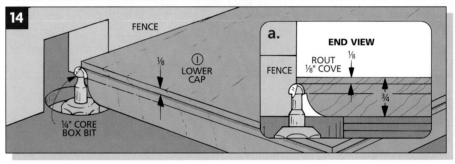

from side to side and front to back. But there's a couple of tricks to achieving a good result when doing this.

Before starting to glue the pieces together, stack them up and check the fit. If you can see gaps around the edges, the pieces aren't flat. To flatten them out, I placed a sheet of sandpaper on top of my table saw and lightly

sanded both sides of each cap (just like you would lap the sole of a hand plane).

When it was time to glue the pieces together, I used small brads to prevent the pieces from slipping under the pressure of the clamps. Just drive a few brads partially into the top of the top panel and the lower cap. Then snip off the heads, leaving about ¹/₄" of each brad *(Fig. 12)*.

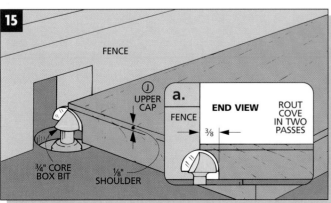

Now that the clock case is finished, all that's left is to build the door and add the glass, hardware, and clock movement.

The construction of the door is similar to the construction of the sides of the clock. The door rails (K) and stiles (L) each have a molded profile routed on the inside edge. And the rails are mortised into the stiles. But there are a couple of differences.

First, the molded profile is slightly different. Instead of a roundover, I routed an ogee on the edge of each door piece after cutting it to width *(Fig. 17a)*.

Then after cutting the rabbets for the glass, the door pieces can be cut to finished length *(Fig. 17)*.

Note: I sized the door pieces to fit the clock opening exactly. Later, after the door is assembled, the top and bottom edges can be trimmed to create a gap.

The other difference is in the mortise and tenon joints. Because the door will be subjected to more twisting and racking than the sides of the clock, I made the tenons a bit longer *(Fig. 17b)*. Otherwise, the mortise and tenon joints are made in the same manner. And like the rails and stiles on the sides, you'll have to miter the molded edges on the door pieces *(Fig. 17b)*.

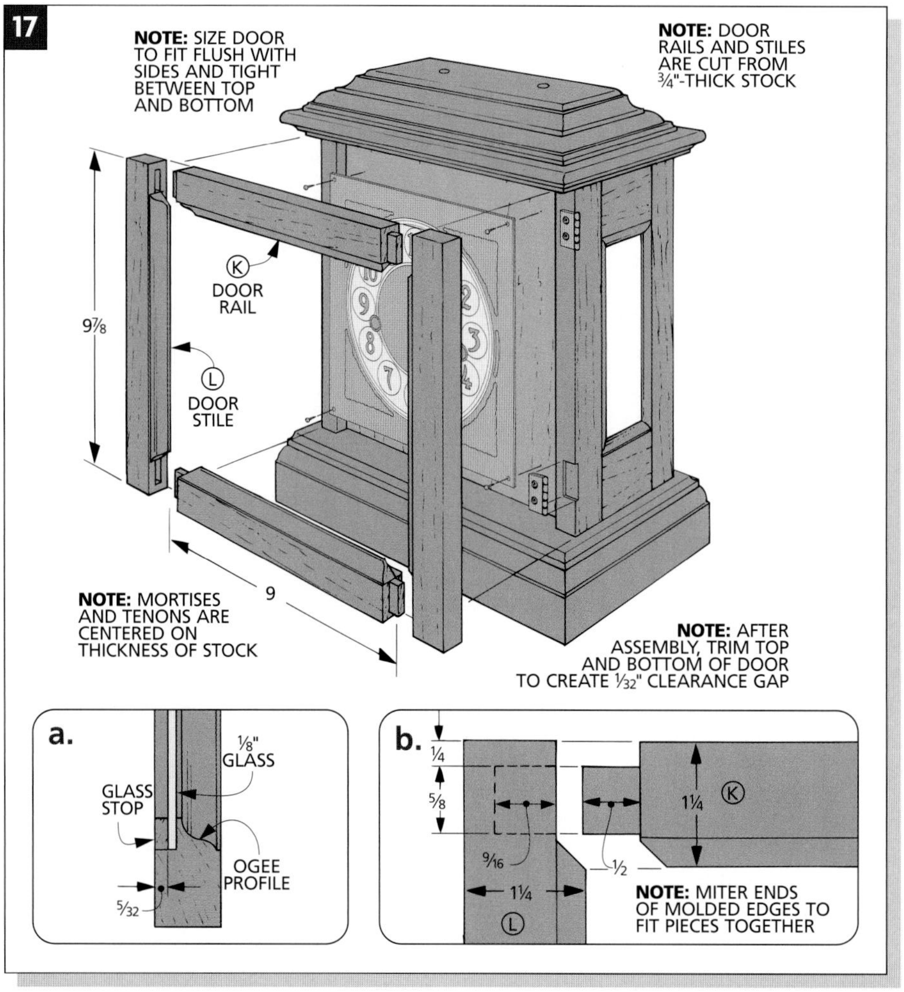

When the joinery is finished, the door can be glued up. (Make sure to check the door for square when clamping it together.)

GLASS STOPS. While the glue is drying, you can make the glass stops (M) for the glass panels in the door and

sides of the clock. These stops are $5/32"$ wide and $9/32"$ thick. After the pieces are cut to length, they are nailed in place behind the glass *(Figs. 18 and 19)*. But since the pieces are so small and there isn't much room to work inside the

clock, I pre-drilled holes in the glass stops for the brads.

HANGING THE DOOR. With the glass in place, you're just about ready to hang the door. But there are a couple of things to take care of first.

17

NOTE: SIZE DOOR TO FIT FLUSH WITH SIDES AND TIGHT BETWEEN TOP AND BOTTOM

NOTE: DOOR RAILS AND STILES ARE CUT FROM 3/4"-THICK STOCK

Ⓚ DOOR RAIL

Ⓛ DOOR STILE

9⅞

9

NOTE: MORTISES AND TENONS ARE CENTERED ON THICKNESS OF STOCK

NOTE: AFTER ASSEMBLY, TRIM TOP AND BOTTOM OF DOOR TO CREATE 1/32" CLEARANCE GAP

a.
⅛" GLASS
GLASS STOP
OGEE PROFILE
5/32

b.
¼
⅝
1¼ Ⓚ
9/16
½
1¼
Ⓛ
NOTE: MITER ENDS OF MOLDED EDGES TO FIT PIECES TOGETHER

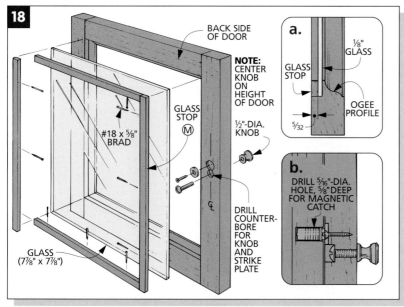

18

BACK SIDE OF DOOR

NOTE: CENTER KNOB ON HEIGHT OF DOOR

GLASS STOP Ⓜ

#18 x ⅝" BRAD

½"-DIA. KNOB

GLASS (7⅞" x 7⅞")

DRILL COUNTER-BORE FOR KNOB AND STRIKE PLATE

a.
⅛" GLASS
GLASS STOP
OGEE PROFILE
5/32

b.
DRILL 5/16"-DIA. HOLE, ⅝" DEEP FOR MAGNETIC CATCH

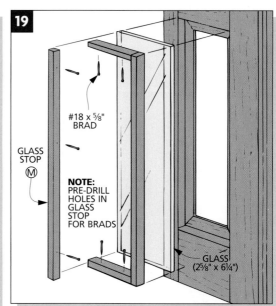

19

#18 x ⅝" BRAD

GLASS STOP Ⓜ

NOTE: PRE-DRILL HOLES IN GLASS STOP FOR BRADS

GLASS (2⅝" x 6¼")

To start, you'll need to trim the top and bottom of the door to create a slight (1/32") gap between the door and the case of the clock. Second, you'll need to drill a couple of countersunk screw holes for the door knob and the strike plate of the catch *(Fig. 18b)*. Once this is done, you can mount the hinges on the door and the side of the clock and then install the rest of the hardware — the door knob, magnetic catch, and handle.

INSTALLING THE MOVEMENT. Next, to install the clock movement, screw the dial to one side of the front panel and the movement to the other side *(Fig. 20)*. When positioning the movement, check to see that the hand shaft and winding arbors are centered in the dial holes.

With the movement in place, set the chime rods inside the clock to determine their position. In order to raise the chime rods just below the level of the hammers, I had to make a chime rod support block (N). It's just a piece of stock cut to match the size of the chime rod base. I lightly chamfered the top edges of the block and then drilled a couple of countersunk screw holes on the underside of the block for the mounting screws. With the chime rods screwed to the block, I then screwed

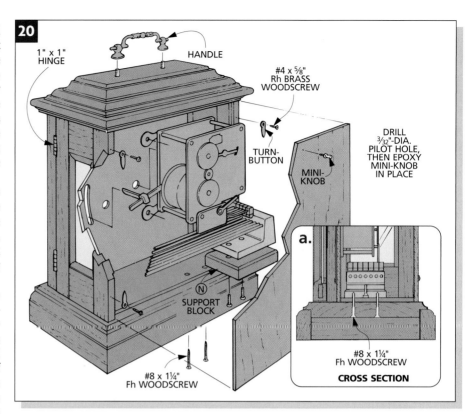

the block to the bottom of the clock case from underneath the clock *(Fig. 20a)*.

BACK. The back of the clock also gets some hardware. First, a mini-knob is added to the back to make it easier to take on and off *(Fig. 20)*. Then, four turnbuttons are added to the sides of the clock to hold the back panel in place. ■

DESIGNER'S NOTEBOOK

Simplifying the top and curving the base of the clock gives it a cleaner, more traditional look.

CONSTRUCTION NOTES:

■ Making this clean, traditional version of the clock is simple, but you could also change the movement or the type of glass in the sides to change the look.

■ Build the side assemblies and front and back panels as before. Be sure to add the hinge mortises to the sides and drill holes for the clock works before adding the panels.

■ The top panel (D) has the same ogee routed on the bottom edges, but now instead of adding the caps and handle, I routed a 1/8" cove in the top edge *(Fig. 1)*.

■ Lay out a curve on the base front molding using the template *(Fig. 2)*. Then use a jig saw (or band saw) to cut the curve, and sand up to the line.

■ Assemble the clock, counterboring and plugging the screws in the top panel.

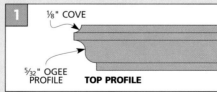

TRADITIONAL CLOCK

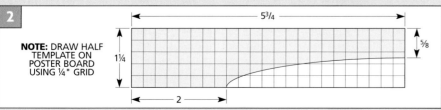

MATERIALS LIST

NO NEW OR CHANGED PARTS
Note: Do not need parts I, J. Also do not need the 4 1/2" antique brass handle with threaded studs and nuts.

Classic Frames

At first glance, it may be hard to believe that these frames were made in a home workshop.
But all you need to make each of them is a table saw to cut coves and a router to shape the moldings.

Over the years, I've made a good number of frames. But none of them have been quite like the ones you see in the photograph above. Most of the frames I've made in the past were built up from small, narrow moldings of various routed profiles.

However, these frames all feature wide, sweeping coves that really set the frames off. But more interesting than how they look is how these coves are made. It may surprise you.

No, they're not made using a router. Instead I used my table saw to hollow out the coves. And it's really not too difficult. By pushing the workpiece over

the saw at an angle, you can create a wide variety of coves.

And if this technique sounds a bit odd or unfamiliar, don't worry. I've included a separate article on how to do it starting on page 74. (You'll want to take a look at that article before building your frames.)

ELEGANT CHERRY FRAME. The first of the frames is made of cherry (the bottom frame in the photo above). The design for this frame makes the mirror look as if it's rising out from the wall.

CLASSIC WALNUT FRAME. Then you'll learn how to build the top frame in the photo above. It's made from walnut.

Here the use of two different coves offers some interesting challenges.

CRAFTSMAN-STYLE OAK FRAME. The third and last frame design is strongly influenced by the Arts and Crafts movement. The use of quarter-sawn white oak complements this timeless style, but just about any wood will do.

MOUNTING. One other thing. I'd strongly suggest that you have your print, artwork, or whatever else you're framing matted and ready to go before you build the frames. This way, you can make sure that your print and glass will fit the opening of your frame. For more on this, see the Technique on page 75.

2

FRONT OF SAW

CLAMP FENCES AT 45° ANGLE TO BLADE

TILT BLADE 45°

CENTER BLANK OVER BLADE

a. END VIEW

1/4

2 11/16

10" SAW BLADE TILTED 45°

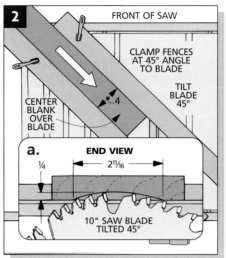

3

TRIM EDGES TO CREATE SHOULDERS

a. END VIEW

1/4

5/16

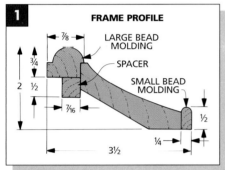

1 FRAME PROFILE

LARGE BEAD MOLDING

SPACER

SMALL BEAD MOLDING

7/8

3/4

2 1/2

7/16

3 1/2

1/4

1/2

ELEGANT CHERRY FRAME

This frame is designed so the outer edge rests flat against the wall, giving the center of the frame a raised-panel look.

My Cherry Frame is not used to frame a piece of art. Instead, I used it to frame a mirror. Construction is the same either way. But, it goes to show that you don't have to be framing artwork to try your hand at these frames.

MIRROR. I purchased the mirror for this frame at a local home improvement center and built the frame to fit around it.

The Cherry Frame is unique because it has two bead moldings. But before getting into how to do this, first take a look at the main section of the frame.

COVE. This frame has a wide, shallow cove which you'll see is slightly asymmetrical *(Fig. 1)*. So to make this cove, you'll first have to tilt the blade as well as set up angled fences to guide the workpiece *(Fig. 2)*. The fences are positioned at a 45° angle to the blade, and the blade is tilted 45°. For more on cutting asymmetrical coves using the table saw, see the Technique on page 74.

Next, trim the workpiece to its final width. But more important than the

overall width is the width of the shoulders on either side of the cove *(Fig. 3a)*.

The last step to complete the cove molding is to rip bevels along all four edges. These bevels aren't difficult to make. I simply tilt the saw blade 30° and re-position the fence for each cut. But the important thing is to rip the bevels in a specific sequence. This way, the workpiece will have at least one flat surface to rest against the fence (or the table) during each cut *(Figs. 4 through 7)*.

Note: To rip the last bevel you'll need to move your rip fence over to the opposite side of the saw blade *(Fig. 7)*.

Once you've completed the coves, they need to be sanded smooth. (For a tip on how to sand coves easily, see the Shop Tip on page 73.)

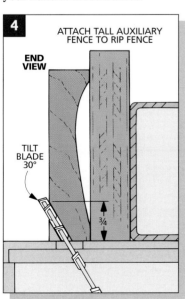

4

ATTACH TALL AUXILIARY FENCE TO RIP FENCE

END VIEW

TILT BLADE 30°

3/4

5

REMOVE AUXILIARY FENCE, FLIP WORKPIECE AND MAKE NEXT CUT

END VIEW

TILT BLADE 30°

7/16

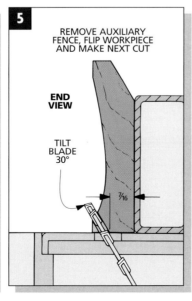

6

LAY WORKPIECE DOWN ON FLAT SIDE TO MAKE NEXT CUT

2 11/16

TILT BLADE 30°

END VIEW

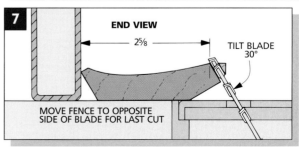

7

END VIEW

2 5/8

TILT BLADE 30°

MOVE FENCE TO OPPOSITE SIDE OF BLADE FOR LAST CUT

LARGE BEAD MOLDING. With all the bevels ripped and the pieces sanded, the next step is to create the large bead molding that is attached to the inside edge of the frame. I used a roundover bit in the router table to make the bead on this piece, leaving a slight shoulder on one edge *(Fig. 8)*. Then rout a rabbet along the opposite edge *(Fig. 9)*. This allows the bead molding to "seat" against the inside edge of the frame.

After the large bead molding is completed, it can be glued to the frame pieces. Because the rabbet in the bead molding helps to position it on the edge of the frame, all you have to do is find a way to hold it in place while the glue dries. I used rubber bands with a length of 1"-dia. dowel underneath them to concentrate the clamping pressure where I wanted it *(Fig. 10)*.

Next you'll want to miter the frame pieces, but there's still one more step to complete. To create a rabbet on the inside of the frame to hold the mirror, I added a spacer. This is just a small, rectangular piece that is glued to the inside corner of the bead molding and edge of the frame *(Figs. 11 and 11a)*.

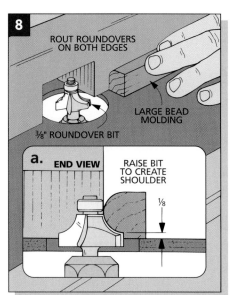

8 ROUT ROUNDOVERS ON BOTH EDGES
LARGE BEAD MOLDING
3⁄8" ROUNDOVER BIT
a. END VIEW — RAISE BIT TO CREATE SHOULDER — 1⁄8

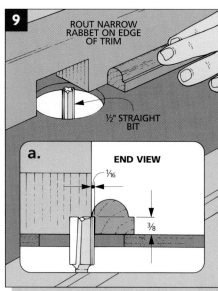

9 ROUT NARROW RABBET ON EDGE OF TRIM
1⁄2" STRAIGHT BIT
a. END VIEW — 1⁄16 — 3⁄8

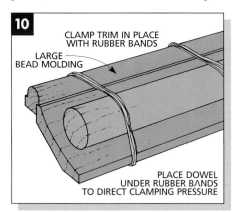

10 CLAMP TRIM IN PLACE WITH RUBBER BANDS
LARGE BEAD MOLDING
PLACE DOWEL UNDER RUBBER BANDS TO DIRECT CLAMPING PRESSURE

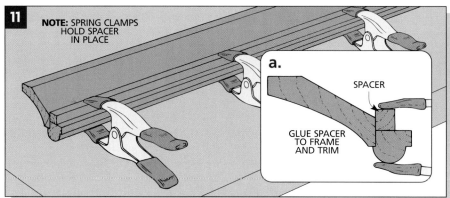

11 NOTE: SPRING CLAMPS HOLD SPACER IN PLACE
a. SPACER
GLUE SPACER TO FRAME AND TRIM

SHOP JIG .... Compound Miter Assembly Blocks

This assembly jig consists of four rectangular scraps, each with four dowels *(Fig. 1)*. The key when assembling each part of the jig is to use a framing square to make sure it will hold the frame pieces square *(Fig. 1a)*.

When gluing and clamping the frames, the band clamp fits against the bottom of the dowels, and these dowels "capture" the top of the frame, keeping the pressure centered *and* keeping the frame from falling apart.

1 5⁄8"-DIA. HARDWOOD DOWEL
3⁄4" MDF
5 1⁄2
6
8
NOTE: MAKE FOUR BLOCKS FOR ASSEMBLY JIG
a. 5 — 1 3⁄4 — 1 3⁄4 — 5
FRAMING SQUARE
TOP VIEW

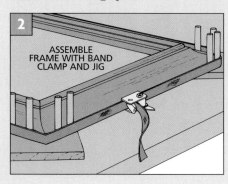

2 ASSEMBLE FRAME WITH BAND CLAMP AND JIG

MITER FRAME. Once the glue is dry, you can miter the frame pieces to length. You'll need to construct a sled to hold the frame molding while cutting the compound miters. For more on how to do this, see the Shop Jig on page 71.

After you've carefully mitered the frame pieces, glue them together using a band clamp and a simple clamping jig. For more details on this, see the Shop Jig on the previous page.

Once the glue is dry, the corners should be reinforced with 4d finish nails. I drilled holes for the nails to prevent them from splitting the wood of the frame (refer to *Fig. 8* on page 73).

Note: I also staggered the nails to prevent them from hitting each other.

At this point, the frame is almost complete. The only thing left to add is a small bead molding all around the outside edge of the frame. Not only does this soften the edges of the frame, but it also covers up the finish nails that you used to reinforce the corners.

SMALL BEAD MOLDING. There's nothing out of the ordinary when it comes to making the small bead molding. As you can see, I started with an extra-wide, $\frac{1}{4}$"-thick blank *(Fig. 12)*. Using a $\frac{1}{8}$"-radius roundover bit, I rounded over all four edges of the blank. Then I switched over to the table saw and ripped the moldings from the blank.

Note: Make sure you use a push block when cutting the moldings.

The bead molding is mitered to length to fit around the frame. In order to help fit the molding, I mitered the end of a scrap piece and clamped it to a corner of the frame. This gave me something to butt the molding up against as I fitted each piece (refer to *Fig. 11a* on page 73.)

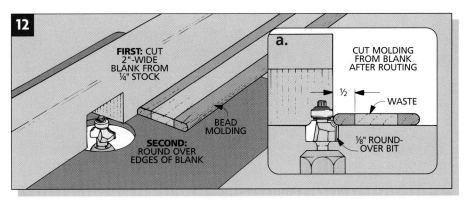

12

FIRST: CUT 2"-WIDE BLANK FROM $\frac{1}{4}$" STOCK

SECOND: ROUND OVER EDGES OF BLANK

BEAD MOLDING

a. CUT MOLDING FROM BLANK AFTER ROUTING

$\frac{1}{2}$ — WASTE

$\frac{1}{8}$" ROUND-OVER BIT

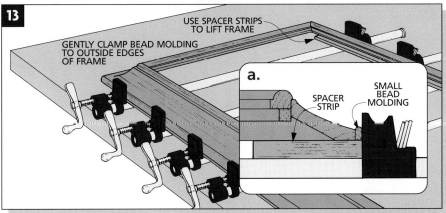

13

USE SPACER STRIPS TO LIFT FRAME

GENTLY CLAMP BEAD MOLDING TO OUTSIDE EDGES OF FRAME

a. SPACER STRIP — SMALL BEAD MOLDING

ASSEMBLY. After the bead moldings have been mitered to length, they can be glued to the outside edges of the frame. To hold them in place, I simply clamped across the frame with several bar clamps *(Fig. 13)*. But in order to center the clamping pressure directly on the bead molding, I placed $\frac{3}{4}$"-thick spacer strips underneath the frame to elevate it *(Fig. 13a)*.

Once the glue was dry, I sprayed on a few coats of lacquer. But for an entirely different look, you might want to try an alternative finish like the ones discussed in the Finishing Tip below.

FINISHING TIP . . . . *Stain & Paint*

By staining or painting the frame a different color, you can achieve a dramatic and interesting effect.

Just be sure to plan out the look you want. Then paint or stain the visible portions of the trim before applying them to the main portion of the frame.

Contrasting colors. *This creates a subtle look. The moldings are finished natural while the main portion of the frame is stained.*

Two-tone effect. *Here the visible portions of the trim were painted black before they were applied to the cove molding.*

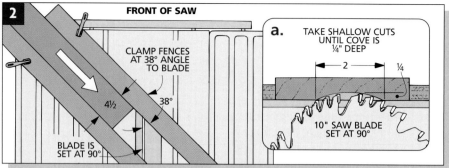

2 FRONT OF SAW

CLAMP FENCES
AT 38° ANGLE
TO BLADE

4½

38°

BLADE IS
SET AT 90°

a. TAKE SHALLOW CUTS
UNTIL COVE IS
¼" DEEP

2   ¼

10" SAW BLADE
SET AT 90°

1 FRAME PROFILE

BEAD
MOLDING

³⁄₈

1³⁄₁₆

13⁄16

2³⁄₄

1¾

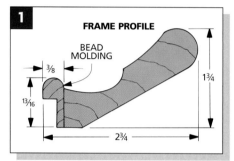

3

TRIM
EDGE OF
MOLDING

a. END VIEW

1

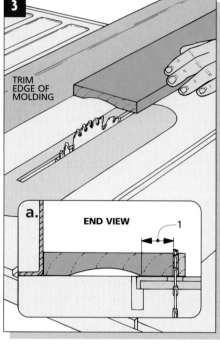

4

CLAMP
FENCES
AT 15°
ANGLE
TO BLADE

TILT
BLADE
30°

FEED WORK-
PIECE INTO
TILT OF
BLADE

a. END VIEW

MAKE SECOND
COVE ³⁄₈" DEEP

1

³⁄₈

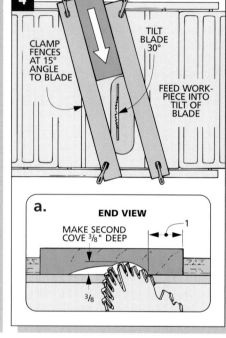

CLASSIC WALNUT FRAME

With the Classic Walnut Frame, I began experimenting a bit by combining a couple of different coves to create a more complex profile *(Fig. 1)*.

COVES. First, I cut a shallow cove down the center (roughly) of the work-piece *(Figs. 2 and 2a)*. Then to make it easier to position the second cove, trim one side of the blank, leaving a 1"-wide shoulder *(Fig. 3)*.

The second cove is cut by setting the fences at 15° and tilting the blade 30° *(Fig. 4)*. But you'll have to pay more attention when positioning the fences for this cove. In order to get the second cove to line up with the first cove, you'll need to position the first fence 1" away from the leading edge of the blade *(Fig. 4a)*.

After cutting the second cove, you can trim the other edge of the blank *(Fig. 5)*.

To create the rounded edge of the molding, use a roundover bit on the router table *(Fig. 6)*. Rout one side, then flip the blank over and rout along the other side to complete the full roundover.

In order to create a flat spot for the frame to rest against the wall, the next step is to rip a couple of bevels along the square edge of the molding. These bevels meet at a 90° angle *(Figs. 7 and 8)*. Once these bevels are cut, the work-pieces can be sanded smooth.

5

TRIM EDGE OF MOLDING
TO CREATE ³⁄₈"-WIDE SHOULDER

³⁄₈

6

ROUND OVER EDGE
OF MOLDING

³⁄₈" ROUNDOVER BIT

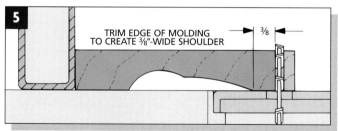

7

³⁄₁₆

TILT
BLADE
30°

NOTE: ATTACH TALL
AUXILIARY RIP FENCE
IF NEEDED

8

MOVE FENCE TO OPPOSITE SIDE
OF BLADE AND TRIM OFF WASTE

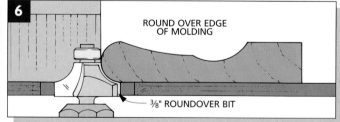

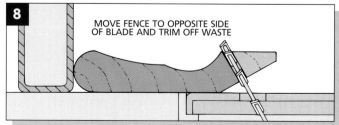

BEAD MOLDING. After sanding everything smooth, I added a rabbet on the edge of the molding to hold the picture.

Because it's difficult (and unsafe) to cut a rabbet on such a small piece of molding, I start with an extra-wide blank and rout roundovers on all four edges *(Fig. 9)*. Next, use a dado blade to cut a couple of grooves at each edge of the blank *(Fig. 10)*. Then, all you have to do is flip the blank over, switch to a regular saw blade, and rip the molding free *(Fig. 10a)*.

Because of the profile of the frame molding, I made a special jig to hold the bead molding and frame pieces together while gluing and clamping *(Fig. 11)*.

COMPOUND MITERS. After the bead is attached to the molding, you're ready to miter the frame pieces to length. But once again, since the molding for this frame doesn't sit flat, you'll have to use the sled described in the Shop Jig below to hold it in position while cutting the miters *(Fig. 12)*.

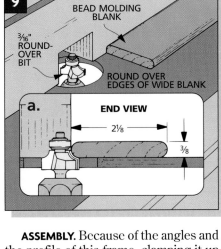

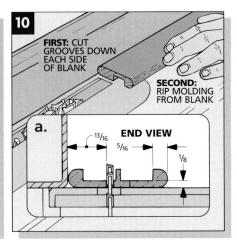

ASSEMBLY. Because of the angles and the profile of this frame, clamping it up is difficult. A band clamp alone tends to pull the miter joints apart as it's tightened. So to support the corners and keep the joints tightly closed, I put the clamping jig used with the Cherry Frame to use again. See this jig and how to make it on page 68.

Once the glue has dried, you can drill some small pilot holes and reinforce each corner of the frame with a couple of 4d finish nails. Just be careful to position the nails so they don't "blow out" of the front or back face of the frame.

After applying a finish to the frame, just fill the nail holes in the corners of the frame with wood filler (or wood putty).

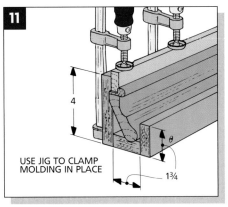

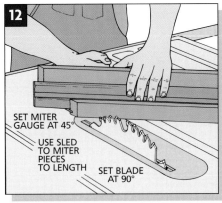

SHOP JIG . . . . *Compound Miter Sled*

Since the picture frame moldings for the Cherry and Walnut Frames don't sit flat, fitting the pieces together means cutting a compound miter.

An easy way to cut a compound miter on a table saw is to leave the blade at 90° and tilt the workpiece. But, the trick to doing this is to hold the workpiece at the same angle that it will be when the frame is assembled.

To do this, I use a simple sled made out of plywood and hardboard (see drawing). The sled attaches to my miter gauge. A lip on the front of the sled helps hold the workpiece in the proper position while cutting the miters (detail 'a').

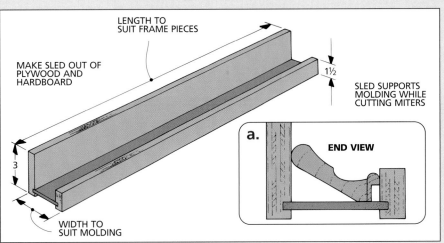

CRAFTSMAN-STYLE OAK FRAME

The Oak Frame is probably the simplest of the three frames, since it's flat and doesn't require any compound miters. I made my frame out of quarter-sawn white oak, but just about any nicely figured wood will do.

Start by cutting the 3/4"-thick blanks for the frame to rough size. I made my blanks 4" wide and about 9 to 10" longer than my matted print. This way, you can trim the frame pieces to exact width and miter them to length after you've created the profile.

CUT COVES. To cut the cove, set up a pair of fences on your table saw at a 30° angle to the blade (*Fig. 2*). Again, refer to the Technique on page 74 for details on how to do this. You want to position the fences so the cove will be roughly centered on the blank.

Note: Unlike the first two frames, the blade here should be square (90°) to the table to cut the cove for this particular frame piece. As before, cut the

cove in multiple passes, taking shallow (1/16") cuts, until the cove has reached the full cove width of 1 7/8" (*Fig. 2a*).

When you've finished cutting the coves, trim the workpieces down to their final width. The thing to watch for here is that the shoulders on either side of the cove end up being the proper width (*Fig. 3*).

CHAMFER. Now take a look at the small profile drawing of the molding (refer to *Fig. 1*). You'll notice that the top inside edge of the workpiece (the shorter of the two flat edges) has a 1/8" chamfer. I made this chamfer on the router table (*Fig. 4*).

While you're at the router table, this is also a good time to cut a rabbet on the back side of the frame. The rabbet will hold the glass and picture. To do this, simply change over to a straight bit and flip the workpiece over (*Fig. 5*).

SAND COVES. Before going any further, you'll probably want to take some time to sand the coves smooth. This can be done many ways, but I decided to make my own "custom-made" foam sanding block. (For more information on how to make this sanding block, see the Shop Tip on the next page.) I started out with 80-grit sandpaper to remove the roughest marks and then worked my way up through 100, 120, and 150-grit papers.

MITER PIECES. Once all the sanding is done, you can miter the pieces to length (*Fig. 6*). There are a couple of things to be aware of here. First, you obviously want the miters to fit together nicely. So spend some time setting up and checking your miter gauge.

Second, you want to make sure that you're cutting the pieces to the correct length so that when the frame is assembled, your glass and print will fit in the opening in the back. For some tips on doing this, turn to the Technique for mounting and hanging on page 75.

ASSEMBLY. Next you'll want to start gluing up the mitered frame pieces. The trick here is to keep all the miters tight. All it takes to do this is a common band clamp to hold the frame square while the glue sets up (*Fig. 7*).

Once the glue has dried completely, I like to reinforce each corner of the frame with a couple of 4d finish nails (*Fig. 8*). But to avoid breaking the glue joint when hammering in the nails, I drill a small pilot hole for each of the nails first.

1 FRAME PROFILE

TRIM

3/4
3/4
1
3 1/4

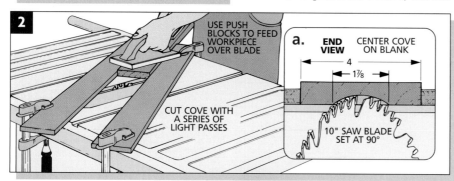

2

USE PUSH BLOCKS TO FEED WORKPIECE OVER BLADE

CUT COVE WITH A SERIES OF LIGHT PASSES

a. END VIEW — CENTER COVE ON BLANK

4
1 7/8

10" SAW BLADE SET AT 90°

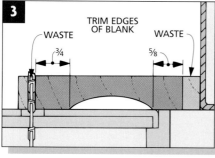

3

TRIM EDGES OF BLANK

WASTE   WASTE

3/4   5/8

4

ROUT 1/8" CHAMFER ON EDGE OF WORKPIECE

5/8

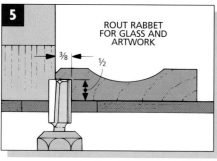

5

ROUT RABBET FOR GLASS AND ARTWORK

3/8   1/2

6

AUX. FENCE

MITER ENDS TO LENGTH

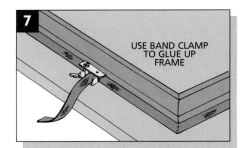

7

USE BAND CLAMP
TO GLUE UP
FRAME

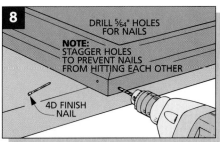

8

DRILL ⁵⁄₆₄" HOLES
FOR NAILS

NOTE:
STAGGER HOLES
TO PREVENT NAILS
FROM HITTING EACH OTHER

4D FINISH
NAIL

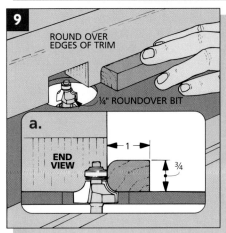

9

ROUND OVER
EDGES OF TRIM

¼" ROUNDOVER BIT

a.

END
VIEW

1

¾

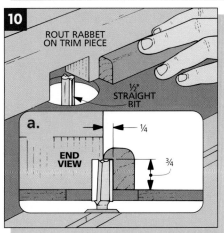

10

ROUT RABBET
ON TRIM PIECE

½"
STRAIGHT
BIT

a.

END
VIEW

¼

¾

11

FIRST: MITER
TRIM PIECES TO
FIT AROUND
FRAME

SECOND:
GLUE AND CLAMP
TRIM PIECES IN PLACE

a.

NOTE:
CUT SHORT
PIECE OF TRIM
TO POSITION MITERS
(SEE DETAIL a)

SHORT
TRIM
PIECE

TRIM. To complete the frame, I added trim pieces all around the outside of the frame. These are just strips of wood that have been rounded over on their two top edges *(Fig. 9)*. Not only does the trim help to dress up the frame a bit, but it also covers the nail holes that you just made in the corners of the frame.

To make the trim, I start by ripping four pieces of ³⁄₄"-thick stock 1" wide. Then, to complete the trim pieces, I simply round over the edges using a ¹⁄₄" roundover bit in the router table *(Fig. 9)*.

To help position the trim, a shallow rabbet is routed on the inside edge of each piece *(Fig. 10)*. Then the trim pieces are mitered to length and glued to the outside of the frame *(Fig. 11)*. To help position the molding around the frame during glue-up, I mitered the end of a small piece of scrap molding to use as a guide *(Fig. 11a)*. ■

SHOP TIP . . . . *Cove Sanding Block*

The best sanding block is one that matches the shape to be sanded. So when it came time to smooth the large coves on the picture frames, I made some custom sanding blocks from 1¹⁄₂"-thick foam insulation board. The three steps below explain a handy way to make a cove sanding block.

1 First trace the outline of the cove onto a small block of 1¹⁄₂"-thick foam insulation board.

2 Next, use a band saw (or even a hand saw and file) to cut the profile to rough shape.

3 Smooth the profile by rubbing it across a piece of sandpaper stuck to the workpiece.

The secret to creating a cove on the table saw is to "scoop" out the wood by running the workpiece over the blade at an angle. To do it safely, first clamp a couple of fences to your table saw to guide the workpiece along the way. And second, remove the material in very light passes.

ANGLE OF APPROACH. The size and shape of the cove you make is controlled by the approach angle (that is, the angle between the blade and the fences) *(Fig. 1)*. A steep angle of approach results in a narrow, elliptical-looking cove. As the angle increases, the cove gets wider and rounder.

ASYMMETRICAL COVES. In addition to changing the approach angle, you can also affect the shape of a cove by tilting the blade. This creates an asymmetrical (skewed) cove *(Fig. 2)*. The more the blade is tilted, the more the cove looks as if it's "leaning" to one side.

Safety Note: When cutting asymmetrical coves, always feed the workpiece into the tilt of the blade.

SETUP. To set up the fences, I initially raise the blade to the desired height (depth) of the finished cove. This makes it easier to determine the angle to set your fences. (If you're cutting an asymmetrical cove, you'll need to tilt the blade first.)

FENCES. With the blade raised to the correct height, the next step is to clamp a pair of fences to the top of the saw. Make sure they have accurate, straight edges and that they're thinner than the workpiece. This way your push blocks won't hang up on the fences (see photo).

The first step in positioning the fences is to determine their angle. For the picture frames, use a protractor or your miter gauge to position the fences.

Note: If you're experimenting with different cove profiles, you'll need to determine the fence angle on your own. But it's hard to "see" what the cove is going to look like. So a trick I like to use is to draw the profile of the cove on the end of my workpiece. Then I place the workpiece behind the blade and kneel down so I can sight down the blade *(Fig. 3)*. Position the workpiece at different angles until the profile of the blade matches the profile drawn on the end of the workpiece *(Fig. 3a)*. Once it does, you can position your fences to match this angle.

To clamp the fences in place, start by positioning a fence in front of the blade

and clamping it down. Then place your workpiece against this fence. Now just butt the second fence against the other edge of the workpiece and clamp it down as well. Lower the saw blade and check to see that the workpiece slides smoothly between the fences without binding, but also without any side to side play.

CUTTING THE COVE. Cutting the cove safely has to be done gradually, in a series of passes. Since you're feeding the workpiece into the blade at an angle, the teeth are only cutting on one side.

I like to start with the blade raised only about $\frac{1}{8}$" for the first pass. Then raise the blade no more than $\frac{1}{16}$" at a time for each successive pass.

Maintain consistent downward pressure on the workpiece, using push blocks to keep it flat against the table.

And, you want to feed the workpiece at an even pace. A slower feed rate has the advantage of giving you a smoother cut, requiring less sanding later.

Finally, make sure that the blank is facing in the same direction for each pass. To keep things straight, I draw a directional arrow on the workpiece. All that's left is to finish sand the cove using a sanding block, as shown on page 73.

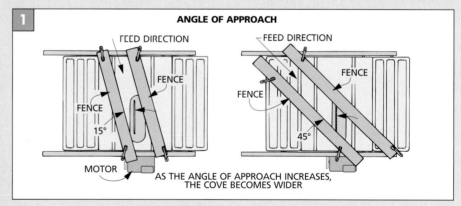

1 ANGLE OF APPROACH

FEED DIRECTION — FENCE — FENCE — 15° — FEED DIRECTION — FENCE — FENCE — 45° — MOTOR

AS THE ANGLE OF APPROACH INCREASES, THE COVE BECOMES WIDER

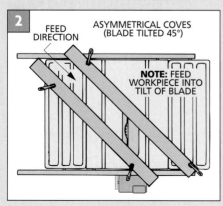

2 ASYMMETRICAL COVES (BLADE TILTED 45°)

FEED DIRECTION

NOTE: FEED WORKPIECE INTO TILT OF BLADE

3 DRAW SHAPE OF COVE ON END OF WORKPIECE

SIGHT DOWN BLADE TO MATCH PROFILE

a. POSITION WORKPIECE SO BLADE LINES UP WITH COVE PROFILE

Before you build your frame, it's a good idea to get your print or artwork matted. This will make it easier when it comes to mitering the frame pieces to length (refer to *Fig. 5* below). For the prints in these frames, I sandwiched the print between a piece of mat board (with a "window" cut out of the center) and a piece of "foam core." Foam core is a polystyrene backing material that cushions the artwork and helps protect it from damage. I purchased both of these items from a frame shop.

Note: If you're not comfortable cutting the mat yourself, order them cut to size — it's not worth risking the attempt to cut them on your own.

MOUNTING THE PRINT. After you've built your frame, you can take it to a frame shop and have your print professionally mounted. Or you can simply purchase the materials and do the mounting yourself. Although professional framers use special tools and fasteners to secure the glass and artwork into a frame, you can do the same thing with some simple turnbuttons, kraft paper, and double-sided tape *(Fig. 1)*.

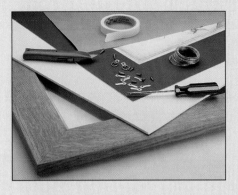

DUST COVER. To protect the print, it's a good idea to add a dust cover to the back of the frame. This is just a piece of brown kraft paper that is attached to the frame with double-sided tape. Once this is in place, I like to add rubber bumpers to prevent the frame from damaging the wall surface.

HANGING THE PICTURE. When it comes to hanging a picture (or any other item) it's important to make sure the hardware you're using is strong enough to support the weight of the object you're hanging. Since these frames are fairly heavy, I used heavy-duty picture wire and two 50 lb. picture hooks for each frame. (You can find these items at most hardware stores.)

Once the print has been mounted and the dust cover is in place, the picture wire can be secured to the frame with a couple of D-rings *(Fig. 2)*. You can also see the special knot that is used to fasten the wire to the ring. After pulling the knot tight, wrap the end of the wire around itself to prevent it from unraveling *(Fig. 3)*. Then, to prevent the wire from scratching or marking up the wall, I like to wrap the ends with floral stem wrap (available at craft stores) or masking tape *(Fig. 4)*.

Note: For another idea for hanging heavy frames, see the Technique article on page 51.

TWO-POINT HANGING SYSTEM. To hang the picture, I prefer to use two picture hooks on the wall. This does a couple of things. First, it evenly distributes the load so all the weight of the frame and glass, as well as the artwork or a heavy mirror, doesn't depend on just a single hook.

And second, it makes it a lot easier to level the picture once it's on the wall. Just install the hooks about 6" apart on the wall. If you have plastered walls, it's best if one of the hooks is driven into a stud. But this isn't necessary if your walls are made of drywall.

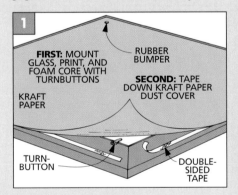

1. **FIRST:** MOUNT GLASS, PRINT, AND FOAM CORE WITH TURNBUTTONS
RUBBER BUMPER
SECOND: TAPE DOWN KRAFT PAPER DUST COVER
KRAFT PAPER
TURN-BUTTON
DOUBLE-SIDED TAPE

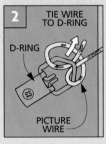

2. TIE WIRE TO D-RING
D-RING
PICTURE WIRE

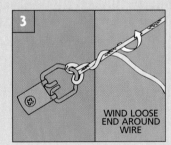

3. WIND LOOSE END AROUND WIRE

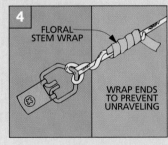

4. FLORAL STEM WRAP
WRAP ENDS TO PREVENT UNRAVELING

CUTTING TO SIZE

When framing your artwork, always have the item on hand before mitering your frame pieces. This way, you can use it as a gauge for marking your frame pieces to length *(Fig. 5)*.

There are a couple of things to consider. First, I like to allow for at least $1/16$" clearance between the edge of the artwork and the frame. Then, even if my glass or mat board is a little oversized it should still fit in the opening *(Fig. 5a)*.

Then, I match the artwork with the size of the opening at the back of the frame. When marking the frame pieces, before cutting them to length make sure to place layout marks on the inside edge of the *rabbet*, not on the inside edge of the frame. Otherwise, you'll end up with a frame that is too large for your artwork.

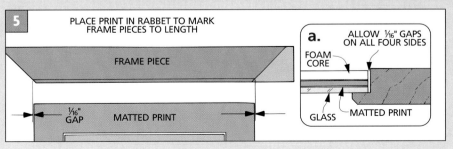

5. PLACE PRINT IN RABBET TO MARK FRAME PIECES TO LENGTH
FRAME PIECE
$1/16$" GAP
MATTED PRINT
a. ALLOW $1/16$" GAPS ON ALL FOUR SIDES
FOAM CORE
GLASS
MATTED PRINT

Book Stand

The features that really stand out on this project are a clever shop-built ratchet that makes the top adjustable and legs that are built in short, easy sections. You can also build square legs to change the look.

Typically, legs like the ones on this Book Stand would be turned from single pieces of stock. But pieces this long (about 40" long, including waste at the ends) are too long to fit on a lathe found in the average wood-worker's shop. Instead, I made each leg from four shorter pieces: two turned sections and two square sections (see Exploded View on opposite page).

To connect the parts of the legs, round tenons on the turned sections fit into round mortises drilled in the square sections. In addition to making the legs easier to turn, this method also makes assembly much simpler.

TOP. The top of the Book Stand is adjustable to several different positions. Thanks to a shop-built ratchet, it can be left flat or opened up to 45° with four positions in between.

That means you can display a large book (like a dictionary or an atlas) at whatever angle makes it easiest to see — depending on your height or the angle of the light in the room. Or if you prefer, you can just lay the top flat with the book rest against a wall to make an attractive side table.

SHELF. Another unique feature of the Book Stand is the shelf — it's made like a breadboard. This design lets the solid

wood shelf expand and contract with changes in humidity without damaging the rest of the stand.

SQUARE LEGS. If you don't own or have access to a lathe, don't worry. A square leg design that doesn't require turning can be built from plans in the Designer's Notebook on page 83.

WOOD AND FINISH. I built the stand from solid plantation-grown Honduras mahogany. It looks almost like forest-grown mahogany but has a slightly pinker color. Rather than waiting a few years for it to darken naturally, I used a deep, dark cherry stain to "age" it and added a satin polyurethane top coat.

EXPLODED VIEW

OVERALL DIMENSIONS:
24W x 16D x 36H

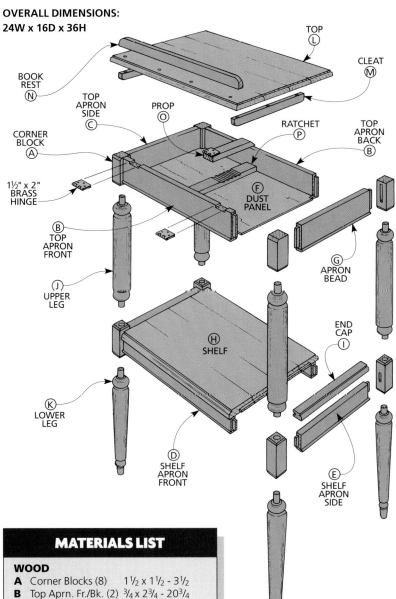

BOOK REST Ⓝ

TOP Ⓛ

CLEAT Ⓜ

TOP APRON SIDE Ⓒ

PROP Ⓞ

RATCHET Ⓟ

TOP APRON BACK Ⓑ

CORNER BLOCK Ⓐ

1½" x 2" BRASS HINGE

DUST PANEL Ⓕ

TOP APRON FRONT Ⓑ

APRON BEAD Ⓖ

UPPER LEG Ⓙ

SHELF Ⓗ

END CAP Ⓘ

LOWER LEG Ⓚ

SHELF APRON FRONT Ⓓ

SHELF APRON SIDE Ⓔ

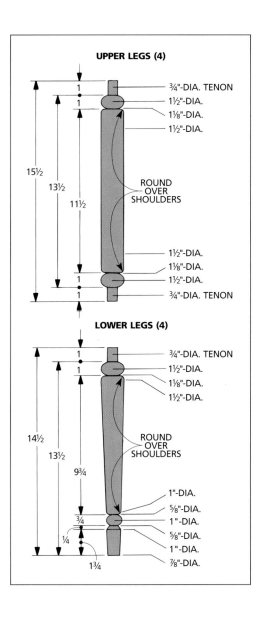

UPPER LEGS (4)

¾"-DIA. TENON
1½"-DIA.
1⅛"-DIA.
1½"-DIA.

ROUND OVER SHOULDERS

1½"-DIA.
1⅛"-DIA.
1½"-DIA.
¾"-DIA. TENON

15½
13½
11½

LOWER LEGS (4)

¾"-DIA. TENON
1½"-DIA.
1⅛"-DIA.
1½"-DIA.

ROUND OVER SHOULDERS

1"-DIA.
⅝"-DIA.
1"-DIA.
⅝"-DIA.
1"-DIA.
⅞"-DIA.

14½
13½
9¾
¾
¼
1¾

MATERIALS LIST

WOOD

A	Corner Blocks (8)	1½ x 1½ - 3½
B	Top Aprn. Fr./Bk. (2)	¾ x 2¾ - 20¾
C	Top Apron Sides (2)	¾ x 2¾ - 12¾
D	Shelf Aprn. Fr./Bk.(2)	¾ x 1½ - 20¾
E	Shelf Aprn. Sides (2)	¾ x 1½ - 12¾
F	Dust Panel (1)	¼ ply - 13¼ x 21¼
G	Apron Bead (1)	¼ x ⅞ -144 Rough
H	Shelf (1)	¾ x 14¾ x 20¾
I	End Caps (2)	¾ x 1⅜ - 12
J	Upper Legs (4)	1½ x 1½ - 15½
K	Lower Legs (4)	1½ x 1½ - 14½
L	Top (1)	¾ x 16 - 24
M	Cleats (2)	¾ x 1 - 11½
N	Book Rest (1)	⅝ x 1¼ - 23
O	Prop (1)	¾ x 1½ - 7½
P	Ratchet (1)	¾ x 1½ - 12¾

HARDWARE SUPPLIES

(8) No. 8 x ¾" Fh woodscrews
(4) No. 8 x 1¼" Fh woodscrews
(6) No. 8 x 1¼" Rh woodscrews
(3) 1½" x 2" brass hinges w/ screws
(4) Figure-8 fasteners

CUTTING DIAGRAM

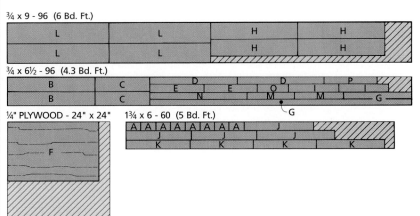

¾ x 9 - 96 (6 Bd. Ft.)

¾ x 6½ - 96 (4.3 Bd. Ft.)

¼" PLYWOOD - 24" x 24"

1¾ x 6 - 60 (5 Bd. Ft.)

I built the Book Stand in four main sections, beginning with the top frame and the shelf frame.

Each of these frames starts with four corner blocks (A). All eight blocks are the same size *(Figs. 1 and 2)*. The main difference between them is the length of the mortises cut in them for the tenons on the aprons *(Figs. 1a and 2a)*.

MORTISES. I used the drill press to cut out the mortises. And, to make cutting them easier, I made up four 7$\frac{1}{2}$"-long blanks, long enough for two corner blocks with waste in between *(Fig. 3)*.

To cut out the mortises, first clamp a fence to your drill press table and adjust it so the width of the blank will be centered under the bit. (See the Shop Tip at right for help in centering the bit.) Then clamp two stop blocks to the fence *(Fig. 3)*. The left stop block determines the right end of the mortise, while the right stop block is for the left end.

Once the stop blocks are in position, drill a hole at each end of the mortise. Then drill out the waste in between.

Now, rotate the blank 90° to cut a mortise on an adjacent face.

Next, turn the blank end for end, and without changing the setup, cut mortises at the other end of the blank to form the second corner block.

The shelf block mortises are shorter than those on the top blocks, so you'll have to change the positions of the stop blocks after cutting the mortises in two of the blanks. Then, cut the blocks to length.

HOLES FOR TENONS. Next, drill holes in the ends of the corner blocks to accept the round tenons on the legs *(Fig. 4)*. The top corner blocks have holes in the bottom end *only*, while the shelf blocks have holes in both ends *(Fig. 4a)*.

To drill the holes, I used a fence and three stops blocks. To do this, center a corner block directly under the drill bit, then clamp the fence and stop blocks around it *(Fig. 4)*.

CHAMFERING. Finally, chamfer the ends of the corner blocks *(Fig. 5)*. But there's a difference between the top blocks and the shelf blocks.

Chamfer all four edges at both ends of the shelf blocks and on one end of each

SHOP TIP
Centering a Mortise

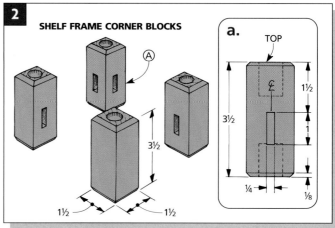

To center a drill bit on thickness of stock, set the fence so a small bit touches the centerline. To re-check, flip stock end for end. Then switch to a $\frac{1}{4}$" mortising bit.

top corner block. But only two of the edges on the top end of each top block are chamfered: the two at the front edges of the front blocks *(Figs. 1 and 5)*. This will allow the top to tip back at an angle.

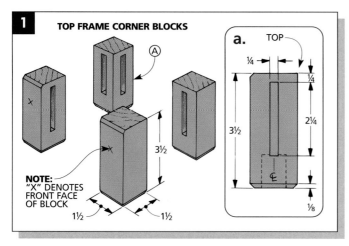

1 TOP FRAME CORNER BLOCKS

a. TOP

NOTE: "X" DENOTES FRONT FACE OF BLOCK

$\frac{1}{4}$ · $\frac{1}{4}$ · 2$\frac{1}{4}$ · 3$\frac{1}{2}$ · $\frac{1}{8}$ · 1$\frac{1}{2}$ · 1$\frac{1}{2}$ · 3$\frac{1}{2}$

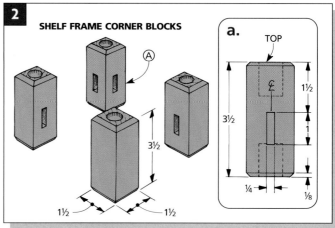

2 SHELF FRAME CORNER BLOCKS

a. TOP

1$\frac{1}{2}$ · 3$\frac{1}{2}$ · 1 · $\frac{1}{4}$ · $\frac{1}{8}$ · 1$\frac{1}{2}$ · 1$\frac{1}{2}$ · 3$\frac{1}{2}$

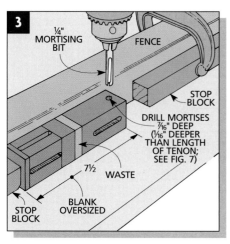

3 $\frac{1}{4}$" MORTISING BIT · FENCE · STOP BLOCK · DRILL MORTISES $\frac{7}{16}$" DEEP ($\frac{1}{16}$" DEEPER THAN LENGTH OF TENON; SEE FIG. 7) · 7$\frac{1}{2}$ · WASTE · STOP BLOCK · BLANK OVERSIZED

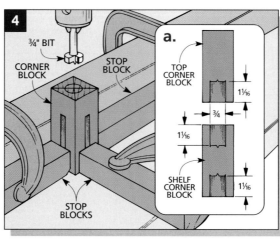

4 $\frac{3}{4}$" BIT · CORNER BLOCK · STOP BLOCK · STOP BLOCKS

a. TOP CORNER BLOCK · 1$\frac{1}{16}$ · $\frac{3}{4}$ · 1$\frac{1}{16}$ · SHELF CORNER BLOCK · 1$\frac{1}{16}$

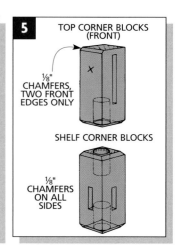

5 TOP CORNER BLOCKS (FRONT) · $\frac{1}{8}$" CHAMFERS, TWO FRONT EDGES ONLY · SHELF CORNER BLOCKS · $\frac{1}{8}$" CHAMFERS ON ALL SIDES

Once the blocks are finished, the next step is to make the four top aprons (B, C) and the four shelf aprons (D, E).

All the aprons are the same thickness and length (including tenons) *(Fig. 6)*. The only difference is their width — the top aprons are *wider* than the shelf aprons.

So begin by cutting the top and shelf aprons to finished size.

TENONS. Next, I used the table saw to cut the tenons on the ends of the aprons, sneaking up on the correct size. They need to fit the mortises on the corner blocks *(Figs. 7, 8, and 9)*.

TOP FRAME. At this point, I set aside the parts for the shelf frame and focused on the top frame. Begin the top frame by cutting a groove on the inside face of each top apron for the dust panel *(Fig. 7)*.

To be sure of a good fit for the dust panel, first dry-assemble the frame and measure the opening, including the depth of the grooves *(Fig. 6)*.

Now cut the dust panel (F) to fit in the grooves. Then, notch out the corners of the panel to fit snugly around the corner blocks *(Fig. 6)*.

HINGE MORTISES. There's one more step before gluing the top frame together — mortising the front apron for the hinges that hold the top of the Book Stand *(Fig. 9)*. The mortises are "nibbled" out in a series of passes on the table saw.

Now you can glue up the top frame. Start by gluing the side aprons and corner blocks together. After the glue is

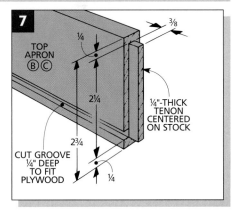

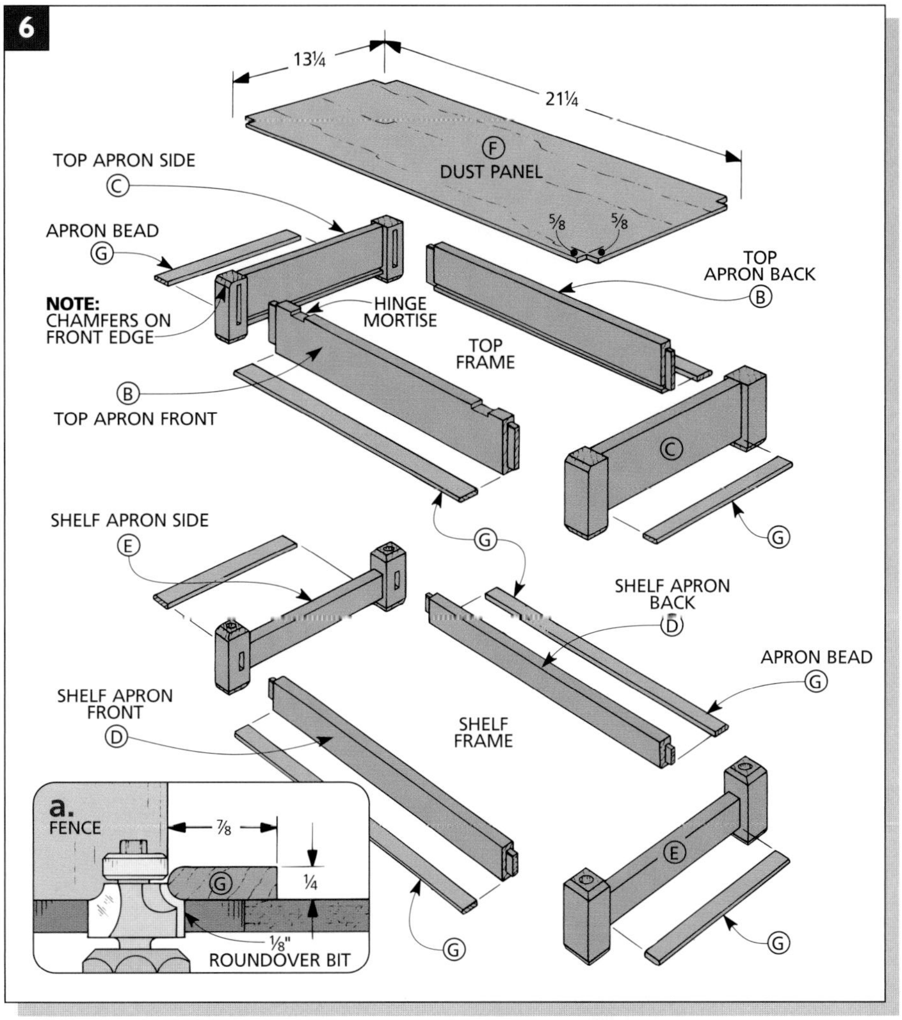

SHOP TIP

Checking for Square

SAWN-OFF CORNER AVOIDS CORNER BLOCKS

A small piece of plywood acts as a substitute where a try square won't fit. Cut the plywood at exactly 90° and trim a corner for clearance.

dry, assemble the sides to the front and back aprons with the dust panel in place, and check the frame for square (see the Shop Tip below left).

SHELF FRAME. The next step is to glue up the shelf frame. It's assembled in the same way as the top frame, except there isn't a dust panel *(Fig. 6)*.

BEADING. Finally, add an apron bead (G) to the bottom edge of each apron *(Figs. 6 and 6a)*. Cut it to fit between the corner blocks, gluing it to the bottom edge of the apron.

6

13¼   21¼

TOP APRON SIDE — C

APRON BEAD — G

NOTE: CHAMFERS ON FRONT EDGE

B

TOP APRON FRONT

SHELF APRON SIDE — E

SHELF APRON FRONT — D

F — DUST PANEL

⅝   ⅝

HINGE MORTISE

TOP FRAME

TOP APRON BACK — B

C

G

SHELF APRON BACK — D

SHELF FRAME

APRON BEAD — G

E

G   G

a. FENCE

⅞   ¼   ⅛"

G

ROUNDOVER BIT

7

TOP APRON B C

⅜   ¼

2¼

2¾

¼

CUT GROOVE ¼" DEEP TO FIT PLYWOOD

¼"-THICK TENON CENTERED ON STOCK

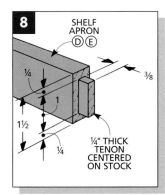

8

SHELF APRON D E

¼   ⅜

1

1½

¼

¼" THICK TENON CENTERED ON STOCK

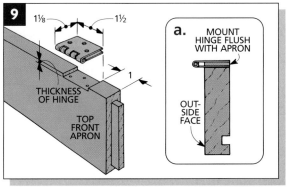

9

1⅛   1½

THICKNESS OF HINGE

TOP FRONT APRON

1

a. MOUNT HINGE FLUSH WITH APRON

OUT-SIDE FACE

When the shelf frame is completed, you can start work on the shelf (H). I used breadboard ends, which allow the shelf to expand and contract with changes in humidity without damaging the stand.

Most wood movement occurs *across* the grain, so the shelf panel can expand and contract — it's not limited by the corner blocks *(Fig. 10)*. The end caps fill in the spaces between the corner blocks. And since wood expands very little *along* the grain, the end caps can safely abut the corner blocks.

SHELF BLANK. Start by cutting a shelf blank to finished width (measure from the outside edges of the aprons and add $1/2$") and length (from corner block to corner block, plus $3/4$" for two tongues) *(Fig. 10)*. Now, cut a tongue on each end of the shelf *(Fig. 10a)*. Then, to allow the shelf to fit between the corner blocks, trim $1 5/8$" off each end of the tongue *(Fig. 11)*.

END CAPS. The next step is to make the end caps (I) to fit between the corner blocks *(Fig. 10)*. Each end cap has a groove centered on one edge to accept a tongue. Place a small dot of glue in the center of each tongue only.

EDGE PROFILE. Next, rout roundovers with shoulders on the edges of the shelf and end caps *(Figs. 12 and 12a)*.

ATTACHING THE SHELF. The last step is to attach thc shclf to thc framc *(Fig. 13)*. I used figure-8 table top fasteners screwed in shallow mortises drilled in the aprons *(Fig. 13a)*.

LEGS & ASSEMBLY

After completing the shelf and the top frame, the next step is to make the upper legs (J) and the lower legs (K). I turned the legs, tapering the lower legs (refer to the Exploded View drawing on page 77).

Note: For legs that don't require turning, see the Designer's Notebook on page 83.

The upper legs have tenons turned on each end. The lower legs have tenons turned on their top ends only. These tenons are sized to fit in the round holes in the corner blocks.

ASSEMBLY. After turning the legs, you can assemble the top frame, shelf, and legs *(Fig. 14)*. I thought this was going to be tricky. But since the tenons fit snugly in the corner block holes, the parts were easy to glue up without clamps.

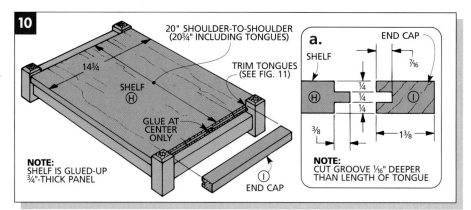

10 — 20" SHOULDER-TO-SHOULDER (20¾" INCLUDING TONGUES)

$14^3/4$

SHELF (H)

TRIM TONGUES (SEE FIG. 11)

GLUE AT CENTER ONLY

END CAP

NOTE: SHELF IS GLUED-UP ¾"-THICK PANEL

END CAP (I)

a. — END CAP

SHELF (H) — ⅞16, ¼, ¼, ¼ — (I)

⅜, 1⅜

NOTE: CUT GROOVE ¹⁄₁₆" DEEPER THAN LENGTH OF TONGUE

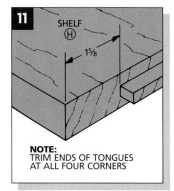

11 — SHELF (H) — 1⅝

NOTE: TRIM ENDS OF TONGUES AT ALL FOUR CORNERS

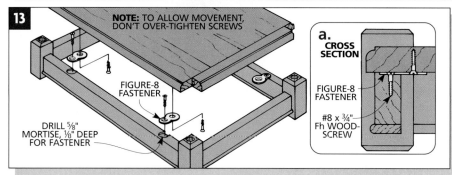

12

a. — ¼" ROUND-OVER BIT — ⅛

ROUT PROFILES ON ALL FOUR EDGES OF TOP FACE

13 — **NOTE:** TO ALLOW MOVEMENT, DON'T OVER-TIGHTEN SCREWS

FIGURE-8 FASTENER

DRILL ⅝" MORTISE, ⅛" DEEP FOR FASTENER

a. CROSS SECTION

FIGURE-8 FASTENER

#8 x ¾" Fh WOOD-SCREW

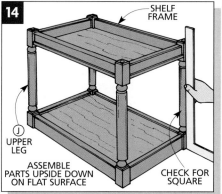

14 — SHELF FRAME

J — UPPER LEG

ASSEMBLE PARTS UPSIDE DOWN ON FLAT SURFACE

CHECK FOR SQUARE

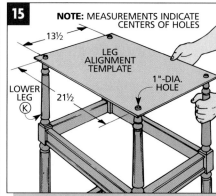

15 — **NOTE:** MEASUREMENTS INDICATE CENTERS OF HOLES

13½

LEG ALIGNMENT TEMPLATE

1"-DIA. HOLE

LOWER LEG (K) — 21½

I found it easiest to assemble the pieces upside down on a flat surface. To begin, apply glue to the tenons on both ends of the upper legs, and insert them into the corner blocks in the top frame *(Fig. 14)*. Then put the shelf on the legs. Now, use a framing square to check that everything is square.

Finally, glue the lower legs to the shelf frame. To help align the legs, I made a plywood template with holes drilled in it to accept the legs *(Fig. 15)*. It holds the legs in the correct positions in relation to each other, and makes it easy to see and correct any racking or twist in the legs.

When turning a spindle on the lathe to match a pre-determined pattern, all you really need is a ruler and caliper.

But, if you're making multiple spindles, like the four legs of the Book Stand, it's simpler and more accurate to transfer the pattern to a full-sized template first. Then turn each leg following the template, and they will all be identical.

TEMPLATE. The template I use is a piece of 4"-wide posterboard cut the same length as the finished leg *(Fig. 1)*.

What makes this template different is that there are marks along both edges.

Along one edge of the template is a line of "tick" marks that serve as a ruler for laying out the pattern. The other edge of the guide has a series of cut-out notches used like a caliper.

PATTERN SIDE. The pattern side of the template shows where the different contours of the leg pattern are to be positioned along the length of the workpiece. By holding this side of the template against the spinning block, the

position of each contour can be marked with a pencil *(Fig. 2)*.

CALIPER SIDE. As the spindle is being turned, the other edge of the template works as an indicator gauge. It shows when you've reached the correct outside diameters of beads, tenons, and tapers, and the correct inside diameters of coves, fillets, and V-grooves *(Fig. 3)*.

A template like this helps ensure all spindles turned from the same pattern look identical (because they're all made using the same template).

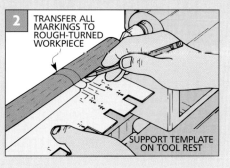

1 MARK POSITIONS OF ALL CONTOURS

CUT NOTCHES TO MATCH DIAMETERS OF ALL CONTOURS

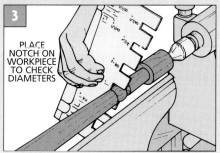

2 TRANSFER ALL MARKINGS TO ROUGH-TURNED WORKPIECE

SUPPORT TEMPLATE ON TOOL REST

3 PLACE NOTCH ON WORKPIECE TO CHECK DIAMETERS

SHOP TIP

Enlarging a Round Tenon

When turning a round tenon on a lathe, it's easy to turn the tenon a little too small, meaning the tenon won't be a perfect fit in the mortise.

So how do you fix it? First plane a thin shaving. Then spread some glue on the tenon and wrap the curled shaving around it (see the drawing below).

When the tenon is glued into the mortise, the shaving becomes part of the joint.

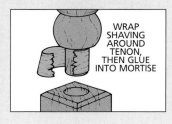

WRAP SHAVING AROUND TENON, THEN GLUE INTO MORTISE

TOP

The last part of the Book Stand to build is the top (L).

To start, glue up a panel and cut it to finished size (16" by 24") *(Fig. 16)*.

EDGE PROFILE. Next, rout a profile along all four edges. I use the same setup on the router table as when routing the profile on the shelf (refer to *Fig. 12a*).

BOOK REST. With the profile complete, screw a $1\frac{1}{4}$" strip as a book rest (N) to the top near the front edge *(Fig. 16)*.

CLEATS. To keep the top flat, I screwed two cleats (M) to the underside of the top (refer to *Fig. 17* on page 82).

Screw (don't glue) the cleats to the top through counterbored oversized

shank holes. The oversized shank holes allow the top to expand and contract with changes in humidity. (If the cleats were glued on, the top might eventually split.)

RATCHET SYSTEM. The angle of the top is changed by adjusting a simple two-part ratchet system. The prop (O) is hinged to the underside of the top (refer to *Fig. 17* on page 82). The ratchet (P) is installed inside the top frame *(Fig. 18)*.

To start, cut the prop to size and cut a 45° bevel at one end. Then screw one leaf of the hinge to the prop at the square end (refer to *Fig. 17* on page 82). The other leaf of the hinge is screwed to the bottom face of the top. Locate the barrel of the hinge $9\frac{5}{8}$" from the back edge, and center it on the length of the top.

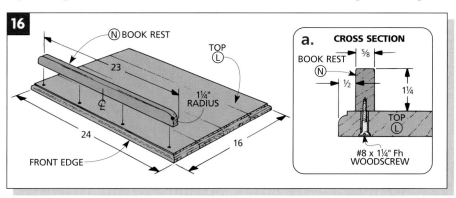

16 N BOOK REST

TOP L

23

$1\frac{1}{4}$" RADIUS

24

16

FRONT EDGE

a. CROSS SECTION

BOOK REST N

$\frac{5}{8}$

$\frac{1}{2}$

$1\frac{1}{4}$

TOP L

#8 x $1\frac{1}{4}$" Fh WOODSCREW

To make the ratchet, cut the stock to length for a close fit between the front and back aprons *(Fig. 18)*. To cut the teeth, I used a ¾"-wide dado blade tipped at a 15° angle in the table saw *(Fig. 18a)*.

After cutting the teeth, glue the ratchet to the dust panel in the top frame, centered on the length of the top frame *(Fig. 18)*.

ATTACHING THE TOP. The last step is to hinge the top to the front apron of the top frame *(Fig. 19)*. To do this, first screw the hinges into the mortises in the apron. Then turn the top and the stand upside down, and position the stand on the top centered evenly between the front, back, and sides.

Now mark the positions of the hinges on the bottom face of the top. This is easier than you might expect, since the hinges stick out ⅜" in front of the apron *(Fig. 19)*. Mark around the sides and barrel of the hinge.

Next, remove the stand and take the hinges off the apron. Now align the hinges with your marks on the top and drill the screw holes *(Fig. 19a)*. Finally, screw the top to the stand.

Note: The stand also makes an attractive flat-top side table, perfect for a hallway or entryway. ■

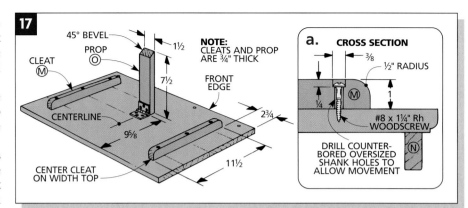

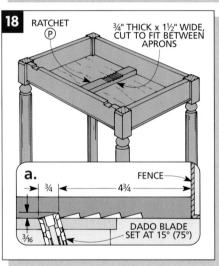

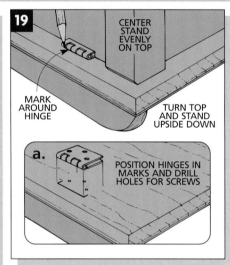

SHOP JIG .... Long Stock Drilling Jig

Drilling a straight hole into the end of a long workpiece can be difficult, so I used this jig for the drill press table to make the job easier.

HOLDING JIG. The jig consists of a block made from 2x6 stock attached to a fence and base *(Fig. 1)*. The jig holds the leg off one side of the table so it's straight up and down under the drill bit *(Fig. 3)*.

BUILD JIG. To make the jig, first I ripped the block and fence pieces to width. Then,

I glued and screwed the fence to the top of a square plywood base *(Fig. 1)*.

Next, cut a brace block from the scrap and glue and screw it to one end of the fence and base, making sure it's square to the fence *(Figs. 1 and 1a)*.

SETTING UP. Now, set the drill press table so it's perpendicular to the drill bit. First, place the jig on the table, take your longest drill bit and align it vertically with both the fence and the block *(Fig. 2)*.

Then, install the bit you'll be using and clamp the piece in the pocket *(Fig. 3)*.

Finally, position the jig on the table so the centerpoint on the bit aligns with the center of the workpiece.

DRILL HOLES. After you're sure that the bit is aligned, clamp the jig to the table and drill the hole.

Note: To drill holes the same depth, set the depth stop on the drill press and align each piece with the top of the jig.

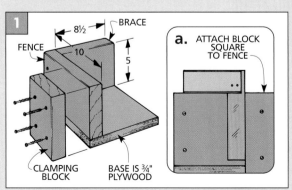

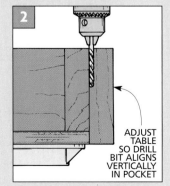

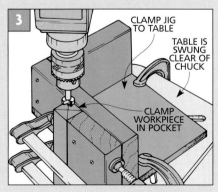

DESIGNER'S NOTEBOOK

*Building this stand with square legs may be your only option if you don't have access to a lathe.
But you won't be sacrificing looks — it's a beautiful piece of furniture either way.*

CONSTRUCTION NOTES:

■ I changed one feature — the legs — on this version of the Book Stand. This meant a redesign of the joinery for the pieces of the leg. Instead of turning tenons on the ends of the legs, I created round tenons by gluing dowels into holes drilled in the ends of the legs (refer to *Fig. 5*).

■ The first step is to cut eight blanks of square stock to finished length *(Fig. 1)*.

■ After the blanks are cut to length, drill the holes in the ends of the legs to accept ³⁄₄" dowels *(Fig. 1)*. To do this on the drill press, see the Shop Jig on page 82.

Note: There's no hole in the bottom end of each lower leg.

You need a good fit between the dowel and the hole, so you may need to buy them a little oversized and sand them down to fit in the holes.

■ The next step is to chamfer both ends of the upper legs, but only the top end of the lower legs *(Fig. 1)*.

■ To give the Book Stand a more delicate appearance, I decided to taper the lower legs, and create a decorative "foot" at the very bottom *(Fig. 1)*.

■ First, cut the taper using a tapering jig on the table saw. Set the jig to begin the taper at the top end of the lower leg.

■ To make the foot on each leg, use the table saw to cut a V-groove 2" from the bottom end *(Fig. 2)*. To set up this cut, tilt the blade to 45° and set it to cut ³⁄₃₂" deep. Use the rip fence as a stop, setting it 2" from the blade *(Fig. 2a)*.

■ You can't use the miter gauge set at 90° when cutting the grooves — the ends of the grooves on the adjoining faces won't align. Instead, tilt the miter gauge so the bottom of the leg is flat against the rip fence *(Fig. 2)*. This is an angle of about 1¹⁄₂°. Now the V-grooves can be cut in the lower legs.

■ Now, the upper and lower legs can be softened by rounding over the edges using the router table *(Fig. 3)*.

■ Once the legs are rounded, use a chisel to cut the chamfers evenly around the corners of the V-grooves *(Fig. 4)*.

■ The last step is to cut the tenons from a ³⁄₄"-dia. dowel *(Fig. 5)*. (Cut them a bit short so they'll come together tight.)

■ Finally, the legs are ready to assemble to the other parts of the stand, just as was done on the Book Stand with turned legs (refer to *Figs. 14 and 15* on page 80).

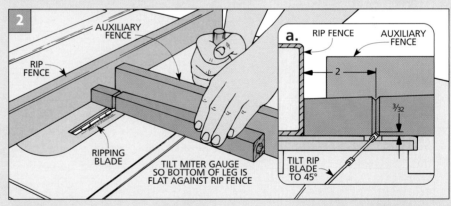

SQUARE LEGS

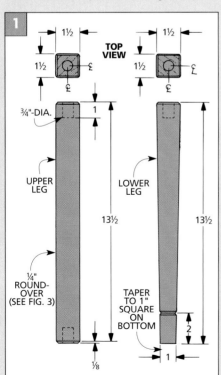

1 TOP VIEW — UPPER LEG, LOWER LEG — 1½, 1½, ¾"-DIA., 1, 13½, 13½, ¼" ROUND-OVER (SEE FIG. 3), TAPER TO 1" SQUARE ON BOTTOM, ⅛, 2, 1

2 AUXILIARY FENCE, RIP FENCE, RIPPING BLADE, TILT MITER GAUGE SO BOTTOM OF LEG IS FLAT AGAINST RIP FENCE — **a.** RIP FENCE, AUXILIARY FENCE, 2, ³⁄₃₂, TILT RIP BLADE TO 45°

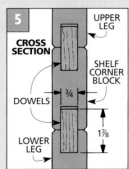

3 ROUTER TABLE FENCE, ROUND OVER EDGES OF LEGS, ¼" ROUND-OVER BIT

4 TRIM CORNERS OF V-GROOVES WITH CHISEL, FOOT OF LOWER LEG

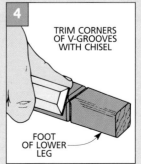

5 CROSS SECTION, UPPER LEG, SHELF CORNER BLOCK, DOWELS, ¾, LOWER LEG, 1⅞

CABINETS

Inspired by traditional cabinets of the past, the pieces in this section offer a wide variety of woodworking challenges and provide an equally wide variety of functions.

Although the designs are inspired by traditional furniture, they have been simplified by the use of some non-traditional materials. Primarily, all three use plywood in some places instead of solid-wood panels. This resolves the issue of wood movement.

Each cabinet offers its own challenges to your skills. The jewelry cabinet's cabriole legs are simpler to make than you might imagine. The chairside chest and the buffet server both feature dovetailed drawers, and each also has a variation of a bead molding to provide visual interest.

Chairside Chest

Handsome from any angle and featuring high-contrast dovetail drawers, this cabinet is a perfect chairside companion. An option for double-deep drawers gives you customized space without changing the look.

One of the most interesting features of this chest is the least obvious — the back of the cabinet is just as beautiful as the top and sides. It's designed to have a finished look wherever it's placed in a room.

The inspiration for this project was an antique spool cabinet. These cabinets displayed and stored thread, and they usually sat on a counter or in the middle of the store. Since they could be viewed from all sides, the back had to look as nice as the front.

DRAWERS. Though frame and panel construction is characteristic of spool cabinets, I've made a couple of changes

from the typical design. First, I increased the drawer height so I could store something larger than a spool of thread. (While I was at it, I came up with an additional design for double-deep drawers that doesn't change the appearance of the chest. Details about this are in the Designer's Notebook on page 95.) The drawers are held together with machine-cut dovetail joints — an attractive feature in these cabinets.

TOP. Another change is the top of this chest. It isn't solid stock, but a walnut frame around a walnut plywood panel. If the top were solid, you'd have to figure out how to anchor it to the case to allow

for expansion and contraction with seasonal changes in humidity. Since a frame and plywood panel won't expand or contract significantly, it can be glued down to the case.

WOOD. I used walnut and walnut plywood to build the chest. The drawer sides and backs are hard maple, as are the interior web frames.

HARDWARE AND FINISH. The knobs on the drawers are classic fluted brass spool cabinet knobs. Many other styles are available (see Sources on page 126).

I finished the chest with two coats of satin polyurethane varnish, sanding lightly between coats.

EXPLODED VIEW

OVERALL DIMENSIONS:
27½W x 17½D x 23H

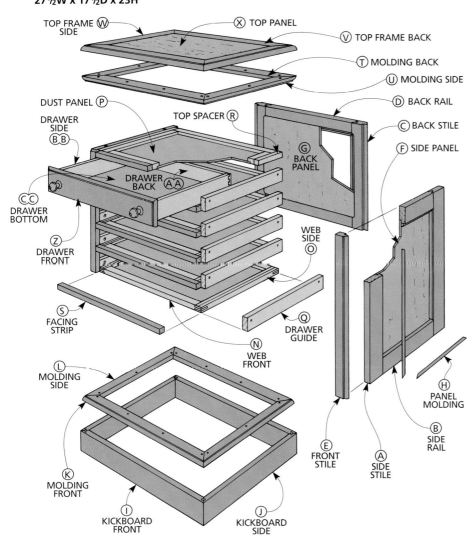

TOP FRAME SIDE (W)
TOP PANEL (X)
TOP FRAME BACK (V)
MOLDING BACK (T)
MOLDING SIDE (U)
DUST PANEL (P)
BACK RAIL (D)
BACK STILE (C)
SIDE PANEL (F)
DRAWER SIDE (BB)
TOP SPACER (R)
BACK PANEL (G)
DRAWER BACK (AA)
DRAWER BOTTOM (CC)
DRAWER FRONT (Z)
WEB SIDE (O)
FACING STRIP (S)
DRAWER GUIDE (Q)
WEB FRONT (N)
MOLDING SIDE (L)
PANEL MOLDING (H)
SIDE RAIL (B)
FRONT STILE (E)
SIDE STILE (A)
MOLDING FRONT (K)
KICKBOARD FRONT (I)
KICKBOARD SIDE (J)

MATERIALS LIST

CASE
A	Side Stiles (4)	¾ x 2 - 18¼
B	Side Rails (4)	¾ x 2 - 12
C	Back Stiles (2)	¾ x 2⅜ - 18¼
D	Back Rails (2)	¾ x 2 - 22
E	Front Stiles (2)	¾ x 1⅜ - 18¼
F	Side Panels (2)	¼ ply - 11¾ x 15
G	Back Panel (1)	¼ ply - 21¾ x 15
H	Panel Molding (2)	⅜ x ⅜ - 192 rough

BASE
I	Kickboard Fr./Bk. (2)	¾ x 3 - 27½
J	Kickboard Sides (2)	¾ x 3 - 17½
K	Molding Fr./Bk. (2)	¾ x 1¾ - 27¼
L	Molding Sides (2)	¾ x 1¾ - 17¼
M	Splines (4)	⅛ hdbd. - ¾ x 12 rough

WEB FRAMES
N	Fronts/Backs (12)	¾ x 1 - 23
O	Sides (12)	¾ x 1 - 14½
P	Dust Panels (6)	¼ ply - 13¼ x 21¾
Q	Drawer Guides (10)	¾ x 1¾ - 14½
R	Top Spacers (2)	⁷⁄₈ x ¾ - 14½
S	Facing Strips (6)	¾ x ¾ - 23

TOP
T	Molding Fr./Bk. (2)	½ x 2⅛ - 27¼
U	Molding Sides (2)	½ x 2⅛ - 17¼
V	Frame Fr./Bk. (2)	¾ x 2¼ - 27½
W	Frame Sides (2)	¾ x 2¼ - 17½
X	Panel (1)	¾ ply - 13 x 23
Y	Splines (1)	¼ hdbd. - ⅞ x 72 rough

DRAWERS
Z	Fronts (5)	¾ x 3⅜ - 25⅝
AA	Backs (5)	½ x 2⅝ - 22⅞
BB	Sides (10)	½ x 2⅝ - 14¾
CC	Bottoms (5)	¼ ply - 14⅝ x 22⅜

HARDWARE SUPPLIES
(14) No. 8 x 1" Fh woodscrews
(18) No. 8 x 1¼" Fh woodscrews
(10) Drawer knobs
(14') Nylon glide tape

CUTTING DIAGRAM

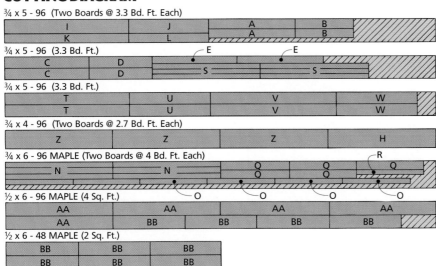

¾ x 5 - 96 (Two Boards @ 3.3 Bd. Ft. Each)
¾ x 5 - 96 (3.3 Bd. Ft.)
¾ x 5 - 96 (3.3 Bd. Ft.)
¾ x 4 - 96 (Two Boards @ 2.7 Bd. Ft. Each)
¾ x 6 - 96 MAPLE (Two Boards @ 4 Bd. Ft. Each)
½ x 6 - 96 MAPLE (4 Sq. Ft.)
½ x 6 - 48 MAPLE (2 Sq. Ft.)

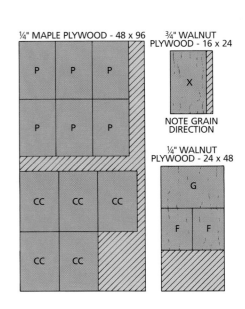

¼" MAPLE PLYWOOD - 48 x 96
¾" WALNUT PLYWOOD - 16 x 24
NOTE GRAIN DIRECTION
¼" WALNUT PLYWOOD - 24 x 48

I began building the Chairside Chest by making the side and back frames of the case. The frames are ¾" hardwood surrounding ¼" plywood panels.

SIDE FRAMES. Start work on the two side frames by cutting the side stiles (A) and side rails (B) to size *(Fig. 1)*.

BACK FRAME. Since the back frame and side frames have to be the same height, I cut the back stiles (C) and back rails (D) at this time (refer to *Fig. 4*).

All three frames are held together with open-ended mortise and tenon joints *(Fig. 1a)*.

MORTISES. I cut the mortises in the stiles with a ¼" straight bit on the router table *(Fig. 2)*. Raise the bit ⁹⁄₁₆" above the table, and position the fence so the bit is centered on the stile *(Fig. 2a)*.

Next, I clamped a stop block to the fence to limit the length of the cut. Position the stop block 2⅛" from the *opposite* side of the bit *(Fig. 2)*.

Note: The mortise only has to be 2" long to accept the tenon on the rail. But I cut it ⅛" longer, so I wouldn't have to square up the rounded end *(Fig. 1a)*.

TENONS. The next step is to cut ½"-long tenons on the ends of the rails. To do this, I cut rabbets on both faces of the rails with a dado blade *(Fig. 3)*.

Sneak up on the depth of cut until the tenon fits snugly into the mortise in the stile. Then cut tenons on all the rails.

FRONT STILES. With the joints completed, I cut two front stiles (E) *(Fig. 4)*. When the case is assembled, these pieces will be glued to the side frames (refer to *Fig. 10* on page 90). But I cut them now since they receive the same

edge profile as the back stiles (C).

EDGE PROFILE. To dress up the edges, rout a roundover (with a shoulder) on the outside corner of each back stile (C) and front stile (E) *(Step 1 in Fig. 5)*.

RABBET. Now, rout a ⅝"-wide rabbet on the inside corner (opposite the roundover) *(Step 2 in Fig. 5)*. The side frames fit into these rabbets when the case is assembled.

ASSEMBLY. Finally, glue and clamp each of the three frames together, checking that they're square.

PANELS & MOLDING

After the three frames were dry, I routed rabbets around the inside face of each frame to accept a ¼" plywood panel (refer to *Fig. 7*).

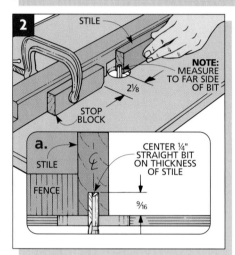

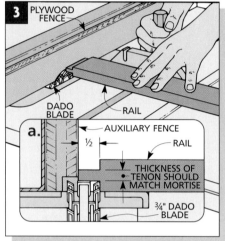

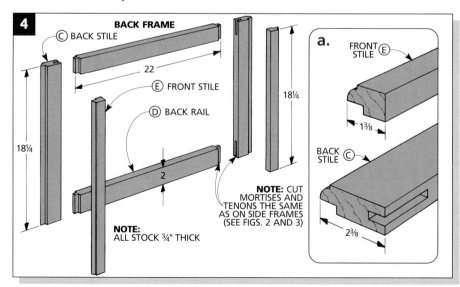

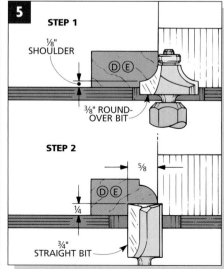

To do this, use a $3/8$" rabbet bit in the router table and raise it to equal the thickness of the plywood *(Fig. 6a)*.

PANELS. Next, cut the two side panels (F) and the back panel (G) to fit between the rabbets.

Note: The grain runs vertically on all three panels.

To make the panels fit, I rounded the corners to match the rabbets *(Fig. 7)*.

MOLDINGS. Once the panels were in place, I glued decorative panel molding strips (H) on the front face of each frame *(Fig. 8)*. To make the strips, cut $3/4$"-thick stock $1 1/4$" wide. Then rout a $3/8$" roundover on each edge *(Fig. 8a)*.

With a zero-clearance insert around the table saw blade, trim a $3/8$" strip off each side *(Fig. 8b)*. And finally, cut each strip $3/8$" wide *(Fig. 8c)*.

Once the molding strips were cut to size, I mitered each end to fit inside the frame (see the Shop Jig below). Finally, glue the strips to the frame and panel.

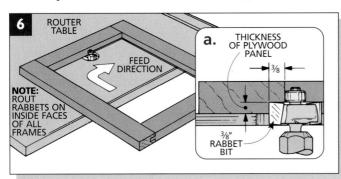

6 ROUTER TABLE

FEED DIRECTION

NOTE: ROUT RABBETS ON INSIDE FACES OF ALL FRAMES

a. THICKNESS OF PLYWOOD PANEL — $3/8$

$3/8$" RABBET BIT

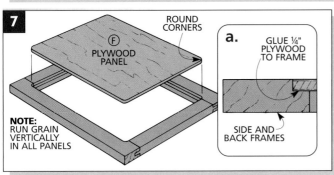

7

ROUND CORNERS

(F) PLYWOOD PANEL

NOTE: RUN GRAIN VERTICALLY IN ALL PANELS

a. GLUE $1/4$" PLYWOOD TO FRAME

SIDE AND BACK FRAMES

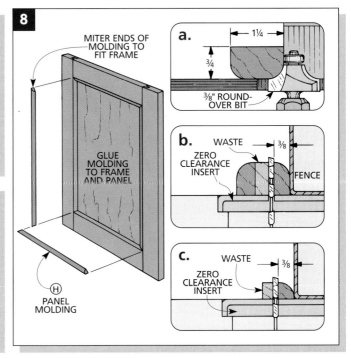

8 MITER ENDS OF MOLDING TO FIT FRAME

GLUE MOLDING TO FRAME AND PANEL

(H) PANEL MOLDING

a. $1 1/4$ — $3/4$ — $3/8$" ROUNDOVER BIT

b. WASTE $3/8$ — ZERO CLEARANCE INSERT — FENCE

c. WASTE $3/8$ — ZERO CLEARANCE INSERT

SHOP JIG .... *Molding Miter Box*

For this project, I built a special miter box for small pieces of molding.

BASE. Start by cutting a base out of $3/4$" plywood *(Fig. 1)*. Then, to hold the fence in place, cut a $1/4$"-deep groove along the base $1/4$" from the back edge.

FENCE. The fence starts out as a block of $1 1/2$"-thick hardwood *(Fig. 1)*.

The width of the fence (its height when mounted on the base) should be $1/4$" taller than the cutting depth of the saw you'll use to cut the miters *(Fig. 2)*.

Next, cut the fence block into three sections at 45° angles, so the left (A) and right (C) sections are both $5 1/2$" long. Save the middle section (B).

ASSEMBLY. To assemble the miter box, follow the sequence in *Fig. 2*.

When using the miter box, I clamp it to my bench to keep everything steady.

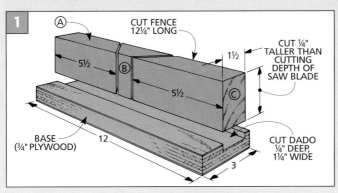

1 (A) CUT FENCE $12 1/4$" LONG

$5 1/2$ (B)

$1 1/2$ CUT $1/4$" TALLER THAN CUTTING DEPTH OF SAW BLADE

$5 1/2$ (C)

BASE ($3/4$" PLYWOOD) — 12

CUT DADO $1/4$" DEEP, $1 1/4$" WIDE

3

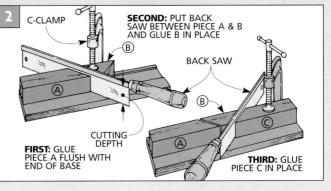

2 C-CLAMP

SECOND: PUT BACK SAW BETWEEN PIECE A & B AND GLUE B IN PLACE

(B)

(A)

BACK SAW

(B)

(A)

(C)

CUTTING DEPTH

FIRST: GLUE PIECE A FLUSH WITH END OF BASE

THIRD: GLUE PIECE C IN PLACE

BASE

The base of the chest consists of a molding frame glued on top of a kickboard frame *(Fig. 9)*.

KICKBOARD FRAME. To build the kickboard frame, start by ripping the kickboard front and back (I) and sides (J) to a uniform width (height) of 3". Then miter the front and back pieces so they measure 27$\frac{1}{2}$" (from long-point to long-point) and the side pieces measure 17$\frac{1}{2}$" *(Fig. 9)*.

To help align the miters and strengthen the joint, I added a spline (M) in each corner *(Fig. 9a)*. So before gluing up the frame, tilt your table saw blade to 45° and cut a kerf in each miter. Then cut splines to fit the kerfs.

Note: Splines can be resawn from solid stock or cut from hardboard. If they are cut from solid wood, make sure the grain direction runs *across* the assembled joint.

MOLDING FRAME. After the kickboard frame is glued together, work can begin on the pieces for the molding frame *(Fig. 9)*. The first thing to do is to rip the front/back (K) and sides (L) to a uniform width of 1$\frac{3}{4}$".

Before mitering the pieces to finished length, I routed a $\frac{3}{8}$" roundover (with a shoulder) on the top outside edge of each piece *(Fig. 9b)*. Also rout a $\frac{5}{8}$"-wide rabbet to fit over the kickboard frame. These are the same procedures as on the front and back stiles (refer to *Fig. 5 on page 88*).

Now you can miter the pieces to finished length so the rabbets in the molding frame will sit on the kickboard once it's assembled.

The base is screwed to the bottom of the case later, but it's easiest to do this if the shank holes are drilled in the molding frame now *(Figs. 9 and 9b)*.

After the holes are drilled, glue the molding frame on top of the kickboard frame. Keep the clamps centered over the edge of the kickboard frame so the top of the molding is square with the front of the kickboard.

ASSEMBLY

After the base is complete, the case sides and back can be assembled and then screwed to the base.

FRONT STILES TO FRAMES. Start assembling the case by gluing the front stiles (E) over the front edges of the

side frames *(Fig. 10a)*. Check that the inside corners are square and that the ends of each stile are flush with the top and bottom of the frames.

SIDE TO BACK FRAMES. Once the stiles have dried, glue and clamp the side frames to the back frame to form a U-shaped assembly that's open in the front *(Fig. 10)*. Again, check that the assembly is square.

SCREW ON BASE. After the glue dries, turn the case assembly over and center the base on the bottom of the case. Then mark the locations of the screw holes on the bottom edges of the case by pushing an awl through the countersunk screw holes in the molding strips.

Finally, drill pilot holes at the marked locations and screw the base to the case with No. 8 x 1$\frac{1}{4}$" flathead woodscrews *(Fig. 10b)*.

WEB FRAMES

With the case screwed to the base, the next step is to build six web frames. These frames connect the cabinet sides and support the drawers. The construction of these frames is similar to that of the case sides and back.

CUT TO SIZE. Begin by cutting all the $\frac{3}{4}$"-thick frame pieces to a width of 1" *(Fig. 11)*. To determine the length of the front/backs (N), measure the dis-

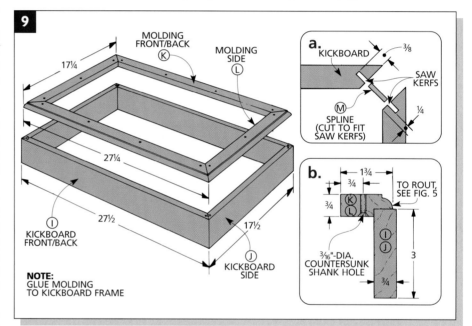

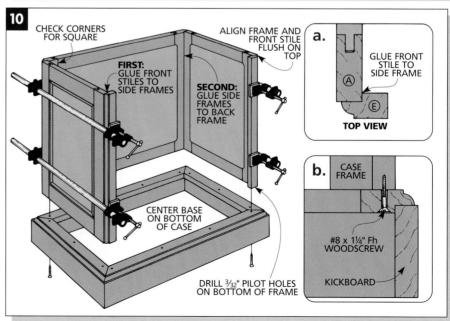

tance between the case sides (24$\frac{1}{2}$" in my case). Then, since drawer guides will be glued to the sides of the frame (refer to *Fig. 14*), subtract the thickness of two drawer guides (1$\frac{1}{2}$"). So I cut twelve web fronts/backs (N) to a length of 23" *(Fig. 11)*.

To determine the length of the web sides (O), measure the distance between the front and back stiles (14$\frac{1}{2}$" in my case). Now cut twelve sides to this length *(Fig. 11)*.

JOINERY. The web frame pieces are joined with open mortise and tenon joints. To make this joint, first cut an open mortise (slot) in each end of each of the web sides (O) *(Fig. 11a)*. Center the mortise on the thickness of the piece, and cut it to depth to match the width of the front/back pieces (1").

Next, I cut a tenon on each end of the web front/back pieces (N) *(Fig. 11b)*. Sneak up on the depth of the cuts until the tenons just fit the mortises.

Now glue and clamp all six web frames together, checking that each assembly is square and flat.

DUST PANELS. To keep a drawer from catching on any items in the drawer below, I glued a $\frac{1}{4}$" plywood dust panel (P) to rabbets routed along the inside bottom edges of each frame *(Figs. 12 and 13)*. Instead of squaring up the corners of the rabbets, I rounded off the corners of the plywood panels.

DRAWER GUIDES

Before installing the web frames in the case, I added drawer guides to five of the frames for the drawers *(Fig. 14)*. (The top frame doesn't need them.) The guides keep the drawer straight as it's moved in and out of the chest. They also provide a way to secure the web frames into the case.

DRAWER GUIDES. The ten drawer guides (Q) are cut to a width of 1$\frac{3}{4}$" and to the same length as the web sides (O) *(Fig. 14)*. Before gluing the drawer guides to the web frames, drill two countersunk mounting holes through each guide *(Fig. 14a)*.

After the holes are drilled, glue the drawer guides to the sides of the web

frame so that they are flush with the ends and bottom edge of the frame. Then, to prevent wear on the frames, I added self-adhering nylon glide tape to the top of each frame *(Fig. 14)*.

TOP SPACER. To keep the top frame the same width as the other frames, glue a $\frac{3}{4}$" x $\frac{3}{4}$" spacer (R) on each side of this frame *(Fig. 15)*.

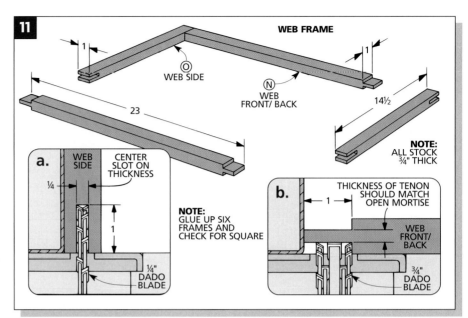

11 WEB FRAME

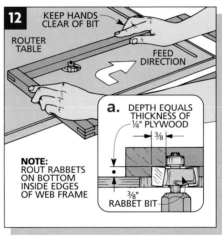

12 KEEP HANDS CLEAR OF BIT

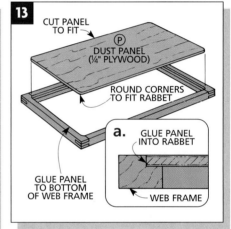

13 CUT PANEL TO FIT

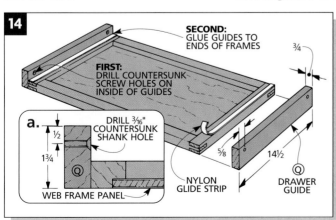

14

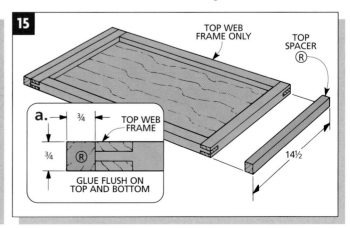

15

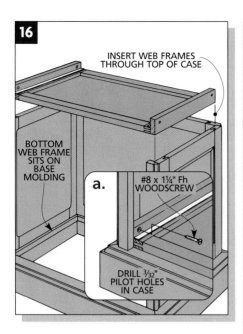

16

INSERT WEB FRAMES THROUGH TOP OF CASE

BOTTOM WEB FRAME SITS ON BASE MOLDING

a.

#8 x 1¼" Fh WOODSCREW

DRILL ³⁄₃₂" PILOT HOLES IN CASE

INSTALLING WEB FRAMES

The next step is to fasten the web frames in the case to form the drawer openings. I used a series of spacers to position the frames and to keep all five drawer openings identical.

BOTTOM FRAME. Start by inserting the bottom web frame through the top of the case until it sits on the base molding *(Fig. 16)*. Now drill pilot holes through the mounting holes, and screw the frame to the case *(Fig. 16a)*.

SPACERS. Next, measure the inside of the case to determine the width of the spacers. (See the Shop Tip above for details on how to do this.)

ASSEMBLY. Once the spacers are cut to the correct height, you can remove them and begin assembly. For each frame, insert two spacers and then a web frame. Then drill pilot holes and screw the frame to the case.

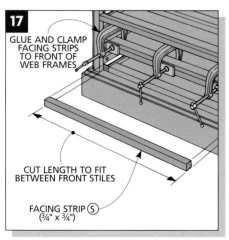

17

GLUE AND CLAMP FACING STRIPS TO FRONT OF WEB FRAMES

CUT LENGTH TO FIT BETWEEN FRONT STILES

FACING STRIP (S) (³⁄₄" x ³⁄₄")

SHOP TIP . . . . Drawer Openings

You can make several drawer openings all the same height by using a simple set of spacers to help position the web frames in the case.

To determine the size of the spacers, measure from the bottom web frame to the top of the case (17½"). Then, subtract the combined thickness of the five remaining frames (3¾").

Now, take this measurement (13¾") and divide it by five (the number of openings). Then rip ten spacers (one for each side of the drawer opening) to this width (2¾") (see drawing).

Next, insert the web frames in the case and separate them with the spacers (see drawing). If the top frame isn't flush with the top of the case, adjust the height of all the spacers.

Note: Keep all the spacers identical.

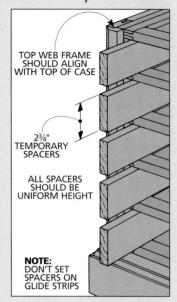

TOP WEB FRAME SHOULD ALIGN WITH TOP OF CASE

2¾" TEMPORARY SPACERS

ALL SPACERS SHOULD BE UNIFORM HEIGHT

NOTE: DON'T SET SPACERS ON GLIDE STRIPS

FACING STRIPS. After all of the web frames are screwed in place, you can remove the spacers and glue a walnut facing strip (S) to the front of each frame *(Fig. 18)*. Cut the strips to fit between the front stiles (E), and clamp them in place with C-clamps *(Fig. 17)*.

TOP

After the web frames and facing pieces are in place, work can begin on the top. This consists of two assemblies.

The top portion is a mitered hardwood frame that surrounds a ³⁄₄" plywood panel (refer to *Fig. 19*).

Underneath this panel assembly is a molding frame. This allows you to add an interesting edge profile to the chest.

MOLDING FRAME. To make the molding frame, start by resawing enough ½"-thick stock for the front and back pieces (T) and two side pieces (U) *(Fig. 18)*. Then rip the pieces to a uniform width of 2⅛".

The next step is to rout a ³⁄₈" roundover (with a ⅛" shoulder) on the bottom edge of each piece *(Fig. 18a)*. Once that is done, you can miter the pieces to length so they're 1¼" longer (long-point to long-point) than the width and depth of the case (27¼" and 17¼").

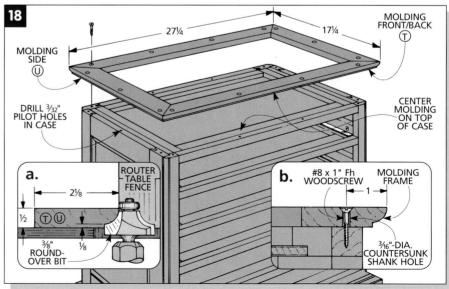

18

27¼

17¼

MOLDING FRONT/BACK (T)

MOLDING SIDE (U)

DRILL ³⁄₃₂" PILOT HOLES IN CASE

CENTER MOLDING ON TOP OF CASE

a.

ROUTER TABLE FENCE

2⅛

½

(T) (U)

³⁄₈ ROUND-OVER BIT

⅛

b.

#8 x 1" Fh WOODSCREW

MOLDING FRAME

1

³⁄₁₆"-DIA. COUNTERSUNK SHANK HOLE

After the frame pieces are cut, screw them down to the top of the case so there's a uniform overhang on all four sides. (In my case, the overhang measured $^5/_8$" on all sides.)

TOP FRAME. Now work can begin on the frame and panel top. To make the frame, start by cutting enough $^3/_4$"-thick stock for a front and back (V) and two side (W) pieces *(Fig. 19)*. Then rip the pieces to a uniform width of $2^1/_4$".

Before cutting the pieces to length, there are a number of routing steps to go through *(Fig. 20)*. First, rout a $^1/_4$" roundover (with a shoulder) on the top edge of each piece *(Step 1)*.

Next, to create a decorative shadow line between the frame and the plywood panel, I used a straight bit to rout a very small rabbet on the inside top corner of each frame piece *(Step 2)*.

To keep the frame pieces and plywood panel aligned during glue-up, I used splines cut from $^1/_4$" hardboard *(Fig. 19)*. To accept the splines, I routed $^1/_4$" slots on the inside edges of the frame pieces *(Step 3 in Fig. 20)*. (Save this router setup for use on the top panel in a later step.)

After routing the slots, miter the frame pieces (V, W) to length so they're $^1/_4$" longer (long-point to long-point) than the molding frame.

PANEL. Next, dry-assemble the frame and cut a $^3/_4$" plywood top panel (X) to fit within the frame. Once the panel is cut to size, rout $^1/_4$" slots on all four edges *(Step 4 in Fig. 20)*.

ASSEMBLY. Now cut the splines (Y) from $^1/_4$" hardboard to a width of $^7/_8$" *(Fig. 19a)*. This allows room for excess glue. Then glue the frame around the panel with the splines in place.

After the glue dries, glue the frame and panel assembly down to the top of the case. Center it on the case so there's a uniform overhang ($^1/_8$") on all four sides *(Fig. 19b)*.

DRAWERS

The last step on the chest is to make the drawers. The fronts are walnut, and the sides and backs are maple. Dovetails are used at each corner. I started by making the lipped drawer fronts.

DRAWER FRONTS. The first thing to do is to determine the size of the drawer fronts (Z). To do this, measure a drawer opening (not including the glide strip) and add $^5/_8$" to the height and width.

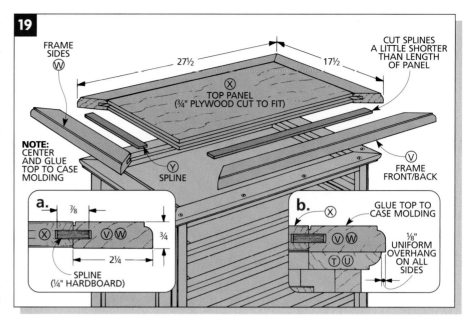

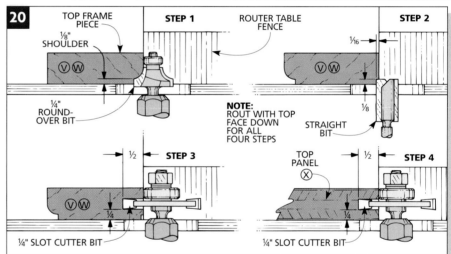

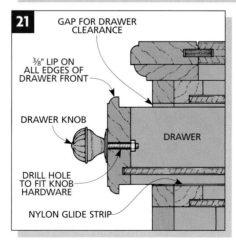

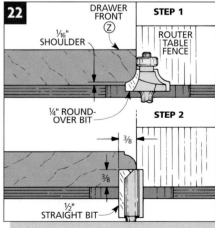

This allows for a $^3/_8$" lip on each edge of the drawer, less $^1/_8$" for drawer clearance *(Fig. 21)*. In my case, the drawer fronts measured $3^3/_8$" x $23^5/_8$" (refer to *Fig. 24* on page 94). Then cut five drawer fronts from $^3/_4$"-thick stock.

PROFILE EDGE. After the drawer fronts are cut to size, rout roundovers with shoulders on all four edges of each drawer front *(Step 1 in Fig. 22)*. Then, to create a lip, rout a $^3/_8$" rabbet on the back side *(Step 2)*.

The contrast between the maple sides and the walnut fronts accentuates the dovetail joints at the front of each drawer.

BACKS AND SIDES. When the drawer fronts are complete, rip $\frac{1}{2}$"-thick drawer backs (AA) and sides (BB) to match the shoulder-to-shoulder width of the drawer front *(Fig. 23)*. (I used maple for these pieces.)

Then cut the five drawer backs (AA) to the same length as the shoulder-to-shoulder length of the drawer front

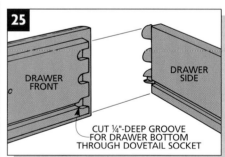

($22\frac{7}{8}$") *(Fig. 24)*. Finally, cut the ten drawer sides (BB) $14\frac{3}{4}$" long.

JOINERY. After all of the pieces were cut, I cut $\frac{1}{2}$" half-blind dovetail joints on the corners. With dovetail joints at the front and back of each drawer, that would be a lot of sawing and chiseling by hand. So I sped up the process considerably by using a router and a dovetail jig to cut them *(Fig. 23)*.

BOTTOM GROOVES. Next, cut grooves in all the drawer pieces to accept the $\frac{1}{4}$" plywood bottoms (CC).

To prevent the grooves from showing on the sides of the drawers, I located it so it would cut through the dovetail sockets in the drawer front *(Fig. 25)*.

This groove has to be in the same location on every drawer front, back, and side. But there's a problem — the drawer lip. It makes the drawer front wider than the other pieces. To work around this, I made an auxiliary fence that fits under the lip (refer to the Shop Tip below). The shoulder of the drawer front (not the lip) rides against the fence. If you use this same fence for all the pieces, the grooves will be cut the same distance from the shoulders on the drawer fronts as it is from the bottom edges of the drawer backs and sides.

Once the grooves are completed, dry-assemble the drawers so you can measure for the drawer bottoms (CC). Then cut the bottoms from $\frac{1}{4}$" plywood to fit the drawers.

PULLS. Before assembling the drawers, I drilled shank holes in the drawer fronts to mount the knobs. Locate the holes $3\frac{1}{2}$" from each end and centered on the height of the drawer *(Fig. 24)*.

Finally, I assembled the drawers and finished the chest by applying a couple of coats of polyurethane. ∎

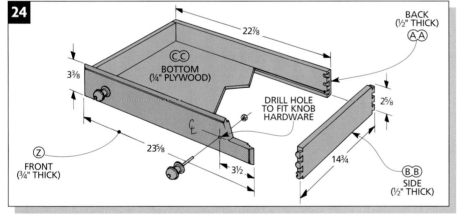

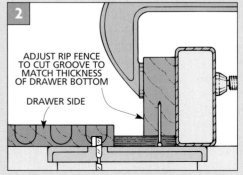

SHOP TIP . . . . *Drawer Bottom Groove*

To align the grooves for the drawer bottom, I clamped an auxiliary fence to the rip fence.

This offset fence is just a piece of $\frac{1}{4}$" hardboard nailed to a scrap block *(Fig. 1)*. Cut a kerf in each drawer piece, then move the fence until the plywood fits the groove *(Fig. 2)*.

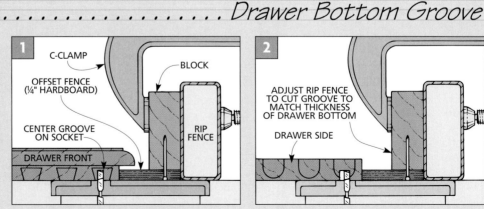

DESIGNER'S NOTEBOOK

Although it looks identical, opening the drawers of this chest will reveal two that are double-deep. The construction is the same, but each large drawer front is made by gluing two shallow ones together.

CONSTRUCTION NOTES:

■ Since there are only three drawer openings, you will only need to make four web frames. The bottom frame is mounted as before.

■ Now you'll have to do a little more math to space the web frames properly. Start again by measuring from the bottom web frame to the top of the case (17½"). Then subtract the combined thickness of the three remaining web frames (2¼"). Now subtract the height of one regular drawer opening (2¾") and divide what's left (12½") in half. This number (6¼") is the spacing between the web frames.

■ I ended up making two 6¼"-high spacers for the double-deep drawers and one 2¾"-high spacer for the regular drawer. Insert the spacers and web frames in the case (as in the Shop Tip on page 92), and adjust the heights of the spacers if necessary.

■ You'll still need five drawer fronts (Z). However, after routing the edge profile, the double-deep (tall) drawer fronts are created by gluing together two regular drawer fronts with a front filler (DD) between them (*Fig. 1*).

■ After the drawer front assemblies have dried, you can rout the lip around the edge (*Fig. 2*).

■ The large drawer backs (EE) and sides (FF) can be cut to size and dovetails routed on the drawer pieces (*Fig. 3*).

DOUBLE-DEEP DRAWER

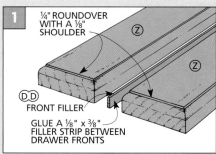

1 ¼" ROUNDOVER WITH A ⅛" SHOULDER

Z
Z

DD FRONT FILLER

GLUE A ⅛" x ⅜" FILLER STRIP BETWEEN DRAWER FRONTS

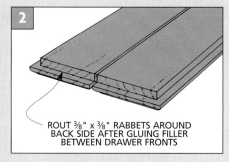

2 ROUT ⅜" x ⅜" RABBETS AROUND BACK SIDE AFTER GLUING FILLER BETWEEN DRAWER FRONTS

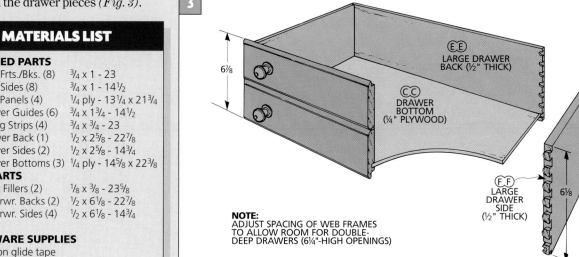

3

6⅛

EE LARGE DRAWER BACK (½" THICK)

CC DRAWER BOTTOM (¼" PLYWOOD)

FF LARGE DRAWER SIDE (½" THICK)

6⅛

NOTE: ADJUST SPACING OF WEB FRAMES TO ALLOW ROOM FOR DOUBLE-DEEP DRAWERS (6¼"-HIGH OPENINGS)

MATERIALS LIST

CHANGED PARTS

N	Web Frts./Bks. (8)	¾ x 1 - 23
O	Web Sides (8)	¾ x 1 - 14½
P	Dust Panels (4)	¼ ply - 13¼ x 21¾
Q	Drawer Guides (6)	¾ x 1¾ - 14½
S	Facing Strips (4)	¾ x ¾ - 23
AA	Drawer Back (1)	½ x 2⅝ - 22⅞
BB	Drawer Sides (2)	½ x 2⅝ - 14¾
CC	Drawer Bottoms (3)	¼ ply - 14⅝ x 22⅜

NEW PARTS

DD	Front Fillers (2)	⅛ x ⅜ - 23⅝
EE	Lg. Drwr. Backs (2)	½ x 6⅛ - 22⅞
FF	Lg. Drwr. Sides (4)	½ x 6⅛ - 14¾

HARDWARE SUPPLIES
8' of nylon glide tape

Jewelry Cabinet

Plywood panels trimmed with solid wood make construction of this case simple. The elegant cabriole legs can be made by following simple step-by-step instructions — or can be purchased ready-made.

Years ago, jewelry was often one of the most valuable things a family owned. So these precious items were stored in a special case or box — something out of the ordinary. That's what I had in mind when I designed this Jewelry Cabinet.

The cabriole legs and curved aprons give the base an elegant look. The case includes built-up moldings at the top and bottom. But I think the most interesting feature is the doors.

DOORS. The doors are L-shaped, so they wrap around the front and sides of the case. Since they're attached at the back, you don't see any hinges. They fold out like wings on each side of the case, revealing a set of drawers and storage for necklaces. The photo shows flat paneled doors, but you may like the look of raised panels instead. The Designer's Notebook on page 105 shows how to build this option.

DRAWERS. The drawers also have some neat features. They can be removed from the case so you can find small items quickly. And the special padded inserts are shop-made.

You might think that all these details require special skills or equipment. But this entire project is built with ordinary woodworking tools and methods.

Even the fancy cabriole legs are straightforward to make. The step-by-step Technique article beginning on page 106 shows you how. Or if you prefer, you can purchase pre-made cabriole legs from one of several mail-order companies (see Sources on page 126 for further information).

EXPLODED VIEW

OVERALL DIMENSIONS:
18W x 12D x 40³⁄₈H

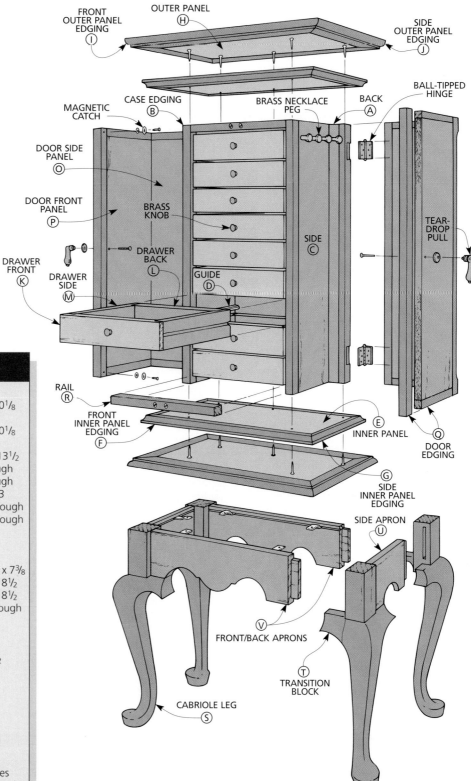

MATERIALS LIST

CASE
A Back Panel (1)   ³⁄₄ ply - 11 x 20¹⁄₈
B Case Edging (4)   ³⁄₄ x ³⁄₄ - 20¹⁄₈
C Side Panels (2)   ³⁄₄ ply - 11 x 20¹⁄₈
D Guides (18   ¹⁄₄ x ⁹⁄₁₆ - 5³⁄₄
E Inner Panels (2)   ³⁄₄ ply - 7¹⁄₂ x 13¹⁄₂
F Fr. Inr. Pnl. Edging (4) ³⁄₄ x ³⁄₄ -16 rough
G Sd. Inr. Pnl. Edging (4) ³⁄₄ x ³⁄₄ -10 rough
H Outer Panels (2)   ³⁄₄ ply - 17 x 13
I Fr. Out. Pnl. Edging (4) ³⁄₄ x 1³⁄₄ - 17 rough
J Sd. Out. Pnl. Edging (4) ³⁄₄ x 1³⁄₄ - 11 rough
K Drawer Fronts (9)   ¹⁄₂ x 2 - 7⁷⁄₈
L Drawer Backs (9)   ¹⁄₂ x 2 - 7³⁄₈
M Drawer Sides (18)   ¹⁄₂ x 2 - 5⁵⁄₈
N Drawer Bottoms (9) ¹⁄₈ hdbd. - 5³⁄₈ x 7³⁄₈
O Door Side Panels (2) ³⁄₄ ply - 6¹⁄₂ x 18¹⁄₂
P Door Fr. Panels (2)   ³⁄₄ ply - 5¹⁄₂ x 18¹⁄₂
Q Door Edging (1)   ³⁄₄ x ³⁄₄ - 192 rough
R Catch Rails (2)   ³⁄₄ x ³⁄₄ - 8

BASE
S Cabriole Legs (4)   3 x 3 - 17¹⁄₄
T Transition Blocks (8) 2¹⁄₈ x 2¹⁄₂ - 1¹⁄₂
U Side Aprons (2)   ³⁄₄ x 4 - 8
V Fr./Bk. Aprons (2)   ³⁄₄ x 4 - 14

HARDWARE SUPPLIES
(6) No. 8 x ⁵⁄₈" Rh woodscrews
(10) No. 8 x 1¹⁄₂" Fh woodscrews
(2 pr.) 2" x 1³⁄₈" ball-tipped hinges
(9) ¹⁄₂" x ¹⁄₂" brass knobs w/ studs
(4) ⁵⁄₁₆"-dia. magnetic catches w/ strikes
(2) 1¹⁄₂"-tall teardrop pulls w/ 1"-dia. back plates
(2) No. 8-32 x 1" brass Rh machine screws
(6) Z-shaped table top fasteners
(4) ³⁄₁₆"-dia. rubber O-rings
(8) 1¹⁄₈" brass necklace pegs

CUTTING DIAGRAM

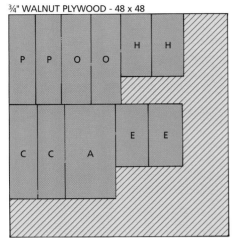

¾" WALNUT PLYWOOD - 48 x 48

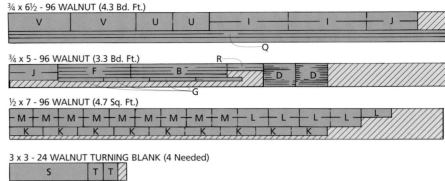

¾ x 6½ - 96 WALNUT (4.3 Bd. Ft.)

¾ x 5 - 96 WALNUT (3.3 Bd. Ft.)

½ x 7 - 96 WALNUT (4.7 Sq. Ft.)

3 x 3 - 24 WALNUT TURNING BLANK (4 Needed)

CASE

This Jewelry Cabinet is constructed in two parts. A storage case containing nine drawers is fastened to a base with cabriole legs. I built the case first, then sized the base to fit.

BACK PANEL. I started with the back (A) of the case *(Fig. 1)*. This is a piece of ¾"-thick plywood cut to size. The sides of this panel are edged with ¾" solid wood case edging (B) to hide the plies. (The edging also provides a solid wood surface for the hinge screws when the doors are added later.) I cut the edging a little thicker than the panel is wide *(Fig. 1b)*. That way, after the glue is dry, the edging can be cut perfectly flush with a flush trim bit in the router.

Next, I cut two ¼"-wide grooves on the inside face of the panel to accept tongues that will be cut on the edges of the side panels *(Fig. 1a)*.

SIDE PANELS. With the back panel complete, I cut two plywood sides (C). But before gluing edging to the sides, I cut a series of dadoes on the inside face

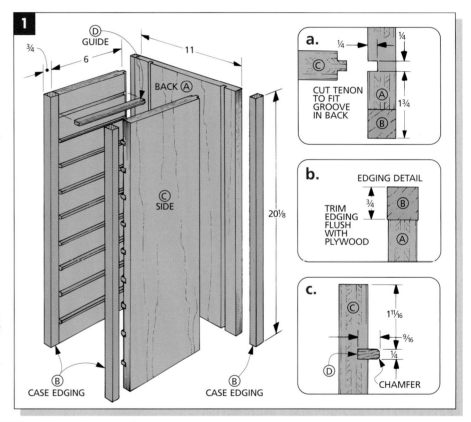

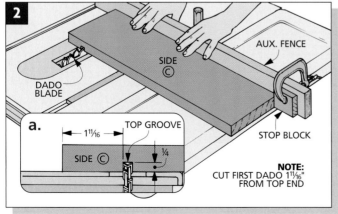

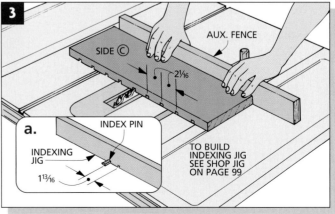

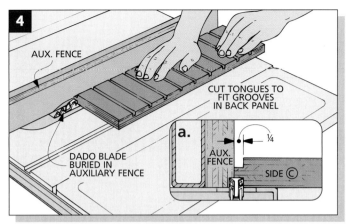

AUX. FENCE

CUT TONGUES TO FIT GROOVES IN BACK PANEL

DADO BLADE BURIED IN AUXILIARY FENCE

a.

¹⁄₄

AUX. FENCE

SIDE C

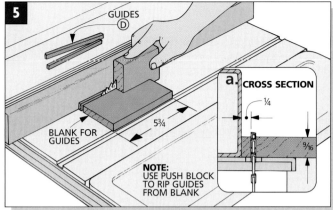

GUIDES D

BLANK FOR GUIDES

5³⁄₄

NOTE: USE PUSH BLOCK TO RIP GUIDES FROM BLANK

a. CROSS SECTION

¹⁄₄

⁹⁄₁₆

of each panel. These ¹⁄₄" x ¹⁄₄" dadoes will hold the drawer guides. In order for the drawers to slide in and out without binding, each pair of guides must line up exactly when the case is assembled.

To accomplish this, I used an indexing jig. (See the Shop Jig box below for details about building this.) But before using the jig, you'll need to cut the top dado on each side (C). This dado is 1¹¹⁄₁₆" from the end *(Fig. 2)*. To ensure that the dadoes would line up between the two sides, I fastened an auxiliary fence to my miter gauge and then clamped a stop block to the fence.

Once these cuts are made, you can use the jig to help you cut the remaining dadoes across the panels *(Fig. 3)*.

After all the dadoes were completed, I cut rabbets on the back edge of each case side (C). This forms a tongue that fits snugly into the groove already cut in the back panel *(Fig. 4)*.

Finally, I added case edging (B) to the front edges of the side panels to hide the plywood edges and the dadoes for the drawer guides *(Fig. 1)*.

DRAWER GUIDES. Before assembling the sides and back, I added drawer guides (D) to the dadoes in the sides

(Fig. 1c). These guides are simply thin strips of solid wood that support and guide the drawers.

To make the guides, I planed down a blank to ⁹⁄₁₆" thick, cut it to length, and then ripped ¹⁄₄"-wide strips from it *(Fig. 5)*. Use a push block to keep the guides from getting pinched between the saw blade and the fence.

After they've been cut to size, the guides are glued into the dadoes, tight against the case edging. Then using a sanding block, I formed slight chamfers on the edges of the guides to help the drawers operate smoothly *(Fig. 1c)*.

SHOP JIG . . . . *Indexing Jig*

With just a piece of scrap and a couple of screws, you can make this simple jig for cutting the dadoes in the sides of the Jewelry Cabinet.

It's just a ³⁄₄"-thick auxiliary fence that's attached to the miter gauge on the table saw. Then a small locating pin is mortised into the bottom edge. Once you've cut the first dado near the top edge of the side panel, the dado is placed over the pin, automatically positioning the workpiece for the next cut.

MAKING THE JIG. To make the jig, start by cutting a shallow notch in the fence that's the same width as the dadoes in the sides of the cabinet (¹⁄₄") *(Fig. 1)*. Cut the notch only ³⁄₁₆" deep to allow clearance between the pin that will be added to the notch and the bottom of the dado in the side panel.

Next, make a pin so it fits snug in the notch and glue it in place *(Fig. 2)*.

SET UP. To set up the jig, temporarily clamp it to your miter gauge *(Fig. 2)*.

Adjust the fence so the indexing pin is 1¹³⁄₁₆" from the blade *(Fig. 2a)*. Then fasten the jig to the miter gauge with a couple of screws.

USING THE JIG. To cut the dadoes, place the side panel against the fence so that the first dado fits over the indexing pin. After running the panel over the blade, move the newly cut dado over the pin. Then just repeat this procedure until you have all the dadoes cut in each of the side panels *(Fig. 3)*.

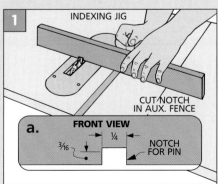

1

INDEXING JIG

CUT NOTCH IN AUX. FENCE

a. FRONT VIEW

¹⁄₄

³⁄₁₆

NOTCH FOR PIN

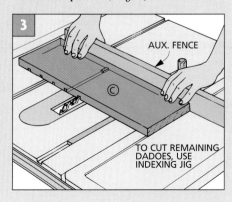

2

FIRST: ADD PIN TO NOTCH

SECOND: CUT ANOTHER NOTCH 1¹³⁄₁₆" FROM PIN

a. FRONT VIEW

PIN

1¹³⁄₁₆

NOTCH FOR PIN

¹⁄₄

3

AUX. FENCE

C

TO CUT REMAINING DADOES, USE INDEXING JIG

SIDE AND BACK ASSEMBLY. With the guides in place, the sides and back panel can be glued together *(Fig. 6)*. To keep the top and bottom edges of the panels flush, I stood the assembly on end as I clamped it together.

Note: To keep the side panels square to the back when gluing them up, I cut a piece of plywood to use as a squaring block.

The top and bottom panels are both made up of an inner and outer layer of edged plywood.

INNER PANELS. The inner panels (E) are made of $^3/_4$" plywood. These panels are wrapped on all four sides with $^3/_4$"-wide inner panel edging (F, G) *(Fig. 6)*. This edging is mitered at the corners and glued in place. Then a cove is routed around one face of the panel *(Fig. 7)*.

Once the edge profiles are routed, attach the inner panels to the case with screws. Make sure to screw into the solid wood edging on the sides and back *(Figs. 6a and 6b)*.

OUTER PANELS. The outer panels are built the same as the inner panels, with a few exceptions. First, the outer panel (H) is slightly smaller than the inner panel *(Fig. 8)*. But once the $1^3/_4$"-wide outer panel edging (I, J) is added, the panel ends up wider and longer than the inner panel *(Fig. 8a)*. The wider edging not only looks better, but it will hold screws more securely when the case is attached to the base.

Another difference is the edge profile. I routed $^1/_8$" roundovers on the outside edges and then $^1/_2$" roundovers on the inside edges *(Figs. 8a and 8b)*. Then the outer panels are simply glued in place *(Figs. 9 and 9a)*.

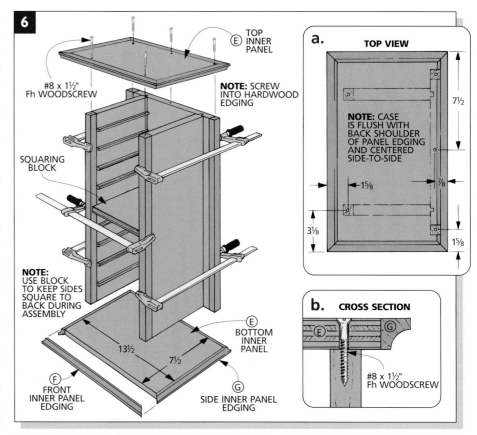

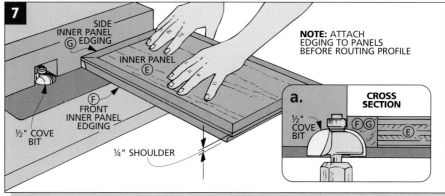

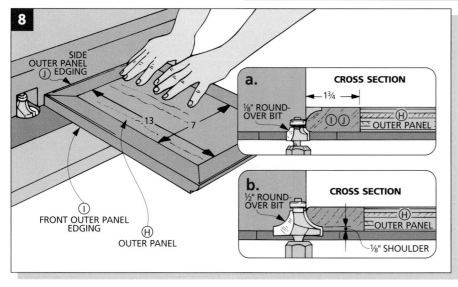

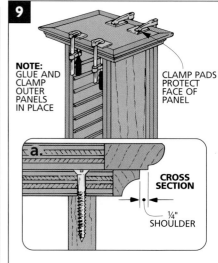

DRAWERS

With the cabinet case completed, I began making the set of nine drawers that fit inside. Since all the drawers are the same size, you can quickly build them in an assembly line fashion.

To start, I cut all the drawer fronts (K), backs (L), and sides (M) to size from $\frac{1}{2}$"-thick stock *(Fig. 10)*.

Note: The drawers are sized to allow for $\frac{1}{16}$" clearance gaps around each drawer. This makes a $\frac{1}{8}$" gap between drawers. (My drawers ended up 2" tall and $7\frac{7}{8}$" wide.)

JOINERY. The drawers are held together with a series of rabbets. First, rabbets cut on each end of the front piece accept the sides *(Fig. 10a)*. And by closing one end of the grooves that are cut in the drawer sides, the fronts also serve as drawer stops.

Next, each side piece receives a rabbet at one end to hold a back piece *(Fig. 10b)*. Then, to allow the drawers to ride on the drawer guides, cut a centered groove along the length of each side piece *(Fig. 10c)*.

After cutting the rabbets and side grooves, I added a $\frac{1}{8}$"-wide groove to each piece for a drawer bottom *(Fig. 10c)*. Now dry-assemble the drawers and cut the bottoms (N) to size from $\frac{1}{8}$"-thick hardboard. Then glue and clamp the drawers (including the bottoms) together. Check each drawer for square as you assemble it.

FINAL TOUCHES. Once the glue had dried, I worked on a few more details on the drawers. First, I routed a $\frac{1}{8}$" chamfer around the inside to soften the sharp edges *(Fig. 10)*. Then using a

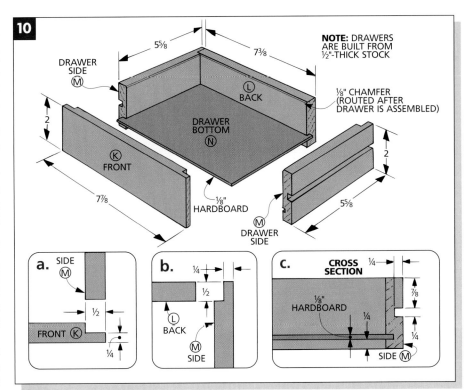

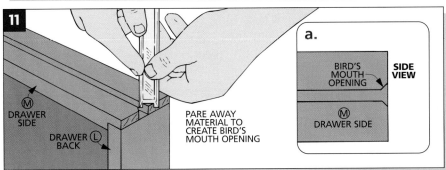

chisel, I created a "bird's mouth" opening at the end of each groove. This makes it easier to place the drawer onto the drawer guides after it has been removed from the cabinet *(Fig. 11)*. And finally, I added velvet-covered drawer liners and ring holders (as shown in the Technique box below).

TECHNIQUE .... *Lining Drawers*

Liners. *I lined some of the drawer bottoms with velvet-covered pieces of posterboard. Mount the fabric with tape and spray adhesive.*

Custom Foam Inserts. *For a couple of the other drawers, I made foam inserts for rings by cutting kerfs in blocks of rigid insulation (blueboard). Then I cov-*

ered the blocks with fabric. Press the fabric into the kerfs with a straightedge and tape it in place. Then carefully slip the inserts into the drawers.

With the drawers completed, the case is ready for the doors (refer to *Fig. 15*). Each door is made up of two pieces of plywood joined together in an L-shape. This way, the doors swing open to allow access to necklaces and other jewelry hanging from the sides of the case.

I started on the doors by cutting side panels (O) and front panels (P) to finished size *(Fig. 12)*. Then to hide the edges, I cut and glued door edging (Q) to the panels.

The front panels are edged on all four sides. But the side panels are only edged on three. Then the side panels are glued to the front panels. I used a square to help glue them together at a perfect right angle *(Fig 12a)*.

Then to complete the doors, I drew layout lines and used a hand-held router to rout 1/8" stopped chamfers on the outside corners *(Fig. 13)*.

HANGING DOORS. Finally, I completed the case of the jewelry cabinet by hanging the doors with 2" butt hinges *(Fig. 14)*. These are mortised into the case back but are simply screwed to the inside faces of the doors.

When hung correctly, the doors should be centered top-to-bottom, and the sides should end up flush with the molded edging on the top and bottom of the case.

MAGNETIC CATCH RAILS. To keep the doors closed, I used magnetic catches. These catches are installed in a pair of 3/4"-thick rails (R) *(Fig. 15)*. The rails fit between the side panels of the case. I

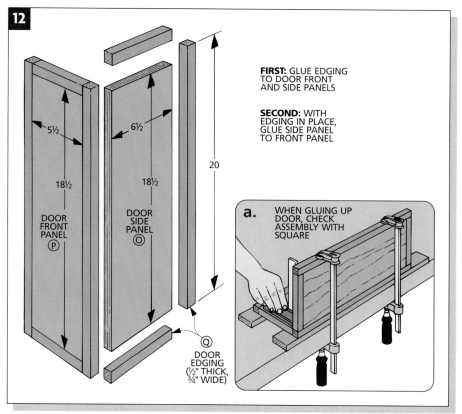

12

FIRST: GLUE EDGING TO DOOR FRONT AND SIDE PANELS

SECOND: WITH EDGING IN PLACE, GLUE SIDE PANEL TO FRONT PANEL

5½
6½
18½
18½
20

DOOR FRONT PANEL (P)
DOOR SIDE PANEL (O)

DOOR EDGING (½" THICK, ¾" WIDE) (Q)

a. WHEN GLUING UP DOOR, CHECK ASSEMBLY WITH SQUARE

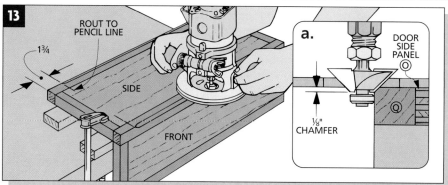

13

ROUT TO PENCIL LINE

1¾

SIDE

FRONT

a.

DOOR SIDE PANEL (O)

⅛" CHAMFER

(Q)

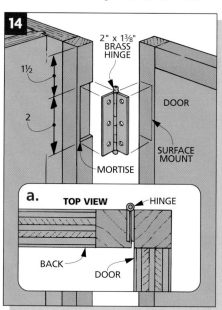

14

2" x 1⅜" BRASS HINGE

1½

2

DOOR

SURFACE MOUNT

MORTISE

a. TOP VIEW — HINGE

BACK

DOOR

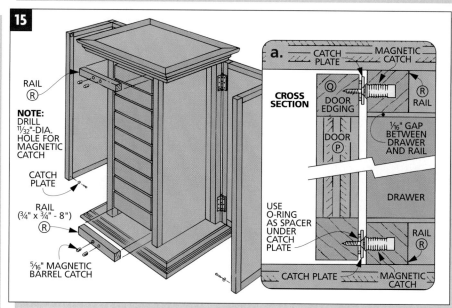

15

RAIL (R)

NOTE: DRILL 11/32"-DIA. HOLE FOR MAGNETIC CATCH

CATCH PLATE

RAIL (¾" x ¾" - 8") (R)

5/16" MAGNETIC BARREL CATCH

a. CATCH PLATE — MAGNETIC CATCH

CROSS SECTION

DOOR EDGING (Q)

DOOR (P)

USE O-RING AS SPACER UNDER CATCH PLATE

RAIL (R)

1/16" GAP BETWEEN DRAWER AND RAIL

DRAWER

RAIL (R)

CATCH PLATE — MAGNETIC CATCH

SHOP TIP

Catch Installation

To get magnetic catches flush with the surface of the rail, use a C-clamp to help press the catches in.

RAIL
®

USE C-CLAMP
TO PRESS DOOR
CATCHES IN PLACE

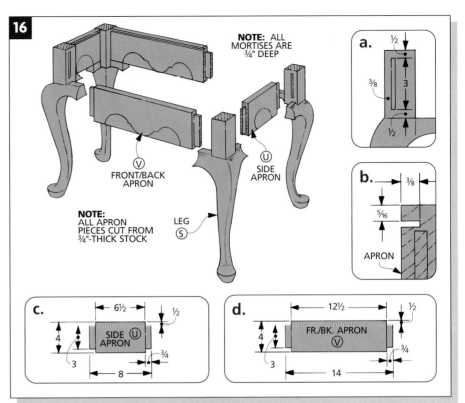

16

NOTE: ALL MORTISES ARE ¾" DEEP

a.

V FRONT/BACK APRON

U SIDE APRON

NOTE: ALL APRON PIECES CUT FROM ¾"-THICK STOCK

LEG S

b.

APRON

c. SIDE APRON U — 6½ — ½ — 4 — 3 — 8 — ¾

d. FR./BK. APRON V — 12½ — ½ — 4 — 3 — 14 — ¾

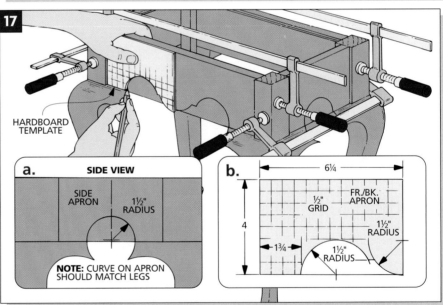

17

HARDBOARD TEMPLATE

a. SIDE VIEW — SIDE APRON — 1½" RADIUS — NOTE: CURVE ON APRON SHOULD MATCH LEGS

b. — 6¼ — ½" GRID — FR./BK. APRON — 4 — 1¾ — 1½" RADIUS — 1½" RADIUS

sized mine to create a ¹⁄₁₆" gap between the rails and the drawers (¾" wide in my case). Before gluing them in place, I drilled two holes for the catches.

I used C-clamps to help install the catches in the holes (see the Shop Tip above). Then I screwed the catch plates in place *(Fig. 15a)*. To adjust the doors in or out, I used a rubber O-ring as a spacer under each catch plate.

BASE

With the case complete, I turned my attention to building the base. There's nothing too unusual about the construction of the base: just four cabriole legs joined by aprons.

LEGS. To make the base, I started with the cabriole legs (S) *(Fig. 16)*. The interesting thing about cabriole legs is that they look a lot more complicated to build than they actually are.

For this project, I kept the legs basic. All you need is a band saw, a drum sander, and some rasps or files — no carving and very little shaping are required. Refer to page 106 for step-by-step instructions.

Note: You can also buy completed legs with all the work done for you (see page 126 for sources).

The legs are mortised to receive the ¾"-long tenons that will be cut on the aprons *(Fig. 16a)*.

APRONS. Once you have the legs ready, they can be connected with side aprons (U) and front/back aprons (V) *(Figs. 16c and 16d)*. I started by cutting these pieces to finished size.

The case will be attached to the base later with metal table top fasteners. To accommodate these fasteners, I cut a ⅛"-wide groove ⅜" deep on the inside face of each piece *(Fig. 16b)*.

After cutting the grooves, tenons are cut to fit the mortises in the legs. I cut them with a dado blade on the table saw.

PROFILE. After cutting the tenons, the next step is to dry-assemble the base and lay out the decorative profiles on the aprons *(Fig. 17)*. The important thing to remember when laying out

these profiles is that they have to match up with the curves on the transition blocks of the legs *(Fig. 17)*.

The side aprons have a simple centered radius *(Fig. 17a)*. This can be drawn right on the aprons, cut out with a band saw, and sanded smooth.

For the front and back aprons, I made a hardboard template that's laid out using a grid pattern *(Fig. 17b)*.

After tracing the pattern onto the front and back aprons, cut the profile with a band saw and sand it smooth.

ASSEMBLY

With the aprons complete, you can glue and clamp the base together. Just check to make sure the base remains square after tightening the clamps.

Once the glue dries, set the case on the base and center it front-to-back and side-to-side *(Fig. 18)*.

Then install Z-shaped table top fasteners in the grooves and attach the other ends to the case bottom with screws *(Fig. 18a)*.

FINISH AND HARDWARE. To complete the Jewelry Cabinet, I applied two coats of varnish that were then rubbed out to a high sheen (see the Finishing article on page 42 for details). Once that was completed, I installed the door and drawer hardware *(Fig. 19)*.

To finish off the cabinet and give it an extra touch of elegance, I used brass hardware. I mounted brass "teardrop" pulls on the cabinet doors *(Fig. 19a)*. The drawers each received a simple brass knob centered on the drawer front *(Fig. 19b)*.

Finally, I added specially designed brass pegs on the case sides to hang necklaces and bracelets *(Fig. 19c* and photo below). These are epoxied into shallow holes.

Note: See page 126 for mail-order sources of pulls and other hardware. ■

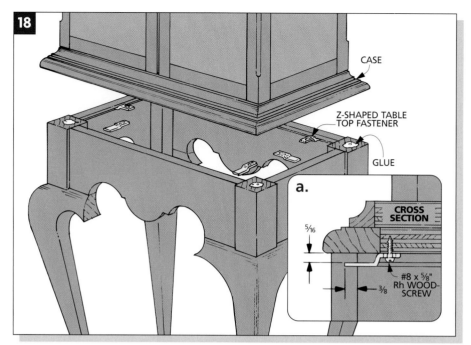
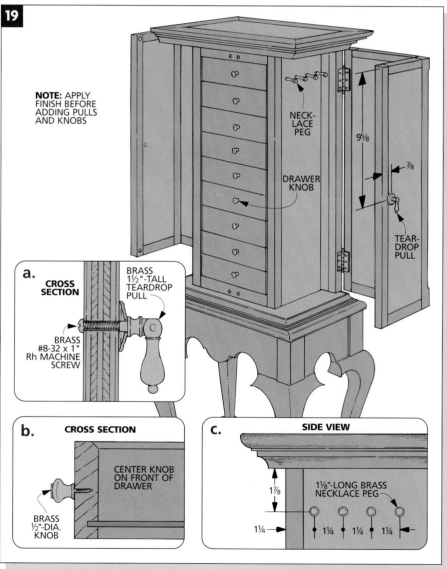

DESIGNER'S NOTEBOOK

Adding raised panels to the door fronts adds an extra touch of character to the Jewelry Cabinet. All you'll need is solid wood instead of plywood and a special bit for the raised panel profile.

CONSTRUCTION NOTES:

■ Adding a little extra character to the face of the Jewelry Cabinet is as easy as replacing the old doors with raised panel doors (see the drawing at right).

Note: This design option calls for solid walnut instead of walnut plywood for the front door panels. You'll need enough for two panels, four stiles, and four rails.

■ Start by making the door side panels (O) the same as before, with $3/4$"-thick edging along the top, bottom, and back.

■ You don't need edging for the door front panels (P), because you'll be making a door frame to hold each one. Start by cutting the rails (X) and stiles (W) to length and width *(Fig. 1)*.

■ Next, cut a groove on the inside edge of each rail and stile *(Fig. 2)*. This $3/8$"-deep groove is offset so it will hold the panel later.

■ Now you can also cut offset tenons on the ends of the rails. These tenons are $3/8$" long to fit the grooves in the stiles *(Fig. 2)*.

■ Now the door frames are complete. It's time to start work on the panels (P).

These raised panels have a specific profile (refer to *Fig. 3*). Start by cutting the panels to finished size (measure the opening in the frame and add $3/4$" to the length and width for the grooves).

■ To rout bevels for the raised panels, use a router table and a $1^7/16$"-dia. raised panel bit (Sears bit No. 25465) *(Steps 1 and 2 in Fig. 4)*. Each bevel is routed in a series of passes.

■ After making a final pass on the bevel, you can complete the profile by turning the panel over and routing a shallow rabbet along the back *(Step 3 in Fig. 4)*.

Note: It's a good idea to finish the panels before assembling the doors. That way no bare wood will show if the panel contracts with changes in humidity.

■ Assemble the doors, but don't glue the panels in the frames (they should float so they can expand and contract). Then add them to the Jewelry Cabinet.

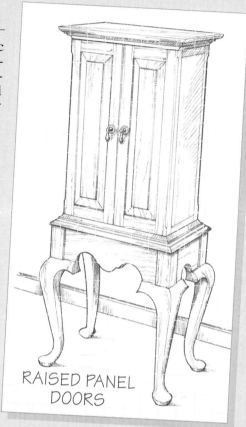

RAISED PANEL DOORS

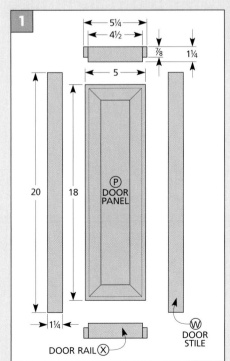

1

DOOR PANEL (P)

DOOR RAIL (X)

DOOR STILE (W)

MATERIALS LIST

CHANGED PARTS		NEW PARTS	
P Door Fr. Panels (2)	$3/4$ x 5 - 18	**W** Door Stiles (4)	$3/4$ x $1 1/4$ - 20
Q Door Edging	$3/4$ x $3/4$ - 7 ft. rgh.	**X** Door Rails (4)	$3/4$ x $1 1/4$ - $5 1/4$

2 TOP VIEW

RAIL (X)

STILE (W)

NOTE: CUT GROOVE ON INSIDE EDGE OF EACH FRAME PIECE

3 PANEL PROFILE (CROSS SECTION)

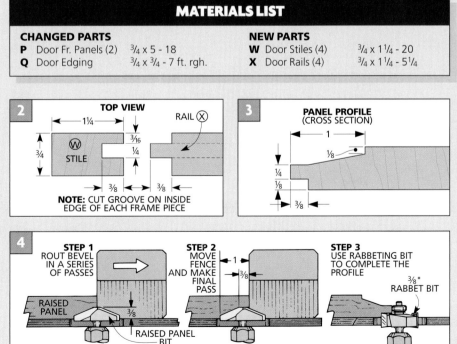

4

STEP 1 ROUT BEVEL IN A SERIES OF PASSES

RAISED PANEL

RAISED PANEL BIT

STEP 2 MOVE FENCE AND MAKE FINAL PASS

STEP 3 USE RABBETING BIT TO COMPLETE THE PROFILE

$3/8$" RABBET BIT

Cabriole legs look more like sculpture than woodworking. And that may scare you away from trying your hand at them. But they really aren't that difficult to make. While some designs can get fancy, I kept these cabriole legs pretty basic. After a few cuts on the band saw, you'll be holding the rough shape of the leg in your hands. Then with some handwork, you can bring the legs to final shape. All you need to do is follow the steps below.

TURNING BLANKS. Cabriole legs start out as thick, square blanks. To avoid joint lines, I don't laminate thinner pieces of wood. I use solid stock to make the legs. The problem is finding pieces that are thick enough.

To get blanks this size, I use 3" x 3" turning squares. I buy them extra long, so I can also cut the transition blocks from the same blank. This makes a nice match in color and grain patterns. Turning squares often come rough cut, so you may need to square them up before you can begin on the legs.

PATTERNS. Once you've squared up the turning blanks, the next step is to create patterns for the leg. (I made mine out of 1/8" hardboard.) There are two patterns: one for the leg *(Fig. 1)* and another that's used for the inside faces of the transition blocks (added later) *(Figs. 2a and 2b).*

Note: Though the same leg pattern works for the Jewelry Cabinet (pages 96-109) and Coffee Table (pages 20-29), the patterns for the transition blocks are slightly different *(Figs. 2a and 2b).*

CORNER POST. After the shape of the leg is laid out *(Steps 1 and 2)*, it's time to work on the blank. I start by drilling the

1

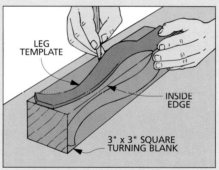

CABRIOLE LEG PATTERN

1¾ · CORNER POST · ¼ · 3 · ⅜ · KNEE · 1½ · TRANSITION BLOCK (SEE FIG. 2) · 18 · 17¼ · FOOT · 3 · 1" LAYOUT GRID

1 To draw the pattern, position template so the back edge of the corner post aligns with inside corner of blank. Flip template and repeat on adjacent side.

LEG TEMPLATE · INSIDE EDGE · 3" x 3" SQUARE TURNING BLANK

2

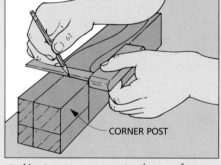

CORNER POST

2 Next, use a square to draw reference lines around all four faces of the blank to indicate where the corner post meets the knee.

3

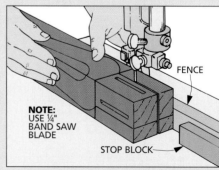

AUXILIARY FENCE · ¼" FORSTNER BIT · **NOTE:** DRILL MORTISES ⅞" DEEP

3 At this point, cut the mortises on the two faces with the patterns. Drill a series of overlapping holes. Then clean up the cheeks with a chisel.

4

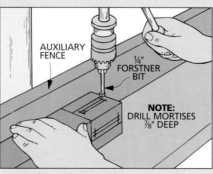

FENCE · **NOTE:** USE ¼" BAND SAW BLADE · STOP BLOCK

4 Set up a band saw to make the face cuts on the corner post. Use a fence to guide the leg and clamp a stop block to the fence to set the depth of cut.

mortises *(Step 3)*. Then two cuts are made on each corner post *(Step 4)*. These cuts stop at the reference lines drawn in *Step 2*.

TRANSITION BLOCKS. Before making the cuts that shape the curves of the legs, you'll have to add two rectangular transition blocks *(Fig. 2)*. These blocks are glued on over the knees of the legs. They should also line up with the reference lines between the corner post and the knee so they end up square.

CUTTING THE LEGS. After the transition blocks are in place, redraw the leg pattern and transfer the transition block pattern to them *(Steps 5 and 6)*. Then make the band saw cuts to complete the corner post *(Step 7)*.

Now, it's time to cut out the leg. This is done in two steps. First, all the cuts are made along one face of the leg *(Steps 8 and 9)*. Since these cuts remove part of the pattern on the adjacent face, you need to save the waste pieces. Then you simply tape them back onto the blank and cut the curves on the adjacent face *(Steps 10 and 11)*.

Now, while the leg is still relatively square, I sand the faces with a drum sander on the drill press *(Step 12)*. (You'll need an auxiliary table to support the leg as you do this.) All you need to do here is sand until the saw marks have been removed.

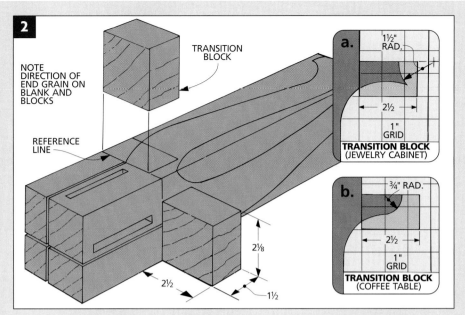

2

NOTE DIRECTION OF END GRAIN ON BLANK AND BLOCKS

TRANSITION BLOCK

REFERENCE LINE

2½

2⅛

1½

a. 1½" RAD.

2½

1" GRID

TRANSITION BLOCK (JEWELRY CABINET)

b. ¾" RAD.

2½

1" GRID

TRANSITION BLOCK (COFFEE TABLE)

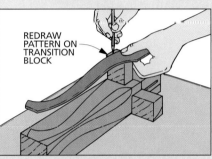

REDRAW PATTERN ON TRANSITION BLOCK

5 Glue on transition blocks, then redraw knee on blocks. Reference line on pattern should align with transition block.

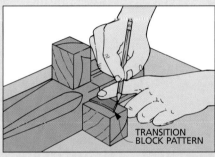

TRANSITION BLOCK PATTERN

6 A second pattern is used to trace profiles on inner faces of transition blocks. Place pattern in corner and mark outline.

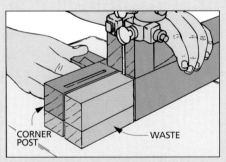

CORNER POST   WASTE

7 Start sawing at corner post by aligning blade with top of transition block. Saw to kerf. Repeat the cut on adjacent face.

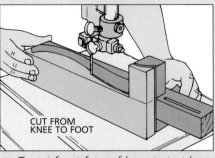

CUT FROM KNEE TO FOOT

8 To cut front face of leg, start at knee and saw around to foot in one smooth pass. Be sure to save the waste piece.

SAVE WASTE PIECES

9 Cut back of leg just like the front. A second cut is needed to form the transition block. Again, save the waste pieces.

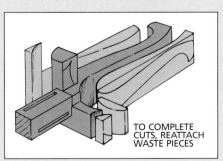

TO COMPLETE CUTS, REATTACH WASTE PIECES

10 The waste pieces are needed when cutting remaining faces of leg blank. Tape the pieces to blank in original positions.

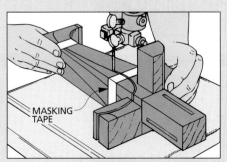

MASKING TAPE

11 Now, finish roughing out leg by repeating cuts on front and back faces. Again, work from the knee down to the foot.

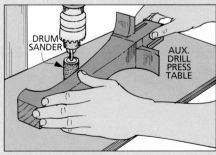

DRUM SANDER

AUX. DRILL PRESS TABLE

12 At this point, the "square" legs can be sanded with a drum sander to remove the saw marks.

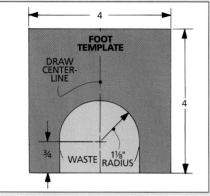

FOOT TEMPLATE

DRAW CENTER-LINE

4

4

¾

WASTE

1⅛" RADIUS

13 To begin shaping the legs, first make a template to help you draw the outline of the foot. This is a piece of ⅛" hardboard with a 1⅛"-radius cutout.

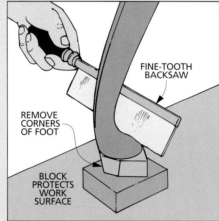

NOTE:
ALIGN CENTER OF TEMPLATE WITH FRONT CORNER OF LEG

FOOT TEMPLATE CENTERLINE

14 Now that the template has been made, the top of the foot can be laid out. Set the template on top of the foot and trace the outline.

At this point, the blanks are beginning to look like cabriole legs. Now it's time to do the final shaping that will soften the square edges.

I work from the bottom up, starting with the foot and moving up to the transition blocks at the knee.

FEET. One of the tricks to making cabriole legs is to get four legs that look similar. And the feet are probably the most noticeable. So I shaped the feet on all four legs and then set them side by side to compare them. If one was noticeably smaller, I worked on getting the others to match it. But don't be too critical. After all, when the project's built, no one will be able to compare them as closely as you can now.

The first step for each foot is to lay out the final radius on the top. Then the corners can be sawed off *(Steps 13-16)*.

To do the shaping, I used a rasp and a half-round file *(Steps 17-19)*. The rasp allows you to remove the wood quickly. But the file gives you a cleaner cut. Both have a curved edge for cleaning up the top of the foot and a flat edge for shaping the sides of the foot.

LEGS. Once the feet were done, I started on the legs. There's not much to these. The front and back corners of the legs get small, tapered roundovers with a file and some sandpaper. But these roundovers aren't the same for the front and back. The front gets rounded over a

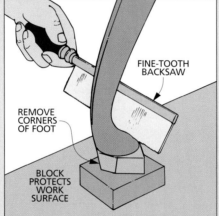

NOTE:
CONNECT CORNERS TO FIND CENTERPOINT

COMPASS

⅝" RADIUS

15 Turn the leg over and find the centerpoint on the bottom of the leg. Then use a compass to draw a ⅝"-radius circle on the bottom of the foot.

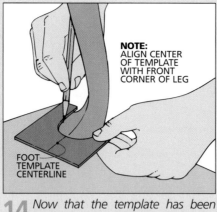

FINE-TOOTH BACKSAW

REMOVE CORNERS OF FOOT

BLOCK PROTECTS WORK SURFACE

16 Next, hold the leg upright and cut away the front and side corners of the foot with a hand saw held at a slight angle. Cut on the waste side of the layout lines.

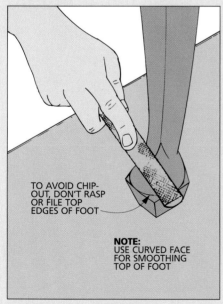

TO AVOID CHIP-OUT, DON'T RASP OR FILE TOP EDGES OF FOOT

NOTE:
USE CURVED FACE FOR SMOOTHING TOP OF FOOT

17 Still holding the leg upright, file the top face of the foot. Remove the sharp lines from the center and feather it out across the top of the leg.

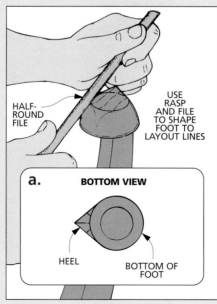

HALF-ROUND FILE

USE RASP AND FILE TO SHAPE FOOT TO LAYOUT LINES

a. BOTTOM VIEW

HEEL

BOTTOM OF FOOT

18 Clamp the leg in a vise and finish rounding the front and sides of the foot, working from the top of the foot to the bottom to prevent chipout.

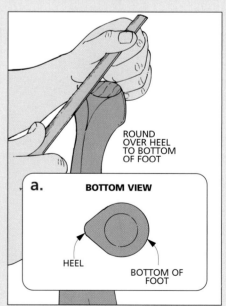

ROUND OVER HEEL TO BOTTOM OF FOOT

a. BOTTOM VIEW

HEEL

BOTTOM OF FOOT

19 Once the sides and front are round, shape the taper on the back of the heel by blending the radius on the bottom of the foot into the back of the ankle.

little more *(Steps 20 and 22)*. The side corners are softened with sandpaper.

To hold the legs during this process, I came up with a shop-made carver's cradle by adding wooden extenders to the jaws of a common ³/₄" pipe clamp (refer to the Shop Jig on page 21).

KNEES. The last area of the leg to work on is the knee, including the transition block. There's not much shaping to do. It's mostly just cleanup.

To begin, I removed the ridge between the corner post and the knee with a chisel *(Step 23)*. But work care-fully — a scratch in the corner post from the chisel will be a chore to remove.

Next, I dry-assembled the aprons and marked the locations of their outside faces *(Step 24)*. Then I rounded over the top of the transition block with sandpaper to blend the edges *(Step 25)*.

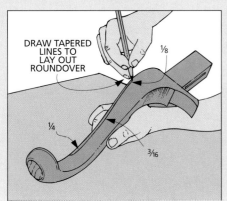

20 Next, lay out marks to show the tapered roundover on the front corner. Connect the marks by drawing lines up and down the leg.

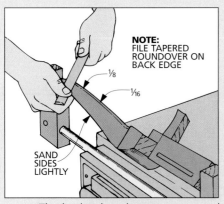

22 The back edge also gets a tapered roundover — though not as large as the front. Lay out guide lines similar to those used on the front edge of the leg.

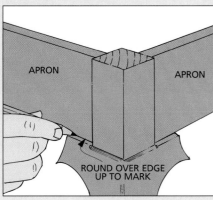

24 Set the aprons in place and trace the front edges onto the leg. Remove the aprons and round over the hard edge to the line with a chisel and sandpaper.

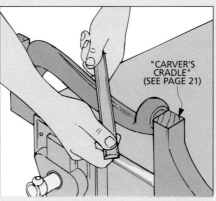

21 Now with a file and some sandpaper, carefully round over the front edge of the leg, until you reach the layout lines that were just drawn.

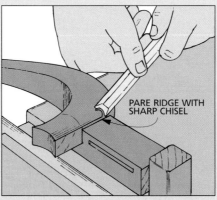

23 Between the corner post and the beginning of the knee, there may be a small ridge. This can be pared away carefully with a sharp chisel.

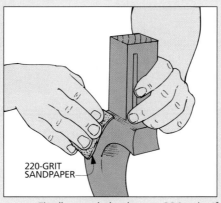

25 Finally, sand the leg to 220-grit. If applying a liquid stain, you might want to use a wood conditioner before staining. See pages 26-27 for more about this.

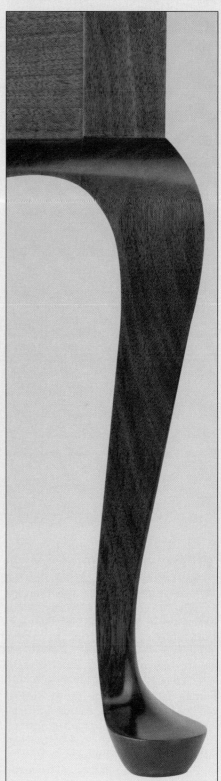

Buffet Server

When it's open, the top provides extra room to set trays and dishes while serving guests. Closed, the cabinet top is smooth and uncluttered. The secret is a special set of hinges that hide out of sight.

It's easy to see how handy this Buffet Server can be. Fold out the top during those large family gatherings so you never have to worry about having enough room at the table. And with the wings folded in, the server doesn't take up much room and still provides plenty of storage.

FOLDING TOP. So how does the folding top work? It's pretty simple really. The top is divided into four parts. The two inside pieces pivot out on hinges and are supported by the two outside pieces (see photos).

But what I really like is that when the top is folded in, you can't see any hard-

ware. That's because I used a special type of "hidden" hinges — Soss hinges. (For step-by-step instructions on installing these, see the article on page 122.)

DOORS. I used another set of non-tra-ditional hinges in this project. The inset doors are mounted on "no-mortise" hinges. Unlike regular butt hinges, these hinges are easy to install and allow for quite a bit of adjustment when it's time to hang the doors.

DRAWER. Although the top and doors use special hardware, I took a different approach with the drawer. I thought

metal drawer guides would look out of place, so I used wooden guides. Traditional dovetail joints are used to fasten the drawer sides to the front.

One problem with wide drawers like this one is that they have a tendency to rack and bind as they're opened and closed. To avoid this, I used runners along both sides and simple guides underneath the drawer.

EXPLODED VIEW

OVERALL DIMENSIONS:
35½W x 21D x 35½H

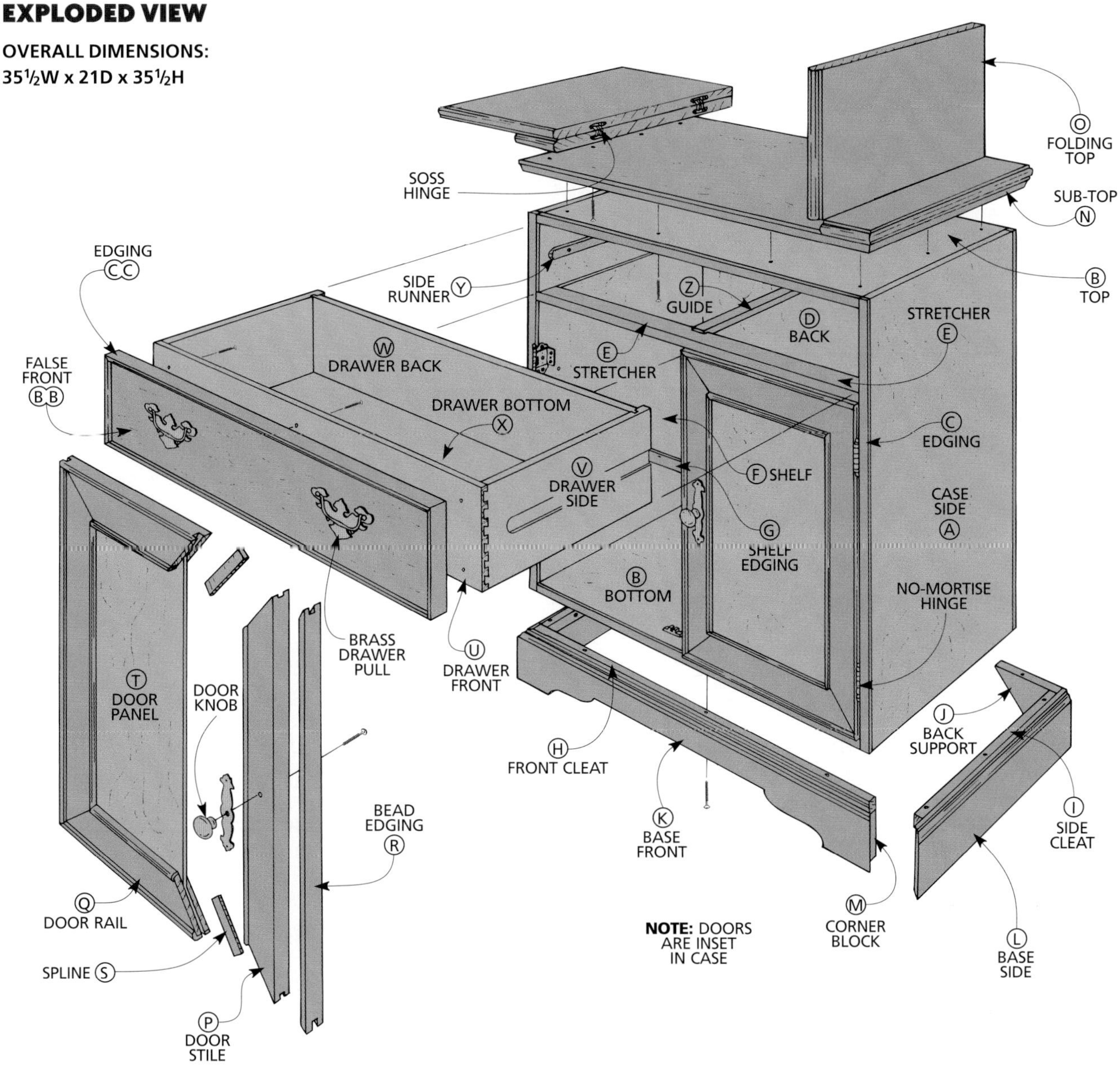

FOLDING TOP — O

SOSS HINGE

SUB-TOP — N

TOP — B

EDGING — CC

SIDE RUNNER — Y

GUIDE — Z

BACK — D

STRETCHER — E

DRAWER BACK — W

STRETCHER — E

FALSE FRONT — BB

DRAWER BOTTOM — X

EDGING — C

CASE SIDE — A

SHELF — F

DRAWER SIDE — V

SHELF — G

BRASS DRAWER PULL

DRAWER FRONT — U

SHELF EDGING — G

BOTTOM — B

NO-MORTISE HINGE

DOOR PANEL — T

DOOR KNOB

FRONT CLEAT — H

BACK SUPPORT — J

BEAD EDGING — R

BASE FRONT — K

SIDE CLEAT — I

DOOR RAIL — Q

SPLINE — S

DOOR STILE — P

CORNER BLOCK — M

BASE SIDE — L

NOTE: DOORS ARE INSET IN CASE

MATERIALS LIST

CARCASE					
A	Case Sides (2)	¾ ply - 19½ x 30	N	Sub-top (1)	¾ x 20⅝ - 34¾
B	Top/Bottom (2)	¾ ply - 19½ x 32¾	O	Folding Top (1)	¾ x 21 - 35⅞
C	Edging (1)	¾ x ¼ - 260 rough	**DOOR AND DRAWER**		
D	Back (1)	¼ ply - 29¼ x 32¾	P	Door Stiles (4)	¾ x 2¼ - 23 rough
E	Stretchers (2)	¾ x 2 - 32¾	Q	Door Rails (4)	¾ x 2¼ - 17 rough
F	Shelf (1)	¾ ply - 17¾ x 31¾	R	Bead Edging (1)	¾ x ¼ - 320 rough
G	Shelf Edging (1)	¾ x ½ - 31⅞	S	Splines (8)	¼ x 3½ - ½
BASE AND TOP			T	Door Panels (2)	¼ ply - 11¹³/₁₆ x 17⅝
H	Front Cleat (1)	¾ x 1 - 33¼	U	Drawer Front (1)	½ x 5¼ - 31⅞
I	Side Cleats (2)	¾ x 1 - 18⅜	V	Drawer Sides (2)	½ x 5¼ - 18
J	Back Supports (2)	¾ x 4 - 6 rough	W	Drawer Back (1)	½ x 4¾ - 31⅜
K	Base Front (1)	¾ x 4 - 36 rough	X	Drwr. Bottom (1)	¼ ply - 17¾ x 31⅜
L	Base Sides (2)	¾ x 4 - 22 rough	Y	Side Runners (2)	¼ x ¾ - 17
M	Corner Blocks (4)	¾ x ¾ - 3	Z	Guide (1)	¾ x 1 - 16¾
			AA	Center Runners (2)	¼ x ½ - 17½

BB	False Front (1)	¼ ply - 5⅛ x 31⅝
CC	Edging (1)	¾ x ¼ - 80 rough

HARDWARE SUPPLIES
(6) No. 8 x ¾" Fh woodscrews
(13) No. 8 x 1" Fh woodscrews
(22) No. 8 x 1¼" Fh woodscrews
(10) No. 8 x 1½" Fh woodscrews
(2) No. 8 x 2" Fh woodscrews
(2) Brass drawer pulls w/ machine screws
(2) Door knobs w/ back plates
(2pr.) ¹³/₁₆" partial-wrap no-mortise hinges
(2 pr.) ⅜" No. 101 Soss hinges
(4) Spoon-style shelf supports
(4) Ball catches

CUTTING DIAGRAM

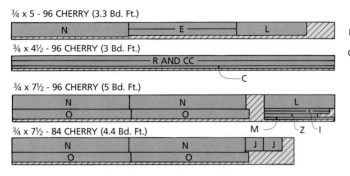

¾ x 5 - 96 CHERRY (3.3 Bd. Ft.)

N | E | L

¾ x 4½ - 96 CHERRY (3 Bd. Ft.)

R AND CC
C

¾ x 7½ - 96 CHERRY (5 Bd. Ft.)

N | N | L
O | O | M | Z | I

¾ x 7½ - 84 CHERRY (4.4 Bd. Ft.)

N | N | J | J
O | O

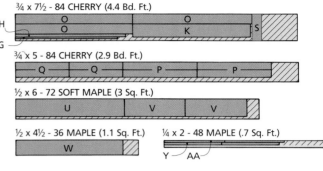

¾ x 7½ - 84 CHERRY (4.4 Bd. Ft.)

H | O | O | S
G | O | K

¾ x 5 - 84 CHERRY (2.9 Bd. Ft.)

Q | Q | P | P

½ x 6 - 72 SOFT MAPLE (3 Sq. Ft.)

U | V | V

½ x 4½ - 36 MAPLE (1.1 Sq. Ft.)

W

¼ x 2 - 48 MAPLE (.7 Sq. Ft.)

Y | AA

¾" CHERRY PLYWOOD - 48 x 96

B | A | F
  | | BB
B | A

¼" CHERRY PLYWOOD - 48 x 48

D
T | T

ALSO NEEDED:
ONE 18" x 32"
PIECE OF ¼"-THICK
MAPLE PLYWOOD

CASE

There are a lot of different parts to this Buffet Server, but the place to start is with the case. Most of the case is made with plywood that's edged front and back *(Fig. 3)*. However, to create the opening for the drawer, there are two hardwood stretchers as well.

SIDES, TOP, AND BOTTOM. To begin construction on the case, I cut the sides (A), and top and bottom (B) to size from ³⁄₄" plywood *(Figs. 1 and 2)*.

Note: When sizing the panels, I allowed for ¼"-thick hardwood edging strips that will be added to the front and back later to hide and protect the edges of the plywood.

But the edging isn't added just yet. A series of ¼"-wide dadoes needs to be cut on the side panels first *(Fig. 1)*. These dadoes will hold the top and bottom and the stretchers.

The next thing to do is to create ¼"-thick tongues on the top and bottom panels that fit into the dadoes on the sides *(Fig. 2a)*. These tongues are cre-

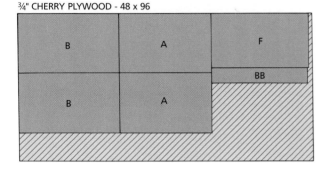

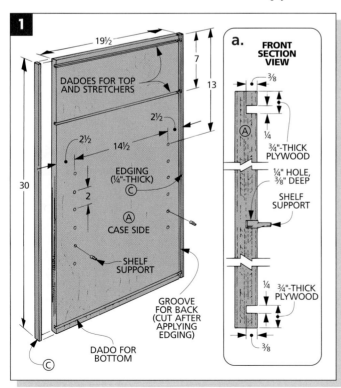

ated by cutting rabbets on the ends of the panels *(Fig. 2a)*.

PLYWOOD EDGING. At this point, the plywood panels are ready for some ¼"-thick edging (C) *(Fig. 3)*. To do this, I glued extra-wide strips to the panels and trimmed them with a flush trim router bit. (See the Shop Tip on the next page for more about this).

Note: The edging doesn't run the entire length of the top and bottom panels. It stops flush with the rabbets on the ends *(Fig. 3a)*.

CASE BACK. After the edging has been trimmed flush on the top and bottom panels, the next piece to make is a ¼"-thick plywood back panel. This piece does more than just close off the back. It also strengthens the case and keeps it square.

To hold the back, first cut ⅜"-deep grooves along the back edges of the sides, top, and bottom panels *(Figs. 1, 2b, and 3b)*. Make sure the width of these grooves matches the thickness of the plywood, which isn't exactly ¼".

After the grooves for the back have been cut, the case back (D) can be cut to size *(Fig. 3)*. To determine its size, I dry-assembled the case and measured the opening. (Just remember to allow for the depth of the grooves.)

STRETCHERS. The last two pieces of the case are the ¾"-thick hardwood stretchers (E) *(Figs. 3 and 4)*. These pieces are ripped 2" wide and are cut to the same length as the top and bottom panels (32¾").

The stretchers fit in the grooves in the side panels just like the top panel — with tongues *(Figs. 3c and 3d)*. Here again, all you have to do is cut rabbets on the ends to create ¼"-thick tongues *(Figs. 4a and 4b)*.

The only difference between the two stretchers is that the one in front also requires a notch in each tongue. This allows it to fit flush with the front of the edging on the sides of the case *(Figs. 3c and 4a)*. This notch is easy to cut — you can use the same fence setting that you used to cut the rabbets. All you need to do is set the stretcher on its front edge and lower the blade so it cuts a notch the same thickness as the edging (¼").

ASSEMBLY. At this point, the case could be assembled, but first I took the opportunity to drill some holes while it's easy to get at the inside faces of the pieces. On the case sides (A), I drilled holes for ¼" shelf pins that will hold a

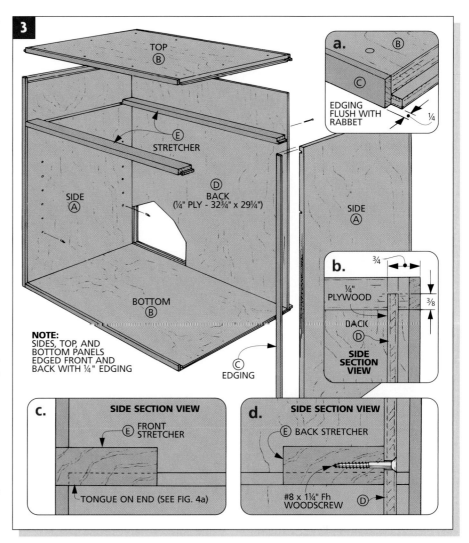

shelf that's added later *(Figs. 1 and 1a)*. Then I drilled countersunk pilot holes in the top panel (B) *(Figs. 2 and 2a)*. These holes will be used to secure the top later on.

Now the case can be assembled. To do this, I laid a side panel down on my shop floor and fit the panels and stretchers into their grooves. Then I added the back and the other side panel on top, stood the case upright and clamped it together. This is not a quick assembly, so be sure to dry-assemble all the pieces first to make sure everything goes together well and use a slow-setting glue. (I used white glue.)

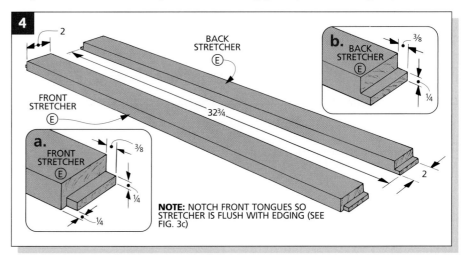

SHELF

With the case assembled, you can step back and take a deep breath. All that's left with the case now is to add a shelf inside *(Fig. 5)*. I ripped the $3/4$" plywood shelf (F) $17^3/4$" wide and cut it to length so there was a $1/16$" gap at each side. (Mine was $31^7/8$" long.) To hide the plies, the front of the shelf is edged like the case panels, except this time, I used $1/2$"-thick edging (G).

BASE

With the case complete, I added the base next (see the photo on the opposite page). It's made up of three pieces mitered to wrap around the front and sides of the case. These pieces have ogee profiles on their top edges, and the front piece has a curved profile cut along its bottom edge.

CLEATS. But you can't simply add the base pieces to the case — you need something to attach them to. So first, I added front and side cleats (H, I) to the

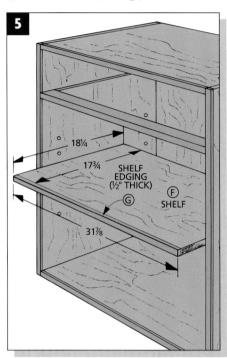

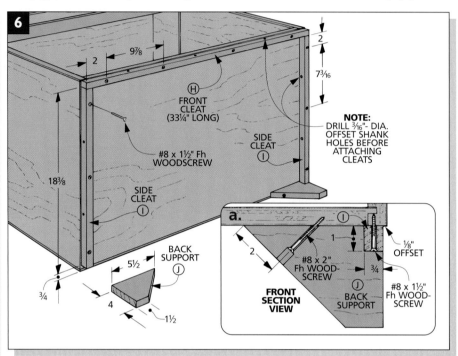

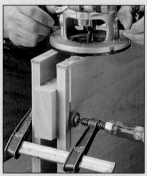

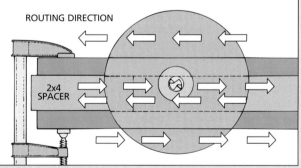

SHOP TIP .... *Trimming Edging Flush*

After the edging is glued to the side panels of the Buffet Server, it needs to be trimmed flush with the plywood. To do this, I used a router with a flush trim bit. But this presented a couple of problems.

First, it's difficult to balance the base of the router on the narrow edge of the workpiece. As a result, it's easy to gouge the edging.

Second, the bearing on the router bit will drop into the dadoes cut on the inside faces of the side panels — which can also gouge the edging.

Fortunately, both problems are easy to solve. To

bridge the gap created by the dado, all that's needed is a filler strip (see photo). Cut the strip so it fits snug in the dado and is flush with the face of the plywood. (I sanded my filler strip to get it flush.)

To create a wider surface for the router to ride

along, just clamp the sides together with a 2x4 spacer sandwiched in between (see photo). The spacer separates the sides so you can rout the edging on both faces of the panel at one time.

One thing to keep in mind is the routing direc-

tion (see drawing). The bit may grab the workpiece if you run the router in the wrong direction.

Finally, after the edging is trimmed flush with the faces, it can be trimmed to length. I use a chisel and carefully pare away the excess on the ends.

An ogee curve at each end of the base front echos the ogee profile routed on the top edge of the base. By cutting away the base between the ogees in a straight line, "toe room" is created. The Shop Tip at right shows how to do this.

bottom of the case *(Fig. 6)*. The cleats are 1" tall and have two sets of countersunk pilot holes drilled in them. One set is for screwing the cleats to the case, and the other is for attaching the base pieces to the cleats.

Note: The holes for attaching the base pieces are countersunk from the back side of the cleat.

The cleats sit back $\frac{1}{8}$" on the front and sides of the case *(Fig. 6a)*. But they stop $\frac{3}{4}$" short of the back edge. This creates room for two back supports (J) that can be added next. These are cut the same height as the base pieces (4").

BASE PIECES. After the back supports are glued and screwed to the case, the

SHOP TIP........ *Straight Guide*

The bottom edge of the base front has decorative curves at each end (see the photo at left). The portion of the base between these curves is straight. Forming this profile is done in several steps.

The curved portions are cut to rough shape on the band saw. Then use a drum sander to sand up to the lines.

To make the edge between the curves as straight as possible, I used a flush trim bit in a router table. However, the bearing of the bit needs a surface to ride on. So I fastened a straight piece of scrap to the base with double-sided carpet tape (see photo above).

You'll still have some touch-up to do since the bit won't reach into the inside corner where the straight portion begins. So stop the cut just short of this point, then complete the profile by using a chisel to square up the corners.

base front (K) and sides (L) can be added *(Fig. 7)*. These $\frac{3}{4}$"-thick pieces are ripped 4" wide. But before mitering them to length, I routed the Roman ogee profile along the top outside edge of each piece *(Fig. 7a.)*

Now the three base pieces can be mitered so they wrap around the case with a $\frac{1}{8}$" shoulder, starting with the base front *(Fig. 7)*. And when the miters on the front corners are complete, the back ends of the sides can be cut flush with the back of the case.

Before attaching the base pieces, I laid out and cut the curved profile on the front *(Fig. 7c)*. The straight section was shaped by roughing out the line with the band saw and then routing it straight with a flush trim bit and a straightedge (see Shop Tip above).

CORNER BLOCKS. When the base pieces have been glued and screwed to the supports, I glued short, $\frac{3}{4}$"-square corner blocks (M) into the front and back corners of the base to strengthen this joint *(Fig. 7)*.

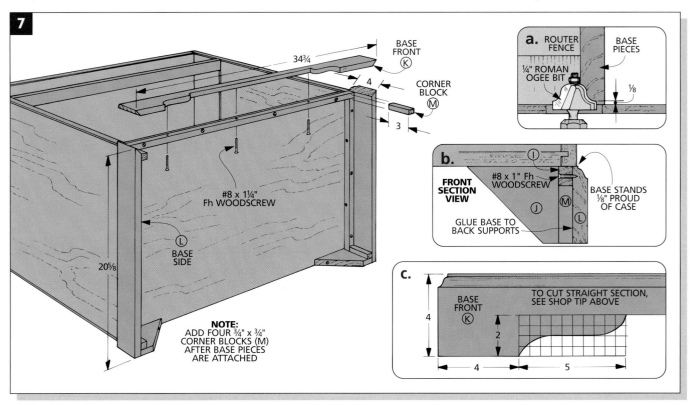

Now the buffet can be set right side up so you can add the top. The top is made up of two hardwood panels: a sub-top and the folding top *(Fig. 8)*.

SUB-TOP. The first thing to do is to glue up a ³⁄₄"-thick panel for the sub-top (N) *(Fig. 9)*. When cutting this panel to size, it should end up flush with the back edge of the case but overhang the front and each side ⁵⁄₈" *(Fig. 9)*. (My sub-top was 20⁵⁄₈" x 34³⁄₄".)

With the panel cut to size, next I routed a ¹⁄₂" cove profile on the front and side edges *(Figs. 9 and 9a)*. Then I drilled four countersunk pilot holes on each end. (Countersink the bottom face.) These are for securing the folding top to the sub-top later.

FOLDING TOP. Next, I started on the folding top (O). It starts out as another long, ³⁄₄"-thick panel *(Fig. 9)*. First I ripped the folding top 21" wide so it would overhang the front edge of the sub-top ³⁄₈" *(Fig. 8a)*.

The folding top overhangs the sub-top ³⁄₈" on the sides, too. But when initially cutting the panel to length, I added ³⁄₈" to the final length to allow for the three saw kerfs that will be made when cutting the panel later. (My panel started off 35⁷⁄₈" long.)

Before cutting the panel, I routed a profile along its front and side edges. Using a ¹⁄₄" roundover bit, the first thing to do is to round over the bottom edge *(Step 1 in Fig. 9b)*. Then flip the panel over for a second pass. But this time, raise the bit to create a ¹⁄₈" shoulder along the top edge *(Step 2 in Fig. 9b)*.

Now the folding top can be cut into four pieces *(Fig. 10)*. To do this, I used my rip fence, cutting the long panel in half first and then cutting off the 4"-long pieces at each end.

TOP ASSEMBLY. Before the folding top can be attached to the sub-top, the two halves of each folding top must be joined with Soss hinges. (For more on installing these hinges, see page 122.)

With the hinges mortised into the folding top, the 4"-long end pieces can be glued and screwed to the ends of the sub-top *(Fig. 8)*. The backs of these panels are flush and the folding top is centered side-to-side. But the important thing here is the gaps between the folding top halves should match the gaps where the halves are joined with the hinges *(Fig. 8a)*.

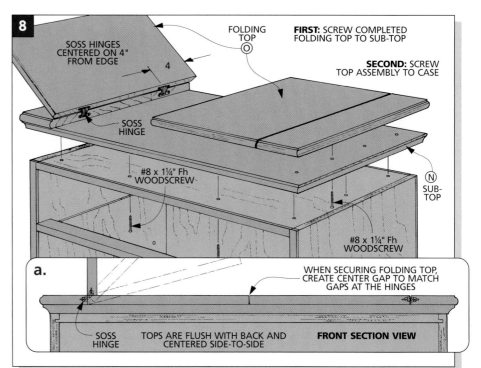

8

SOSS HINGES CENTERED ON 4" FROM EDGE

FOLDING TOP (O)

FIRST: SCREW COMPLETED FOLDING TOP TO SUB-TOP

SECOND: SCREW TOP ASSEMBLY TO CASE

SOSS HINGE

#8 x 1¼" Fh WOODSCREW

(N) SUB-TOP

#8 x 1¼" Fh WOODSCREW

a. WHEN SECURING FOLDING TOP, CREATE CENTER GAP TO MATCH GAPS AT THE HINGES

SOSS HINGE

TOPS ARE FLUSH WITH BACK AND CENTERED SIDE-TO-SIDE

FRONT SECTION VIEW

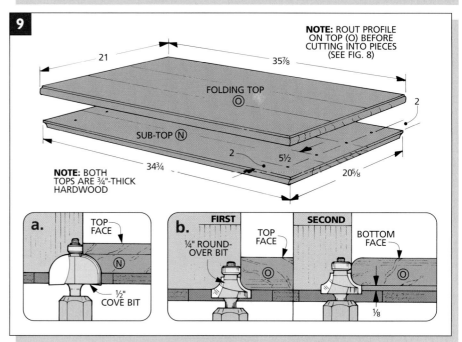

9

NOTE: ROUT PROFILE ON TOP (O) BEFORE CUTTING INTO PIECES (SEE FIG. 8)

21

35⁷⁄₈

FOLDING TOP (O)

2

SUB-TOP (N)

2

5½

34³⁄₄

20⁵⁄₈

NOTE: BOTH TOPS ARE ³⁄₄"-THICK HARDWOOD

a. TOP FACE (N)

½" COVE BIT

b. FIRST

¼" ROUND-OVER BIT

TOP FACE (O)

SECOND

TOP FACE

BOTTOM FACE (O)

¹⁄₈

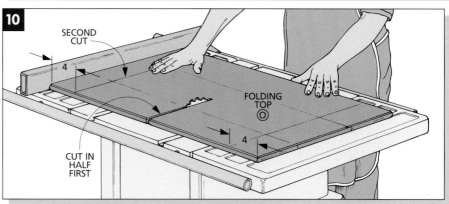

10

SECOND CUT

4

FOLDING TOP (O)

4

CUT IN HALF FIRST

With the folding top and sub-top screwed together, all that's left is to screw them to the case, making sure the tops overhang the case the same on each side *(Fig. 8a)*.

DOORS

Next I turned my attention to the two doors *(Fig. 11)*. These doors are inset, and their frames are joined with reinforced miter joints. A bead edging wraps around the door frame.

FRAME PIECES. To build the doors, I started with the frames. The stiles (P) and rails (Q) are cut to width ($2^1/_4$") from $3/_4$"-thick stock (refer to *Fig. 12* on next page). But before these pieces can be cut to length, you need to make and add the bead edging (R) to both edges (see the Technique box below).

After the edging is on and has been trimmed, the stiles and rails can be mitered to size *(Fig. 12)*. When doing this, I allowed $^1/_{16}$" gaps around and between the doors *(Figs. 11a and 11b)*.

Usually I build an inset door to fit its opening exactly. This way, I can trim it slightly so the gaps around the doors are all the same. But this method won't work with these doors.

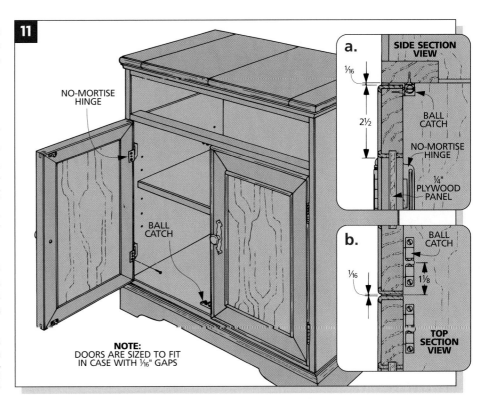

NO-MORTISE HINGE

BALL CATCH

NOTE: DOORS ARE SIZED TO FIT IN CASE WITH $^1/_{16}$" GAPS

a. SIDE SECTION VIEW

$^1/_{16}$

$2^1/_2$

BALL CATCH

NO-MORTISE HINGE

$^1/_4$ PLYWOOD PANEL

b. BALL CATCH

$^1/_{16}$

$1^1/_8$

TOP SECTION VIEW

The reason these doors can't be trimmed much is because of the bead edging that's applied around the edges. It's too thin to allow you to trim much off without it being noticeable (or worse yet, cutting right through the molding). So when mitering the rails and stiles to finished length, you need to be as accurate as possible so any trimming will be kept to a minimum.

TECHNIQUE .... *Bead Edging*

The trick with the bead edging is attaching it to the frame pieces so it stands proud the same amount all around the door. But I came up with a simple solution: I used a groove to "lock" the edging in position. Then after the edging is attached, the excess can be trimmed on the table saw.

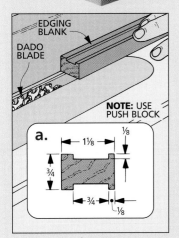

EDGING BLANK

DADO BLADE

NOTE: USE PUSH BLOCK

a. $1^1/_8$ | $^1/_8$

$3/_4$

$3/_4$ | $^1/_8$

1 First, cut $^1/_8$"-deep grooves on both faces of a $3/_4$"-thick blank. Size the grooves to hold the door pieces.

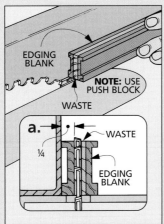

EDGING BLANK

NOTE: USE PUSH BLOCK

WASTE

a. WASTE

$^1/_4$

EDGING BLANK

2 Next, rip two $^1/_4$"-thick edging strips from each blank. Use a push block when making this cut.

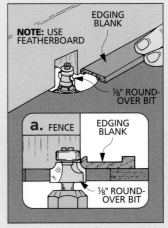

NOTE: USE FEATHERBOARD

EDGING BLANK

$^1/_8$" ROUND-OVER BIT

a. FENCE | EDGING BLANK

$^1/_8$" ROUND-OVER BIT

3 Now, using a $^1/_8$" roundover bit and the router table fence, rout both outside edges of each strip.

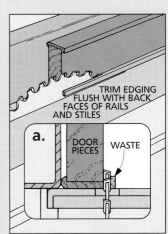

TRIM EDGING FLUSH WITH BACK FACES OF RAILS AND STILES

a. DOOR PIECES | WASTE

4 After the edging is glued to the rails and stiles, trim the back edge of the molding flush, using the table saw.

SPLINES AND DOOR PANELS. With the door pieces cut to size, the next thing I did was cut some $1/4$"-deep grooves along the inside edges and along the ends of each piece *(Figs. 12 and 13)*. The grooves on the edges will hold a $1/4$" plywood panel. And the grooves on the ends will hold some splines, which will strengthen the miter joints.

Unfortunately, to cut these grooves, you can't use a dado blade because $1/4$" plywood is just a little bit less than $1/4$" thick. So for each groove, I made two passes with a regular blade *(Fig. 13)*. And because of the bead molding on the edges, the inside face has to stay against the fence. So to sneak up on the final width of the grooves, you need to make a pass on the edge and end of each piece before nudging the rip fence over a bit for the second pass.

Note: As I cut the grooves in the door frame pieces, I also cut a groove in a piece of scrap. Then I used the scrap as a test piece to help position the fence properly for the second pass.

Cutting the grooves on the long edges of the frame stiles and rails is easy *(Fig. 13)*. But when it's time to cut the grooves on the ends, the pieces are too narrow to pass over the blade safely. So I decided to add a little extra support. The Technique box on the opposite page shows how I did this.

Once the grooves are cut on the edge and ends of each piece, dry assemble the door frames and measure for the plywood panels (T) *(Fig. 12)*. Be sure to figure in the depth of the grooves in the rails and stiles. (My panels were $11^{13}/_{32}$" x $17^{5}/_{8}$".)

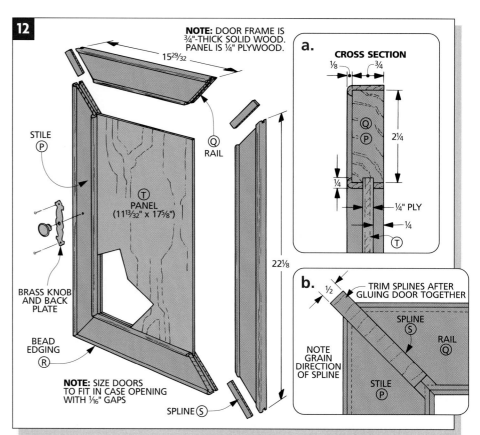

12

NOTE: DOOR FRAME IS $3/4$"-THICK SOLID WOOD. PANEL IS $1/4$" PLYWOOD.

$15^{29}/_{32}$

STILE Ⓟ

RAIL Ⓠ

PANEL Ⓣ ($11^{13}/_{32}$" x $17^{5}/_{8}$")

BRASS KNOB AND BACK PLATE

BEAD EDGING Ⓡ

NOTE: SIZE DOORS TO FIT IN CASE OPENING WITH $1/16$" GAPS

SPLINE Ⓢ

a. CROSS SECTION

$1/8$ — $3/4$

Ⓠ Ⓟ

$2^{1}/_{4}$

$1/4$

$1/4$" PLY

$1/4$

Ⓣ

$22^{1}/_{8}$

b. $1/2$ — TRIM SPLINES AFTER GLUING DOOR TOGETHER

SPLINE Ⓢ

RAIL Ⓠ

NOTE GRAIN DIRECTION OF SPLINE

STILE Ⓟ

13

NOTE: TO CUT THE GROOVES ON THE ENDS OF THE PIECES, SEE TECHNIQUE ON PAGE 119

DOOR RAILS AND STILES

a.

CUT TO FIT $1/4$" PLY

Ⓟ Ⓠ

$1/4$

$1/4$

NOTE: CUT GROOVES IN TWO PASSES

NOTE: TO CUT THE GROOVES ON THE ENDS OF THE PIECES, SEE TECHNIQUE ON PAGE 119

HARDWARE .... *No-Mortise Hinges*

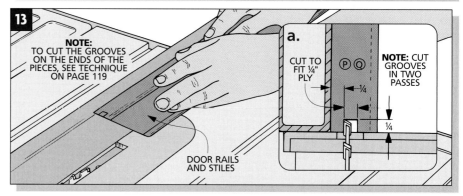

One problem with traditional butt hinges is that they require some precisely cut mortises. So with this project, I tried a type of hinge I hadn't used before: a no-mortise hinge. With these, the leaf attached to the case fits around the leaf attached to the door. So there are no mortises to cut.

But what I really like is that there's some built-in adjustment. The hinge has slotted shank holes in the leaves that allow you to move the door side to side and up and down. This is very useful when fitting inset doors.

INSTALLATION. To mount these hinges, I screw them to the case first. Next, I set the door on a couple of $1/16$"-thick shims inside the case opening. This sets the gap along the bottom of the door, so you can reach inside and mark the position of the slotted pilot holes on the back of the door.

Now, the pilot holes can be drilled, and the door can be mounted in the case. Next, you need to step back and check the gaps around the door. And if needed, you can even out the gaps by adjusting the hinge screws.

When the door fits, the last two screws "lock" the door in place.

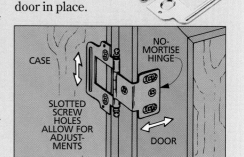

CASE

NO-MORTISE HINGE

SLOTTED SCREW HOLES ALLOW FOR ADJUSTMENTS

DOOR

Cutting a groove in the end of a work-piece for a splined miter joint is usually pretty simple. All you have to do is make a couple passes over the table saw, flipping the piece between each pass to center the groove.

But cutting the grooves on the ends of the door frame pieces of the Buffet Server is a different story. For starters, I was concerned about keeping the long mitered pieces steady while at the same time keeping the end flat on the table as it passed over the blade.

Fortunately, the solution to this problem is simple. I just clamped a scrap to the workpiece to act as a runner along the top of the rip fence

(Fig. 1). I used a wood clamp pad to avoid damaging the bead molding.

And to prevent chipout as the blade exits the workpiece, I clamped a mitered scrap block to the runner, behind the workpiece.

The bead molding on the edges of the mitered pieces raised another concern. Because this molding stands proud of the front face of the frame piece, only the back face can be placed against the rip fence of the table saw. This keeps the groove centered on the thickest portion of the workpiece.

Note: In order to cut a groove on the opposite end of each workpiece, you'll have to unclamp the backer block and

flip it around so the workpiece is angled in the opposite direction *(Fig. 2)*.

I found it was easiest to cut the grooves in the ends while I was set up to cut the grooves in the edges. This way the grooves for the splines and the door panels will align. Start by making a single pass on each edge and end of the frame pieces. Then instead of flipping the workpiece to widen the grooves, you'll have to reposition the rip fence.

After making the initial pass on each of the ends, reposition the fence to sneak up on the final width of the groove *(Fig. 1a)*. Once the fence is set and locked, finish cutting the rest of the grooves on the edges and ends.

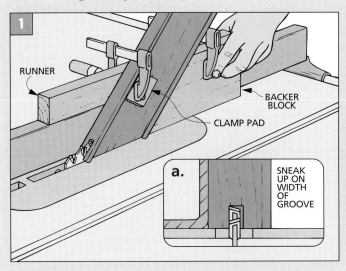

RUNNER

BACKER BLOCK

CLAMP PAD

a. SNEAK UP ON WIDTH OF GROOVE

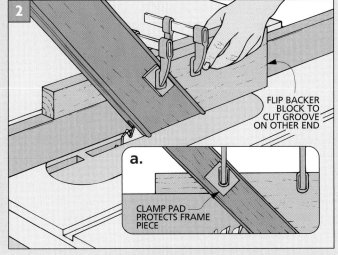

FLIP BACKER BLOCK TO CUT GROOVE ON OTHER END

a. CLAMP PAD PROTECTS FRAME PIECE

ASSEMBLY. Before gluing the doors together, I made hardwood splines (S) to fit the grooves in the corners. These can be planed and cut from scrap, but to make them as strong as possible, make sure the length of the grain runs *across* the joint *(Fig. 12b)*.

As you position each spline, be careful that it doesn't extend into the grooves on the inside corner of the workpieces. Otherwise, the plywood door panel won't fit in. The splines should stick out along the outside corners of the door frames *(Fig. 12b)*. This allows you to trim them perfectly flush with a chisel and some sanding after the doors are assembled.

I glued and clamped the doors together on a flat surface so I could check for any twist in the frames.

MOUNTING THE DOORS. Now that the doors are completed, the next step is to mount them in the case. Since these are inset doors, it's important that they end up with even gaps all the way around. To make this part of the job easier, I used no-mortise hinges, which allowed me to adjust the position of the doors somewhat. (There's more about this in the Hardware box at left).

HARDWARE. With the doors mounted in the opening, I added the other pieces of hardware. First, I mounted brass knobs with back plates to the inside door stiles *(Fig. 12)*. Then to hold the doors closed, I added double ball catches at the top and bottom of each door (refer to *Figs. 11a and 11b* on page 117). For sources of hardware, refer to page 126.

A hardwood spline at each corner of the door frame helps reinforce the miter joint, since this is an end grain to end grain joint. The splines are planed to thickness from scrap to fit the grooves cut in the ends of the frame pieces.

DRAWER

All that's left now is to add the drawer. The trick with adding a wide drawer is to get it to slide in and out smoothly. To make this work, the weight of the drawer is supported at the sides, but the drawer is guided in and out of the opening by a couple of runners on the bottom of the drawer that straddle a drawer guide fastened to the case.

FRONT AND SIDES. The first thing to do is to measure the opening in the buffet. (Mine was 5½" x 32".) The front (U) and sides (V) are ripped ¼" shorter than the opening (5¼") *(Fig. 14)*. (A false front will be added later.) And the front (U) is cut ⅛" less than the width of the opening (31⅞").

To join the front and sides of the drawer, I routed ½" half-blind dovetails with a dovetail jig *(Fig. 14b)*. Then to hold a ¼" plywood drawer bottom, cut a ¼"-deep groove along the bottom of each piece. Just as you did for the door frames, these grooves are cut by making two passes over the saw blade.

Then, to hold the back between the sides, cut a ¼"-wide dado across each side toward one end *(Fig. 14a)*.

BACK AND BOTTOM. Now the drawer back (W) can be cut to size from ½" stock. It doesn't match the height of the sides. The back is only 4¾" high because it stops flush with the groove at the bottom. And it's cut to length to fit between the dadoes in the sides.

Note: When the drawer is assembled, the back sits on top of the drawer bottom. This makes a smooth surface the depth of the drawer for attaching the runners later (refer to *Fig. 17*).

To get the back to fit between the sides, cut a rabbet on each end of the back piece to create tongues that fit in the dadoes *(Fig. 14a)*. Then I dry-assembled the drawer and cut a bottom (X) from ¼" maple plywood.

Before gluing the drawer together, rout a stopped groove on the outside of

each side piece to accept some side runners *(Fig. 14)*. Then the drawer can be glued together.

SIDE RUNNERS. To mount the drawer, the first thing I did was add the ¼"-thick side runners (Y) to the case. These hardwood runners support the weight of the drawer *(Fig. 15)*. Round the front ends of the runners to match the grooves in the drawer sides *(Fig. 15a)*.

To allow the drawer to slide smoothly, the runners have to be positioned so the drawer will sit just above the stretchers. The easiest way to do this is to cut a spacer to set the runner on (see the Shop Tip at right). (The runners butt against the back of the case.)

GUIDE. The next piece to add is the ¾"-thick drawer guide (Z) inside the case *(Fig. 15)*. It's cut 1½" longer than

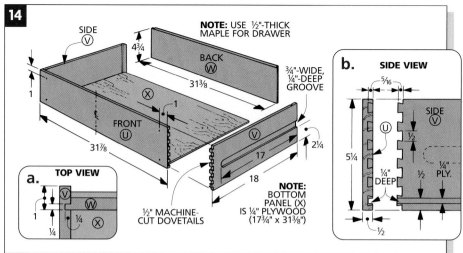

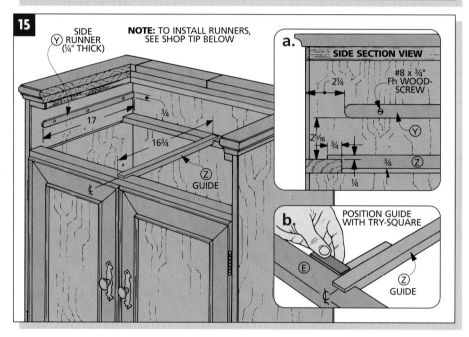

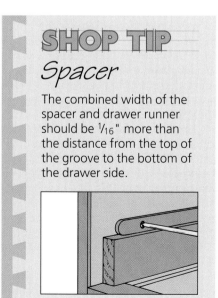

SHOP TIP

Spacer

The combined width of the spacer and drawer runner should be ¹/₁₆" more than the distance from the top of the groove to the bottom of the drawer side.

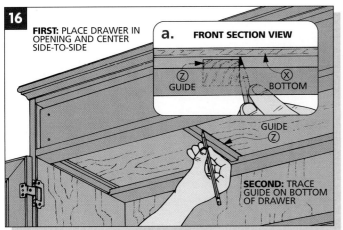

16 **FIRST:** PLACE DRAWER IN OPENING AND CENTER SIDE-TO-SIDE

a. FRONT SECTION VIEW

Z GUIDE
X BOTTOM
GUIDE Z

SECOND: TRACE GUIDE ON BOTTOM OF DRAWER

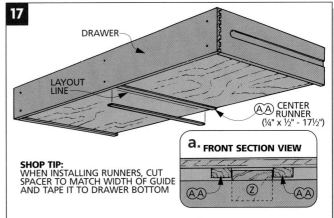

17 DRAWER

LAYOUT LINE

AA CENTER RUNNER
(¼" x ½" - 17½")

SHOP TIP: WHEN INSTALLING RUNNERS, CUT SPACER TO MATCH WIDTH OF GUIDE AND TAPE IT TO DRAWER BOTTOM

a. FRONT SECTION VIEW

AA Z AA

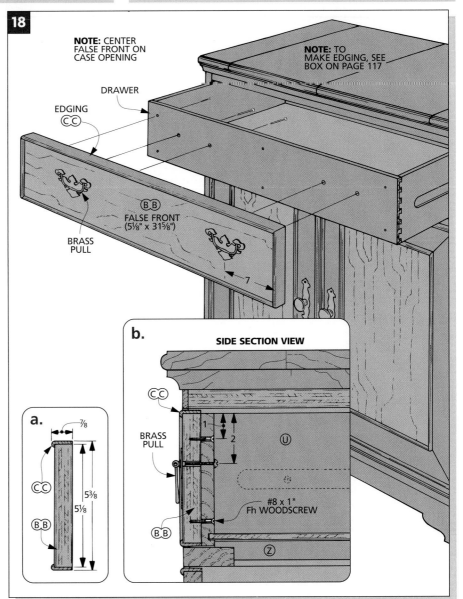

18 **NOTE:** CENTER FALSE FRONT ON CASE OPENING

NOTE: TO MAKE EDGING, SEE BOX ON PAGE 117

DRAWER

EDGING CC

BB FALSE FRONT (5⅛" x 31⅝")

BRASS PULL

7

a. ⅞

CC

BB

5⅜
5⅛

b. SIDE SECTION VIEW

CC

BRASS PULL

1
2

U

#8 x 1" Fh WOODSCREW

BB

Z

the distance between the front and back stretchers (E). Then a ¾" x ½" rabbet is cut on each end *(Fig. 15a)*.

To add the guide, all you need to do is center it in the opening and glue it in place. The critical thing is that it's parallel to the sides and square to the stretchers *(Fig. 15b)*.

CENTER RUNNERS. The guide (by itself) doesn't keep the drawer aligned as the drawer moves in and out. To complete the guide system, you need to add two center runners (AA) to the bottom of the drawer. These ¼" x ½" pieces are easy to make, but positioning them takes a bit more work.

To do this, I set the drawer in place and centered it side-to-side. Then I reached inside the case and traced the guide onto the drawer bottom *(Fig. 16)*. After removing the drawer, I cut a spacer the same size as the guide and clamped it between the layout lines. Now it's a simple matter to glue the runners in place *(Fig. 17)*.

FALSE FRONT. All that's left now is to add the false front (BB) to the drawer. The trick is cutting it to final size. That's because you have to account for the ⅛" edging just like on the doors.

To do this, I started with the drawer opening (5½" x 32") and then subtracted from each edge ¹⁄₁₆" for the gap between the drawer and case and ⅛" for the edging.

With the false front cut to size, I added the edging (CC) around the outside *(Fig. 18a and the Technique box on page 117)*. (This is similar to the edging on the doors, but this time, the strips have to be mitered to final size before they're glued in place.) Once the edging is applied, you can center the false front on the drawer front, screw it in place, and add the pulls *(Fig. 18b)*.

Now all that's left is to add the finish. I removed the hardware and stained the buffet with a cherry stain. (This evens out any color differences between the plywood and solid wood.) Then I applied a few coats of a wipe-on polyurethane finish. This provides a durable finish on the buffet top.

When it came to selecting hinges for the folding top of the Buffet Server, I was concerned with two things — strength and appearance. So I selected Soss hinges.

Soss hinges are a type of "invisible" hinge. Instead of a hinge pin, the two leaves of the hinge are connected by a "knuckle" made of interlocking fingers. When the hinge is closed, the knuckle joint folds into itself, within a pocket in the hinge (see photo). The result is a concealed hinge that provides strong mechanical support.

MORTISES. Like a butt hinge, a Soss hinge fits into a pair of mortises cut on each piece. But that's where the similarity ends. Instead of a shallow, square mortise, a Soss hinge requires a rounded, deep mortise (see photo on opposite page).

Normally, I would make each mortise by drilling a series of holes on a drill press and then cleaning up the mortises with a chisel. But because the folding top pieces of the buffet that receive the hinges are too tall to be supported on a drill press, I had to use a hand-held drill. This created some interesting challenges (more on that later).

LAYOUT

To help lay out the holes that create each hinge mortise, Soss provides a paper template (see drawing at left).

To use the template, simply fold it over on the line and place it on the edge of the workpiece where you wish to install the hinge *(Step 1)*.

Just keep in mind that since the mortises aren't centered on the thickness of

the top, the template should always be placed on the *outside* face of each workpiece.

Note: To position the template, I drew a line on my workpiece to align with the template's centerline.

With the template in place, mark the four hole locations for each hinge with a sharp awl *(Step 1)*.

TRANSFER LOCATIONS. After marking the centerpoints of the holes, use a square and a sharp pencil to draw guidelines through each centerpoint *(Detail 'a' in Step 1)*. These lines are needed later for aligning a dowel jig.

Now the hole locations can be laid out on the other piece. But this calls for some creative thinking. In order for the two pieces to line up once the hinges are installed, both sets of hinge mortises must be laid out identically. But using a tape or ruler to lay out identical hole locations isn't a reliable method, since it's easy for errors to creep in.

Instead, I transferred the hole locations directly from the first piece to the second piece. To do this, hammer four small brads halfway into the hole locations on the first workpiece. Then snip off the heads of the brads, leaving about $1/4$" exposed *(Step 2)*.

Now to transfer the hole locations, simply place both workpieces on a flat surface against a straight edge. (I used the rip fence on my table saw.) The fence ensures the ends of the pieces are flush. A quick rap with a mallet trans-

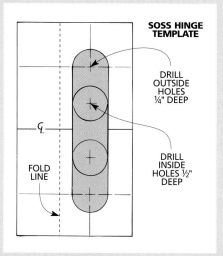

SOSS HINGE TEMPLATE

DRILL OUTSIDE HOLES ¼" DEEP

DRILL INSIDE HOLES ½" DEEP

FOLD LINE

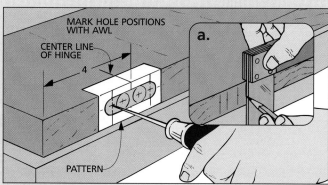

MARK HOLE POSITIONS WITH AWL

CENTER LINE OF HINGE

a.

PATTERN

1 *Place the template on the edge of the workpiece and use an awl to mark the four hole locations for each mortise. To aid in positioning a dowel jig later, draw layout lines on the edge of the board through each of the holes (detail 'a').*

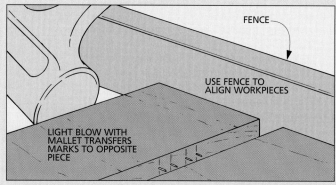

FENCE

USE FENCE TO ALIGN WORKPIECES

LIGHT BLOW WITH MALLET TRANSFERS MARKS TO OPPOSITE PIECE

2 *To transfer the hole locations, drive a small brad into each of the holes made by the awl. After snipping off the heads of the brads, butt the mating workpieces together and tap them with a mallet to mark the locations on the adjoining workpieces.*

fers the locations from one to another *(Step 2)*. Then remove the brads.

INSTALLATION

Now that the layout is complete, you can begin drilling the mortises.

DOWEL JIG. When it comes to drilling the holes for the mortises, there are three things to look out for. First, the holes have to be drilled to the right depth. Second, they have to be parallel with the face of the workpiece. And finally, they have to be drilled straight. Instead of trying to steady the workpieces on edge while drilling the mortises on the drill press, I used a hand-held drill and a dowel jig *(Step 3)*. The dowel jig keeps the holes lined up and prevents the drill bit from wandering in the tough end grain of the workpiece.

Note: If you have a self-centering type of dowel jig, you'll need to place a spacer between the jig and your workpiece in order to drill off-center holes.

DRILLING THE HOLES. The waste is drilled out in two steps. Shallow holes are drilled at each end of the mortise

first *(Detail 'a' in Step 3)*. Then a series of deeper holes are drilled in the center. (For the hinges used on the buffet, I used a ³⁄₈"-dia. drill bit.)

The depth of the shallow end holes is important since they determine the position of the hinge once it's installed. (The hinge should sit just a hair below the surface.) Unfortunately, there isn't any way to test the fit until after the mortise is completed. But if you drill the end holes ¼" deep, the hinge should sit at just the right height.

Note: I wrapped a piece of masking tape around my drill bit to serve as a depth guide *(Detail 'a' in Step 3)*. And once I had the tape positioned correctly, I drilled the end holes for all the mortises at this time.

The center section of the mortise is deeper than the ends to provide room for the main body of the hinge (see photo at right). This pocket is created by drilling three ¹⁄₂"-deep holes to remove the waste *(Step 4)*.

Note: The depth of these holes isn't as critical. Just make sure they are at least ¹⁄₂" deep.

Stepped mortise. *A Soss hinge is mortised into the edges of mating workpieces. Each mortise is "stepped." It's deeper in the middle to accommodate the body of the hinge.*

Once all the holes have been drilled, clean up the sides of the mortise carefully with a chisel *(Step 5)*.

Note: To prevent splitting the thin wall of the mortise, I clamped the workpiece and a support board in a vise.

Installing the hinges is simple — it's just a matter of inserting each leaf into a mortise and using the screwholes as a guide for drilling pilot holes *(Step 6)*. Then screw the hinges in place.

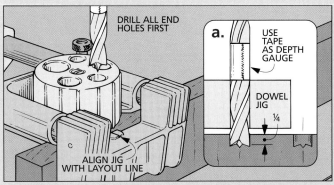

3 *Align the dowel jig with the first layout line. Then using a ³⁄₈"-dia. brad-point bit, drill a ¹⁄₄"-deep hole. Use a piece of masking tape on the bit as a depth gauge. Drill all the end holes for all hinges before readjusting the masking tape depth gauge.*

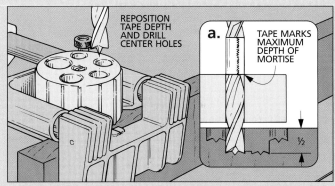

4 *After drilling the end holes in all the pieces, reposition the tape depth stop to drill a ¹⁄₂"-deep hole. Then drill out the waste in the center of the mortises, again using the layout lines to align the dowel jig.*

5 *After drilling all the holes, the mortise can be cleaned up with a chisel. To prevent splitting the thin sidewall of the offset mortise, clamp a scrap piece to the side of the workpiece for additional support.*

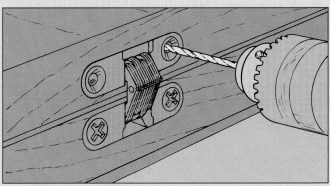

6 *To install the mounting screws (No. 5 x ³⁄₄"), place the hinge in the mortise and drill pilot holes, using the hinge itself as a guide. Be careful not to overtighten the screws or the threads will strip out the end grain.*

DESIGNER'S NOTEBOOK

Simple things change the look of the buffet server entirely, like adding muntins to the door panels and using stub tenons and grooves to connect the rails and stiles. New hardware completes the design.

CONSTRUCTION NOTES:

■ The base front (K) and sides (L) on this mission-style buffet server will stay the same as before, except that the base front (K) has a different profile *(Fig. 1)*. Start by making this profile before cutting the miters on the ends *(Fig. 1)*. Once that's complete, rout $1/2$" chamfers along the top edge of the base front and sides, see chamfer detail below.

Note: See page 115 for a tip on using a straight guide to keep the newly cut edge of the base piece straight.

■ Next, make the sub-top (N) with the same $1/2$" chamfers that were added to the front and side base pieces *(Fig. 2)*.

■ After the folding top (O) has been cut to size, use sandpaper to ease the sharp edges all the way around *(Fig. 2)*. Then cut it into four pieces as before, and add the hinges.

■ The new drawer false front (BB) will have a routed raised panel. The edging (CC) is removed as well *(Fig. 3)*.

■ First, make the drawer false front (BB) from solid wood, crosscutting and ripping it to size. To determine the size of this version, add $1/8$" to the width and $1/4$" to the length of the drawer front (U). (My false front is $5^3/8$" x $31^7/8$".)

■ To cut the raised panel, I rabbeted the false front using a $3/4$" straight bit in my router (mounted in a router table). Partially bury the bit in the router fence, leaving $1/2$" exposed. Raise the bit to the desired height ($1/8$") above the table and rout the rabbet *(Fig. 3)*.

Note: Rout the end grain of the drawer first, using a piece of scrap to back it up to minimize chipout.

MISSION-STYLE BUFFET SERVER

MATERIALS LIST

CHANGED PARTS

K	Base Front (1)	$3/4$ x 4 - $34^3/4$
L	Base Sides (2)	$3/4$ x 2 - 22 rgh.
P	Door Stiles (4)	$3/4$ x 2 - $22^1/8$
Q	Door Rails (4)	$3/4$ x 2 - $12^3/4$
T	Door Panels (2)	$1/4$ ply - $12^3/4$ x $18^7/8$
BB	False Front (1)	$3/4$ x $5^3/8$ - $31^7/8$

NEW PARTS

DD	Vert. Muntins (4)	$1/4$ x $1/2$ - $18^1/8$
EE	Horz. Muntins (4)	$1/4$ x $1/2$ - 12

Note: Do not need parts R, S, or CC.

HARDWARE SUPPLIES

Need two pair of 2" butt hinges and four mission-style ring pulls w/ #8-32 x $1^1/2$" machine screws.

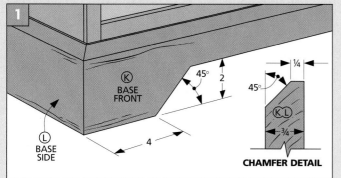

1

ⓀBASE FRONT

ⓁBASE SIDE

45° — 2

4

CHAMFER DETAIL

45° — $1/4$

Ⓚ Ⓛ

$3/4$

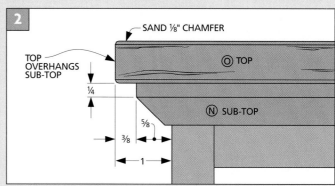

2

SAND $1/8$" CHAMFER

TOP OVERHANGS SUB-TOP

Ⓞ TOP

$1/4$

Ⓝ SUB-TOP

$5/8$

$3/8$

1

■ Now center and mount the drawer false front as before, making sure to leave $1/8$" reveals at the top and sides.

■ Finally, lay out the location of the mission-style ring pulls and drill the holes for the mounting screws *(Fig. 3)*. Add the pulls after the finish has been applied.

■ I also changed the look of the doors. Once again, I eliminated the bead edging (R). And instead of framing the door panels with mitered rails and stiles, I used stub tenons and grooves.

■ Start by ripping and crosscutting the stiles (D) to length *(Fig. 4)*. They're sized to leave $1/16$" gaps at the top and bottom, once the doors are installed.

■ To determine the length of the rails (Q), measure the width of the door opening and subtract the combined width of the four stiles. Divide this number by 2 and add $3/4$" to their length to allow for the stub tenons *(Fig. 4)*. (My rails were $12^3/4$".)

■ Once the rails and stiles are cut to length, cut centered grooves on their inside edges. These grooves will accept the stub tenons and the door panel. I cut each groove in two passes using a regular saw blade in my table saw. It's sized to hold the $1/4$" plywood panels.

■ Now cut the stub tenons on the rails, sizing them to fit the grooves *(Fig. 4a)*.

■ Next, cut the door panels (T) to size and glue up the doors *(Fig. 4)*.

■ Before going on to the muntins, you'll have to mortise the doors to hold the door hinges *(Fig. 4)*. The mortises are the full depth of the hinges. I laid them out (as shown in *Fig. 4b*), and cut them with a sharp chisel.

Note: You may have to trim $3/64$" from the inside edges of the doors to fit the opening of the server. You want to end up with a $1/16$" gap between the doors after mounting the hinges.

■ Next, I made the vertical (DD) and horizontal (EE) muntins. They're ripped from solid stock. An easy way to do this is to use an extra-wide blank for all of the muntins and then cut the half-laps across the blank before ripping them to size.

■ To locate the half-laps, set the table saw's rip fence to cut the first half-lap. After cutting a half-lap on one end of the muntins, flip the piece end-for-end to cut the half-lap on the other end. Finally, rip the muntins to width *(Fig. 5)*

■ Now all that's left is to glue the muntins to the door panels *(Fig. 5a)*. Once the glue for the muntins has set up, you can add the door and drawer hardware and hang the doors.

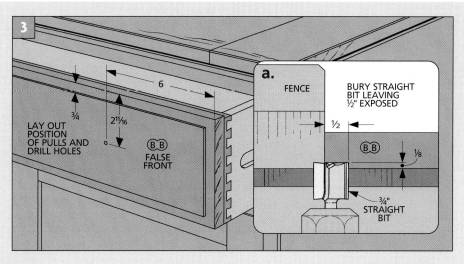

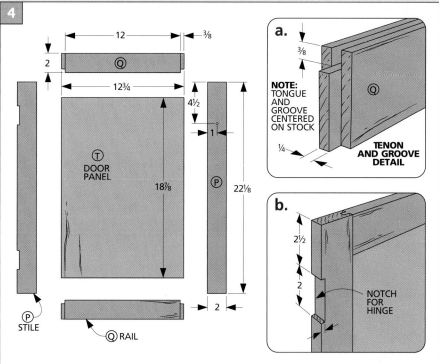

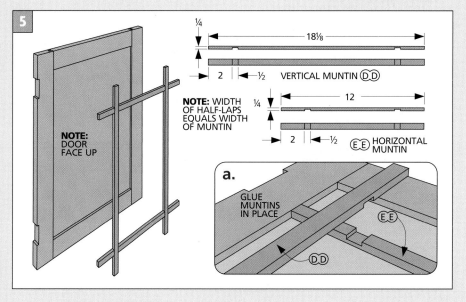

One of the first things we take into consideration when designing projects at *Woodsmith* is whether the hardware is affordable and commonly available. Most of the hardware and supplies for the projects in this book can be found at local hardware stores or home centers. Sometimes, though, you may have to order hardware through the mail. If that's the case, we've tried to find reputable sources with toll-free phone numbers and web sites (see the box at right).

In addition, *Woodsmith Project Supplies* offers hardware for some of the projects in this book (see below).

Note: We strongly recommend that you have all of your hardware and supplies in hand before you begin building any project. There's nothing more discouraging than completing a project and then finding out that the hardware you ordered doesn't fit or is no longer available.

WOODSMITH PROJECT SUPPLIES

At the time this book was printed, the following project supply kits and hardware were available from *Woodsmith Project Supplies*. The kits include hardware, but you must supply any lumber, plywood, or finish. For current prices and availability, call toll free:

1-800-444-7527

Coffee Table
(pages 20-29)

This kit contains full-size patterns for the apron and table top.
.....................................No. 8005224

Mantel Clock
(pages 56-65)

This kit contains only the shop drawings. Clock works can be obtained from sources listed at right. ....No. 7119250

Chairside Chest
(pages 86-95)

The nylon glide tape is available by the foot. ....No. 1006104

KEY: TL10

MAIL ORDER SOURCES

Some of the most important "tools" you can have in your shop are your mail order catalogs. The ones listed below are filled with special hardware, tools, finishes, lumber, and supplies that can't be found at a local hardware store or home centers. You should be able to find many of the supplies for the projects in this book in one or more of these catalogs. Many even offer online ordering.

Note: The information below was current when this book was printed. August Home Publishing does not guarantee these products will be available nor endorse any specific mail order company, catalog, or product.

THE WOODSMITH STORE

2625 Beaver Avenue
Des Moines, IA 50310
800-835-5084
Our own retail store with tools, jigs, hardware, books, and finishing supplies. We don't have a catalog, but we do send out items mail order.

CONSTANTINE'S

1040 E. Oakland Park Blvd.
Ft. Lauderdale, FL 33334
954-561-1716
www.constantines.com
One of the original woodworking mail order catalogs. Find hinges, pulls, and finishing supplies including gel stains and rubbing compounds.

ROCKLER WOODWORKING & HARDWARE

4365 Willow Drive
Medina, MN 55340
800-279-4441
www.rockler.com
A very good catalog of hardware and accessories, including dovetail jigs, pulls, hinges.

WOODCRAFT

560 Airport Industrial Park
P.O. Box 1686
Parkersburg, WV 26102-1686
800-225-1153
www.woodcraft.com
Almost everything you'd need, from layout to hardware to finishing supplies. A good selection of hinges and router bits, plus dovetail jigs.

LEE VALLEY TOOLS LTD.

P.O. Box 1780
Ogdensburg, NY 13669-6780
800-871-8158
www.leevalley.com
Several catalogs actually, with tools and hardware. In the hardware catalog you'll find pulls, hinges, magnetic catches, and necklace pegs.

WOODWORKER'S SUPPLY

1108 North Glenn Road
Casper, WY 82601
800-645-9292
www.woodworker.com
You'll find a good selection of pulls and hardware, router bits, and magnetic catches.

VAN DYKE'S RESTORERS

P.O. Box 278
Woonsocket, SD 57385
800-558-1234
www.vandykes.com
An amazing collection of reproduction hardware, plus cabriole legs, finishing supplies and lots more.

ADAMS WOOD PRODUCTS

974 Forest Drive
Morristown, TN 37814
423-587-2942
www.adamswoodproducts.com
They specialize in turning blanks and cabriole legs of all sizes and in many types of wood.

BLACK FOREST IMPORTS

22865 Savi Ranch Pkwy., Unit "D"
Yorba Linda, CA 92887
800-824-0900
www.blackforestimports.com
A wide variety of traditional clock works and accessories.

INDEX

AUGUST HOME
PUBLISHING COMPANY

President & Publisher: Donald B. Peschke
Executive Editor: Douglas L. Hicks
Project Manager: Craig L. Ruegsegger
Creative Director: Ted Kralicek
Art Director: Doug Flint
Senior Graphic Designer: Chris Glowacki
Assistant Editors: Joel Hess, Joseph E. Irwin
Graphic Designers: Robin Friend, April Walker Janning, Stacey L. Krull,
Vu Nguyen
Design Intern: Heather Boots, Matt O'Gara

Designer's Notebook Illustrator: Mike Mittermeier
Photographer: Crayola England
Electronic Production: Douglas M. Lidster
Production: Troy Clark, Minniette Johnson
Project Designers: Chris Fitch, Ryan Mimick, Ken Munkel, Kent Welsh
Project Builders: Steve Curtis, Steve Johnson
Magazine Editors: Terry Strohman, Tim Robertson
Contributing Editors: Vincent S. Ancona, Jon Garbison, Brian McCallum,
Bryan Nelson
Magazine Art Directors: Todd Lambirth, Cary Christensen
Contributing Illustrators: Harlan Clark, Mark Higdon, David Kreyling,
Erich Lage, Roger Reiland, Kurt Schultz, Cinda Shambaugh, Dirk Ver Steeg

Corporate V.P., Finance: Mary Scheve
Controller: Robin Hutchinson
Production Director: George Chmielarz
Project Supplies: Bob Baker
New Media Manager: Gordon Gaippe

For subscription information about
Woodsmith and *ShopNotes* magazines, please write:
August Home Publishing Co.
2200 Grand Ave.
Des Moines, IA 50312
800-333-5075
www.augusthome.com/customwoodworking

Woodsmith® and *ShopNotes*® are registered trademarks of August Home
Publishing Co.

©2002 August Home Publishing Co.
All rights reserved. No part of this book may be reproduced in any form or by
any electronic or mechanical means, including information storage and retrieval
devices or systems, without prior written permission from the publisher, except
that brief passages may be quoted for reviews.
First Printing. Printed in U.S.A.

Oxmoor House®

Oxmoor House, Inc.
Book Division of Southern Progress Corporation
P.O. Box 2463, Birmingham, Alabama 35201

ISBN: 0-8487-2684-7
Printed in the United States of America

To order additional publications, call 1-800-765-6400.
For more books to enrich your life, visit **oxmoorhouse.com**